2-26-62

American Enterprise:

THE NEXT TEN YEARS

THE MACMILLAN COMPANY
NEW YORK · CHICAGO
DALLAS · ATLANTA · SAN FRANCISCO
LONDON · MANILA

IN CANADA
BRETT-MACMILLAN LTD.
GALT, ONTARIO

American Enterprise:

THE NEXT TEN YEARS

EDITED BY *Martin R. Gainsbrugh*

From the Proceedings of the Forty-Fourth Annual Meeting of the National Industrial Conference Board

New York | **THE MACMILLAN COMPANY**

Library of Congress catalog card number: 61-15159

The Macmillan Company, New York
Brett-Macmillan Ltd., Galt, Ontario

PRINTED IN THE UNITED STATES OF AMERICA

Foreword

11'71849

THIS VOLUME presents the considered views of more than 60 leading
business executives, government officials, and economists and other
scientists on the nation's economic outlook for the current decade.
This select group was brought together on May 19-20, 1960 to apply
its collective talents to the central theme of the Board's Third
Annual Economic Conference: "American Enterprise: The Next
Ten Years." Representatives of The Macmillan Company who
attended the Conference were so impressed with its high quality
and timely character that they invited The Conference Board to
join with them in publishing the proceedings. To this the Board
gave its assent, in the belief that not only did the proceedings
merit publication in permanent form but also the problem areas
intensively explored by these authorities were—and are today—
much in the mind of the American public.

Economic growth is no longer simply a matter of academic
interest. Instead, our current and prospective rates of growth have
become the subject of intense public discussion and, indeed, growing national and international concern. These appraisals, in turn,
involve such vital matters as the international outlook, the future
of technology and productivity, and the adequacy of our savings
and financial resources to meet the job requirements of an expanding population—to say nothing of the consumption explosion

this nation's greatly enlarged labor force would generate, providing it continues to be employed productively.

Much has already been made of the sharp contrast between the high expectations surrounding our entrance into the 1960's and the harsher economic realities of the initial 12 to 18 months of that decade. No attempt has been made here, however, to remove the impress of time from the discussion. The participants were primarily concerned with the longer run, so that relatively little attention was devoted to events of the day. Where such references occur, they were allowed to remain. The reader can thus observe to what extent, if any, such transient factors may have influenced the given individual's judgment of future trends.

As of mid-1961, however, the departure from the collectively high expectations for the decade is deemed to be more cyclical than secular. Some builders of economic models, their faith renewed by the current recovery, foresee a return to the long-term trend line by the year-end or in 1962, at the latest. Others, their enthusiasm moderated by the recession experience, tend to believe that their earlier projections may require some modest scaling down. Few, if any, accept the recent recession as evidence of the onset of economic stagnation. In general, the anticipations upon which the longer-range plans of American business are based in the summer of 1961 remain largely those discussed in this volume.

The Conference Board is grateful to the outstanding authorities who contributed their experiences and ideas to the appraisal of America's economic potential. In each instance, the individual gave his views as an authority in his own right and not necessarily as a representative of the organization with which he was affiliated. These affiliations, it should be noted, are shown as they were at the time of the Conference.

This project was conceived (and delivered) by the Board's Economic Divisions. The staff organizers of the panels for the four major problem areas were: J. Frank Gaston, "America and the World"; Albert T. Sommers, "Domestic Markets: The Demand Ahead"; Daniel Creamer, "Technology and Its Impact: The Promise and the Problems"; and Morris Cohen, "Financing National Growth." Martin

R. Gainsbrugh, the Board's Chief Economist, edited the proceedings
and delivered the Conference's closing address, which now appears
as a preface to this volume.

JOHN S. SINCLAIR
President

July, 1961

Preface: Economic Growth in the 1960's: Prerequisites, Potentials, Problems

THE COURSE OF ECONOMIC EVENTS in 1960 suggests that economists have far from mastered the short-term outlook. Hence it is with due humility that we here approach the task of commenting on the outlook for economic growth in the decade ahead. The task, however, is made easier for us—and more palatable for the reader —by drawing heavily upon the analyses already prepared by others who have been busily exploring the economic environment of the 1960's. In this study we have borrowed freely from the long-term projections made by the staff of the Joint Congressional Economic Committee, the United States Bureau of the Census, and the United States Bureau of Labor Statistics—to name just a few. The economic fraternity has indeed made a historic joint effort to provide its followers with more detailed projections for the 1960's than for any earlier decade in U. S. history. No greater collection of economic talent has ever been assembled by The Conference Board in the quarter-century I have been associated with it to deal with the problems of longer-range projections.

By way of placing the 1960's in proper economic perspective, let me first sketch briefly for you the "middle years" thesis I began to advance about 1955. The essence of this thesis was that growth would be harder to come by as the artificial stimuli of the postwar recovery gradually wore off. Among such stimuli were included the hyperliquidity of financial institutions, the accumulated backlogs of domestic demand of both consumers and industry, and the lush world markets with limited foreign competition.

As we entered the 1960's, the economic environment still closely corresponded with this "middle-year" period. The bulk of the nation's financial institutions were "loaned up." Capacity has now outstripped market demand in industry after industry, not only domestically but in a great many countries abroad. Idle capacity brings with it intensified price competition. The postwar price tilt no longer bails out poor investment or managerial decisions. Intensified world competition has drastically altered our balance-of-payments position. Labor as well as management senses this changing economic environment and the increasingly sterner disciplines of the market place that are making themselves felt, as competitive pressures mount, month by month and year by year.

That the postwar inflationary tide has receded is quite apparent in the record of aggregate price indexes. Wholesale price indexes are no higher now than when recovery began in April, 1958. In contrast, may I remind you, in the first two years of the 1949-1953 recovery, wholesale prices rose 16%; and in the first two years of the 1954-1957 recovery, the same indexes rose by 4% to 5%.

With the perspective of hindsight, it is becoming increasingly clear that the inflation generated by World War II, and recharged a bit by the Korean War, reached a crest in the middle 1950's. Rising prices by that time had cut deeply into the purchasing power of liquid assets accumulated during the war. Industrial capacity was becoming ever more adequate to meet prevailing demand. Monetary and fiscal policy grew increasingly conservative as public concern mounted over the toll of inflation. The weight of this evidence clearly suggests that our hyperstimulated postwar boom ended with the start of the 1960's, if not some years before.

Output rates no longer press rigidly against capacity. Instead, costly excesses of capacity now overhang the market place. Growth in output and rising prices combined have raised the dollar value of output to a far more normal balance with the nation's money supply. That balance is being held by firm, conservative monetary and fiscal policies, with broad public support and understanding. Many countries with historically lower labor costs have now with our aid gained the technology and capital required to improve their productivity. For a growing number of products, their total production costs compare most favorably with our own.

Finally, even as the band of unused industrial capacity widened, so, also, has the rate of unemployment risen. The hyper-full employment levels of earlier postwar years have given way to more slack in the labor markets. Since 1956, average hourly earnings have risen about 3% to 5% annually, as compared with as much as 10% in 1951. Profits, too, are much harder to come by. The rates of return on investment now run sharply below early postwar experience in virtually all industries.

That is the setting in which we found ourselves as the 1960's began. The economic climate of the new decade is thus very different from the "hothouse" atmosphere of the first 10 to 15 postwar years. Dramatic and historic changes have marked the very beginning of the decade. These are often mistaken as signs of cyclical or temporary weakness. Instead, they are precursors of deep-rooted secular change. The most sweeping of these changes is that the stimulus for growth in the 1960's must come from current market forces rather than from the artificial stimuli of war-induced shortages, inflation, unbalanced budgets, or excessive wage increases passed through in the form of price increases, irrespective of our position in world markets.

In the morning of the 1960's, World War II and its aftermath appear not in our economic statistics but in a set of national habits and attitudes developed during a decade and a half of postwar prosperity and inflation, of artificial stimuli to markets, and of frequent recourse to government for the redressing of supposed imbalances.

To paraphrase Toynbee, no decade is without its challenge. We more than met the production challenge of the 1940's and the 1950's. To that our present abundance testifies. The challenge of the 1960's is the final severing of our ties to postwar artificialities. We must now rediscover—and here harsh actualities underscore this conclusion—the normal, vigorous but hard-to-come-by incentives for growth and efficiency that have been present in our free enterprise system throughout our history.

The charts that follow amply document the growth potentials ahead. The challenge of the 1960's, to repeat, is to achieve this economic growth potential without inflation and without the sacrifice of individual freedoms.

Toynbee also tells us that as one previous civilization after another died, the challenge to which they failed to respond in every instance was from within rather than external. I think the challenge of the 1960's is, again, far more internal than external.

For the countries that were the battlefields of war, postwar recovery was a heroic struggle to rebuild standards of living quite literally from the ground up. In America, however, the economic costs of the war, while tremendous in terms of dollars, took the form mainly of interruptions and distortions rather than massive destruction. The economic aspects of postwar recovery, with its related phenomena of inflation, rising debt, and rapidly advancing living standards, took hold early in America, while Europe was still struggling to its feet.

In the American economy of the early 1960's, the traces of war and of postwar recovery are no longer easy to find. Living standards have reached historic peaks; productive capacity is adequate or abundant in virtually all industries; our level of private debt has been rebuilt to a normal if not liberal proportion of our national income; and we have absorbed (partly through inflation) the excesses of money supply created by wartime and postwar deficits.

Now for a short corollary that flows from the conclusion that the 1960's promise to be a decade of sweeping change. Quantitative forecasts for the next ten years, relying primarily upon projections of the first decade or so of postwar experience must, therefore, be treated with more than usual caution.

In the first dozen postwar years, the swollen levels of demand prevailing throughout the American economy acted to make both the businessman and the economist demand conscious. The stimulation of investment, as distinct from demand, was relatively unimportant. Here is a second fundamental distinction between the past postwar period and the decade which lies ahead. The fundamental incentives which have led to increased investment over long stretches of more normal times have been largely neglected. One of the major problems already visible for the 1960's is this: the need for a high and rapidly rising level of investment if growth and efficiency is to be secured and productive jobs created for the millions who will be flooding into the labor force in the decade ahead.

Forecasting practices of the postwar years have developed primarily around projections of demand and output potentials. The economic arithmetic involved is to multiply the increased inputs of labor by the prospectively higher output per man-hour, thereby yielding the impressive projections of national output by 1970. Virtually all of these projections assume that the required incentives for investment will be automatically forthcoming, thereby enabling the gains in productivity and output to materialize. Our own charts present a broad range of output projections for the United States economy for the next decade. These projections, all of them based on long-term historical trends, yield results for 1970 ranging from as little as $625 billion (the 1909-1959 trend)—or about 25% above the current rate of output—to as high as $860 billion, or 70% above the current rate of output. To achieve this growth in the decade ahead will require an environment that not only stimulates current levels of demand, but also widens the investment perspectives open to industry. The more favorable the investment environment, the more likely is the achievement of the higher end of this range.

Economic growth has characterized the performance of the American economy ever since its founding. This growth has been persistent and also irregular (Figure 1). Over the long term, the growth rate has averaged about 3% a year. In the past 30 years, 1929-1959, the rate averaged more than 4%, in part because the period begins with the Great Depression of the 1930's and ends with postwar prosperity. In the postwar years, 1947-1959, national

---

Figure 1 (opposite). National economic growth in terms of output per hour, employment and gross national product, 1909-1970.

NATIONAL GROWTH: RETROSPECT AND PROSPECT

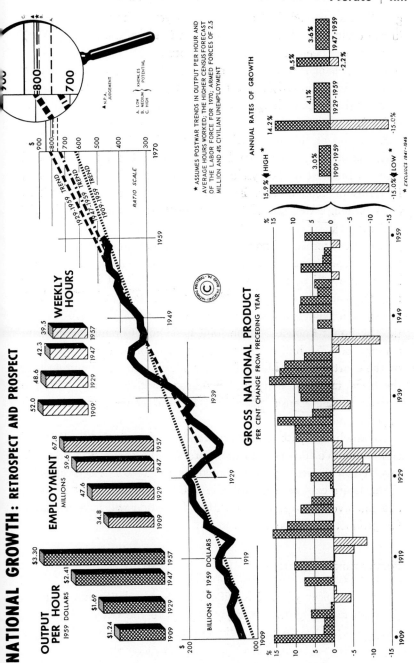

★ ASSUMES POSTWAR TRENDS IN OUTPUT PER HOUR AND AVERAGE HOURS WORKED; THE HIGHER CENSUS FORECAST OF THE LABOR FORCE FOR 1970; ARMED FORCES OF 2.5 MILLION AND 4% CIVILIAN UNEMPLOYMENT

OUTPUT PER HOUR
1959 DOLLARS

EMPLOYMENT
MILLIONS

WEEKLY HOURS

ANNUAL RATES OF GROWTH

GROSS NATIONAL PRODUCT
PER CENT CHANGE FROM PRECEDING YEAR

BILLIONS OF 1959 DOLLARS

RATIO SCALE

growth has proceeded at about 3.6% a year. The rate was higher in the early part of the period (which includes the Korean War) than it has been in more recent years.

Annual changes in the rate of national output have ranged from about + 16% to − 15%. In the postwar years, the range of annual changes has been sharply narrower, running from + 8.5% to − 2.2%.

Projection of this historical experience into the future yields a wide variety of results from 1970. Extending the 1909-1959 trend through the next decade yields an output for 1970 of $624 billion, in terms of 1959 dollars. Extension of the postwar trend yields $724 billion. Extension of the 1929-1959 trend would yield $806 billion.

Current forecasts of national output in 1970 tend to fall in the upper range of this spectrum, recognizing that growth rate in the labor force will be more rapid in the 1960's than it has been over the long run. The "judgmental" forecast of the National Planning Association points to $802 billion; projections of the 1970 "potential" by James Knowles, of the Joint Economic Committee, indicate a range of $754 billion to as high as $837 billion. Also indicated on the chart is a $796 billion forecast. This is obtained by projecting the trend in productivity and hours of work, combined with the Bureau of the Census projection for the labor force, and 4% unemployment.

So much for past aggregate trends and their implications, if continued. We turn next to the more specific economic arithmetic involved in estimating the potentials of the 1960's. A typical point of departure explores the probable trends in population, workforce, and the levels of skill and education the nation will have available for production in the 1960's.

Population Growth

Since the early years of the 1940's, U. S. population has resumed the high rate of growth it enjoyed prior to the Great Depression (Figure 2). Despite the tragic loss of life and the deferrals of

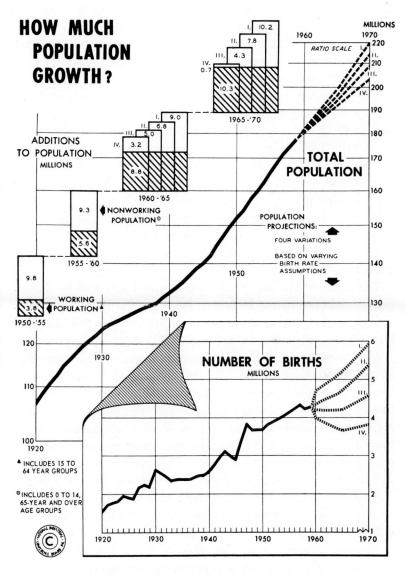

Figure 2. U.S. population growth, 1920-1970.

marriages and births resulting from war in the first half of the decade, the population rose by about 18 million in the 1940's, or roughly twice as rapidly as in the depression-ridden decade of the 1930's. In the 1950's, another 30 million Americans were added.

The resumption of rapid population growth in the past 15 years reflects a record number of births. These exceeded 4 million annually in the last six years of the 1950's. In turn, the high birth rate has meant a large addition to the population below the working-age level. Roughly one-half of the net addition to population during the 1950's was in the age groups under 15 years.

Total population growth in the 1960's depends, of course, on the prospective birth rate. Four projections of the birth rate, on varying fertility assumptions, are shown in the lower insert of Figure 2. These alternative birth-rate projections suggest total population additions for the decade as a whole of 25 million to as much as 40 million. (Population forecasts in the past have usually tended toward understatement.)

The level of economic well-being in the 1960's will be an important influence on the birth rate, and hence on the rate of population growth; conversely, the rate of population growth will doubtless influence demands for a broad range of goods and services.

All of the variation in the 1970 forecasts is, of course, concentrated in the age groups below ten; the working-age, marrying age, buying-age population of the 1960's is already born. In the first half of the 1960's, increases in these age groups will approach 2 million, as contrasted with a decline of over one million during the entire decade of the 1950's; this population segment will grow even more rapidly in the last half of the decade. In these years, the full force of the postdepression population wave will reach the labor market and the markets for family goods.

There is little possibility of error in the projections of those who will be adult consumers in the years ahead, since the underlying population is already here. This estimate does not involve speculation about the future birth rate. Population increases over the next decade should thus provide a major increment to the market for consumer goods and services.

The Expanding Labor Force

As the 1960's wear on, the number of young adults in the population will expand sharply, echoing the advancing birth rate of the late 1940's and early 1950's. This dimension of the population outlook is also a firm actuarial statistic, free of economic influence. That population is also here now. Regardless of changes in business condition, the number of young adults in the age groups 20-34 will rise by almost two million in the first half of the 1960's, and by more than that in the last half of the 1960's. Never before has this nation been asked to find productive jobs for so many young people in so short a period of time.

The ascending birth rate of the 1940's and early 1950's will be reflected in a sharply rising workforce during the 1960's. In the past ten years, the aggregate addition to the workforce was less than 9 million; in the next ten years, it may be as much as 13½ million, and the annual rate of additions will be accelerating throughout the decade (Figure 3).

Particularly striking will be the uptrend in male additions to the workforce. During the 1950's, under conditions of high prosperity and a small supply of male entrants into the labor market, job opportunities for women were unusually good and the labor force participation rate for married women entered on a pronounced rise. In the past ten years, net additions of women to the workforce actually exceeded the additions of men, although men constitute roughly two thirds of the total labor force. In the 1960's, the rate of male entrants into the workforce will advance sharply; in the last half of the decade the increase will be more than twice as great as in the last half of the 1950's, and will substantially exceed the increase of women in the workforce.

Because the dominant influence on the labor force of the 1960's is the rising birth rate of the 1940's, additions to the workforce will be concentrated at younger ages—in the 20-34-year age groups. In the more mature age groups, in fact, net increases in the labor force will be smaller than they were in the 1950's; this itself is a reflection of the low birth rates prevailing in the 1920's and 1930's.

THE EXPANDING LABOR FORCE

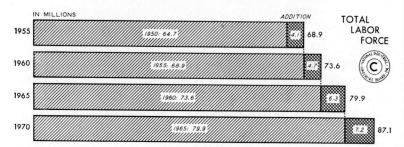

ADDITIONS TO THE LABOR FORCE: A RISING TIDE OF YOUNG MEN

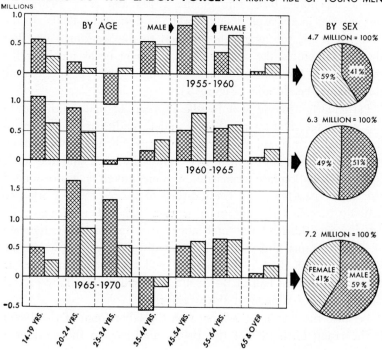

Figure 3. Additions to U.S. workforce, 1955-1970.

The workforce will thus grow younger, as well as bigger. While the prospective growth in the total will be substantial, the reservoir of mature workers for higher managerial positions will rise little from its present level. In particular, the net increase in the male workforce in mature age groups will be small in the first half of the decade, and negligible in the last half.

EDUCATIONAL INPUTS

Finally, under the heading of probable human inputs by 1970, we can count on a much higher level of skills within the labor force. This is still another form of investment that we must begin to provide funds for increasingly in the 1960's. Over the long term, the proportion of unskilled workers and farm laborers in the American economy has been declining sharply, while the proportion of professional and service workers has been rising. At the same time, the training level of the new entrant into the workforce has been rising. During the 1960's, projections by the Bureau of Labor Statistics suggest that the number of entrants into the labor force who have a high school diploma will be almost 60% greater than in the 1950's, while the number with no high school education at all will be one-third smaller (Figure 4).

The consist of the United States labor force has been molded by the increasingly complex character of economic activity and the higher educational standards required of worker and manager. The consequence has been a wide disparity in the growth rates of the labor force classified by skills. The absolute number of unskilled workers in the labor force is now substantially lower than 20 years ago, although the total labor force has increased by almost 30%. In contrast, the number of professional, technical, and managerial workers has very nearly doubled over the past 20 years.

Between these two extremes of the skills spectrum, a variety of other influences is reflected in the composition of the labor force. The number of service workers has risen steadily and rapidly, reflecting the growing share of the so-called service industries in

MORE JOBS AT HIGHER SKILLS

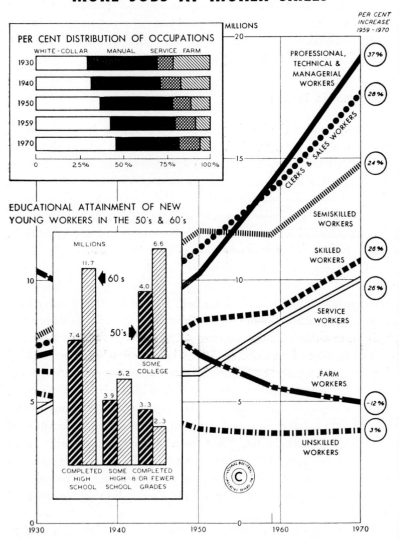

Figure 4. Educational attainment and levels of skills in U.S. labor force.

the total economic activity of the nation. The number of clerks and sales workers has likewise advanced rapidly, as the marketing, distribution and planning aspects of business activity have risen in importance. And the number of farm workers has declined dramatically.

These broad trends in the structure of the human inputs are expected to continue in the coming decade. Between 1959 and 1970, the professional, technical and managerial workforce is likely to increase by more than 5 million, or about 37%. At the other extreme, the number of unskilled workers is likely to show little if any change, and farm employment is expected to decline another 12%.

This restructuring of the labor force in the direction of higher skills implies an ascending level of educational attainment on the part of new entrants into the labor force. The rising tide of the workforce itself, coupled with an upward shift in skills required by a more complex, more highly mechanized productive system and a higher level of educational attainment on the part of new workers, is one of the great economic promises of the new decade.

A problem that I have underscored from the outset is the required capital inputs if these human inputs are to be transformed into an increasingly productive economic resource. Will these human inputs be used ever more efficiently and productively in the 1960's? Can the postwar crop of babies as they mature in the 1960's keep themselves in the style to which we have made them accustomed?

Among the basic unknowns of the next decade—and here we are exploring almost virgin territory—is the amount and quality of the production equipment that will be made available to this growing labor force. The gross stock of business plant and equipment is worth about $700 billion currently (Figure 5). This is equivalent to about $11,000 per worker in the private sector— the value of the resources we now supply to lengthen the arm of the worker. The rate at which this supply of tools grows may well be the primary determinant of the prospective trend of output per worker in the 1960's and hence of total output.

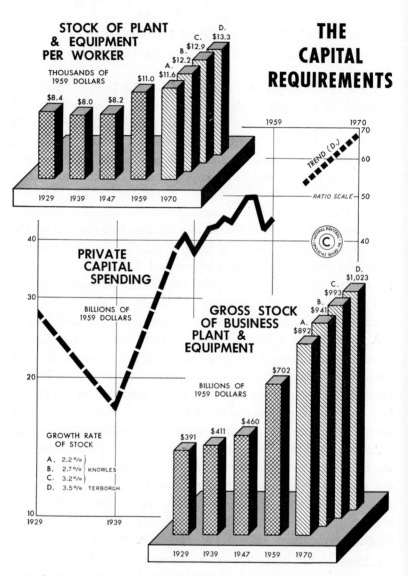

Figure 5. Gross stock of business plant and equipment and plant investment per worker.

CAPITAL REQUIREMENTS

To do the production job of the next decade—to sustain or improve on the historical growth rate of output in the American economy—will require far more private capital in the form of fixed investment in productive facilities. A substantial increment in investment will be required to equip perhaps 13 million new workers for efficient production; and still more capital will be required to continue the historical uptrend in the productive efficiency of all workers.

Our stock of business, plant and equipment, in real terms, is almost 80% greater than in 1929. The great bulk of the addition has been made in the postwar years; during the depression the available fixed capital hardly increased at all, and the rate of addition during the war was limited by the overwhelming needs of defense. In the postwar years, the stock of productive capital has risen rapidly, since annual capital outlays have run at about double the rate at which these facilities were being used up.

In the coming decade, the gross stock of capital assets must advance sharply. Several estimates for 1970 drawn from differing assumptions of growth rates of the stock range from a little less than $900 billion to over $1,000 billion. To achieve the highest of these projections, annual capital spending for new facilities will have to run substantially above its level of the 1950's, averaging almost $58 billion annually, and reaching nearly $70 billion near the end of the decade. (The spending projection was prepared by the Machinery and Allied Products Institute; it differs somewhat from the Department of Commerce's historical series mainly in that it excludes certain farm plant, investment of nonprofit institutions, and petroleum- and gas-well drilling.)

The supply of productive facilities in 1947 was actually less per worker in the private business sector than in 1929, but it has since grown rapidly. The several estimates of the growth rates of fixed capital over the next decade point to a level per worker of $11,600 to $13,300 by 1970, as contrasted with about $11,000 currently. To reach and maintain an annual rate of private investment of $70 billion will obviously require levels of corporate earnings materially higher than those experienced in recent years. This again underscores the emphasis I have placed upon the need to heighten the incentive for investment in the decade ahead.

We are laying the base for a vigorous technological advance. Witness the curve for research and development outlays. This base for rapid technological advance is being forged in the research and development facilities of private industries as well as by government, universities, and nonprofit institutions (Figure 6). We are now spending over $12 billion a year for technological research. (The rapid growth of R&D outlays in recent years has drawn heavily from the reservoir of technological advances developed during World War II. That may be another of the artificial stimuli being withdrawn from the economy as we enter the 1960's.)

INVESTMENT IN RESEARCH AND DEVELOPMENT

In 1947, research and development was still a small dimension of the American economy, accounting for $2 billion of spending, only a little less than 1% of national output. By the end of the Korean war, the spending rate had reached $5 billion. Current estimates place the present rate at over $12 billion, or about 2.5% of national output. While these estimates are general and have been revised considerably in the past, there is little doubt that R&D spending has entered on a sharp uptrend, with dramatic implications for the future. For the closing years of the 1960's, one source has estimated that R&D outlays will be more than double their present annual rate. If so, something like 4% of national output will be finding its way into reinvestment in this most vigorous of all "seed money."

Currently, the federal government is still providing more than half of the funds for research and development, although it actually expends only about 15% of total R&D outlays. Industry is now spending roughly three fourths of the total and providing three eighths of the funds. As of 1957—the latest year for which industry detail on R&D spending is available—about three eighths of the total was in the aircraft industry (where it doubtless reflects

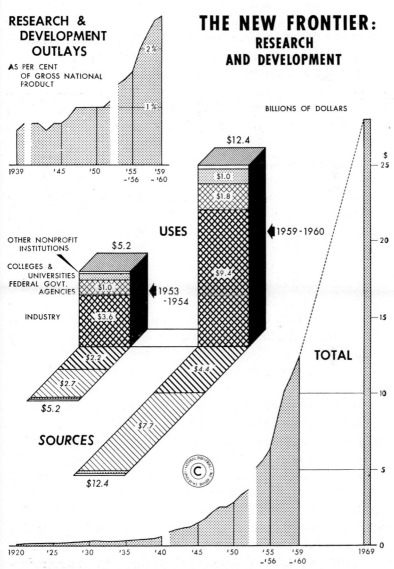

Figure 6. Research and development expenditures.

missile and space research). About 16% of the total was spent by electrical equipment producers, and something less than 10% each by the machinery and chemicals industries. Do we have, or can we develop, the proper incentives to induce expanded research outlays of this dimension in the future? Another of the problem areas of the 1960's may stem from our having largely exploited the technological breakthroughs of World War II. Growth in the next decade would thus be far more dependent upon new ideas and techniques now germinating in our research laboratories.

Productivity Projections

Research outlays and capital spending are among the primary determinants of a nation's productivity. What of productivity in the 1960's? Over the past 50 years, output per man-hour in the private economy has advanced at about 2.3% per annum (Figure 7). In the postwar years, the rate has risen to 3.1% per annum. Much but not all of this improvement can be traced to a spectacular increase in agriculture, which has been undergoing a technological revolution of its own. Even excluding agriculture, however, the rate of rise in output per man-hour has shifted significantly upward.

In its most recent projection, the Bureau of Labor Statistics forecasts an aggregate rate of increase slightly lower than the postwar average, but with all of the decline in the agricultural sector. Even among specialists there is a broad range of opinion on the productivity outlook, some maintaining that at least a modest further acceleration should be expected, others arguing that the postwar rate benefited from the exceptional circumstances and can hardly be maintained over the next decade.

In the postwar years, output per man-hour in the manufacturing sector has risen by about 3.7% per annum, if only production workers are taken into account, and 2.9% per annum on the basis of all employment. The difference reflects the fact that nonproduction workers' employment in manufacturing has risen considerably more rapidly than that of production workers. In nonmanufactur-

PROJECTING PRODUCTIVITY: TRENDS IN OUTPUT PER MAN-HOUR

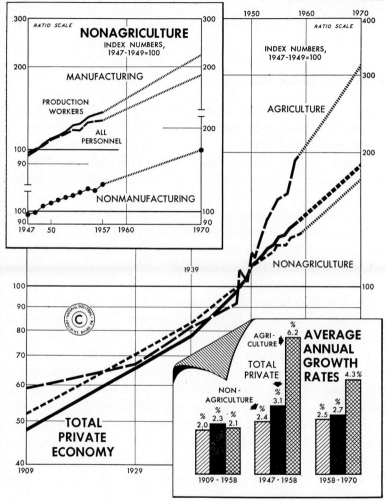

Figure 7. Output per man-hour and average annual growth rates.

ing, nonagricultural industries, output per hour has been rising at about 2.3% per annum. Projections of productivity at these rates of growth suggest that by 1970 output per hour in manufacturing industries may be about 85% greater than in the early postwar years; in other nonagricultural industries, it may be about two thirds greater.

POTENTIAL YIELDS, 1970

After this brief review of probable human and capital inputs, we are in a position to combine the various factors affecting national output and determine their potential yield in 1970. The long-term projections of national output to which reference was made initially are essentially an exercise in combining a limited number of assumptions. These assumptions include output per man-hour, length of the workweek, size of the workforce and volume of unemployment. A variety of combinations of these assumptions are shown in Figure 8, together with the results they yield for national output in 1970. While the combinations presented far from exhaust the possibilities, the range of the findings is strikingly wide. The $200 billion gap between the lowest and highest result is, in fact, about equal to the gap between the present level of output and the lowest forecast for 1970.

The highest projection assumes continuation of the postwar rate of increase in output per man-hour and of the present length of the workweek, the "high" labor-force estimate devised by the Bureau of the Census, and an unemployment rate of 3%. It yields a gross national product in 1970 of $860 billion (in 1959 dollars). The lowest of the projections assumes a rise in output per hour at the long-term rate, a decline in the workweek at its postwar rate, the lowest of three labor-force forecasts by the Census Bureau and a 5% unemployment rate. It yields little more than $660 billion.

Particularly significant is the impact of changes in each of the four sets of assumptions on the total result. In the ranges used here, a shift in the labor-force assumption or the unemployment assumption yields differences in results of around 2%. Changing

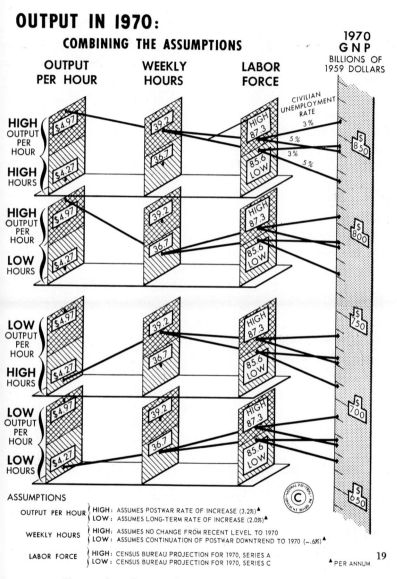

Figure 8. Estimated 1970 gross national product.

the workweek assumption yields a difference of 7%. The difference in results yielded by the postwar productivity rate on the one hand, or the long-term rate on the other, is fully 16%. The trends in productivity and in the length of the workweek thus dominate the prospective growth in national output during the 1960's.

The embarrassingly broad range of these potentials highlights the extreme importance of the productivity assumption. Switching from the first productivity assumption to the second yields a difference in the gross national product, or $110 to $120 billion by 1970. This again illustrates how much the rate of economic growth depends on developments in technology and even more in point the rate at which these developments will be stimulated by and translated into investment.

My emphasis thus far has been almost exclusively upon product and investment rather than upon markets in the next decade. It is time now to correct this lack of balance. The market implications of cumulative national growth over a ten-year period are very dramatic indeed. Assuming a national output in 1970 of about $800 billion would mean that roughly $300 billion more of goods and services would be taken off the market place by consumer, business and government in 1970 than in 1959 (Figure 9). On the further assumption that these markets will maintain their relative size, the accompanying charts portray these increases in market demand and what they would mean for each major sector of the economy.

AN ADDED MARKET DEMAND OF
$300 BILLION

More specifically the assumptions employed are: (1) that the total labor force will reach the higher of the Census projections for 1970; (2) that unemployment will amount to 4% of the civilian labor force; (3) that average weekly hours of work will continue to decline at the postwar rate; and (4) that output per man-hour

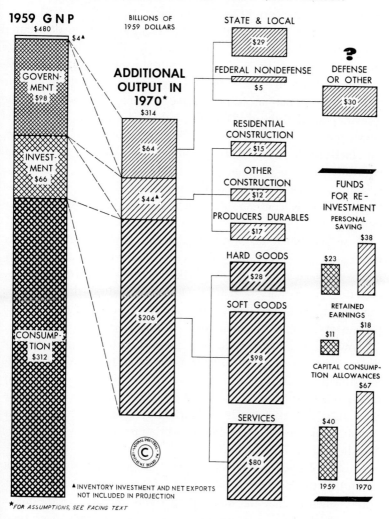

Figure 9. The projection of U.S. national output in 1970.

will continue to rise at the postwar rate. These assumptions yield a national product of $796 billion (in 1959 dollars) for 1970. This is an increase of 66% and implies a net addition of a little over $300 billion to the current level of output.

The addition to the total volume of output is then distributed among the various types of expenditures in 1970, on the assumption that the relative structure of expenditures will remain approximately as it was in 1959. While this procedure is hardly more than a first approximation, it puts some striking dimensions on the growth potential ahead. Thus the indicated increase for personal consumption is equal to the total of all consumer outlays in 1946; the increase in demand for producer durables is roughly the equivalent of the addition of an entire industry the size of the present automobile industry; the combined increase in construction demand is considerably larger than the present residential building industry.

These and other increments to demand assume a proportionate increase in the requirements of defense. To the extent that developments between now and 1970 make such an increase in defense spending unnecessary, a portion of the allotted $30 billion would presumably become available for distribution to other forms of private and public spending or investment.

Shown at the lower right is a proportionate reconstruction of the saving flows required to finance the projected levels of private investment. By 1970, the annual volume of personal saving may be approaching $40 billion, and the retained earnings of corporations may be nearing $20 billion. Most strikingly, capital consumption allowances (including noncorporate as well as corporate) may be nearing $70 billion.

The use of the relative disposition of output currently as a guide for cutting the 1970 pie is the crudest of approximations. However, history suggests that the broad proportions allocated to the major sectors of the American economy change only slowly over time, except for periods of war and severe depression. Even after such abnormal developments, the proportions appear to revert to something like a long-term norm.

SECULAR TRENDS IN OUTPUT
AND EXPENDITURES

With isolated exceptions attributable to war and severe depression, the underlying composition of American output and expenditures has tended to change only gradually, in a long evolutionary process. The distribution of output among goods, construction and services, and its allocation between the two major private sectors was not radically different in the late 1950's from what it was in the late 1920's (Figure 10). The burden of proof thus rests with those who expect a dramatic alteration in basic distribution and production patterns over the next ten years.

One exception to this slow evolution has been a pronounced expansion in government's share of total national expenditures. Even here, however, the expansion has largely reflected the growth of federal spending for defense. Other, slower changes in the structure since 1929 are: construction expenditures have risen faster than expenditures for goods and services; investment expenditures have risen more rapidly than consumption expenditures; hard-goods output has advanced relatively to soft-goods output; and the rate of investment in machinery and equipment by business has risen somewhat more rapidly than its investment in construction.

As measures of postwar rather than long-term trends, the value of services output has advanced more rapidly than total output, and government expenditures more rapidly than private expenditures. Consumption spending and investment spending have changed about proportionately; hard-goods output has outpaced soft-goods production; federal outlays since the end of the Korean War have subsided as a percentage of total government outlays. Actual construction outlays of business have increased more than equipment outlays.

The comparisons are in current dollars and thus reflect relative changes in prices. In particular, the rising share of construction in the postwar economy is influenced by the relatively rapid rise in construction costs; and the rising share of services reflects a

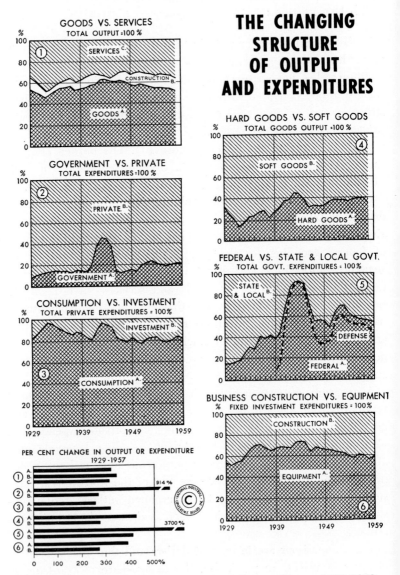

Figure 10. Changes in U.S. output and expenditures, 1929-1959.

persistent uptrend in rentals from the artificially low, controlled rents of the war and early postwar years.

INNOVATIONS AND NEW PRODUCT DEVELOPMENT

Beneath this secular stability, however, there will again occur sweeping, seething changes in internal composition of the major sector accounts as new products and some markets multiply with others not growing at all or subsiding. These are the localized dislocations that have always existed within the relatively unaltered allocations account of the national product.

While the broad structure of the economy has changed only gradually over the long term, there has been plenty of room, and evidently plenty of incentive, for local revolutions within the evolving totals. In the postwar years, the quickening technological pace has left its mark in a series of dramatically growing individual industries and products. The list of such products could be extended to great length; a selection of some of the more important industrial growth trends of the past 15 years is shown in Figure 11. It is noteworthy that these come largely from the electronics and chemicals sectors, where outlays for research and development have risen extremely rapidly. One of the great challenges of the 1960's is the preservation and strengthening of the incentives that initiated such revolutions.

Postwar socioeconomic changes have also taken on dramatic proportions. The total population has increased about 25% over the past dozen years. But the number of families with incomes of over $6,000 (in 1959 dollars) has about doubled, the coverage of private pension plans has almost tripled, the volume of air travel has more than quadrupled, and the number of OASDI beneficiaries has increased almost sevenfold. In the past seven years, the number of shareowners in United States corporations has about doubled.

Rapid change in the production mix, and in the social characteristics of the American economy, has thus occurred within a generally stable institutional framework. Innovation and social change will doubtless continue to alter and enrich the mixture.

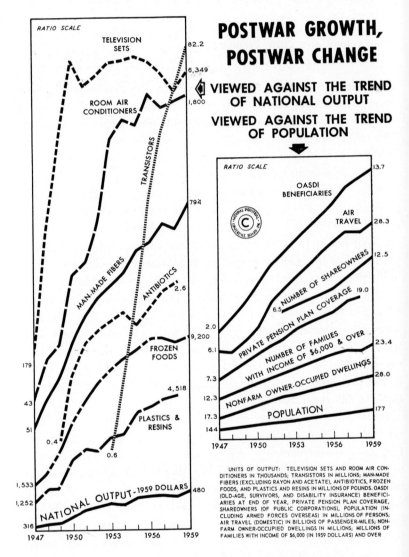

Figure 11. Postwar growth and change in U.S. output and population trends.

Sweeping Demographic Change

Dramatic demographic change will also affect market patterns in the decade ahead. As the wave of young adult population approaches crest in the late 1960's, the household and family formation curves will be drastically altered. In 1959, United States households numbered 51 million, roughly 8 million more than in 1950. Throughout the decade of the 1950's, the household formation rate fluctuated erratically around an average of about 860,000 a year. Available forecasts for the 1960's suggest a rising trend in the rate of household formation during the decade, but the estimates cover a wide range. The high forecast for 1970 envisages 63 million families; the low forecast calls for 59 million (Figure 12).

The case for an ascending rate of household formation in the Sixties, perhaps considerably sharper than is suggested by the five-year averages is clear enough on demographic grounds. Household formation is normally closely correlated with the rate of marriages. Statistically, marriages depend on the number of women of marriageable age, and this number is in for an unprecedented expansion in the 1960's as still another consequence of the birth-rate wave shown in an earlier chart. The annual number of marriages at the end of the 1960's may well be fully 50% higher than currently. If so, the "high" forecast of household formation could be much nearer the mark than the "low" forecast.

Since the 1920's, the number of housing starts and the rate of increase of automobiles in use have been related to the rate of household formation. This relationship is quite precise for housing, and less so for automobiles in use (which were also profoundly affected by depression, war, and postwar rebuilding of the car stock). Considerable future benefits will accrue to both of these markets from a high and rising rate of household formation over the next decade.

For the same reason, the late 1960's may see mounting pressures for sharply higher rates of spending by state and local governments for the facilities associated with rising family and household formation.

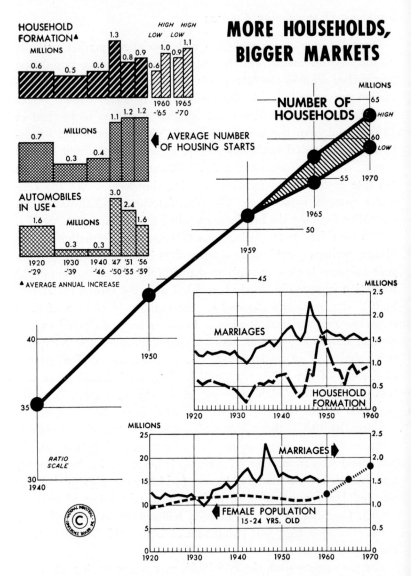

Figure 12. Housing starts and increase in automobile use versus household formation.

Economists as custodians of the long-term trend are congenitally full-time worriers. Glowing as are the economic potentials of the 1960's, the economic fraternity is deeply concerned about the many problem areas already visible as we enter the 1960's—as well as some just looming over the horizon. Many of these are analyzed at length in the commentaries that follow this general review. One such major problem area is the wage-cost-price dilemma.

The Wage-Cost-Price Dilemma

The United States money supply rose precipitously as wartime deficits became monetized. Initially the network of wartime controls over prices and wages tended to suppress the inflationary consequences of the rise in money supply. When the war ended, the relationship of money supply to the value of national output was about as high as at any time on record.

A persistent economic trend of the postwar years has been the gradual unraveling of this monetary imbalance. While there was a further moderate increase in the money supply, the value of output entered on a steep and almost uninterrupted ascent, reflecting increased production of goods and services and a pronounced rise in prices. The ratio of money supply to GNP has drifted gradually back to about the levels prevailing in the first three decades of the century (Figure 13).

As the value of output has approached a more normal relationship to the money supply, interest rates have worked their way irregularly upward from the artificially low levels of the war and early postwar years. At the same time, the rate of price inflation, which has moved in a series of well-defined waves, has gradually assumed diminishing proportions.

At the start of the 1960's the monetary environment of the United States economy had largely emerged from the inflationary excesses that characterized the 1940's and most of the 1950's. With the exception of the service area, prices themselves have been stable across a broad front for much of the past two years.

The monetary causes of inflation thus appear to have been largely

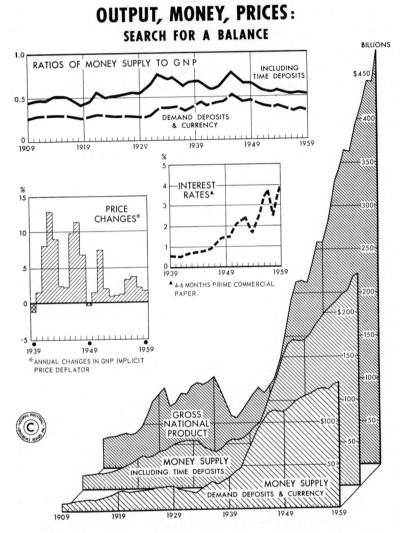

Figure 13. Ratio of money supply to gross national product, 1909-1959.

eradicated as the new decade begins; the exuberant, if unhealthy, atmosphere of inflation has departed, at least temporarily. One of the sharpest challenges of the 1960's may be the readjustment of patterns of costs and prices, and of collective bargaining, to a stabilized monetary environment.

AGRICULTURAL SURPLUSES AND SUBSIDIES

A second problem area, as yet unresolved, is to be found in agriculture. American agriculture has taken some giant strides toward efficiency and prosperity in the past 25 years. Since the mid-1930's, total agricultural output has been rising at about 2¼% per annum, while farm employment has been declining at about the same rate. Real product per man-hour in agriculture has been rising by better than 4% annually in the past 25 years; in the postwar years, the rate of increase has been fully 6%. Today, the output of a farm worker supports 25 persons, compared with ten persons in the mid-1930's (Figure 14).

Contributing to this spectacular increase in productive efficiency have been massive mechanization, integration into fewer but larger farms, more intensive use of much-improved fertilizers, better feeds and better seeds. There is little indication of any marked slowing in the dramatic rates of change in agriculture over the next decade: agricultural economists expect the rise in farm output and the decline in employment to continue at least through 1970.

In the course of the agricultural revolution shown in Figure 14, the farmer has been the recipient of an extraordinary federal subsidy, accompanied by the inevitable federal controls. Price supports encouraged levels of output for many agricultural commodities (notably wheat, cotton and corn) substantially in excess of real demand. The resulting surpluses now held by the Commodity Credit Corporation total $9 billion. Nearly 70% of the estimated $5.1 billion expenditures for agriculture and agricultural resources in the federal budget for the current fiscal year reflects the cost of farm price support and related programs.

Maintaining the pace of the agricultural revolution and the gen-

AGRICULTURE IN TRANSITION

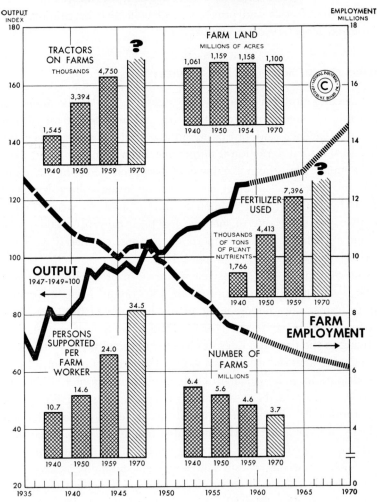

Figure 14. Farm employment and output, 1935-1970.

erally prosperous level of the farm sector while at the same time minimizing the subsidy costs, the surpluses and the controls over agriculture constitutes another of the challenges of the 1960's.

BALANCE-OF-PAYMENT DIFFICULTIES

Most urgent currently of these problem areas is the deterioration of our international balance of payments. Not only is this one of our most serious economic problems, but it may very well become a major political issue in the years immediately ahead. How will we as a people resolve the attrition of our gold reserves that have now reached disturbingly low levels? In the past 15 years our exports of goods and services have considerably exceeded our imports (Figure 15). The excess was particularly great in the early postwar years, in 1951 and in 1956-1957, reflecting economic aid, the Korean War and the temporary closing of the Suez canal respectively. Our economic relations with the rest of the world continue to suggest that we held a strong if not dominant position in world markets. Even so we have had a deficit in our balance of payments (as measured by the outflow of gold and liquid assets) every year in the last decade with the exception of 1957.

In 1958, as our commodity exports subsided, our imports continued firm (they have usually tended to decline in recession years). In 1959 our exports failed to rise while our imports advanced sharply, reflecting a rising tide of finished manufactures entering the country. (In 1959, finished goods accounted for 35% of our total imports, as compared with 17% in 1947.) The pronounced alteration in the trade balance between 1957 and 1959 was the major influence in a rapid increase in net outflow of dollars and gold. This gold and dollars outflow has focused attention much more closely on our economic relations with the rest of the world.

We remain a substantial net investor in the world economy, and our income from investment abroad is several times the income from foreign investments here. At the same time it is clear that respectable competitors for the world market, as well as for our own domestic market, have arisen in Europe and Asia. In this area,

THE U.S. IN THE WORLD

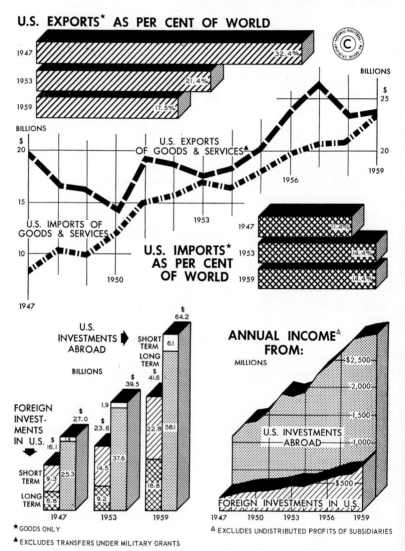

Figure 15. U.S. exports and imports, 1947-1959.

too, the decade of the 1960's contains a challenge not present in the 1950's: many of the nations we have helped to their feet through aid are now ready and willing to trade. This imposes a new set of restraints on the American economy. We cannot legislate a trade balance, or inflate world demand for our goods by expanding our domestic money supply. Efficiency and competitive costs are the ultimate tools for defending our position in the world economy.

This again serves to underscore the emphasis given at the outset to this review, namely the desirability of providing greater tax incentives for investment in the 1960's. Such investment will not only contribute toward restraining the wage-cost-price push at home, but through improving this nation's technological superiority would help to redress the lack of balance in our world trade position.

In closing, in terms of the SEC prospectus, it should be understood that the economic arithmetic computed here for 1970 is meant to be illustrative. The statistics are used solely as a means of describing the economic environment in which the decade begins, its changing character and the trends inherited from the past and their promise for the future. No attempt is made to provide a forecast in terms of specific dimensions.

The models drawn give no assurance that the economic potentials of the next decade will be reached automatically. They do indicate that there is gold in the far-off hills of 1970. But the road is likely to be strewn with as many casualties as in any earlier gold rush. We must assume, too, that the golden 1960's will wend its way through a few recessions as has been true of the decades past. The potentials of the next decade are dramatic. The initial assay is high; the actual yield should be rich and rewarding, provided we respond, as I believe we will, to the challenges and the problems of the 1960's, particularly the creation of an economic environment conducive to an accelerated rate of private investment.

MARTIN R. GAINSBRUGH
Chief Economist
National Industrial Conference Board

Table of Contents

xlvii

INTERNATIONAL
COMMODITIES:
A World
Supply-and-
Demand
Outlook

Charles A. Wight
CHAIRMAN

THREE KEY AREAS:
Growth Rates and
Trade Potentials

Robert J. Dixson
CHAIRMAN

Part Two: **OUR DOMESTIC MARKETS: The Demands Ahead**

CONSUMER
MARKETS
OF THE FUTURE

M. C. Mumford

CHAIRMAN

THE LONG-TERM
BUSINESS
OUTLOOK:
President's Panel

Robert E. Wilson
CHAIRMAN

Part Three: **TECHNOLOGY AND ITS IMPACT: The Promise and the Problems**

THE
TECHNOLOGICAL
HORIZON

G. W. Chapman
CHAIRMAN

PRODUCTIVITY
AND WAGES:
The Outlook
and
the Implications

Donald F. Valley
CHAIRMAN

ABSORBING
TECHNOLOGICAL
CHANGE:
The Employment
Problem Ahead

J. E. Jonsson
CHAIRMAN

Part Four: **FINANCING NATIONAL GROWTH**

CONSUMER

FINANCE

IN THE 1960'S

L. W. Lundell
CHAIRMAN

FINANCING
BUSINESS
IN THE 1960'S

Murray Shields
CHAIRMAN

Part One

AMERICA AND THE WORLD

THE INTERNATIONAL OUTLOOK

E. V. Huggins
CHAIRMAN

1

Martin R. Gainsbrugh
CHIEF ECONOMIST
NATIONAL INDUSTRIAL CONFERENCE BOARD

Introduction

IN NO SECTOR of its economy has the United States experienced such changes as in its international economic relations in the past 15 years. Further, this area promises to remain in ferment in the decade ahead. Even before the war terminated, plans were laid for the establishment of two large financial institutions, designed to meet the major expected economic problems of the postwar era. These two institutions, the International Monetary Fund and the International Bank for Reconstruction and Development, required, along with other institutions, an investment by the federal government of nearly $5 billion up to early 1960. These two institutions constitute only a small number of the various banks, finance corporations, loan funds and the like, to which the United States has been a huge contributor. Our membership in these institutions constitutes one of many manifestations of a growing awareness and willingness of this country to partake in those activities designed to facilitate world trade and investment.

In addition, the United States engaged in the postwar years in a huge program of economic aid at a cost of $34 billion. This was undertaken first for the purpose of re-establishing the war-devastated European economy and then was shifted to aid the growth of underdeveloped nations of the world. The essence of all this was the shipping of goods for reconstruction and development of foreign nations without expectation of repayment.

3

During the early part of this period we enjoyed a growing share of world manufacturing production and trade. Because of the inability of Europe to supply manufactured goods, those nations seeking to buy had to turn to the United States. This was true even of most of the nations of Latin America where war devastation was not a factor. The gold and dollar reserves that these countries built up during the war years were spent buying the goods that they couldn't purchase earlier. As a result, U. S. manufacturers enjoyed a swift growth in exports in the early postwar years without serious competitors.

Starting mainly in 1953, this easy, temporary advantage steadily gave way to the re-establishment of European industrial capacity. American manufacturers began to feel the pinch, first of shrinking overseas markets and then of competition within their own borders.

The continuation of rapid industrial growth in Europe and the increasing difficulty of U. S. producers in foreign markets are important factors in the most recent outflow of gold and liquid dollar balances. Our balance of payments, at one time so favorable, has been reversed so as to constitute a serious threat to the nation's financial structure—and the end is not yet in sight. Shrinkage of our international reserves and the accumulation of liquid balances by foreign nations may well constitute a grave problem through most of the 1960's.

A new element which has not yet had an opportunity to make itself felt completely in international economic relations is the formation of several regional blocs throughout the world. Of these the European Common Market is the most prominent as well as the most ambitious in its aims. Of growing importance also is the newly formed Free Trade Association consisting of Great Britain, Sweden, Norway, Denmark, Portugal, Austria and Switzerland. Others, particularly in Latin America, have been planned and are in various stages of development. The precise impact of these regional organizations upon the United States is not entirely clear. From one point of view they clearly represent forces that will intensify the struggle of United States exporters for world markets. From another, they may provide the needed institutional stimulus to growth in member countries and hence become a profitable market for our exports and investment.

At the same time that the United States has been meeting growing competition abroad, its imports have been increasing. These imports represent both shifts in personal consumption and the growing relative shortage of raw material within the borders of the United States to meet its huge industrial requirements. For many of its raw materials, this country must now look beyond its borders to supply its needs. The minerals output of the United States, for example, which comprised 52% of the world total in 1948 (excluding USSR) shrank to approximately 40% by 1958.

This background of international developments led the Board to bring together this group of distinguished experts to appraise our country's international position currently and in the 1960's. Of the many facets of international economic affairs, three are examined in depth: First, our export-import trade, as well as direct investment, and the significance of both for domestic industries; second, the world outlook for important raw materials; third, and last, the outlook for selected areas of the world of special significance to the United States.

2

E. V. Huggins

**VICE PRESIDENT AND CHAIRMAN OF THE
EXECUTIVE COMMITTEE
WESTINGHOUSE ELECTRIC CORPORATION**

The International Outlook

EVERYONE who has given much thought to the international outlook—many people have not—has a firm opinion about it. I don't know of anybody who is lukewarm one way or the other. The problems that exist are complicated by a great many imponderables and uncontrollable factors, insofar as our country's participation in world trade is concerned. These include varying costs and prices; different types and levels of national economies; varying types of government supports, open or otherwise; the Soviet trade threat; and present government lending policies. We also have the problem of the dollar deficit in our balance of payments—a matter of considerable significance, although in terms of foreign trade only one of the factors that must be considered.

Then we have the fact to which my friend Professor Vernon may take exception: our foreign trade policies are treated as part of our over-all foreign policy and are under the control of the State Department. This Department has no real responsibility for and, in the opinion of many, has no regard for or understanding of the effects of its policies on the nation's domestic economy.

Another factor has been the opening of the St. Lawrence Seaway. I understand this permits the laying down of foreign steel in Chicago at less than competitive domestic prices. We also have the

Common Market in Europe and regional blocs in other areas; a very good job of selling these institutions has been done in the United States.

There are, of course, many other factors that becloud the future. We have experts here to consider these international problems and maybe they can pull out one or two worms so that those of us who have to make a living in this area can catch a fish or two.

3

Emile Despres
VISITING RESEARCH SCHOLAR
CARNEGIE ENDOWMENT FOR INTERNATIONAL PEACE

The U.S. Share in World Trade: Underlying Factors

IN DISCUSSING the outlook for the United States' share of world trade, I shall deal chiefly with the export side, leaving the import side to Professor Vernon. The first point is this: it has been exceedingly difficult in the past few years to get a sober appreciation of the underlying trend of our efforts, for the reason that, to an exceptional degree, U. S exports from quarter to quarter and from year to year have shown exceptionally wide fluctuations for essentially temporary reasons. The result is that there was, I believe, exaggerated pessimism about American export prospects last year.

In 1957 for a combination of special reasons, of which the Suez crisis was the most important, our exports were extremely high and, as was to be expected, the drop was extremely sharp. In the first half of 1959 our exports, on a seasonally adjusted basis, were running at the annual rate of $15.7 billion per annum as compared with $19.5 billion in the year of 1957. This drop of almost $4 billion a year led to a great deal of concern both about our balance-of-payments position and about our general position in world markets.

I have the impression that the concern about this has abated a good deal during the past few months, owing, I think, to the behavior of exports in that period. They seem to be running currently in 1960 at the annual rate of a little over $18.5 billion annually, which, you see, is quite a comeback. But just as the pessimism before was excessive, the calmer attitude today may be too much influenced by short-term factors.

Looking at the recovery in exports since the middle of 1959 one finds a number of temporary factors: First, our sales of jet aircraft have been large. Second, exports of agricultural commodities for special reasons have been unusually heavy. Third, the business cycle has operated in our favor to some extent. The expansion of demand abroad, and particularly in Western Europe, has outrun the expansion of domestic demand. The American economy seems to have been moving more or less sideways, whereas the Western European economy has been going up. The effect of this is an increase in American exports of steel, steel scrap and a good many machinery items.

If one abstracts all of these temporary factors, I don't think our exports would be running as high as $18.5 billion a year.

I am at this point reminded of a story told by a friend of mine who was a student of the late Lord Keynes. He was asked by Keynes to write a paper on the outlook for interest rates. He wrote a paper on the outlook for the next three months. When Keynes saw the paper, he said, "If economists can say anything at all, they can say something about the outlook over the next ten years, but they certainly can't say anything about the next three months."

I would like to proceed to the subject I was really assigned— namely, the fundamental factors and the long-term outlook. And for this purpose one ought to take a longer historical perspective.

The share of our exports in total world trade was a little over 16%, or about one sixth, in 1959. This was, surprisingly enough, only moderately lower than the share in 1950, which amounted to 17.6%.

In 1959 we had a somewhat larger share than in 1938 and about the same share as in 1928. And actually, if one takes the figures for the first quarter of 1960, our share of world exports today is fairly close to 18%, an apparently far-from-depressing picture.

Our exports of manufactures, as a percentage of world trade in manufactures, is higher than it was before World War II or in the 1920's. It is appreciably higher than the prewar period. This percentage has, of course, been declining during the 1950's, as one would expect in view of industrial developments in Western Europe and in Japan. The fact ought to be kept in mind in interpreting these comparisons that our exports today are bolstered by a sizable amount of foreign aid.

The important matter, however, concerns the underlying trends. What of the longer-term future?

The first thing I'd like to say about this is that we have not been pricing ourselves out of world markets as this term is usually understood. I think the people who say this usually mean that, because of domestic inflationary pressures in the United States, the rise in the prices of our goods has impaired our competitive strength.

If the general price indexes for the United States are compared with the movements of the price level as a whole in other industrial and manufacturing countries, it will be found that inflation has been at least as great elsewhere as it has been here. In this sense, we have not been pricing ourselves out of world markets.

What has been happening is that price relationships in the United States have been altered in comparison with the corresponding movements in Western European countries, particularly since the middle 1950's. The prices of machinery and metal products have increased in the United States in relation to prices in general; the opposite has been occurring abroad.

In a number of manufacturing lines the technological gap between the United States and other manufacturing countries has been closing or at least narrowing for a number of products. There are really two significant things to consider in examining the outlook for American exports: What is happening to our underlying competitive strength in various lines of products as influenced by productivity changes here and abroad? What is happening, in other words, to what economists call the structure of comparative advantages? And, secondly, what is happening to trade barriers?

To answer the first question—the main trend is that advanced industrial technology is spreading. The really puzzling thing in comparing American and European industry is not why the technological gap is narrowing, but why it persisted so long in the past. Now it has been narrowing, especially in the machinery and metal products lines. There are a number of lines where this hasn't taken hold yet.

When I talk about the spreading of advanced industrial technology I mean not only what is happening in other advanced industrial countries—Western Europe, Japan—but also the industrialization of the underdeveloped countries.

I think this is a long-term trend which is bound to affect our relative competitive position and the structure of our exports. We are going to continue to have an intensification of competition in a number of manufacturing lines. The American manufacturers who are exposed to this may not be fond of it, but from the point of view of the economy as a whole it is a salutary force. The effect in the past few years has been basically and very powerfully anti-inflationary in the United States: it has injected a growing cost consciousness in American industry; caused a re-examination of price policies; injected a new note in the wage negotiations and, please note, it has been an important influence in inducing the large equipment expenditures for modernization purposes which are planned this year. In other words, it has been in a number of aspects a healthy spur, even if not an altogether pleasant one.

An implication of this increased competition is undoubtedly going to be that our manufactured exports will tend to be more and more concentrated in highly advanced technological products, such as jet aircraft and computers—keeping ahead of the game. Even in routine things we are likely to feel increasingly the pressure of intensified competition abroad.

In some respects our most sophisticated product is what is vaguely called our know-how, technology and organization. It seems to me that our production of and sale of capital goods to underdeveloped countries can be very greatly increased if we combine these with a number of other important facilities—managerial training services, repair facilities, and so on. I don't think the opportunities here have been exploited to the full.

While developments abroad have caused a narrowing of the technological gap in a number of manufacturing lines, there is one extremely important field where our productivity has been advancing for the past quarter century on the whole a great deal more rapidly than productivity abroad. If trade followed the lines of comparative advantage, we would have a booming export market in this field.

I am referring, of course, to agricultural products. One of the main reasons for our balance-of-payments difficulties today is that the natural adjustment of trade to changing competitive strength is being inhibited in the case of agricultural products, not only by some of our own domestic agricultural policies which we try to offset by export subsidies, but especially by agricultural protectionism abroad. Here is one point on which the United States ought to make a very strong stand, however embarrassing it may be for us to do so, since we have always argued in trade negotiations that agriculture should be an exception to trade liberalization. Nevertheless it will be extremely difficult for us to get anywhere unless we take this kind of a stand on the matter of agricultural protectionism abroad. One cannot stress the importance of this too greatly.

As to the matter of trade barriers to manufacturers, there has been a substantial liberalization and relaxation of import quotas abroad in the past few years. So far as manufactured goods are concerned, apart from agricultural products and coal, one can say that by the end of 1961 the import quota type of restriction of these American exports will be almost entirely gone. This has already happened to a large extent. The full benefit has not yet been reflected in our export trade, so that this factor is favorable only to a limited extent.

The tariff picture, on the other hand, is less encouraging. During the period of world dollar shortage we did reduce our tariffs on European manufacturers considerably. I think one can say we are today a moderate-tariff country. There haven't been any reductions of importance in our import duties since about 1952, but the subsequent expansion of our imports has been in part the result of these earlier tariff reductions.

Owing to the change in the United States balance-of-payments position, the shoe is now on the other foot—regrettably, of course, since one would like to refer to the European Common Market as a factor in the direction of trade liberalization. It remains to be seen whether this will be the case, whether the common external tariff around the Common Market will be high or low. I have tried to look into the recently announced acceleration of the movement toward the common tariff. The publicity that has been given to this is misleading. Without going into the technical details, what it amounts to is this:

There will be quite sizable increases in the Belgian and Dutch tariffs against outside goods at the end of this year and a sizable increase in the German tariff at the end of this year. There will be quite modest reductions in the French and Italian tariffs. On balance at a time when their balance-of-payments position should justify a rather substantial lowering of external tariffs, a new net barrier to imports into Western Europe is actually being imposed.

In conclusion, I want to say something about the possible consequences of the Paris Summit fiasco.

First, if war fears should become pronounced, one would obviously expect inventory accumulation. This will affect both our exports and our imports, particularly our imports. If this should happen—and I certainly hope it won't—it would provide a golden opportunity for the liquidation of some of our top-heavy government stockpiles if there should be a rush of private speculative buying.

The other point is that an increase in the rate of military spending may occur now. If it does, it is likely to be a larger increase in military spending here than in Western Europe, and the effect on our balance of payments would be adverse.

4

Dr. Raymond Vernon

PROFESSOR OF INTERNATIONAL TRADE AND INVESTMENT
GRADUATE SCHOOL OF BUSINESS
HARVARD UNIVERSITY

Trends and Implications of Import Competition in the U.S. Market

THIS SUBJECT of import competition is always one calculated to stir men's souls.

Today our reasons for being uneasy about import competition are perhaps a little stronger and more obvious than they have been at any time in the recent history of the United States.

For one thing, the world has shrunk considerably. The possibility of bringing textiles or clothing or electronic products or toys from any corner of the globe on a short pipeline with good timing for a prospective market in the United States has increased manyfold over the situation which existed, say, a couple of decades ago.

For another, the possibility of quickly determining the feasibility of setting up a textile mill in Liberia or an aluminum plant in Nigeria is much greater. The lag between planning and execution is shorter and the possibility that a new source of cotton cloth or white metal may appear in a few years instead of several decades is greater.

Finally, of course, there is the problem of the return of the Soviet bloc into international markets. Here is a monolithic trade adversary of a new sort. We haven't discovered a set of rules in the game or a means of protection which satisfies us. And so we worry.

Anyone who tries to appraise what these developments mean for United States imports has to make a projection about United States

14

import policy. My assumption is that United States import policy will muddle along at the liberal end of the spectrum; that we will not revert to a very high order of protectionism; that we will continue to cling to a variety of protectionist techniques which we now employ; and in general that our behavior with respect to import policy will not be very different from what it is now. I find myself at home with this assumption, partly because I fail to see the sharp distinction between the Republicans and the Democrats in trade policy which once existed. There are differences within each party, to be sure, but the net effect of the balance of forces is that each of the parties follows a kind of restrained liberalism with respect to imports.

Now, if you will allow me this assumption, then perhaps there are some things that I can say about a likely pattern of future trade.

First, let me go back to the Soviet bloc and say one word very briefly about this, leaving the bulk of the discussion to Mr. Schwartz.

My own expectation is that Soviet exports to the United States don't really constitute a serious problem for us. The Soviet re-entry into world markets on a somewhat increased scale may represent a problem in other countries but not, I think, in the United States proper.

One means by which the Soviet bloc could conceivably affect the United States' internal economy is by dumping primary products in other markets, and thus depressing prices without necessarily exporting directly to the United States. My own assumption is that the Soviet Union is not engaged in a devious plot to wreck capitalist markets in primary products; that she is engaged in some flatfooted and clumsy selling from time to time; but that by and large she has patched up her errors, as she has seen them, as rapidly as she could, once the errors became visible. The latest step of the Soviet Union in joining forces with that archetype of capitalism, the DeBeers diamond syndicate, suggests that the U.S.S.R. will sell at the best price it can get. That is a very short statement on a very long subject, but Mr. Schwartz can either supplement or demur on this point.

Now let us turn to the role of the underdeveloped countries with respect to imports on the part of the United States. Here I see rather considerable change. First, on the assumption of a generally liberal United States trade policy, I anticipate a modest increase in United States imports of raw materials from underdeveloped countries—lead, zinc and petroleum particularly, but others as well. To be sure, these imports will be kept under control and some variant on the lead and zinc quotas may continue to exist. But under the pressure of internal exhaustion of raw materials, more particularly the pressure of rising internal costs, I expect to see some modest liberalization of the imports of a considerable variety of raw materials which are competitive with United States raw materials.

Where I see the exciting change is in the manufacturing field— exciting in more than one sense with regard to many U. S. manufacturers. Textiles are the prototype of a much larger group of commodities which the underdeveloped areas of the world are going to be in a position to export. What is it about textiles that makes them exportable?

In the first place, for many types of textile operations, one can take the technology of a developed country and transfer it bodily into an underdeveloped area without too much concern for the fact that the environment external to the textile plant may be of a low order of development. This isn't true of every type of manufacturing, of course. In most manufacturing processes it is essential to have a fairly well-developed environment to operate in order to draw on necessary elements such as a predictable source of power and transportation system. With textiles this is not true to the same extent as, for example, it would be for some complex chemical product.

There is another aspect about textiles which makes them and a great many similar products a natural medium for underdeveloped areas. This is the fact that the processes inside the factory are highly standardized and repetitive and demand a minimum of training for most workers.

The third aspect of textiles is that labor costs are still a significant part of the total cost of these products, even though they are standardized in their operation. With the high degree of price competition in the textiles field, the producer is anxious to find a location which would reduce his labor cost. And while this is not true of all products, it is particularly true of textiles and many other items in which price competition is severe.

The last characteristic one has to look for in order to identify the products of which I am speaking is the question of transport cost for the finished product. This cost must be of little significance. To put it a little differently, the product has to be high in value per pound so that the cost of moving the goods from the under-developed producing area to the industrialized markets is not great. We can develop quite a list of products which fit this criterion.

Apply the four criteria and I suspect you can identify a list of products which the underdeveloped industrialized areas of the world will be exporting in a much larger quantity in the next decade. From the point of view of the United States these are par-ticularly sensitive products. They are products which, in many cases, have been involved in internal shifts in U. S. movements from the high-wage North to the lower-wage South, because firms in the United States have been responding precisely to the set of pressures I have described, the need to reduce their labor cost. Some of the industries which have been moving South will, I sus-pect, be moving to the Philippines, Ghana and Algeria, shipping their products to the United States.

We must not assume, however, that there are no trade advan-tages for the United States in these developments. The whole pur-pose of the stepped-up exports of the developing countries will be precisely to buy more goods from the industrialized areas, includ-ing the United States. The critical question for our country, therefore, will be whether it can remain competitive in the capital-goods and intermediate industrial products needed by underindus-trialized countries, which are exporting goods in order to buy them.

Let us now consider competition on the part of the industrialized countries as typified by Western Europe and Japan. Professor Despres had some interesting observations to make in the context of United States competition in third-country markets. I can only carry his views a step further by offering some suggestions as to our competitive position in our own home markets.

To me, the reason why the United States has so long been ahead technologically in its competitive relationship with, say, Western Europe does not seem quite so mysterious as Professor Despres suggests. For one thing, I do not think the reason is that we have been brighter, wiser—more on our toes—than our Western competitors. I think this is a myth we have created which has given us a sense of false superiority in certain areas.

Partly because of the size of our market, but even more importantly because of the height of our average level of income, we have generated in the United States a mass demand for new products before any such mass demand could possibly have developed elsewhere. At an earlier stage here than in Western Europe, therefore, it has paid our businessman to "engineer" a product idea into a production line. Thus repeatedly, with one product after another, we have made the investment in the engineering processes which has made possible the mass production of a test-tube idea.

I am therefore implying that at the point at which the Western European businessman could see a large tangible market for that same product in Western Europe, he, too, had the skill and the technical ability to engineer that product into a production line. The catch-up in living standards and the liberalization of trade in Western Europe have had the effect of closing the technological gap, primarily because it has become perfectly clear that it is worthwhile to engineer many products into large-scale production for the Western European market. Once that decision is taken, of course, the next decision of the producer is that he can export the product as well, operating upon the low cost created by the large internal market.

That is what we are faced with. A catch-up in living standards in Western Europe has generated a large market in Western Europe in many products for which there was not a large market before. Once facilities were in place, producing for that large market, it has been fairly easy to sell to the rest of the world, including the United States.

What are future developments likely to be? First of all, I think that the Western Europeans—precisely because they are catching up and are enjoying increases in living standards—will begin to lose their cost advantage in some of the markets we have recently entered. We begin to see the signs in Holland and Germany of a narrowing of the cost advantage they once enjoyed. This is one trend that will continue, I am sure, reducing the advantage of Western European countries selling products in the American market, although probably not obliterating the advantage in many such products.

The other thing that will happen—and this is something that we do not place enough stress on in our own thinking—is that the higher living standards of the United States will continue to generate new products and new opportunities for large-scale production which will put us temporarily, but only temporarily, in an advantageous position in a new range of commodities. For a while we will enjoy a competitive advantage in these new commodities until Western Europe enjoys a large enough internal market to get into these; then she may begin to push on these products as well.

In sum, I envisage a change, a constant pressure upon us, generated partly by the underdeveloped areas and partly by the industrialized areas of the world. This pressure will demand constant shifts from the United States, requiring us to relinquish the standardized, the repetitive, the high-labor-cost products to our competitors and constantly to engineer new products to fill the new demands of our own people. I see a changing import mix and a constant need for adjustment. At the same time, the opportunities for increased exports should keep pace with the increased imports these pressures reflect.

CHAIRMAN: That was an excellent analysis of the problems that United States industry faces and will continue to face. I want to warn you, Professor Vernon, that I have a question to ask along those lines that you didn't get around to answering; it has some political overtones, also about labor union pressures.

We hear next from Mr. Schwartz on the "Soviet Bloc as a Trade Competitor." Could you preface your discussion, Mr. Schwartz, by some brief comments on the implications of the collapse of the Summit talks in Paris?

5

Harry Schwartz
SPECIALIST ON SOVIET AFFAIRS
THE NEW YORK TIMES

The Soviet Bloc as a Trade Competitor

I WELCOME Mr. Huggins' invitation to say a few words about the political aspects of what has happened in Paris. It seems to me that here again, as so often happens quite in contradistinction to the Marxist thesis of the primacy of economics, we have seen the primacy of politics over economics. If you want to understand that vividly, think about being in the shoes of a gentleman who last February signed a contract for the large-scale import of Soviet automobiles into the United States.

The real question is why did Nikita do it? What he did, I think, is well known to everyone in this audience. He has completely blown apart the entire political conception of the framework under which the world has operated since last September and he has called into question every possible conception regarding the future, and not just the future of American-Soviet relations. He has certainly raised the possibility that all projections of the future are perhaps meaningless because there may not be any future in the event of a nuclear war. We certainly can't rule out the possibility of nuclear world war in the next few months. I don't expect it, but you at least have to reckon with the possibility.

Well, as far as why he did it, I have only a couple of guesses. I'd like to suggest that first the U-2 incident did have something to do with it. Before we get overly sanctimonious, which is one of our prime national failings, we ought to recall or reflect upon what our reaction would be if a Russian plane had been shot down over St. Louis and if the Soviet Government had made admissions (a) that the plane had been sent over on an espionage mission, and (b) that the Soviet Government has been sending such planes over for many years, and (c) that it intended to continue doing so.

Beyond the U-2 incident I believe it was even obvious on April 30 before Mr. Powers took off on his ill-starred flight that things were going very badly. The reasons we can see that were roughly these:

First, Mr. Khrushchev was faced with the fact that he was getting very little or nothing from his policy of relaxing international tension. As early as January 1960 the United States had again made abundantly clear that it wasn't going to pay a bribe in the form of a loan of several billion dollars, such as Mr. Khrushchev has been hoping for since at least mid-1958. Our refusal to discuss such a loan is what blew up the negotiations in trying to settle the Lend-Lease debt which now is 15 years old.

On Berlin, the speeches of Secretary of State Herter and Mr. Dillon and the conclusions of the NATO Ministers' Conference (all in April) made clear that rather than planning to hand West Berlin over to Mr. Khrushchev on a silver platter we have actually withdrawn those concessions in the Berlin matter that we offered in Geneva in 1959 at the Foreign Ministers' Conference.

In other words, he was faced by the prospect that he was going to return from the Summit with very little or nothing at all. Beyond that, Mr. Khrushchev was finding domestic pressures building up. The standard line of Soviet propaganda is that everybody in the Soviet Union lives in the happiest of all possible worlds, but since Soviet citizens are human beings and human beings are by nature unhappy and greedy, there is reason to doubt the truth of such propaganda. There has certainly been a lot of evidence of mounting pressure on Soviet leaders.

In the fall of 1959, when Mr. Khrushchev returned from America and China and toured the Soviet Far East and Siberia, there were a number of incidents which suggested this pressure was mounting rapidly. In one place where he made a speech the workers interrupted him to say, in effect, "Well, it doesn't matter, all these things you are talking about. When are you going to lower prices? When are you going to cut the prices on consumer goods we have to buy?"

We know that in the fall of 1959, at the building site of one of the largest metallurgical plants in the Soviet Union (and perhaps in the world) there was a major strike provoked by dissatisfaction with living conditions; some reports, which I gather are true, indicate that the strike almost took the form of an armed revolt. At any rate, the Soviet Government had to send troops and use bullets to put down this strike.

More recently there apparently have been strikes in Kemerovo Province in Siberia, and also some statements in the Soviet press about strikes over labor dissatisfaction in other widely scattered areas.

We have to remember that the Soviet people have had a look at the outside world in the past several years such as they have not had for a long time. Thousands of Soviet citizens have traveled abroad and have come back and told their friends privately—they haven't made speeches—about what they saw. The American Exhibition at Moscow last summer was seen by three million Soviet visitors. In general, the Soviet people have begun to get an idea of what they have been missing. And what they have been missing from the consumer point of view has been quite a lot.

So when you look at this picture of rising dissatisfaction and link it with the greater knowledge by the Soviet people of the nature of the outside world, you can understand there were reasons for Mr. Khrushchev to have second thoughts about his policy of encouraging peace, greater contacts and generally lowering the Iron Curtain, and to cause him to re-examine the wisdom of permitting a growing knowledge among his own people of life in the outside world.

And, finally there is the fact that Mr. Khrushchev always has an opposition to the policy of relaxing tension. The opposition has been clearest on the part of the Chinese Communists. Perhaps the most startling spectacle has been Mr. K. spreading one line while the Chinese Communists—in speeches, radio broadcasts, and newspaper articles—are spreading a completely different line. Mr. Eisenhower has been a key to this really unprecedented debate. Until the last few days, Mr. Eisenhower—as depicted in Soviet propaganda —has been a man of peace, good will, a reasonable fellow with whom you can negotiate. But in the propaganda of the Chinese Communists, Eisenhower has always been just another reactionary capitalist and imperialist who has been mouthing words of peace for tactical reasons but is always plotting aggression.

If nothing else, the events in the last few days show that the Chinese Communists have won out. Mr. Khrushchev has taken over the Chinese Communist line, and, for all of his apparent good humor when he holds a press conference in a cow barn, has suffered a major political defeat. His entire policy has now been repudiated —a policy which his opponents in the Communist camp warned him for many months could lead only to disaster.

Whether or how Mr. Khrushchev will ride the storm of this reversal I don't know. But we shouldn't lose sight of the fact that in part his anger and intemperate language may be caused by chagrin over the humiliating defeat he has suffered at the hands of Mao Tse-tung. Of course, Mao has allies in the Soviet leadership, certainly within the Presidium of the Soviet Party, and also within the top leadership of the Soviet Army.

So much for the political background. At least some of the things I have mentioned must play a role. Perhaps all of them do.

What, then, are the implications of this on the economic scene? What kind of policy has the Soviet Union been following? How may this policy be altered, if at all, in the light of the new political atmosphere?

The policy of the Soviet Union on the economic front has been compounded of a number of elements.

Number one, of course, has been the effort to get maximum rapid growth of production. I suppose that everybody has heard *ad nauseam* all of the statistics about how the Russians are growing at 8, 9, 10, or 12% a year while the United States is growing at 1, 2, or 3% a year. If you project these growth rates into the future, somewhere in 1970, or 1975, or 1980 Russia will equal and go ahead of us in industrial production. At any rate, this has been the notion Mr. K. has had. His first thesis has been he wanted a relaxation in international tension, during which he expected to defeat us by purely economic competition by showing us that his society simply works better than the tired old nag which is what he considers the capitalist society to be. Certainly over the past two years there has been a contrast between the very rapid growth of the Soviet economy which has continued into the first quarter of this year and the rather complex movement of American economy and production. (Perhaps a stronger word than complex should be used in a week when steel production falls to only 70% of capacity.)

Along with this growth of production has come a much greater increase in Soviet international trade for at least two reasons. First, the Russians have simply had a great deal more to sell than ever before, in both quantity and in variety of goods. With the growth of their output has come increased opportunities for export. But there is another element in the Russian thinking, something that goes beyond the field of international trade. This is the incredible increase of interest in what we might call the rational direction of the economy.

Under Stalin the economy was more or less run by the seat of Stalin's pants. Comrade Stalin's intuition ran the Soviet economy. In the last few years Soviet economists have been turned loose to read the books of Western economists. The Soviet economists accordingly have awakened to the fact that the Western economists had a lot of good ideas which could be used to increase productivity, efficiency and output, and reduce costs in the Soviet economy. One of the ideas that the Soviet economists succeeded in selling at least partially to the Soviet leadership is the notion that there is such a concept as comparative advantage, and that there is an international division of labor from which all participants may benefit. As a result, there are today a whole series of statements by Khrushchev and Mikoyan extolling the international division of labor in terms that would have been very familiar and acceptable to men like Adam Smith.

So, for both of these reasons—the increase in export possibilities and the realization that international trade and comparative advantage can bring gains—the Russians were interested in international trade.

Professor Vernon has suggested that the Russian conduct in international trade was probably based very largely upon ignorance. Well, in the case of any human being you can't dismiss ignorance. I must say, however, that I myself am impressed in recent years not so much by Russian ignorance but rather by the fantastic detail with which they try to follow every possible development in the world market in every commodity.

There are a number of publications in the Soviet Union which for the breadth and thoroughness of their coverage of economic developments in different countries have no parallel in the United States. There are people in the United States who subscribe to those publications simply because they want to obtain more detailed information on the world economy than is possible to get from any single periodical appearing in the United States or Great Britain. So I would not overplay the ignorance aspect.

Actually, of course, they have been following a series of different policies. I think this can be explained in terms of different situations and different pressures. I suppose these policies can be summarized by citing three case histories—in aluminum, oil and diamonds.

As Professor Vernon has already indicated, the diamond policy represents one extreme possibility. The Russians in effect have "joined the gang." They have made an agreement with DeBeers to sell their diamonds only through the DeBeers marketing group. Thus they have joined the monopoly, if you will, and are not going to cause trouble. Any young ladies in this world who may have thought they could get cheaper diamonds when they got engaged because the Russians were going to break the diamond market are apparently going to be disappointed, unless, of course, Mr. Khrushchev's recent words signify a new tack which might see the Russians repudiate that agreement. So politics again must be remembered.

In the case of aluminum, we have a situation where the Russians started off in late 1957 and 1958 with an unbeatable sales offer. Some people went around offering to sell aluminum at a cent-and-a-half less than it could be had from any other producer. They sold a lot of aluminum and the big aluminum companies in the West were forced to reduce their prices. But the Russians then agreed upon a quota of a certain number of tons a year, and they have been observing that quota. Just a few days ago Mr. Irving Lipkowitz, an executive of the Reynolds Metals Company, testified before a Congressional Committee that the quota seems to have worked out. So in a certain sense the Russians have "joined the boys" in the case of aluminum as well, although since the market situation is more complex it is not as formal as the diamond situation.

Finally, in petroleum, the Russians apparently are following a different policy. There are some markets where they are simply selling at the posted price, some markets where they are selling at more than the posted price, and some markets where they are offering oil at substantial discounts from posted prices. My assumption is that this kind of policy will continue and that the real problem in oil will grow in a number of ways because they are going to increase their oil supplies; they are also interested in increasing their political power in the undeveloped countries where oil is produced. The chief challenge to oil companies is not so much the Soviet threat of oil price-cutting as that the Communists will take over Saudi Arabia or Iraq.

What are the implications of the recent political developments to this kind of pattern?

In the first place, there is nothing that has happened in the last few days that should diminish in the slightest Mr. Khrushchev's intention to increase his production. He will go on increasing production rates if he can. The real question that arises is, will he change the pattern of this production? Or, to put it in another way, is he going to embark on a rearmament program? Will he stop the demobilization of the 1,200,000 soldiers and increase the Soviet Army beyond its present size? Is he going to increase the production of planes and rockets and tanks? That is the key variable we should look at. If he does embark upon a rearmament program, one of the consequences will be that some of the resources he now has available to compete with us abroad will no longer be available for that purpose.

There is another possibility in the present situation, particularly because of the apparent Chinese ideological victory. The Chinese may now be able to get a substantial increase in the amount of Soviet economic aid. What I am trying to suggest is that if worse comes to worst, short of all-out war, the problems we have been worrying about in terms of economic competition may be somewhat transformed. It is possible that the purely economic aspects of Russian competition may diminish as Russia diverts resources to make herself even stronger militarily than she is now, and—more important—to make Communist China progress more rapidly in every way.

AUTHOR'S POSTSCRIPT: The above speech was delivered immediately after Premier Khrushchev had torpedoed the Paris Summit conference and created greatly increased tension throughout the world. At that time it appeared that the Chinese Communists had won in the internal struggle within the Communist world. Subsequent events, particularly Premier Khrushchev's efforts to reduce the tension he had created in Paris, showed that this was not entirely true. Therefore the speech should be read as an assessment of the then-existing world situation, and of Soviet policy at a crucial point in world history when the tide of Western peace hopes was at low ebb. Fortunately Premier Khrushchev retreated from the possibilities he himself had opened up.

CHAIRMAN: The last member of our Panel to speak is Professor J. Herbert Furth, who will talk about United States Foreign Investments.

6

J. Herbert Furth

ASSOCIATE ADVISER
DIVISION OF INTERNATIONAL FINANCE
BOARD OF GOVERNORS OF THE FEDERAL
RESERVE SYSTEM

The United States as a World Investor

FIRST, what follows is personal opinion and not necessarily the views of the Board of Governors of the Federal Reserve System.

Second, I must emphasize that I am not blessed with a gift of prophecy and therefore shall not try to read the future but only discuss some trends which may be apparent today.

From the point of view of world trade, which I suppose is our main concern here, there are two types of foreign investment. The first tends to stimulate foreign trade, the second tends to reduce it. The first type is represented by investment that serves to develop and exploit national resources or, more generally, encourages the growth of less-developed areas in a way that will lead to an increased participation of those areas in world commerce. The second type is represented by the transfer of enterprises to fully developed countries that are protecting themselves against imports so that goods are now produced within the borders of those countries instead of entering world trade.

Recent experience suggests that the factors favoring investments of the first type are not as strong as those that seem to favor investments of the second type.

I shall first summarize some basic facts and then try to review very briefly recent developments in the various types of United

States direct investment in foreign countries other than Canada. I shall not consider investment in Canada because I believe that it is in many respects more akin to domestic than to foreign investment.

The outstanding amount of direct investments of United States capital in foreign countries, excluding Canada, has been estimated at nearly $20 billion. About half of that sum is invested in petroleum and mining and smelting; nearly half of the investment in these industries is located in Latin America, and most of the rest in other less-developed areas. Of the amount invested in other industries, again about half is located in Latin America, but most of the rest in Western Europe.

Net earnings of these investments transferred to the United States have recently amounted to about $1¾ billion annually. Net outflows of investment funds from the United States have fluctuated between $¾ billion and $1½ billion annually. In every recent year the net outflow has thus been considerably smaller than net earnings; this relation has also been true for most individual areas and industrial sectors. Reinvested earnings have amounted to about $1 billion annually. The fluctuations in the net outflow of funds have occurred primarily in the petroleum industry, where the annual sums have varied between $1 billion and less than $½ billion.

The future of investments in the petroleum industries seems particularly uncertain. For the first time since the war, oil is believed to be in heavy surplus. In 1958 the net flow of United States funds into these industries was less than half of the amounts of 1956 and 1957, although still larger than in other recent years. The industry breakdown for 1959 is not yet available, but the country breakdown suggests a further decline. The only factor tending to stimulate investment, at least west of Suez, seems to be the political threat regarding future availabilities of Near Eastern oil to the Western world. As you probably know, the experts now believe that unexploited resources of petroleum are far larger than had been previously estimated. This change in opinion may increase expenditures on exploration but it may also (in my opinion more likely) put a further brake on such investments because of the threats to oil prices which is inherent in the expected rise in supplies.

The factors influencing investments in *mining and smelting* are somewhat similar. Prices of many basic metals have not recovered from the decline of recent years. On the other hand, racial unrest in Central and South Africa may jeopardize the future of that source of supplies and thus stimulate investments in other parts of the world.

Investment in *European manufacturing* has recently been attracting attention somewhat out of proportion to the actual flow of United States funds. While the industry breakdown for 1959 is not yet available and may indeed register some increase, the figures through 1958 show that until that year U. S. net investments in European manufacturing never reached as much as $100 million annually, and were regularly about one third less than net earnings of United States capital invested in European manufacturing.

The most important factor likely to influence the future volume of such investments is the character of the European efforts toward regional integration. If these efforts are realized without a significant rise in tariff barriers against imports from the United States, it is clear that the incentive for U. S. producers to jump over those tariff barriers will be less than if United States exporters are hurt, not only by the discrimination inherent in any customs union or free-trade area, but also by absolute increase in tariff duties.

The future direction of European integration will, obviously, depend on the decision of the Europeans themselves. However, I do not doubt that the national policy can influence those decisions, and if the United States makes it clear that we will resist any attempt to make the regional organization of Europe "inward" instead of "outward" looking, our exports will have a better chance and there will be less need and incentive for investments in Europe as substitutes for exports.

Another factor that has loomed large in recent public discussions is the alleged inability of our exporters to compete with European producers. It is obvious that any failure on our part to avoid inflation would lead to further cost and price increases and thus result in a further decline in our exports and in a shift of some export industries to foreign locations. However, as Professor Vernon has emphasized, it seems that the United States is realizing this danger, and the movement in our balance of payments for the first quarter of 1960 is consistent with the expectation that we will remain competitive with Europe.

As Professor Despres and Professor Vernon have told you, wage rates in Europe are lower than in the United States, as they have been for centuries. The only question is whether the ratio between wage differentials and productivity differentials has recently shifted significantly in favor of Europe. Moreover, competitive positions depend not only on relative costs and prices but also on the ability to adapt export goods to the special needs of the customers and to anticipate changes in such needs. In many respects Europe may have caught up with the United States, but the question remains whether the United States will stay ahead in flexibility and in inventiveness. Obviously, the more competitive we remain, the smaller will be the incentive to transfer factories to Europe.

New investments in Latin America, quite apart from declines in petroleum, mining and smelting, have dropped considerably, largely because of unsettled political situations in some important countries. However, a number of factors may help to reverse this trend. In many countries there is a growing awareness of the need to restore and maintain financial stability in order to attract foreign capital. The activities of such institutions as the Inter-American Development Bank may well help Latin Americans think and act as creditors and investors rather than exclusively as debtors. Finally, new investments may be stimulated by the endeavors of some Latin American countries to set up common markets or free-trade areas in imitation of the European example. Much will depend, however, on the outcome of the Cuban experiment. If it becomes clear that its anticapitalist economic policy does not succeed, even in a short run, the attitude of other Latin American countries toward foreign investment may actually improve. However, if Cuba receives enough aid from sources unfriendly to the United States, and if its leaders are sufficiently ruthless to reduce consumption so much that internal investment is raised and development furthered in spite of the drop in national income, the repercussions on the rest of Latin America may be very serious indeed.

The rest of the world has so far been of little importance for investments in industries other than petroleum, mining and smelting; moreover, a large part of the sum of $50 million annually, reported for all areas outside of Western Europe and Latin America, is going to such countries as Japan or Australia rather than to less-developed areas. In many of these less-developed areas, nationalistic and socialistic tendencies make the outlook for investments even less reassuring than in Latin America. However, there are some brighter spots. India, Pakistan, Malaya and Thailand, for instance, appear to be veering toward greater understanding of the importance of private enterprise and foreign capital for economic development, and may well provide new opportunities for investment, especially with the aid of our program of government guarantees against political risks.

There has been much talk about forcing investment in less-developed areas by tax advantages and other types of government assistance going beyond guarantees against political risks. It would certainly be convenient if private capital could relieve the government of some of the burden of its foreign aid program. However, few observers believe that anything except full government guarantees against all risks (which would make investment private in name only) would induce investors to direct large sums to those countries that are in particular need of foreign help.

In summary, the prospects for new investments seem to be brightest in Western Europe, the area in which the inflow of foreign capital is least needed and where it is least likely to stimulate foreign trade.

However, even if we should not expect a substantial rise in private investment in less-developed areas, a moderate flow may suffice to benefit all parties concerned. Economic history indicates that development is not so much the result of a massive inflow of foreign capital as of a change in basic attitudes, and especially of the growth of a domestic entrepreneurial class. Such changes can be accelerated by technical assistance, which does not require the transfer of large funds. It is the autonomous development of industry abroad, rather than the transplantation of American factories, which may be expected to determine the growth of the less-developed areas of the free world, and thereby insure the continuing expansion of world trade.

CHAIRMAN: As I indicated earlier, I am going to use the prerogatives of the Chairmanship to ask a question. As a prelude to it I would like to pull together two or three statements that were made by our various speakers.

Various comments were made to the effect that we have lost our technological advantages as compared with our Western European and Japanese competitors. It is recognized that there is a cost variance between these competitors and United States manufacturers. Professor Vernon used the textile industry as a good example of the impact or potential impact on United States trade of developing the underdeveloped countries.

I would like to submit that that impact has long been felt even before the exports of textiles from those countries to the United States. When those textile industries were developed, frequently with U. S. loans, they removed a market from traditional suppliers. Those traditional suppliers then turned to the United States where they could undersell United States producers, so that its impact has long since been felt. When these underdeveloped countries start exporting there will be an additional impact. That is not limited to the textile industry, but perhaps that is a good illustration to use.

Professor Vernon indicated that the traditional party policies of the Republicans and Democrats were so similar that you could not expect much difference. On the other hand, I don't think anybody is going to argue with the fact that a strong United States is essential to the entire Western world. The impact of foreign competition is being felt more and more by basic industries and accordingly by more and more people.

Professor Despres indicated that this problem has gotten into the labor discussions. Certainly labor unions are becoming more and more concerned. There is, I believe, a growing protectionist feeling within the United States, both on the part of industries affected and on the part of labor.

I would like to ask Professor Vernon to comment upon the political aspects of this problem from the standpoint of increasing demands for some type of protection for United States industry to prevent what seems to me an assumption, on the part of our experts here, that there will be a substantial transfer of United States manufacturing activity overseas.

The impact of this on the United States economy and the United States approach to world trade is something I would like Professor Vernon to elaborate on, not only from his present position, but from his background in the State Department.

PROFESSOR VERNON: Mr. Huggins and I reminded each other that we have been having these delightful discussions sporadically over a period of something like ten years and I am glad to renew the discussions in public.

There was an assumption in the Chairman's question that the trends that I and some of my colleagues here on the platform were tracing out were in some sense bad for the United States economy. This is an assumption that I want to dispel, if I can.

I suggested that there is likely to be an increase in the competition in U. S. markets for standardized products, products bearing the characteristics which I summarized during my talk. Now, what does this mean to the United States? Well, in the case of the underdeveloped countries, one can see the related possibility for expanding exports to those markets—and exports in the lines in which, generally speaking, the United States has the most rapid productivity increases.

In short, when one says that the United States is going to face increased import competition, this is only half the story. The rest of the story is that opportunities for greater export possibilities will open up at the same time. The one model that can't stand up, the model you must dismiss from your minds as a possibility, is one in which the United States imports more and more and exports less and less. This can't happen. A number of forces intervene to prevent this before it has gone very far.

One of the forces in the case of the industrialized countries exporting to the United States is an increase in their cost and a decline in our costs such that our competitive position begins to be changed once more. I see that tendency already beginning to occur in Western Europe. As for the underindustrialized countries that are selling us more products, their whole purpose in selling is to buy.

The critical challenge to the United States is this: Does it attempt to retain its domestic markets unchanged by keeping out foreign competition and by concentrating on those lines in which it has been facing the severest competition? To put it in extreme terms—terms which are perhaps a little unfair but which I shall use to make a point—do we propose to remain a nation of glass blowers and hat manufacturers or do we propose to get into the new chemicals, the new machinery lines and the new know-how for export?

Now, for the individual manufacturer the problem is not all that simple. He may be progressive, and may be exploiting every technological and market opportunity, and still he may be confronted with competition from sources which look to him to be unfair. In individual cases such as this, my whole reaction has been one of sympathy, but not sympathy to such a degree that I would have the United States stand still. At the point at which the interests of such individual manufacturers clash with those of the United States as a whole, the response of the United States has to be a shift into the more highly productive, more advanced products, and the maintenance of its exports along those lines.

Let's change the scene for just a moment. What do I expect the United States political response will be to these imports? I don't know. I said I was assuming—and I was prepared to bow to anyone else's opinion in this regard—that we would not engage in substantially more protectionism as an answer to these increased imports. I assume that because we are a nation of sensible, pragmatic people and a nation which realizes that to grow we must change. I hope that assumption proves right.

CHAIRMAN HUGGINS: Thank you, Mr. Vernon. An advantage of

these panel discussions is that you can disagree with a speaker. I have even heard international bankers who, five years ago, were all in favor of liberalized trade, now say we would have to do something to protect the heavy investments and jobs of people in basic industries. You can't blithely change your domestic products quite that fast. Instead of being a problem ten years from now, this is a problem for a great many people today. I have yet to hear any suggested answer to it other than protection. I don't think that there is anybody that wants that, but nonetheless I am afraid, Professor Vernon, that forces are building up so that there is not much that anybody can do about it when jobs and basic investments are threatened.

7

Discussion

QUESTION: Professor Furth, some fear has been expressed that in the next recession the Federal Reserve authorities may be somewhat hampered or handicapped in pursuing as easy a money policy as they might desire because of the loss or drain of gold to foreign nations. Assuming, for example, that we get into a recession and other nations are expanding and their interest rates are substantially above ours, what substance is there to this fear? His answer is of course as an individual rather than as a member of the Board.

PROF. FURTH: I hope you won't expect me to predict the policy of the Federal Reserve. However, speaking as an economist and not as a member of the Staff of the Federal Reserve, I can tell you that there is by and large no conflict between policies that are needed for domestic and for international reasons. For both domestic and international reasons the Federal Reserve must always try to stabilize the flow of spending. This means that in a recession it will be expanding and in prosperity it will be tightening.

In general, an outflow of gold occurs primarily when our exports are lagging because of recession abroad and our imports are booming because of prosperity at home. That was the case when our upswing started after the 1957-1958 recession, at a time when there still was a recession in Europe.

If by any chance there should be a temporary situation in which this rule doesn't hold true, we must expect this situation to be temporary, and so short that it doesn't need to affect basic policies. And I want to remind you that for the last eight months our gold losses have been very small. We still have a deficit in our balance of payments, and I hope very much that it will be further reduced; but I have no doubt that, under the proper policies, we will be able to reach equilibrium before the next recession.

QUESTION: Mr. Schwartz, you said that the Communist control of increasing supplies of petroleum would be the biggest worry for the companies. With the new shift in the Soviet political policy, won't Western markets be more resistant to receiving supplies from an undependable source; secondly, won't the shift in Soviet policy cause more oil to be used for internal development—that is, for the entire Soviet bloc; thirdly, you mentioned increased supplies controlled by the Soviets from the Middle East. Isn't it true that if the Soviets go into the Middle East that would surely mean war, in which case those supplies would not enter the competing markets?

MR. SCHWARTZ: There are a number of points you have raised. Let me try to answer them in the reverse order.

In the first place, so far as the Middle East is concerned, I did not state that I anticipated the Soviet Army would march into the Middle East and seize the oil for the Soviet Union. If that were to happen it would be part of a much larger event—World War III—in which case all bets are off.

I said that the real challenge was the possibility that in the new climate of the world, the new Cold War, the Soviet Union may be more interested in inducing the indigenous forces in the Middle East—I mentioned Iraq, for example—to seize the oil deposits there from their present operation and control by foreign investors. That may not provoke war. If the Iraqi Government seizes oil or if the Saudi Arabian Government does it, we could not go to war with Russia. It would not be a logical thing to do. I think there was misunderstanding on that point.

Now, you have raised the question whether Western markets would be receptive to Soviet oil in the face of the kind of blow-hot, blow-cold political situation; that it might be an unreliable supplier.

I certainly don't claim to be an expert in petroleum marketing, but I don't see why the factor of price wouldn't play a role. If the Russians offer oil cheaply enough I assume they can sell it in almost any country. If oil can be bought today for two cents a gallon cheaper than anybody else offers it, are many people going to worry what's going to happen six months from now? I don't know. I say I'm not an expert on petroleum marketing, but I want to emphasize that the Russians have this tremendous advantage. They don't have to pay any dividends to stockholders. There aren't any stockholders and as far as I know they can repudiate bonds if they feel like it. They did it a couple of years ago. And they don't have to show a profit. They have a lot of levers and a lot of freedom of action.

With respect to the middle point, I tried to suggest in the close of my remarks that one consequence of this new shift in policy might be a reorganization of the Soviet economy and of Soviet activity abroad that would require more of the Soviet resources internally within the bloc. With respect to oil, the problem is which might happen faster—the increase of Soviet oil production or the increased need of oil within the bloc? And on that point I must regretfully tell you that oil production has been one of the most rapidly increasing fields in the entire Soviet economy.

QUESTION: On the price part of it, if it is for the national good, in those countries where imports of petroleum are vital, then would these governments allow the independents to accept the lower price of the Soviet import? Would the national governments allow the petroleum to come in even at the lower prices if it endangered the source of supply of petroleum from the major markets, the major companies?

MR. SCHWARTZ: Is that really something on which we can make a general statement? There are so many different countries and so many different internal, political and economic supply-and-demand situations, the only thing I can say is that the reaction would be different in different countries.

CHAIRMAN HUGGINS: One answer might be that Egypt did not hesitate to let Russia build the great Aswan dam with the consequent control, if you will, of the basic power supply of Egypt and all the implications that follow. Surely the dam is going to be there and the generators and all the rest of it will require maintenance. I wouldn't be surprised if the Russians control the maintenance. Egypt, for political or other reasons, accepted Russian help in an area where there are certainly far fewer alternatives than there would be in the supply of petroleum, considering the availability of petroleum today.

MR. SCHWARTZ: May I remark that I would be very much surprised if the Egyptians would go in on the basis you suggest? It seems to me a fundamental feature of every Soviet contract is that Russians also agree to train indigenous personnel.

CHAIRMAN HUGGINS: I admit that unquestionably the Russians agree to train indigenous personnel. But when you get down to the real experts and to the problem of where the spare parts needed to maintain it are concerned, you have something else. Russia will control these.

MR. SCHWARTZ: Spare parts are a different item. I agree.

CHAIRMAN HUGGINS: The Russian in charge of the Aswan project in Egypt is a real smart fellow. I would be a little bit surprised if the Russians didn't, by one means or another, exercise very substantial influence in Egypt for a long time to come, simply because they are building the dam and bringing in the power equipment.

QUESTION: If we are giving up our comparative competitive advantage in machine building, for example, and we perhaps have the greatest area of progress in the agricultural field, what will happen to our country ultimately when we transport all of our know-how overseas? What happens to our technological know-how when someone decides to drop a bomb over here and we have to go to Nigeria's machine shop to get something to retaliate with? I just don't see the logic of your point of view, Mr. Despres.

MR. DESPRES: This isn't an all-or-nothing kind of a situation. I do not envisage an exclusively agrarian, underindustrialized America. If that appeared to be the implications of my remarks I would like to correct it now. The point is this: We are living in a world of changing competitive underlying strengths and this, in the long run, is just as favorable to our export position as it is to our import position.

We have two alternatives open to us. One is to try to fight the trend. This will hamper our economic growth. It will hamper the world's economic growth. The other is to try to make the best use of the trend. And this means, as Mr. Vernon pointed out, that there will be lots of lines where we are ahead in the nonroutine things.

If you look at the position today, we have to say that the adjustment is not going to take place wholly within manufacturing. An increase in our agricultural exports has to be an important part of the adjustment process. Canada and Australia, which are high-income countries, are industrial manufacturing countries if you look at their domestic economy, but their exports are to a large extent primary products. There is a widespread notion that if you export agricultural goods or other primary products you are backward. This just doesn't hold water. New Zealand, Australia and Canada and so on prove just the opposite.

There is one point, however, that I would like to add to this about the adjustment process.

We are today feeling the effects of this changing world competitive position more sharply in the form of increased imports and of increased competition in export markets than we are in these beneficient forms of expanding world demands benefiting other export lines. As a matter of fact, a large part of today's balance-of-payment problem is a reflection of this fact.

Now, the counterpart of our balance-of-payments difficulties from a worldwide point of view is that a few other industrial countries have not yet taken up the effects of their rising productivity in any form other than increasing their gold reserves. I have in mind particularly West Germany and Italy. So long as this remains the case ours will be an unbalanced situation. Although I am entirely in agreement with Mr. Vernon that we ought to hold the line on a moderately liberal import policy, I do think that we ought to insist very strongly today on a further relaxation of barriers abroad which are hampering the adjustment process to the new competitive situation.

I don't feel that we ought merely to say automatic forces will take care of this whole thing. I think we ought to put very strong pressure to accelerate this process.

So far as the underlying situation is concerned, I would emphasize this: American manufacturers by and large are much more concerned apparently by a 1% loss of markets due to imports than they are by a 10% loss of markets due to any domestic cause. If you talk about the effects on jobs, profits, output in the United States, there can be no question that the lagging growth of domestic demand in the United States since 1955—we have had some growth but it is much lower than the growth of our capacity—has affected profits and jobs adversely by a higher multiple than any export competition. I just can't share the kind of alarm that you express.

QUESTION: I appreciate your reply, but I am not thinking of our country today. We as a nation are where we are today because of the heritage set up for us by our predecessors. If we as managers of businesses transfer our know-how, our technology overseas for a picayune 10% royalty or set up jobs overseas, our concern should be to our children and their children and their children, not to our immediate balance-of-payments situation.

CHAIRMAN HUGGINS: Let me answer that. The initial question started on the problem of the question of agricultural exports and machinery imports. There is a case history on that north of the border where some very basic Canadian industries are, in effect, obsolete because Canada is primarily an exporter of grains and metals. To export them, Canada must let their primary product customers import into Canada. As a result, some Canadian industries which have been in existence there for many years are in practically a no-profit or even a loss position. Japan has just let it be known in Canada that, since they are buying large amounts of wheat in Canada today, they expect to sell substantial amounts of equipment. That isn't going to make it any easier for the manufacturing fraternity north of the border.

MR. DESPRES: Let me just answer the one about the concern with your children and grandchildren and great-grandchildren. If you are concerned not about your own problems but your children's and grandchildren's and great-grandchildren's, I think I can be very reassuring about this.

It is inconceivable that the rest of the world is going to imitate our technology—I agree with Professor Vernon about this—or let's say cut to our level of productivity and stay at their present level in real income and living standards. The idea that their desire is only to export and not to import is a contradiction. I am worrying about the problems in the next few years. If we adapt to those in what I consider to be the wise way—and this isn't wholly an American problem, but a problem particularly for the other advanced industrial countries—I have no doubt that our grandchildren as well as theirs will not be looking for jobs but they will have much higher living standards.

In other words, I think the fallacy of your position is that you think of it only as competition on the selling side. What you omit is growth in production, in real income, growth of buying power, growth of imports as well as exports.

Now, as I said before, there has been a lag—I would describe it as no more than a lag—in the case of Italy and West Germany, but this is a problem for the next few years and not for your grandchildren.

QUESTION: I would like to compliment you on that fine summary. I think in the long run one of the main factors will be the shrinking resources base in relation to the population increase. That means that the world will be subdivided into blocs and regions which will compete between themselves. Can we be sure that the alliance of the fast-growing populations will not pre-empt what the other countries are now trying to accomplish through their increased productivity?

One of the problems that confronts us is how to correlate these two influences, the resources exploitation and the participation in economic productivity.

There is one more question, Mr. Chairman, which relates to this chain of questions. What part will American business take in this contest which, as I see it, is a contest between American corporations and Russian commissars?

CHAIRMAN HUGGINS: I think American business will participate wherever it sees a reasonable chance of a reasonable profit. Once you get outside of the profit motive, American business does not have the capabilities. There is no single company—neither General Motors nor any other—that has the capabilities to get into a contest with the Soviet Union or any other controlled or semicontrolled economy. Would you like to comment further, Mr. Schwartz?

MR. SCHWARTZ: I had an unhappy feeling as I heard Mr. Huggins make his remark right now. The question, as I understood it, was what would be the contributions of American business in the struggle for survival against the most dangerous enemy to free society that has ever existed. And Mr. Huggins' answer, given in all candor, was that American business will contribute to the extent that it can make a buck. My only comment would be, if this is all we can expect, can we really hope to survive?

CHAIRMAN HUGGINS: I was referring to individual corporate contributions from their own treasuries. American business will contribute in many, many respects, but no one business has the ability to determine basic policy to meet the Russian threat. Certainly in the Cold War picture, American businessmen will contribute just as any other loyal American would. They are perhaps better able to contribute because they are used to taking risks. But we still are motivated by the profit element. This country has been built on it. I believe it will stay strong because of it. I do not think that it is any reflection on American businessmen to say they will invest where they can see the possibility of making a reasonable profit. That is why they are hired as managers; that is their duty to their stockholders. As corporate members of our society they will play very major parts in the over-all countering of the Russian threat.

PROF. VERNON: It's too bad one of the most critical questions arises so late in the meeting. One observation I want to make is that we generally tend to underestimate the attractiveness which the enterprise system has in the newly developing areas of the world. This is not to suggest that they will ultimately develop into a pattern precisely in the United States model. But countries like India, Pakistan and others contemplate a substantial place for private enterprise in their developing economies. There is a big but, however, which is of tremendous relevance to American business.

In order for these countries really to develop on patterns which are tolerable, they have to have export markets. There is no projection of the future of India or Mexico or Pakistan or Turkey which contemplates both a tolerable growing rate and a stagnation of exports. They simply must have more exports in order to grow at a tolerable rate.

The challenge to conscientious American business therefore is: What does the individual American businessman do when these exports confront him with the need to change his own business? If his response is "I'm for enterprise, I'm for competition," then the corollary of that response must be, "I'll not use my political power to exclude those exports; I'll use my productive power to meet the competition or make other items."

There is another problem confronting the thoughtful American businessman. It may well be that we will have to improvise new kinds of measures to tide over countries that are being threatened with trouble because of their trade relations with the Soviet Union. In those circumstances, the challenge of conscience to American enterprises is: Do we allow the United States Government to do things that are unorthodox in terms of our classic philosophy of the roles of government and business in order to meet the threat, if such measures are our only apparent response? Do we also, on occasion, make a generous gesture by opening up our markets on some extraordinary basis to hard-pressed countries like Iceland or Egypt?

These are the challenges for U. S. business. To meet them will require a willingness to accept change—change of products and change in the role of government. But I see no alternative for survival.

QUESTION: Mr. Schwartz, in view of our suspicions that Russia has a gold supply and in view of export controls discouraging Russia from purchasing the goods she wants, why does she seem to be concerned with obtaining long-term credits?

MR. SCHWARTZ: Well, of course, I think you have to understand that the Russian leaders always consider themselves to be really in a state of war. In a state of war the general is always most solicitous about his reserves and tries to avoid committing his reserves except under the most dire emergency conditions possible. The Russians apparently consider their gold reserves as that kind of reserve, something to be used only in the event of a dire emergency. Therefore, if they can get a loan, they would much rather have it than spend any of their gold. There is one part of the answer.

The other part is that the Russians have said they are looking forward to making the ruble a convertible currency, and want to have a very good gold supply to back it up.

So those are the reasons they prefer to shoot for loans rather than spend their gold thoughtlessly at the present time.

INTERNATIONAL COMMODITIES:
A World Supply-and-Demand Outlook

Charles A. Wight
CHAIRMAN

Charles A. Wight

PRESIDENT
FREEPORT SULPHUR COMPANY

1

Introduction

Very grave and interesting problems confront us in connection with the world supply and demand of commodities. The situation concerns all of us, not only those of us who are actually engaged in the production of commodities, but also those who are concerned with their consumption. It concerns the whole public, for commodities affect the fabric of our entire economic society.

There is, unquestionably, one common problem in connection with world commodities, and that is oversupply. One member of our panel at lunch today expressed it as "too much." Using "commodities" in the everyday sense, I am sure we have too much of almost all our commodities; on the other hand, there is no such thing as really having "too much" of any commodity when one considers the long-term demand and the fact that in most commodities one can see the eventual end of supplies.

Rather, the problem of "too much" seems to me to center more around "too much at a given moment" than "too much in total quantity."

Mr. Stewart Coleman, who was to be our first speaker this afternoon, is ill and is unable to be with us.* He will be represented by Mr. George Piercy, who is the Deputy Manager of the Coordination Department of the Standard Oil Company of New Jersey.

* Mr. George Piercy delivered Mr. Coleman's speech.

2

Stewart P. Coleman
VICE PRESIDENT
STANDARD OIL COMPANY (NEW JERSEY)

Petroleum

THERE IS no subject more appropriate than petroleum in a discussion of international commodities. It comprises in value about 5% of all international exchange—double that of the next closest items. Its tonnage alone equals that of all other items in international trade. Petroleum has enjoyed a spectacular growth. It has become a most important raw material source for the production of specialties and a host of chemicals. Petrochemical tonnage now amounts to 30% of all U. S. chemical production, yet only 2% of U. S. crude oil is sufficient for the production of this immense quantity of chemicals. The vast bulk of petroleum finds an outlet as a source of energy.

Oil and gas, of course, are only two of several sources of energy. Thus, in evaluating potential petroleum demand we must first appraise the potential for total energy requirements as well as petroleum's competitive position.

OUTLOOK FOR ENERGY

Energy has been aptly described as "the go of things" and the struggle for existence has been defined as "the struggle for the energy with which to do work." The need for energy to lighten man's burdens has increased incessantly. In the last ten years the

Free World's total energy consumption has increased 50%. This year it will reach approximately 45 million barrels per day of oil equivalent.

Over the next decade, Free World total energy demand is expected to grow at an average rate of 3% per year. This increase, expressed as oil equivalent, will amount to an average annual growth of 1,700,000 barrels per day. Actually, this estimate may well be on the low side, since it implies only a slight improvement in the Free World's average per capita energy consumption. Currently per capita energy consumption in all Free Foreign nations is only one tenth of that in the U. S.; in Asia and Africa it is only one twenty-fifth. This disparity gives an idea of the potential which is available. If economic activity and standards of living in these foreign areas are improved beyond the modest degree assumed here, the impact on total energy demand will be tremendous.

Outlook for Growth of Petroleum

The question of importance to the petroleum industry is just how much of this energy demand will be supplied by petroleum. Oil and gas have inherent qualities of efficiency, cleanliness, convenience, economy, and ease of transportation which enhance their competitive position. In the past decade these two sources have increased their combined percentage share of the world's energy market from 43% to 56%.

Looking to the future, oil will remain the primary source of energy for transportation for many years to come. As a source of energy for stationary installations, the advantages of oil and gas over coal in many locations will persist. Reassessments of the cost keep delaying the widespread use of nuclear energy. All these factors point to petroleum supplying about two thirds of incremental energy demand in the coming decade, thus raising its market position to nearly 60% (16% supplied by natural gas and 44% by oil).

For the entire Free World, gas could conceivably increase from 36 to 54 billion cubic feet per day and oil from 19,000,000 to

26,000,000 barrels per day. We look for the Free World's combined oil and gas growth in demand over this period to average about the same as experienced thus far in the postwar period. This will amount to an annual increase of nearly 800,000 barrels per day of oil, and 2 billion cubic feet per day of gas. Naturally, the percentage growth rates will be somewhat abated because of the ever increasing base.

Are these forecasts of growth optimistic? Not at all. Let us first consider the United States. Many of us who live in congested areas are apt to assume that motor fuel consumption has reached its peak. This is not true. First of all about one quarter of the families of this nation do not own a car. In addition, our population is growing at about 1.5-2% per year, which will mean millions of new motorists. Also, we are rapidly becoming a nation of families having more than one car; today 17% of all car-owning families have two or more cars compared to 7% in 1950.

Although demand for home heating oil is now growing slowly due to competition from natural gas, the demand for similar products for use as automotive diesel and jet fuels is increasing rapidly.

Over-all, we expect the U. S. demand to continue at a healthy pace—resulting in an increase of about 270,000 barrels per day each year. Since we are working from a very high base, the percentage rate will be less than we have experienced in the past.

The opportunity for improvement in petroleum demand is even more pronounced abroad. Many factors, such as common markets and foreign-aid programs, are working to stimulate economic activity and raise the standard of living. This requires energy and, in particular, petroleum energy.

Anyone who travels abroad quickly notices the need for better transportation. European visitors to the United States are usually amazed to see the tremendous parking lots which adjoin our American factories. Some who come here for the first time have trouble believing that ordinary workers own those modern cars and drive to their jobs. In the U.S. there is now one passenger automobile for every 3 persons, whereas in Western Europe there is only one for each 18 persons. Should Europe attain our automobile saturation, it is obvious that demand for motor gasoline would increase tremendously.

Take the example of central heating for homes and the need for more of it in northern Europe. A central heating system is so commonplace in the U. S. that most of us have forgotten the inconvenience of a pot-bellied coal stove or a kerosene space heater.

In Europe and the U. K. there are some 71 million dwelling units of which only 8 million, or 11%, have central heating systems. And of these only 3 million, or 4%, are heated by oil. Here is a great opportunity for oil to expand. Other opportunities, such as the mechanization of agriculture and industry, exist in most nations.

The average annual per capita consumption of all the Free Foreign nations is only a fraction of that of the U. S.—1.6 barrels per person per year, compared to 19 here. Even in highly developed Western Europe, the consumption is only 3.8 barrels per person per year.

This means that a tremendous potential market for petroleum exists abroad. Raising the per capita oil consumption of the free Eastern Hemisphere to an appreciable fraction of the U. S. level would require staggering quantities of oil. If the 1.5 billion people of the free Eastern Hemisphere used even one fourth as much oil per person as we do, their consumption would amount to about 20,000,000 barrels per day—substantially more than the entire world consumption last year.

SUPPLY

Looking at the supply side, there certainly is no need to fear that we will run out of petroleum for many years to come. Estimates of proved reserves in the Free World today exceed 260 billion barrels. This represents an inventory amounting to 40 years' supply at current production levels. During the postwar period the Free World has consistently added more to reserves each year than it has withdrawn by production, so that the "supply ratio" has been successively improved. In 1948, for example, we had only a 21-year supply and this was based on a production level only 50% as great as today's.

It should be noted that these are *proved reserves* only; in other words, they are a conservative estimate of the volume of oil discovered to date by actual drilling and known to be recoverable under today's conditions of price and technology. They are by no means the limit of our supply, and it should not be inferred that the Free World will exhaust its reserves in 40 years. Ultimate reserves—those believed to exist but not yet discovered—are the basic source of supply. In the U.S., for example, proved reserves are currently carried at 38 billion barrels, whereas estimates of ultimate remaining reserves run in the neighborhood of 400 billion barrels, with several times that amount abroad.

Two things serve to make our reserve position even better. For one thing, these estimates of recoverable oil are based on an expectation of being able to recover only 25 to 30% of the oil in a given pool. The industry is currently developing new methods which will improve this rate substantially.

Secondly, there are roughly one trillion barrels of oil available in sedimentary deposits of oil shale in the U. S. alone—almost four times current Free World proved reserves. Also, there are additional staggering amounts of oil available in the Canadian tar sands. To date both of these sources have remained untapped because of the high costs of recovery and processing. However, work is currently going on to develop more economic techniques and these supplies might be an economic reality before the decade is past.

Now I am certain that all of you have heard statements these days to the effect that the oil industry is in a serious state of excess capacity. To be sure, there is currently more capacity than actually required for flexible operations. The industry entered the postwar period with virtually no spare capacity in any of its three principal functions—certainly an undesirable position. Consequently, a program of rapid expansion was undertaken and through 1956 the industry was barely able to keep up with the requirements of an ever-increasing demand. Today we are overbuilt. In 1959 some 26% of Free World producing capacity was shut in; refineries ran at 83% of capacity; and in transportation some 350 tankers were tied up, representing 13% of the available fleet.

Since these figures may be misleading, however, I believe it is necessary to look more thoroughly at each one in order to see the true picture. The pace with which we have recently developed our producibility is certainly not without purpose. For one thing, the expansion of producibility is quite different from expansion of refining or transportation capacity. We can design and build tankers or refineries of exactly, or at least very close to, the level which we estimate we need. In producing, however, it is not that simple. The success of exploration and development ventures is erratic and unpredictable. Thus, we must each year carry on enough exploration programs so that with probable success ratios we will discover sufficient reserves to meet our needs. In the past few years these operations have been more successful than normally expected so that we have added more producibility than actually required. Equally important, it is imperative that the Free World have proved reserves located strategically and in volumes which are consistent with military and "emergency" requirements. The existence of some shut-in wells is the price we must pay for this necessary flexibility.

In transportation, idle tankers are primarily the result of improved technology which permits the operation of vessels three to five times as large as the 16,000-ton T-2. Since the cost savings are large, operators are forced to build these new, larger ships even though present ships have many years of useful life. By constructing these new supertankers we are lowering cost, thus enhancing the competitive position with regard to other sources of energy. Again, the existence of tankers in tie-up is the price we must pay for progress.

Finally, current excess refining capacity in the U. S. is due to the fact that our industry generally overestimated its requirements. Abroad, spare capacity has been brought about by the insistence of many consuming nations that refineries be built within their national boundaries. These new plants have duplicated facilities already existing elsewhere in the historical exporting areas. This refinery spare capacity may be worked off, however, as demand catches up.

Actually, there is a hidden blessing in this spare capacity situation. The intense competition has caused most companies to markedly improve their efficiency. I am confident that we in the oil industry will all come out of this situation with "tighter ships."

No appraisal of the prospects of the oil industry would be complete without a consideration of the impact of Soviet oil exports on Free World markets. Soviet bloc oil exports to the Free World last year averaged 300,000 barrels daily. Since virtually all of this export volume has been developed in the short space of about six years, it has received a great deal of publicity, and fears have been expressed that a flood of cheap Soviet oil may be about to engulf the Free World oil industry.

Now I do not want to minimize the competitive problems posed by the existence of Soviet supplies on world markets, but it is essential that we keep them in perspective. In the first place, the 300,000 barrels daily that the Soviets exported last year came to less than 2% of Free World demand. Thus, Soviet bloc supplies are still very far from attaining the proportions of a "flood." Secondly, we must remember that both the Eastern European satellites and China have ambitious economic development plans and that they, too, are looking to oil to satisfy the bulk of their incremental energy requirements. Moreover, these countries are oil-deficient as a group and will be looking to the Soviet Union to satisfy their ever growing import requirements. Thus, even if Soviet oil production targets are attained, it is possible that the rapid growth in internal Soviet bloc requirements will limit the size of any future exportable surpluses.

Lastly, there is every indication that the bulk of Soviet oil exports to date have been commercially rather than politically motivated. The Soviets are using their oil as a relatively efficient means of obtaining imports of commodities which they vitally need for their internal development. In an effort to obtain outlets for their oil they have had to offer price discounts, but these are generally no greater than any new entrant would have to offer in today's highly competitive market.

In short, Soviet competition causes problems wherever it appears but, at the moment, it is just one additional element in a highly competitive situation and one which may become relatively less important as time goes on.

Now I would like to conclude with a brief summary. Petroleum can look forward to the coming decade as one of dynamic growth. Over this entire period the Free World demand for gas could increase at an average rate of about 2 billion cubic feet per day each year and Free World demand for oil could increase at an average rate of 800,000 barrels daily.

Petroleum, because of its convenience, cleanliness, and cost, continues to be preferred for many energy needs. There are ample supplies. In fact, right now oversupply is a problem in this competitive industry. The industry is aggressive and modern and the present readjustment that it is going through should strengthen it for future competition with other sources of energy. All in all, the 1960's will unquestionably be years of prosperous growth for the petroleum industry.

3

F. W. MacMullen

GENERAL MANAGER
INTERNATIONAL DIVISION
STAUFFER CHEMICAL COMPANY

Chemicals

A FEW DAYS AGO a very distinguished chemist and Chairman of the Board of Monsanto Chemical Company, Dr. Charles Thomas, gave an excellent address before the National Federation of Financial Analysts Societies. I think that it is worth repeating here a few of Dr. Thomas' remarks. Discussing the future of export sales with the maturing of the European Common Market, the Outer Seven, and similar blocs now forming in Latin America Dr. Thomas said:

> Our feeling is that, while shipments of bulk chemicals may decrease, and while export sales may shrink as a percentage of our total sales, their dollar volume will not necessarily decrease. Movement of the more sophisticated groups of specialty chemicals is increasing. These require greater technical sales effort, but command higher profit margins.

I heartily concur with Dr. Thomas' remarks. However, one factor in the world may mitigate against even this trend of increased sales of specialty products from the U. S. This factor is the nationalism that exists in many parts of the world and which demands that specialty products be produced locally to save foreign exchange and increase national prestige. I wager that not a day passes that the International Divisions of U. S. chemical companies are not faced with pressure from various markets either to produce a specialty product locally or to license some local manufacturer to produce the product.

The pharmaceutical division of the chemical industry has been faced with this pressure for some years now. They have solved the problem fairly well by a variety of techniques including:

1. Setting up local subsidiaries to manufacture
2. Forming joint-ventures with local manufacturers, and
3. Licensing local manufacturers

I am convinced that, sooner or later, other segments of the chemical industry will be faced with the same problem, probably to the same extent as the pharmaceutical industry. They, of course, will solve the problem in much the same fashion. In fact, with the advent of the European Market, most of the American chemical industry is pretty well represented in Europe with local manufacturing operations.

The president of one large European chemical company bitterly complained to me that the only one to benefit from the Common Market would be the Americans. It was his opinion that American knowledge of marketing in a large market would enable them to outstrip their European counterparts. It was this factor that played a major role in his decision to form a joint venture with an American company.

This brings me to another point made by Dr. Thomas. He cited the following six opportunities for the chemical industry investment abroad:

(1) Participating in markets and profits which import quotas, tariff barriers and foreign currency shortages otherwise would deny you.

(2) Tapping additional foreign markets by exporting to other countries within an established trade area, such as the British Commonwealth or the European Common Market.

(3) Exchanging know-how for equity or licensing it for royalties.

(4) Providing an outlet for intermediate chemicals of the parent company, and, the other side of the coin, securing raw materials needed by the parent company.

(5) Broadening the parent company's over-all knowledge of international commerce. Each foreign nation has its particular manufacturing, marketing and distribution techniques.

(6) Providing additional breadth to the parent company's basic fund of technical knowledge through overseas research.

I don't believe these points need any further elaboration.

I shall now discuss the chemical industry in three of the main areas of the world other than the U. S., namely, the United Kingdom, West Germany and Japan.

BRITISH CHEMICAL INDUSTRY 1958

British production and exports of chemicals leveled off in 1958 after a prolonged steady advance since World War II, but regained some of the lost ground in 1959. Production losses were attributed largely to a recession in heavy industries, and centered in the products consumed by those industries. Petrochemicals, plastics and synthetic detergents continued to advance. Although some investment projects lagged slightly because of the brief recession, by mid-1959 massive investment programs were again in full swing. The manufacturers who are concerned that the European Economic Community (EEC) will work to their disadvantage doubt that the seven-nation European Free Trade Association will offer sufficient advantages to compensate for membership in the Community. They also anticipate more difficult trade conditions in other export markets, but foresee sustained and growing demand for chemicals resulting from a resumption of domestic economic growth.

THE INDUSTRY'S SIGNIFICANCE
IN THE ECONOMY

The industry has been one of the prime leaders in rehabilitating the economy after World War II and in restoring equilibrium to the United Kingdom's international trading position. Its postwar growth rate has been high, and its heavy investment programs have created markets for British machinery and construction industries, assisting both to attain efficiency high enough to promote overseas contracts. By supplying basic chemicals at reasonable prices to industry as a whole, manufacturers have assisted the British export drive. The development of new products, particularly petrochemicals and plastics, has led to the establishment of numerous new firms using these products, many of which have succeeded as exporting industries, thus contributing to the economy's over-all growth rate.

Before World War I, the British chemical industry ranked considerably below its great continental competitor, Germany, which hampered it considerably in the war effort. Immediately after the war, spurred by tariff protection, the industry grew rapidly but was preoccupied with meeting domestic requirements.

After World War II, chemicals became major exports, rising from 6.9% of total exports in 1953 to more than 8% in 1958. The only exports that surpass them to any large extent are all machinery except electrical, which in 1958 accounted for 17.7% of the total. Exports of chemicals totaled £263 million ($736 million) in 1958, 8.2%, only slightly below exports of cars, trucks, and related equipment (9.4%), slightly above textile products (8%), and electrical machinery (7%), and substantially greater than aircraft (4.8%).

Chemical production represented 2.6% of gross domestic output and 7.3% of gross manufactured output in 1958. But chemicals accounted for 9.8% of all exports of manufactured goods. The industry employed 357,000, or 1.5% of the total British labor force, about one third being administrative, technical and clerical personnel. Since the end of World War II special attention has been given to increasing productivity. The industry also has extended considerably the scope of its research, and expenditures on research and development have risen steadily.

Investment

Investment in the chemical industry, according to the British Report on the Chemical Industry in Europe submitted to OEEC (OEEC Document CP [59]4), totaled £124 million ($347 million) in 1958, compared to £128 million in 1957 and £127 million in 1956, about a 3% reduction. The report also shows a lag in new investments in the first few months of 1959. This development may signal the beginning of a leveling off from the $350-million annual rate of the past 3 years.

The 1957-58 reduction was due partly to the short recession in the fall of 1957. In that period, for the first time since World War II, production in most chemical lines fell well below capacity, unquestionably causing some firms to delay projected investments and making it more difficult for the smaller and/or less efficient producers to obtain credit for large expansion projects. However, the plans of Imperial Chemical Industries (about 40% of the total industry) probably were not immediately affected, and the largest British oil companies, Shell and British Petroleum, may well have been stimulated to increase their investments in chemicals as a hedge against an apparently more serious lag in growth possibilities for petroleum.

British manufacturers were more perturbed about the marketing outlook at the end of 1958, questioning whether the United Kingdom would be able to share in EEC benefits and visualizing increasingly difficult export marketing in continental Europe.

On the other hand, domestic prospects are good. The industry has probably built up enough momentum in the past 15 years to withstand any immediate marketing difficulties. Some firms have established highly efficient and profitable lines and will continue to expand them. Firms that are making substantial profits each year usually plow back their earnings even though they anticipate more difficult conditions. Other firms plan to develop complementary lines for better over-all operating efficiency. All large firms have important research programs, and "breakthrough" discoveries will doubtless lead to investment in large new facilities. Progressive development of the Common Market may stimulate other British industries in addition to oil companies to expand into chemicals, the chemical industry probably being better equipped than most others to compete in third countries with firms operating in the Common Market.

New Facilities

Most of the major expansion is in the fields of petrochemicals, especially thermoplastics, pharmaceuticals, and basic coal-derived products. Other projects of particular interest are increased fertilizer capacity by ICI, Shell and Fisons; expanded capacity for materials used to produce synthetic fibers; and additional capacity for new metallic products—tantalum-niobum, silicones, and beryllium—and for oxygen.

Production and Prices

According to the Organization for European Economic Cooperation (OEEC) Report on the Chemical Industry in Europe (OEEC Document CP [59]4), British chemical production totaled £1,300 million ($3,640 million) in 1958, compared with £1,315 million in 1957 and £1,234 million in 1956. Inasmuch as the index for wholesale prices for chemical and allied products fell 1% during the year, apparently the 1958 volume differed only marginally from that of 1957. In fact, consumption of chemicals by volume probably increased in 1958 as compared to 1957, because imports rose by £5 million and exports declined by £4 million, making available for domestic use an additional £9 million ($25.2 million) worth.

Foreign Trade

The chemical industry ranks as the United Kingdom's third largest exporter, accounting for 8% by value of all its exports. Exports were down some 2% in 1958, from £267 million ($747 million) in 1957 to £263 million ($736 million), whereas imports rose by 5%, from £114 million ($319 million) to £120 million ($336 million). Nevertheless, the United Kingdom continues to be a large exporter of chemicals, accounting for more than 15% of the world's total, and the long-term trend seems to be toward an increase of about the same proportions as that of imports. However, the United Kingdom has lost to West Germany its postwar position as the world's second largest exporter, and the industry's leaders do not expect to regain it immediately. If inter-EEC trade is ultimately categorized as domestic, the United Kingdom could well recapture that position, but most businessmen do not foresee that the six countries will operate as a single trading unit for some time.

By commodity groups, export losses were especially evident in inorganic chemicals, down about $6 million from 1957; dyestuffs, $3 million; pharmaceuticals, $5 million; and soaps and detergents, $7 million. These reductions were compensated somewhat by an increase of some $10 million in miscellaneous chemicals and $4 million in fertilizers.

WEST GERMAN CHEMICAL INDUSTRY

The West German chemical industry reports generally good years in 1958 and 1959. Its importance in the national economy remained high despite a slackening in its growth trend. Increases in production and sales were about double the averages registered for all industries. Foreign sales of inorganic industrial chemicals decreased, and domestic sales, following the normal trend after periods of rapid growth, leveled off.

Developments in the organic industrial chemicals sector clearly reflected the sales crisis in coal mining as production of coke and coke by-products and coal-tar derivatives (pitch and phenol) declined. Sales volume in this sector was generally satisfactory, but profits were uniformly lower. Heavy investment, expansion and new construction characterized the petroleum branch. The increase in production of major aliphatic chemicals except ethylene oxide was considerably lower than in 1957.

Owing principally to direct subsidies and high exports of nitrogenous fertilizers, total fertilizer production increased, although development by product was widely uneven; the nitrogenous group soared, phosphoric fertilizers rose very slightly, and potash dropped. The industry counts on a good crop year and increased domestic consumption to offset anticipated declines in foreign sales—which weigh heavily in this branch—but is not too optimistic.

Production of dyestuffs, also heavily dependent on foreign sales, declined slightly in the face of the world-wide textile recession, and no improvement is foreseen for 1959.

Pharmaceuticals production, spurred largely by the substantially increased output of human pharmaceutical specialties, advanced by 7% to DM 1.7 billion (1 Deutsche mark = U. S. $0.238). Production of antibiotics declined, whereas sales of tranquilizers reportedly increased. The uptrend in domestic consumption, which absorbs about 75% of total production, and the sound reputation and generally competitive prices of West German pharmaceutical products in the international market are expected to ensure future growth for this branch at a rate exceeding that of the chemical industry as a whole.

The soaps and other washing agents branch lost the slight gains registered in 1957; volume dropped by 2% and value remained about the same.

Sharper competition in the international market exerted considerable pressure on exports, a very important sales outlet for the chemical industry; they advanced by only 2.5% to DM 4.62 billion. Exports of inorganic industrial chemicals declined, whereas organic industrial chemicals and chemical specialties (particularly plastics, pharmaceuticals, nitrogenous fertilizers and photochemicals) advanced. Exports to European countries increased, accounting for more than 61% of the total. Trade with the American continent declined, owing chiefly to an 8% drop in exports to the United States; foreign sales to other areas remained at about 1957 levels, although marked changes occurred in trade with individual countries.

Imports continued to advance faster than exports, rising by 7% to DM 1.74 billion. They accounted for 11% of domestic consumption during the year. Purchases from the American continent advanced substantially, to 33% of the total, largely owing to a 15% increase in imports from the United States. Other leading suppliers were OEEC (Organization for European Economic Cooperation) members, whose share in total imports was almost 49%.

Foreign investment increased as the Big Three in particular expanded their overseas interests. Recent measures to liberalize the outflow of capital are expected to result in further increases.

Although the Common Market has become a reality, its effect on the chemical industry during the reporting period was slight. Establishment of international secretariats for pharmaceuticals and general chemical associations within the area and the impetus given to developing petrochemical facilities in the Federal Republic —anticipating competition from other EEC (European Economic Community) countries which have cheaper raw material sources)— promise to influence future developments.

Within the framework of expected national economic growth, trends apparent in the chemical industry should continue. Production and sales will probably rise but at a slightly slower rate. Sharper divergencies among sectors seem likely, and production of chemical specialties and organic chemicals will increase their leads over industrial and inorganic chemicals. Trade with Europe and the United States is expected to increase and the Federal Republic will remain a net exporter of chemicals. Competition will probably be even sharper and accompanied by increasing pressure on prices, and the industry will respond with greater efforts to rationalize. The Big Three are looking forward to a good year which will tend to benefit the industry as a whole.

PRODUCTION AND SALES

Sales advanced by 5% to a record high of DM 18.05 billion in 1958 from DM 17.19 billion in 1957, which was an 11% increase over 1956. Total sales for all industry increased by only 2.8% to DM 205 billion. Chemical output volume rose more steeply than did sales, owing to intensified price competition in both domestic and international markets.

INVESTMENT

Investment in the chemical industry reportedly continues to occupy first place among all West German branches. Since the currency reform it has totaled DM 8 billion and in 1958 approached DM 1.50 billion, which exceeds the amount invested in 1956 and 1957 (DM 1.45 billion) and accounts for about 8% of all chemical sales. The trend, apparent since 1956, of directing investment principally toward rationalization, modernization of existing facilities, and automation continued in 1958, particularly in the consumer chemical specialties sector. Investment for new facilities was concentrated in basic chemicals (especially petrochemicals), plastics and noncellulosic fibers. Although expenditures for research vary widely from sector to sector, they average approximately 4% of sales. Existing capacities were utilized satisfactorily during the year, indicating the absence of any sizable misdirected investments in recent years.

The industry has above-average capital investment per worker; the proportion of salaries and wages to turnover equals 15% as against the over-all industrial average of 18%. Despite relative price stability, the industry succeeded in maintaining a good level of profitability owing chiefly to increased efficiency.

JAPANESE CHEMICAL INDUSTRY

The Japanese chemical industry, which grew at a prodigious rate between 1950 and 1956, continued to expand in 1957 but leveled off substantially in 1958. Production increased 21% in 1956 and 11% in 1957. In 1958 the increase rate slowed to a mere 2%, according to preliminary Economic Planning Agency data, apparently owing partly to overexpansion and overproduction in 1956-57. At a time when a recession abroad prevented exports from increasing as fast as anticipated, producers were left with excessive inventories and a general price decline followed.

In a field as diversified as chemicals, the various component sectors fared unevenly in the two-year period. The pharmaceutical branch, which is not included in the production index data on which the above percentage changes are based, increased production rapidly in 1957 and probably led in size of percentage increase in 1958. Production of urea, ammonia, butanol and calcium carbide also showed above-average gains. On the other hand, polyvinyl chloride, which had had the most rapid increase in recent years, suffered a 28% drop. Alkalis, other inorganic chemicals and synthetic dyes and intermediates also decreased.

Although chemical exports are not large in relation to total exports, they are of considerable importance to some producers. The 1957 and 1958 totals of $125.9 million (f.o.b.) and $138.9 million (preliminary) accounted for less than 5% of all Japanese exports. Chemical exports were concentrated in a few lines, particularly fertilizer. Imports of chemicals other than raw materials fell from $183.4 million in 1957 to $166 million in 1958 (c.i.f.).

The general trend of investment in the industry is upward, from $178.7 million in fiscal year 1956 to a record of $207.6 million in 1957. It decreased to approximately $193.7 million in 1958, but a perhaps too optimistic figure of $253.4 million is planned for 1959. Although some facilities, especially fertilizer, appeared overexpanded at the end of 1957, others, including petrochemicals, synthetic resins, and organic synthetics, are increasing rapidly.

The most important new development in the period under review was in the petrochemical industry. By the end of 1958, 13 companies were pushing toward completion their First-Phase programs in this new area of Japanese industrial growth. The following petrochemicals are now in quantity production: Ethylene, ethylene oxide, ethylene glycol, polystyrene, polyethylene, isopropanol, acetone, phenol, secondary butanol, methylethyl ketone, benzol, toluol and xylol.

INVESTMENT

New investment in the fiscal years 1957 and 1958 fell considerably short of plans for those years, owing to a shortage of funds resulting from the Government's deflationary monetary policy. Productive capacity in some sectors had expanded far beyond the growth of domestic and export markets, and investment programs were accordingly curtailed, notably in the case of fertilizers. Programs in other areas, such as caustic soda, were postponed until the market returns to normal. The investment goal of more than $253 million for fiscal 1959, which is $45 million larger than in any of the three previous fiscal years, provides an increase, to $106.6 million, for petrochemicals and synthetic rubber and a revival of the soda industry's program, $16 million. Construction of facilities for the new synthetic rubber industry began in 1958, but production is not expected until late 1959 or early 1960.

Investment in the related synthetic and chemical fibers industry decreased from a high of $174.9 million in the fiscal year 1956 to an estimated $94.3 million in 1958. An increase to $127.3 million is scheduled for 1959, large portions going to synthetic fibers and cellulose acetate.

It may be of interest to compare the growth rate from 1938-1958 of the chemical industry in various chemical-producing countries of the world.

Country	Per Cent Growth
United States	7.3
Italy	6.6
Canada	6.1
Great Britain	5.8
Japan	5.8
France	4.9
West Germany	4.8

The poor showing of West Germany can be explained. Having already reached a position of great importance in 1938, it suffered setbacks during the war and early postwar years which it has not yet entirely overcome.

Now let us compare the export statistics of the three major chemical-producing countries of the world for the years 1957-1958.

Country	1957	1958
United States	$1,376,000,000	$1,343,000,000
West Germany	1,072,500,000	1,100,000,000
United Kingdom	747,000,000	736,000,000

It is interesting to note that in 1958 only the West German exports increased, while both the British and American exports felt the effects of the depression. The 1959 figures indicate substantial increases in exports for all three countries.

Rather than try to cover superficially, in the allotted time, the world supply-and-demand picture for all the various categories of chemicals, I have decided to discuss in some detail the plastic category. Plastics represent the largest single category in terms of dollar sales, and show the most spectacular growth since the war.

PLASTICS

Not so very long ago plastics were considered little more than curiosities, yet today they are valued mass goods and the plants making them approach those of the heavy chemicals industry in size. This is particularly true in the United States where the output of plastics has reached vast dimensions, making the output of individual European countries seem rather trivial. The picture is different if one considers Western Europe as a whole, but is it possible to speak at all of "European plastics production"?

Yes, for European plastics producers are among industrial leaders in breaking through national economic boundaries. Joint production ventures inside and outside Europe, joint license agreements, joint raw materials procurement, joint endeavors to expand exports and, not least, a common interest in meeting growing American competition in Europe have already brought about extensive integration within many sectors of Europe's plastics industry. Nor is this integration limited to narrower communities such as the Common Market and the Outer Seven; rather it is continent wide.

Competition will always exist between individual producers in any liberally conceived economic community, and indeed is desirable in the interests of continuing technical and industrial progress. But producers have and always will have mutual interests. These no longer stop at national boundaries today, but extend over the whole European market.

This is the background which justifies treating the European plastics industry as an entity.

Comparison of European and U. S. figures clearly shows that the European plastics industry has been catching up to the American during the last few years. The U. S. growth rate was 9.0% in

1956-57 and 6.8% in 1957-58; in Europe the gains were, respectively, 19.2% and 16.5%. The growth is also greater in Europe on an absolute scale. It was 229,194 tons (U. S., 146,900 tons) for 1956-57 and 232,588 tons for 1957-58. In the latter year, U. S. growth (121,600 tons) was lower than in 1956-57.

The production of the Six has advanced more steeply than that of the Seven; the gains were, respectively, 18.5% and 9.0% in 1958. But then the Common Market includes three major producers, Germany, France and Italy, whereas the United Kingdom is the only major producer among the Seven and with an output less than that of Federal Germany alone.

Plastics production throughout the world increasingly favors the thermoplasts (thermoplastic resins, softened by heat) and OEEC figures mirror this trend. Thermoplasts accounted for 48.3% of 1958 production, thermosets (thermosetting resins, solidified by heat) 40.0%, cellulosic resins 11.5% and the casein resins 0.2%.

The summary of PVC (polyvinylchloride) producers shows that Europe's gross capacity has almost reached that in the United States. No precise information is available on American PVC capacity, but the 1958 output was 394,000 tons and assuming that facilities were 80% employed, this would indicate a gross installed capacity of 490,000 tons per annum. The European capacity of approximately 414,000 tons is thus already quite comparable.

Almost three quarters of capacity lies in the Common Market. The Solvay concern stands out among individual producers and with its six plants throughout Europe may well be the leading manufacturer, particularly when one remembers that Solvay also has an interest in Britain's largest producer, Imperial Chemical Industries, Ltd. (ICI).

U.S. WELL AHEAD IN POLYSTYRENE

The European polystyrene picture is far less favorable. Against American capacity of approximately 400,000 tons per anum, Europe has to offer only 148,000 tons, of which 108,000 tons lie within the Common Market.

EUROPE THE HOMELAND OF POLYETHYLENE

Although polyethylene originated in Europe, here, too, American capacity far outstrips European. But European producers have recently been gaining ground and the dynamics of expansion continues. Since a number of plants are approaching completion at this very moment, it seems appropriate to set out capacities at the beginning of 1960. Further plants are planned or under construction, as provisional capacity figures for the end of 1961 indicate.

In contrast to PVC and polystyrene, individual polyethylene plant capacities are largely known, so that national production figures can be taken as very substantially accurate.

Because of the large ICI contribution, the Seven show up much better on a capacity comparison than they do for PVC and polystyrene. But expansion is being especially pushed within the Common Market, so that by the end of 1961 the Six should be well ahead.

A comparison between installed capacities for high-pressure and low-pressure resins is interesting. The Seven lead at present in high-pressure polyethylene (again because of ICI) whereas the Six outweigh in low-pressure resin by 4.5:1. But there should be some leveling off by 1961. On the one hand the countries of the Common Market are expanding high-pressure polyethylene capacity strongly, on the other the United Kingdom is pushing ahead with plants to make low-pressure resin.

MANY COOPERATIVE VENTURES IN EUROPE

The concept of a West European Market is further accentuated by many companies having underpinned marketing of their products through production units in other countries.

These units may be operated by wholly owned subsidiaries, but the course increasingly favored is to seek out a partner in the land in question with market experience and a captive supply of raw material. In other words, the enmeshing of raw material producers is being duplicated on the resin manufacturing side, either through participations or joint ventures.

To take only a few examples: Solvay not only has straight sub-sidiaries, but is enmeshed with ICI; BASF works in France with Kuhlmann and in Germany with Shell.

EUROPEAN PLASTICS IN WORLD MARKETS

The European plastics industry has been able not only to keep pace with its sharpest competitor, the United States, but also to forge ahead. Comparable U. S. figures are unfortunately available only for 1956, but these show that the export advance was less over two years, both relatively and absolutely, than between 1957 and 1958 in Europe.

The Six, excluding Belgium-Luxemburg, were able to advance their exports substantially more than were the Seven; France and Germany enjoyed the largest growth rates. Indeed, the less important producers of the Seven were forced to reconcile themselves to declining exports, though excepting Austria which was able nearly to double shipments. The advance in British exports was also relatively small. Europe predominates in all group markets, with the exception of Latin America.

As is only natural, the greater proportion of British exports go to the Commonwealth; France, too, ships substantial quantities to the Communauté. It is interesting that Italy makes the greatest deliveries to the U. S., and these may well largely comprise polypropylene which has figured in a lively U. S. advertising campaign by Montecatini.

Federal Germany is strongest in Eastern Bloc trade, followed by the United Kingdom and Italy. Austria, whose shipments are recorded under "remainder of the Seven," also exports to the Eastern Bloc. But to Eastern Bloc exports must also be added the major part of goods shipped to Hong Kong, which is an entrepôt for the China trade. The United Kingdom is strongest here, but the U. S. also sends by no means unimportant quantities.

PRODUCTION OVERSEAS

Export figures alone give an incomplete picture of the importance of Europe's plastics in the World. European firms have, indeed, a not unimportant foothold in American production via subsidiaries or participations. Whereas British companies rather naturally play a dominant part in the Commonwealth, it is German and French firms which have been able to contribute to technological development in the countries of Latin America, by establishing manufacturing plants there.

But even this does not exhaust the potential of the European plastics industry. One must not forget "intellectual cross-fertilization," which in most cases also has a background chink of coin. Under this heading comes the numerous license and technical assistance agreements which European firms have entered into with overseas partners. Undoubtedly the leading entrant is polyethylene, now made throughout the world essentially under European licenses. The high-pressure resin, developed independently by BASF of Germany and ICI of England, and the low-pressure resins of Professor Ziegler, have each secured a leading place among plastics. Also processes for polypropylene—which promises to become a serious competitor to polyethylene in the near future—originated in Europe. They were developed by Professor Ziegler and Professor Natta and are licensed overseas by Montecatini.

U.S. Seeking European Markets

A compilation of American plastics exports to Western Europe is most informative. While American and Canadian exports to non-European markets rose by 11% over the course of two years, exports to Europe—and here effectively only the Six and the Seven come into question—advanced by 20% within a single year! The Six were particularly affected with an advance of 22% (only 13% in the case of the Seven).

Britain, in fact, imported less plastics from the United States in 1958 than in 1957. Instead she experienced a new competitor, Japan, who has so far only sampled the rest of the European market. British PVC sales suffered especially from imports of each Japanese resin.

But the United States does not limit itself to pushing physical exports. Producers are throwing their most significant export commodity—capital—into the balance in order to establish production actually within Europe. American capital has brought positive gains for its European partners. They have benefited from American processes and American know-how and have been able substantially to increase their share of the market and to diversify their range of products.

On the other hand, many European enterprises have come to recognize that alone or in partnership with other European undertakings—either of the Six or of the Seven, it is immaterial—they already have sufficient economic strength to carry on the European plastics tradition.

CONCLUSIONS

This survey of the plastics industry serves to illustrate the truly international character of the chemical industry and the techniques used to penetrate the world markets.

Our conclusion is that the outlook for the chemical industry is bright. There are some gloomy factors, such as nationalism and competition from the Iron Curtain countries. However, the chemical industry of the Western world is strong, imaginative, aggressive and resourceful, and should have no difficulty in overcoming these gloomy factors. Fortunately, labor costs are not an important factor in the chemical industry so that it does not face the strong competitive factors from low-wage areas of the world that some industries face.

The United States, which now enjoys the commanding position in the world chemical industry, should continue to maintain this position in both the near and long-term future. However, to maintain our position we must take an even more aggressive approach in our export sales. We can no longer indulge in the luxury of allocating products for export when domestic sales slump and withdrawing the allocation when domestic sales are good. We must also staff our export departments with competent sales people and devote the same intelligent effort to export sales as we do to our domestic sales. The European and Japanese companies have learned this lesson and we would do well to copy their methods. American investments abroad are likely to increase substantially, particularly in the underdeveloped areas of the world. These investments will be largely in the form of wholly owned subsidiaries and joint ventures with local producers.

Hon. Felix Edgar Wormser
CONSULTING MINING ENGINEER
FORMER ASSISTANT SECRETARY OF THE INTERIOR

Nonferrous Metals

ALUMINUM, copper, lead, nickel, tin and zinc are well-known common nonferrous metals, but those of you who attended the session on the impact of technology on our society (p. 257) must have been impressed with the number of nonferrous metals bearing unfamiliar labels that are now being put to work. Only recently has science been able commercially to recover the scarcer metals, the rare earths (some not so rare after all). It would take a book to cover the probable future of all the nonferrous metals including antimony, beryllium, cadmium, cobalt, columbium, chromium, germanium, hafnium, lithium, manganese, mercury, molybdenum, selenium, tellurium, thorium, titanium, tungsten, uranium, zirconium and about fifteen others. We can only make a few general observations.

Periodically the public press will be found to carry rather alarming analyses to show that the United States is a "have not" nation in metals and minerals, by which is meant that our domestic supplies, heretofore ample, will soon run out. This fear has been accentuated by occasional shortages that result in a scramble for metal. But our mineral resources are far from being exhausted. We are even creating relatively new mining industries. Titanium and uranium are good examples of what I mean.

Titanium is a common constituent of rocks but it has been costly and difficult to extract in metallic form. Because of its unique properties, especially its corrosion resistance and ability to withstand high temperatures, the federal government provided attractive incentives to stimulate the production of titanium for military application. Excellent plants were built by private enterprise, but so swiftly and sharply does technology progress in our age that the program was hardly under way when government plans were altered, eliminating the need for large quantities of titanium in military apparatus. In a few years production had risen dramatically from about 1,000 to 17,000 tons of sponge annually by 1957 but the yearly output now is back to roughly 4,000 tons. In the meantime, however, the price of titanium sponge has declined from $5 to $1.60 per lb.—still too high for widespread use, but giving much promise for the future.

Uranium is a good answer to those who contend we are a "have not" nation. As we enter the atomic age, uranium will have an increasingly significant part to play. Long a mineralogical curiosity with a small production from the Rocky Mountains, the metal has become of incalculable importance to the nation's future security. Uranium mining is a new industry with large reserves in sight. Seven years ago only 1,000 tons of U_{238} were produced in the United States. In 1959 over 19,000 tons were shipped with an estimated value of $135,000,000. Obviously the industry has been enormously assisted by the federal government's fixed-price purchase program, but it demonstrates the effect of a good market upon the potential supply of a metal or mineral. By the same token, the uranium mining industry faces an uncertain future after government purchasing ends in 1966.

It is true we experience shortages from time to time. Producers as well as consumers are disturbed over those events. Shortages are disruptive of carefully cultivated markets. A serious scarcity of lead and zinc a few years ago was damaging to the outlets for those metals. But mineral shortages, or rather scarcities, are usually dissipated with surprising suddenness and may bring about such an abundance that trouble arises. We had an acute shortage of nickel four years ago. Now we have more than enough in sight. Sulphur (not a nonferrous metal, of course) was in desperate demand a few years ago. Mexican production plus submarine recoveries in the Gulf of Mexico have changed the picture drastically for a long time to come.

Where do we stand looking towards the future of the nonferrous metals? The basic facts are these:

(1) The world's use of metals and minerals is growing. Because of business ups and downs, it is growing erratically, but it is growing nevertheless.

(2) The easily discoverable metal and mineral deposits of the world are behind us. It is becoming increasingly difficult to find the metals that are important to industry and mankind.

(3) Mining is a one-crop business. Metals can only be mined once, but many can be reused over and over again. The reclamation of scrap metal is a useful and increasingly important industry.

(4) The world's mineral resources are enormous, but

(5) The grade of the ores commercially treated is becoming lower and lower. However, our extractive technology is constantly improving.

Put all of these assertions together and the conclusion is that we shall have adequate supplies of the metals and minerals we need but that we can anticipate higher prices for the older common metals, and lower prices for the newer ones. The long-range future of the nonferrous metals appears brilliant, with ample supplies to serve civilization as far ahead as anyone can see.

A fundamental change has taken place in the position of the United States mineral economy. We used to lead the world in the production of most nonferrous metals. That is no longer true. Moreover, the American appetite for nonferrous metals and minerals has grown so great that the domestic mine supply has generally been able to furnish only a diminishing fraction of the requirements of industry. We are on an import basis for practically the entire list of nonferrous metals. Without needed imports industry would suffer. Only three major mineral products are exported from the United States. They are coal, sulphur and molybdenum. Our nation has been thrust squarely into the international mineral picture. This is not a new experience. But the implications in some of our comparatively recent history are rather sobering in looking at possible future international trends. To illustrate:

After World War II an International Materials Conference was organized. This was set up to allocate, on a world-wide basis, country by country, available supplies of copper or other materials then in short supply. The expression was then coined, "Entitlement for Consumption." That is, each nation was entitled to so much copper or other mineral allocation.

Conference personnel decide what share of available metals and minerals each nation was to receive. This philosophy met with the approval of some officials of the United Nations who complained about the unparalleled growth in the economy of the United States, and contended that we ought to slow down while the rest of the world caught up to our standard of living. Their ingenious method for achieving this objective was to limit the supply of necessary foreign raw materials imported into the United States, thereby restricting our growth! Fantastic, but true. I am glad to report the International Materials Conference was killed in 1953 by an act of Congress.

Not every country feels as we do that the greatest benefit to mankind arises from freedom, freedom in the market and open competition. Cartels are common abroad. Moreover, a tendency towards the formation of international government commodity cartels was quite noteworthy prior to the advent of the Eisenhower administration. In an effort to curb often-violent fluctuations in world commodity markets, international commodity agreements were proposed.

A tin agreement was actually drafted after seven years of work, with the assistance of the United States. Thanks in part to the recommendation of the Randall Commission on Foreign Trade, which pointed out the rigidities of any international governmental commodity control, the United States did not go along with the tin agreement. Nevertheless it seems to be functioning to the satisfaction of many of the producers in the tin industry, and some consumers. However, the period of time in which it has been in existence has not been long enough to place sound judgment on its merits.

I merely mention a possible trend to commodity agreements because efforts may be made to apply them to other metals. Indeed, government officials on an international basis may try to usurp the function of a free market as they have in the past. I doubt, whether any group of governmental officials has the wisdom to discharge a market price responsibility as well as a free market. I know nothing better than the unfettered operation of the law of supply and demand to bring about a speedy adjustment of an unbalanced commodity situation.

Another feature of our international markets which will affect the source of mineral supplies is the reduction in trade barriers now slowly taking place all over the world, largely initiated by the United States under the Reciprocal Trade Agreement Act and illustrated also by the development of the Common Markets abroad, the Inner Six and the Outer Seven. A sharp reduction in the United States tariff structure on metals and ores has made it difficult for some of our domestic mineral industries that have traditionally depended upon tariff protection to survive. The government is currently using other means such as quotas to help them.

We are living in an age characterized by monetary manipulation to control trade to a degree unique in the history of the world, so that the tariff itself now occupies a subordinate position, as an international trade impediment, to monetary manipulation such as currency devaluation, quotas, and other devices to direct trade in various channels.

The development of a European Common Market should have beneficial results similar to those which accrued to the United States from the freedom of trade among the 50 states. If there is any validity in the Reciprocal Trade Agreement philosophy for the liberalization of world trade, it would seem that North America offers an exceptionally fine opportunity to apply this policy between Canada and the United States. The unfortified military border from coast to coast is an example to the rest of the world how two great nations can live in friendship and peace. Living and labor standards are parallel. Both countries would profit markedly if all the trade barriers between the two nations were gradually extinguished over a period of 10 to 15 years. This is an excellent place for free trade to be applied internationally, but I do not expect to see this occur for political rather than economic reasons.

I have not mentioned the beneficial impact of technical research on the world's future supply of metals and minerals. The general public does not realize the great amount of progress that has been made in improving our technology for the recovery of metals and minerals or in successfully treating low-grade ores. Nor does it realize the fact that we have an abundance of new metals and minerals that are quite common but either haven't appeared commercially, or are just beginning to appear.

Our scientists, through the United States Geological Survey, have made a scientific analysis of the composition of the Earth. They tell us the most abundant nonferrous metal in the Earth's crust is aluminum,* 8.1%; then calcium, 3.63%; sodium, 2.8%; potassium, 2.6%; magnesium, 2.1%; then a big drop to titanium, 0.44%.

We take another sharp drop down to manganese, 0.1%. Now we come to one that I doubt many of you have heard about—rubidium, the next most abundant metal in the earth's crust, 0.03%; then strontium, 0.03%; barium, 0.025%. We then note another metal just beginning to appear as a valuable raw material for industry—zirconium, 0.022%.

Admiral Rickover called me up a few years ago when I was in government to thank the Bureau of Mines for the work they did in developing the means of producing commercial zirconium. He told me he would have had difficulty in designing the *Nautilus* if he hadn't had a metal such as zirconium available.

As a by-product of zirconium, we get hafnium, another metal

* More abundant than iron.

further down the list. I will just mention quickly some others: chromium, 0.020%; vanadium, 0.015%; zinc, 0.013%; then nickel, 0.008%; copper, 0.007%. That is where my list terminates.

Delve into the whole gamut of the metals and see how far down some common ones are listed. The percentages seem small, but the aggregate is gigantic considering the weight of the earth.

Government and private industry are doing an enormous amount of technical and commercial work in the field of rare metals. Industry has developed means for producing extraordinarily high temperatures and pressures, not to mention chemical developments, all of which promise to improve metallurgical and mineral techniques. Mineral technology will make many low-grade uncommercial ores eventually profitable. In fact, the U. S. Geological Survey expects to see, some years from now, the mining of entire geological formations. To illustrate, the phosphoria formation in Idaho contains phosphate but also many trace metals which will ultimately permit the entire formation to be mined for its combined mineral value. One gigantic untapped source of all metals and minerals is the ocean. We are already deriving a supply of one metal commercially and profitably from the sea—magnesium.

We are also obtaining from the ocean another useful element, bromine (not a nonferrous metal). I am sure the profitable recovery of other mineral products will follow. Many rare metals will become household words in the future as they are mined and refined, and their properties prove to be useful, particularly germanium, cerium, selenium and tellurium.

Some government action under existing statutes not intended primarily to benefit the mineral industries, oddly enough, has helped to provide a stockpile of useful metals and minerals which should comfort those who remain disturbed about prospective, adequate nonferrous metal supplies. I refer to the acquisition of metals and minerals by the Department of Agriculture through the barter of surplus wheat, cotton and corn under the provisions of Public Law 480.

One may well ask what better use for our easily replaceable agricultural surpluses than to exchange them for irreplaceable one-crop mineral products produced abroad? A large stockpile of useful metals and minerals accumulated from abroad is essentially a transfer of foreign mineral deposits to our shores. Some barter has already been done. Unfortunately, there are many complexities and much international hostility to barter because of the potentially demoralizing character of barter transactions on world wheat and cotton markets. Hence I do not anticipate too much barter for minerals being done.

A few thumbnail observations about the major nonferrous metals follow:

Aluminum. Its growth has surpassed other major metals but it must find new uses or expand existing ones to keep abreast of production from new plants.

Antimony. Largely a by-product metal from lead refining and recovery from scrap storage battery plates. Imports necessary.

Cadmium. A by-product of zinc smelting. A useful plating metal and paint pigment.

Chromium. Domestic producers subject to high costs in exploration and beneficiation of low-grade ores. Large imports required.

Copper. Highly competitive with aluminum, steel and plastics. Variations in supply have tended to favor competition. Ample supplies for the foreseeable future.

Lead. Although currently in excess world supply, new discoveries of lead deposits are conspicuous by their absence. Subject to intense competition but has large outlets in metal and chemical form.

Magnesium. A metal of the future because of inexhaustible supply.

Manganese. Indispensable in some uses. Relatively inexpensive. U. S. dependent upon imports.

Mercury. Essentially noncompetitive markets and unique properties insure an attractive future.

Molybdenum. Mines subject to competition from by-production of copper mines.

Nickel. Despite its relatively high cost the outlook is excellent for both peace and wartime application.

Titanium. A metal of the future because of potentially great supply and useful properties. High unit cost gradually declining. A promising outlook.

Tungsten. Extremely useful properties, especially resistance to high temperatures, and alloying qualities. Domestic mines subject to much low-cost foreign competition.

Uranium. A metal of the future. No substitutes as a basis for nuclear fuel. Wholly dependent today on government purchases at fixed price.

Vanadium. A metal with useful alloying properties restricted in application by relatively high cost.

Zinc. Large potential supply of this important metal. Subject to strong competition in both metallic and chemical form. Low price should generate enlarged markets.

In conclusion, I hope I have left the impression that I have no anxiety about the adequacy of our future nonferrous metal supplies. Government intervention may occasionally cause trouble for sellers and buyers, but scientific evidence tells us that mineral products are available for mankind's benefit to a degree that makes them inexhaustible.

Continuation of a free market, nationally and internationally, is the best assurance to commerce and industry that any metal or mineral will be produced in the quantities required by mankind.

5

Henry L. Griffin
ECONOMIST
UNITED GRAIN GROWERS LIMITED

Grains

GRAINS GENERALLY are presently in abundant supply, and that situation is likely to persist.

Of all grains, principally wheat warrants detailed discussion. Much more than any other grain it is a commodity of trade being grown mainly for sale. Corn, in contrast, is produced mainly to be fed where grown. It is mainly wheat which presents problems and complications.

As everyone knows, the world is abundantly supplied with wheat now, and the surplus is concentrated in North America, predominantly in the United States. That surplus is costly to maintain, impossible to sell and difficult to give away. It has developed during the past seven years as the world shifted from a state of wartime and postwar scarcity of food to a state of abundance. Nothing now in sight warrants a prediction of early change.

If we seek for light we shall not find it by studying market reports. No longer is there a closely integrated international wheat market, with quotations at Liverpool, Chicago and Winnipeg sensitive to every changing circumstance affecting demand and supply throughout the world. Nor can we reach conclusions by laborious compilation of statistics. That is only partly because accurate figures are difficult to come by for vast areas such as Russia, China and India. It is largely because the forces affecting wheat are not primarily economic but are political. National policies of different governments, international politics and even local elections all play a part.

You may ask how is it possible to have a superabundance of wheat when the population of the world has been increasing at an alarming rate, frequently described as explosive. The number of living human beings did not exceed one billion until well past A.D. 1800. Now there are 3 billion of us. By the end of this century there may be 7 billion. The Malthusian doctrine that population is due to outrun food resources has become almost commonly accepted in recent years. In consequence, the presently existing wheat surplus demands explanation.

(1) Since the end of World War II available food has kept well ahead of population. We must conclude that in the past, total food resources have been underestimated. So, also, has the rate at which it is possible to increase these.

(2) Agriculture is vastly more efficient now than only a few years ago. Each acre and each hour of human labor on the farm produces more than used to be thought possible and the improvement goes on at an accelerating rate. The process has been described as the agricultural revolution, not less important than the industrial revolution of the early 19th century. Mechanization has been one factor, but there are a multitude of others. Weeds are controlled by chemicals and insects by other chemicals. Plant breeders are constantly producing new varieties designed to be immune from various diseases, and breeders of animals and poultry are providing new strains that use feed more efficiently. Animal diseases are checked by antibiotics. The science of animal feeding has so progressed that more meat, more milk and more eggs are forthcoming from a given area for a given number of livestock. Artificial fertilizers are applied to land more abundantly and more skillfully. In the United States their total use is approaching an annual value of $1½ billion. Corn yields have increased enormously from the use of hybrid seed and the technique of hybridization is extending to other fields. Progress has not been confined to this part of the world; it is widespread.

Beneficent as this progress is for human welfare, it carries troubles in its train. Proportionately to the whole, the farming population has to shrink and redundant farmers transfer or be transferred to other occupations. The transfer is often difficult and sometimes painful. It gives rise to social problems and to attempts to alleviate these by political means.

(3) The horse and mule have disappeared as sources of motive power, and petrol has been substituted for hay and oats as a source of energy. A great area of land formerly devoted to the sustenance of these animals, not less than 60 million acres in North America alone, is now available for human food. Correspondingly nylon and rayon have relieved agriculture from the task of providing a great deal of clothing. Otherwise, land now producing food would be required for linen, cotton and wool.

(4) The traditional eaters of bread (with which we may include spaghetti) in North America and in Europe now need less wheat per capita than 50 years ago. With muscle power losing its importance, the intake of high-energy foods has been reduced. So also increased prosperity and rising standards of living have made possible more varied diets in which the importance of bread steadily declines. For example, in Canada the total consumption of white flour has tended to remain fairly constant over a long period despite a great increase in the country's population.

In the United States, according to a milling authority, the annual use of wheat is less by 115 million bushels because of a drop during recent years of 40 lbs. in the annual per capita consumption of flour. That fact alone is sufficient to account for much of the current wheat surplus in the United States.

Elsewhere a rising standard of living may mean an increased consumption of white flour. Also, to some extent, wheat is becoming a regular article of consumption for people who formerly used it little or not at all. But to find such new customers and to develop trade with them is not easy, and if the people in question live in remote Asiatic villages it may be impossible.

Among political forces affecting wheat is the direct participation of governments in wheat trade. Years ago a student commencing to study international trade would be told that nations as such do not trade; instead international trade is carried on between individuals residing in different countries. Such is no longer true of wheat. No bushel now moves from one country to another unless the government of at least one of them is involved in the transaction. Frequently both are and quite often there have been intergovernmental negotiations as to prices and quantity.

This advent of governments into merchandizing has resulted in various problems and difficulties and in conflicts of interests.

For example, European countries, noting that large stocks of wheat are held under governmental control in Canada and the United States, have been inclined to see in this fact a concerted effort to hold up prices to their disadvantage and to plan defensive measures. These might be to increase their own wheat production, reducing their need for imports, or at times to buy wheat from Russia as a demonstration of independence.

There is sales competition between exporting governments and fears are sometimes expressed that this may develop into cutthroat competition, for which of course the responsibility would always lie with some other country than one's own. The United States Department of Agriculture must constantly keep its collective eye upon prices quoted by the Canadian Wheat Board. The latter is concerned with every adjustment in subsidies on grain exports from the United States. Both countries are concerned when in the British markets they meet competition from subsidized wheat exports from France. And all other exporting countries are constantly concerned as to how much grain the Soviet Union has to export and as to how urgent is that government's desire to market surplus grain.

This business of merchandising by governments is so new a thing that there is neither an accepted nor an expected pattern of behaviour. There are conventional methods for dealings between different governments on political matters; there are normal expectations of reactions of producers, consumers and merchants in an ordinary market. These have not yet had time to develop with respect to governments in trade. Consequently, although what one's own government does in buying or selling may seem proper, reasonable and wise, it may be difficult to predict or to understand the trading policy of another country.

There is, for example, a trade practice described as "dumping," thought reprehensible, against which most industrialized importing countries have restrictive legislation. It means selling abroad at prices less than those prevailing in the domestic market. It has become common practice with wheat and to a certain extent with other grains, through subsidized exports. Let me admit at once that if my own country has not yet adopted it and maintains domestic and export prices on the same level, the so-called "two-price system" is frequently advocated in Canada. On occasion Canada has sold abroad certain quantities of dairy products at distress price levels.

An international transaction in wheat presents different aspects when viewed from different angles, as, for example, the recently announced arrangement for some 600 million bushels of United States wheat to be supplied to India during a four-year period in return for Indian currency. To some it will appear as a step to get rid of a burdensome surplus. True, it may tend to prevent the North American surplus from further growth during the next four years. It does not, however, promise a reduction in that surplus, because wheat so shipped is likely to be replaced by new production. Here we may hope for a permanently expanded market in India. That country seeks only a breathing spell of four years during which to develop her own agriculture and to eliminate need for further imports. Australia and Canada see the transaction as limiting outlets for their own wheat.

An arrangement just concluded between Canada and Norway is interesting because of its concept more than because of its size. A limited quantity of Canadian flour is to be supplied free of charge, except for transportation, to Norway. That country undertakes to maintain a flour reserve for an indefinite period. Assured of an emergency supply in case of need, Norway will be less likely to stimulate her own grain production. Other countries of Western Europe have not yet responded to suggestions to set up food reserves under a somewhat similar plan. Were they to do so, they might feel under less pressure to stimulate wheat growing within their own boundaries for fear of food shortages in the event of war.

That fear of possible food scarcity is only one of several reasons prompting different countries to resist the import of a comparatively cheap wheat available from North America and to obtain wheat supplies from their own farmers at much higher costs. One such reason is the generally benevolent attitude towards domestic agriculture to be found in most countries, a feeling in continental Europe that a prosperous peasantry must be maintained or, as in England, a feeling that the natural resources of soil fertility must be fully exploited.

Then there is the need, or rather the belief in the need, to limit expenditures for imports in order to protect the exchange value of a country's currency. Until a short time ago that was summed up in the phrase "dollar shortage." The condition so described has been disappearing. Nevertheless, its consequences continue.

In theory, everyone believes in international trade. Largely that is only partial belief, a belief in that half of international trade represented by exports from one's own country. Belief in the other half, that represented by imports, is much more lightly held.

Wheat tends to attract action by governments because of the ease of intervention. It is correspondingly difficult to let go. Intervention often means price guarantees, frequently at the cost of the national treasury. To benefit, the farmer must not only grow wheat; he must bring it to market. He refrains from feeding wheat on his own farm; others refrain from buying it for feed because in the domestic market wheat has become more expensive than other grains. Farmers in parts of England, for example, have been heard to complain that instead of keeping their land in grass, as they would prefer, they must grow and sell wheat to benefit from government assistance.

Human consumption of wheat is quite inelastic and in total volume is comparatively little affected by price fluctuations. But the use of wheat for livestock feeding is extremely elastic and has been greatly restricted as an unintended result of various governmental policies.

Wheat policies of a government, of whatever country, are not to be considered fixed and unchangeable. The government in Great Britain, instead of buying all imported cereals as formerly, withdrew completely from direct trading in grain after a Labor administration was replaced by a Conservative one. It has, however, continued measures to promote domestic production. The government of Argentina has withdrawn from participation in the business of exporting wheat, which under a previous administration was monopolized, for a special reason of its own, the control of exchange.

A change is currently taking place in the Common Market countries of Western Europe, which are promoting grain transactions with each other and endeavoring as a whole to become independent of imports from outside. This threatens to reduce outlets for North American wheat.

Intervention by governments in wheat, once commenced, tends to persist. It builds up vested interests resistant to change. These are not confined to farmers. They may include agencies and manufacturers of machinery or fertilizers.

Almost all governments are sensitive to farm opinion in their own countries. They do not respond to foreign criticism of their policies. For example, the International Wheat Agreement of 1959 expressed concern that measures should be taken towards correcting the present world wheat surplus situation. But it also declared the complete liberty of each country to determine and administer its internal agricultural and price policies.

We must expect that sometime or other there will be a change from the present world situation of a surplus of wheat. It may come about through steady increase of human population. It may come from other causes. For all that can be seen at the moment, the existing surplus is likely to be with us for some time ahead.

6

Israel Rogosin
PRESIDENT AND CHAIRMAN OF THE BOARD
BEAUNIT MILLS, INC.

Fibers

THE FIBER INDUSTRY and my company will prosper only if the United States prospers. I have heard for too many years that the textile industry is the first to suffer from low-cost importation. Heavy-industry producers supposedly have gained by the loss of the textile industry: they have been paid for their products through the importation of textile products. The poor textile manufacturers have been made to appear unintelligent—even stupid. The major industries of this country have kept selling the public the idea that they must have an open door for world products, deluding themselves with the idea that it is to the interest of the American public for their industries to prosper by being able to sell their products abroad.

Now, however, all industries are being threatened, including steel, motors, chemicals, and machinery. If they wait long enough, they, too, will lose out, as other industries did during the past fifty years when they ignored the threat of low-cost competition. An indication of how serious this situation has become is the fact that all of the newest fibers, nylon, polyesters, and acrylics are being imported in yarn and fabric. Foreign producers are underselling this country. When foreign countries build up production capacity beyond the requirements of their home markets, we will be swamped by their competition. Before long, we will have the same situation with the polypropylene and other chemicals.

American companies, now recognizing the threat to their continued profits, are either setting up factories to manufacture abroad or buying component parts throughout the world. They are making arrangements with foreigners to give them help in merchandising and manufacturing international products. Part of their profit will come from European companies. In short, the individual company will profit, but the United States will lose out. This individual effort to retain a profit will result in unemployment of American labor. Our economy is being threatened by the low-cost producing countries in fibers, fabrics, metals, machinery, chemicals, and all other products. We need knitting machines for a new plant in the United States, as well as additions to old plants. Our company is buying abroad all the machines to be installed here.

We must move either to lower our costs of management, research, production, and labor to meet conditions in the world or to protect our market. We must recognize that, with our cost of production, we cannot expect to retain any portion of world markets, but we should at least retain our own market for ourselves. In the past, technical knowledge of chemicals, dyestuffs, and textiles was found only in certain countries in the world. Now that position has changed and technical know-how has spread to almost every country of the globe.

Low-cost producing countries also have adopted mass-production methods. They produce per manhour as much as we do and are a threat to world markets and our own markets. I am not guessing at this. I visited large plants in Japan, one of them with 4,000 employees, making the same product that we do—paying their standard of wages and their standard of salaries for scientists and researchers. We gave them some of our know-how. They are now making the same number of pounds of synthetic fibers per manhour that we are. They are not merely benefitting from cheap labor.

During the past 30 years we have lived by the philosophy of the student rather than by the philosophy of the realist. We can no longer, however, give away our strength and remain prosperous and respected. We have the natural resources and sufficient ingenuity to cope with these problems. If we wake up now, we shall not be surpassed by anyone.

THREE KEY AREAS:
Growth Rates and Trade Potentials

Robert J. Dixson
CHAIRMAN

1

Robert J. Dixson
CHAIRMAN OF THE BOARD AND PRESIDENT
JOHNSON & JOHNSON INTERNATIONAL

Introduction

THE SESSION we are about to open should provide an appropriate balance in the international picture, and should prove helpful to all whose interests lie in Western Europe, Latin America and Canada. The events occurring in Paris during the past few days portend difficulties and uncertainties and, as Prime Minister Macmillan said in his report to Parliament, they may have grave implications. But it is too early to assess the motives of the Soviet Union. I should prefer to leave the interpretation of the results and the happenings in Paris to others who are more expert in this field than am I. Therefore let us turn to the brighter side and rely on several basic assumptions that have been widely accepted by men of authority in business and in government.

The first is that there will be no major war in the 1960's and, with God's help, this will be so. The second is that there will be an ever-expanding world economy, which, in itself, will help the world to avoid a conflict.

The third assumption is that we will not be faced with a major world-wide economic recession. The fourth is that the economic lessons of the last 15 years have been learned and currency stability will replace the debilitating inflations of the past.

If we are right on all counts, there will, in fact, be a new set of political and economic dimensions in the world of the future.

We can only hope and pray that we shall have the chance to prove the accuracy of these assumptions.

The three areas selected for discussion today are important to the United States in its international relations. This is not to say that other areas are unimportant, for clearly the industrial expansion in Japan poses a problem of some importance for some and, perhaps, many United States manufacturers.

The emergent states in Africa hold out a promise of the development of that huge and largely unknown continent. Peculiar problems of the Near East also exist that require specific analysis and treatment. But there is a need for sharpness of focus and, in that respect, the three areas scheduled for discussion represent ones of particular importance to the United States, each in its own separate way.

Before anyone develops the feeling that he is being shortchanged by a selection of only three areas, let me remind him of the extensive coverage that is involved herein. Canada has a land mass that exceeds that of continental United States. This is likewise true of Latin America, which also has a population in the aggregate which exceeds that of the United States and Canada together.

With respect to Western Europe, the land mass obviously is not as extensive but the population is considerably greater and the industrial base is nearly as large as that of the United States. Without attempting to anticipate the specific remarks of the distinguished speakers that we have here today, I would like to point out some of the important features that distinguish the areas with which we are concerned.

Western Europe, as already mentioned, contains a concentration of industry that, in size, complexity and variety, comes close to matching that of the United States. While large parts of the area are still agricultural, its industrial base is extensive and accounts for the major share of the income of most countries. Of particular importance has been the very rapid growth in industrial production even after the early period of reconstruction.

Since 1953, industrial production in Western Europe has increased approximately 50%. This has been a matter of some satisfaction, then concern, and then reason for sober analysis by American businessmen. More recently, the nations of Europe have banded together in two large organizations, the Common Market and the Free Trade Association, designed in large measure to remove the barriers to foreign trade that still remain in the form of tariffs and quotas.

These two organizations, while they have the laudable intention of removing barriers to trade, also present particular problems to American businessmen. The existence of two organizations rather than one may provide the setting for rivalry of a possibly harmful variety. Such organizations, of course, also present an opportunity, by virtue of the stimulus that they provide to the expansion of local markets, but it is an opportunity that one must be inside in order to take advantage of.

It is conceivable in a few years—and I might say, parenthetically, that I am among the very few people who believe in this possibility —that these two groups may have reconciled their differences and abolished import barriers against a significant group of countries within Western Europe. The proposal to indefinitely postpone imposition of prejudicial tariffs against the Outer Seven with the complete acquiescence of Bonn is significant.

Even though this month's budget has been fashioned to prevent an overstraining of the country's resources, price mechanism and balance of payments, Britain enters this new decade with a profile of over-all financial stability unmatched in modern history. In 1955, it was authoritatively predicted that Britain would double its national standard of living in 25 years. At the end of this decade, it is now expected that England will have achieved 60% of the goal that was originally forecast for 1980.

We must remind ourselves of suggestions appearing in the German press for greater trade relationships between Britain and Germany.

In Latin America we have a very expansive land with a large population dependent, for the most part, for its livelihood on agriculture and primary production. Such materials as copper, petroleum, iron ore and foodstuffs such as bananas, coffee and sugar are all closely associated with Latin America, often as a main source of supply for the United States.

For the most part, Latin America is regarded as an underdeveloped area of the world, although in many instances substantial progress has been made toward industrialization. The average per capita income in Latin America is less than about one quarter of that in the United States. Latin America, as we all know, is a land of many sharp contrasts. The Amazon Valley of Brazil contains some of the most dense tropical forests in the world, parts of which have not yet been completely explored.

In the southern portions of the area, Argentina has a climate that comes very close to that which we enjoy here in the northern section of the United States. Going still farther south, the tip of South America contains some of the chilling climate similar to that of the Arctic areas. In elevation, the contrasts are just as sharp, from the 24,000-ft., snow-capped Aconcagua peaks in the Andes to the plains of Argentina and the flatlands of the Amazon Valley.

Within each nation there are sharp contrasts in wealth and plane of living. Virtually each country has a large urban population living in surroundings where architecture, culture and conveniences match that existing almost anywhere else in the world. But, side by side, there are some of the most wretched poverty-stricken areas to be found any place in the world.

From the point of view of the United States, the ties with our neighbors to the south are many: military, economic and political, but above all cultural. As a site for United States direct investment, the nearly $9 billion invested there places it just below our investments in Canada.

In Canada, we have a very close neighbor, spiritually and physically. We have a common unguarded border of several thousand miles. In the organization of United States businesses, the Canadian market is often looked upon as an extension of that in the United States, however false or however inaccurate that may be as an accurate base for operations.

Another example of the closeness with which we regard our Canadian friends is the huge growth that has taken place of United

States investments, portfolio and direct, in that area. Such a development speaks volumes for the confidence that we have in that country, for nowhere else in the world, except fairly recently in Europe, have United States investors increased their investments with such rapidity.

Canada is a nation that has grown tremendously since the war and it obviously has a potential for much more growth. From its own point of view, it would like to continue the advances it has enjoyed, take from the United States the ideas, incentives and practices that it regards as being applicable to the people in Canada and, at the same time, wishes to avoid being swamped in any sense by its neighbor to the south.

Donald F. Heatherington
DIRECTOR, EUROPEAN DIVISION
NATIONAL FOREIGN TRADE COUNCIL, INC.

2

Europe Looks Forward

SEVERAL among you may recall that on a like occasion only a year ago, you were exposed to my views on the dimension of the European market. Now on rereading last year's notes, I must say that I find no reason to quarrel with myself, and nothing shouts for revision. Since this is a rather rare experience, the temptation is to repeat myself, and give you last year's speech all over again.

But our concern then was primarily with current conditions, with the immediate circumstances of Europe. Today the topic assigned requires that we look ahead, that we assess as best we may the growth trends and trade potentials of the 1960's. Somehow the act of moving into a new decade always seems to call for such an appraisal, even though in most instances one decade shades imperceptibly into the next. Indeed, as the eminent British economist, Professor C. F. Carter, lately observed when similarly set at the task of charting the prospects, "The most important thing that we know about the future is that it will be full of surprises." To which he added the equally pertinent comment: "There is often confusion, too, between estimates of what is *attainable* (that is, within the bounds of possibility if everything goes well) and estimates of what is *likely*." This, I think, is a significant distinction, and one well worth keeping in mind as we consider the outlook for Western Europe as it travels toward 1970.

It has been only a few days since we observed the 15th anniversary of V-E Day. While time, unhappily, has robbed the date of much of its early and essential meaning, it is still the base point from which to measure the first steps toward the physical reconstruction and regeneration of Western Europe. There is little doubt that over what must be regarded as a relatively brief span the European economic pattern has been materially transformed, not merely restored. It is, moreover, an accepted and evident fact that Western Europe is now healthier and stronger than at any time within the last 30 (some would say 40) years. Thus Per Jacobsson, not only the Managing Director of the International Monetary Fund but also a long-time student of Europe, is able to speak of a situation having been reached "in which the European countries have attained an economic position which in all essential respects can be said to be better than at any time in Europe's history." He reminds us further that in October, 1959 the Conservative Party in Britain fought an election with the slogan "You Never Had It Better," and adds "that is, I think, true for Europe as a whole."

The outward expressions of this newly acquired strength are observable everywhere; in the widely heralded and familiar output and production records, in the substantially expanded volume of both internal and external trade, in the vastly improved position of the various currencies, in the ability and willingness to liberalize trade and remove restrictions, and in a greater over-all stability.

In a sense, Western Europe entered the 1950's a weak, hesitant, uncertain convalescent, still dependent on outside support and stimulants, still a bit fearful of what might happen when these would be withdrawn. It emerged as a vigorous, assertive, dynamic presence with a desire and demonstrated capacity for sustained growth. Few, I venture to guess, would be inclined to dispute the proposition that Western Europe, standing on the threshold of the 1960's, is the most rapidly growing political and economic power in the world picture, and a force to be reckoned with.

Western Europe has entered the 1960's under virtually a full head of steam. Last year total output for the area as a whole rose by more than 4% and industrial production by 7%. France, Germany and the Netherlands all had increases in their gross national product of better than 5%, while Italy had a gain of 6%. As a result, full-employment and full-capacity levels in many instances have been all but reached.

In an interesting exercise, the Secretariat of the United Nation's Economic Commission for Europe recently classified these countries according to their individual margins for short-term economic expansion; that is, their capacity to meet an increase in domestic demand from domestic output in the first instance and from external sources in the second.

On this basis, Finland, France, Western Germany, the Netherlands, Norway, Sweden, Switzerland and the United Kingdom are all considered to have a "narrow" margin for domestic expansion in the near term; Austria, Denmark, Greece, Ireland, Portugal, Turkey and Yugoslavia each have a "medium" margin for expansion. Only Belgium and Italy have wide margins. Taking into account their exchange reserves and current balance-of-payments positions, three of the countries with a "narrow" margin for internal domestic expansion—Western Germany, the Netherlands and Switzerland—have "wide" margins on the external side. In other words, they can, without fear of exchange strain, allow rising demand to be met through imports. France, Norway, Sweden and the United Kingdom, on the other hand, have narrow margins on both accounts. Italy alone has wide internal as well as wide external margins.

While measures of varying severity have been taken in many of these countries to contract credit, curb or moderate demand pressures and maintain price stability, the general expansionary trend is likely to continue through the year, although perhaps not at the 1959 rate. Officials of the Common Market predict a further 5 to 6% rise in the combined gross national product of the Six, which is in line with estimates that have been made in and for the separate countries. They also foresee increases in consumer spending, industrial investment, and imports, especially in consequence of rising wages and salaries. Since it is acknowledged that industrial production may not be sufficiently flexible to keep pace, imports of finished capital and consumer goods are almost sure to go up, as are imports of raw materials and semimanufactures in response to a build-up of inventories.

Turning to the longer-term outlook, various opinions have been expressed as to the likely pace at which Europe will be expanding. We shall here note only two of these. First, in the course of a more general study of Europe made for the Senate Foreign Relations Committee last year, the Corporation for Economic and Industrial Research, better known as C-E-I-R, projected a 5½% average annual rate of growth for Western Europe and an increase in total GNP of more than 100% between 1957 and 1970. C-E-I-R qualified the 5½% rate, however, conceding that it might prove too high, "especially if, as incomes rise, the U. S. pattern of a low rate of saving manifests itself." Almost in the same breath, C-E-I-R went on to note: "Yet the rate could be higher."

The second and perhaps most elaborate, detailed and authoritative estimate—if any economic forecast which ranges so far ahead can be so described—is one recently made by the members of the OEEC Secretariat at the request of the Energy Advisory Commission of that organization and covering the period 1955-1975. Assuming that a reasonably high level of activity and a high level of capital investment will be maintained, the OEEC group puts the average annual rate of growth in GNP for the entire OEEC area taken as a whole at approximately 3.15% between 1955 and 1965, and at 3% between 1965 and 1975. These rates compare with an annual average of 4.7% over the years 1950-1955.

The projections, it might be observed, are based in turn on the expectation of a substantially smaller increase in the labor supply than occurred between 1950-1955, or roughly a gain of about 2% between 1955 and 1965. Allowing for some reduction in hours worked, no change in the labor supply is anticipated in the succeeding period from 1965 to 1975. The OEEC forecast also reflects an annual increase in productivity per man-hour of just under 3%, compared with 3.1% between 1950 and 1955. This would be entirely consistent with the accepted presumption that there will be at most only a slight change in the rate of capital formation and in the output per unit of new investment during the whole of the period.

These OEEC projections point to a probable increase in private consumption, both in actual outlays and as a share of gross national product. In the latter case, the change would be from approximately 65% in 1955 to 70% in 1975. Independent calculations also suggest an increase of 40% in per capita expenditure on food, of 80% on clothing, of 53% on housing and of 160% on consumer durables. This last category includes "transport equipment," presumably consisting mainly of automobiles on which per capita expenditures rise by the same percentage as the entire class—in other words, 160%. The estimated rise in the per capita cost of "operation of transport equipment" comes to 260%.

Supplementary projections by OEEC point to an increase in net imports of primary products from the outside world of a trifle over 43% between 1955 and 1965, and of nearly 40% between 1965 and 1975. On the same basis, imports of manufactures would rise by about 90% during the first period and by 40% in the second. In order to continue an over-all current surplus in the balance of payments of about $1.5 billion at 1955 prices, total exports would have to expand by 85% while manufactured exports would have to more than double over the 20-year period from 1955 to 1975. The OEEC staff concludes that, insofar as supply is concerned, such an expansion does not present any particular problem, especially since industrial production is also expected to more than double.

On the demand side, if the share of the OEEC countries in world trade in manufactures were to remain constant, this trade would need to about double in twenty years. It is observed, however, that "in the light of recent trends and future prospects, it seems that world trade in manufactures will considerably more than double between 1955 and 1975, so that OEEC's trade may be expected to increase by more than the minimum figure necessary."

There are obvious uncertainties and imponderables surrounding these projections. Certainly not the least among them is the ultimate impact of the regional economic integration movement of which your chairman has spoken. One of the members of the Common Market Commission has cited an estimate that, in the absence of the Economic Community, the gross national product of the Six would have increased by 90% between 1953 and 1955 and between 1973 and 1975, but now, as a result of the creation of the Common Market gross national product may be expected to expand by 120 to 150% over the same period.

The European Economic Community, and to a somewhat lesser extent the Free Trade Association, unquestionably will be stimulating influences, sparking a more rapid rise in both output and productivity. But to achieve an increase of this magnitude—that is, of 120 to 150%—in the gross national product would require a rate of economic growth considerably in excess of most expectations, including apparently those of the OEEC group. Moreover, if the present division of Western Europe continues for any extended period, it could have inhibiting effects on economic expansion in both sectors.

We have neither the occasion nor the time to embark on an extended and detailed inquiry into the various aspects and potential implications of European integration. All that need be said here is that conceptually the Economic Community is clearly intended, as is the Free Trade Association in a looser, less emphatic manner to open the way and set in motion the forces which will spur economic growth.

Western Europe is obviously most anxious to succeed in this endeavor, however brought about, to improve materially the standard of living and to develop a mass-consumption economy. The question now is no longer whether these aims can be accomplished, but how rapidly, at what price and under what conditions.

Whether the exact rate of economic growth be 3, 4 or 5%, there can be no doubt that for Western Europe the next ten years will be an extremely significant, extremely critical period, constituting a formative period during which there will be marked and material changes.

What will this mean to the United States? First, it will mean increased strength for the Free World. A prosperous, expanding

Europe will add, in Jean Monnet's phrase, a "second pillar of the West." Secondly, it will mean intensified competition in the United States home market. Thirdly, it will offer new and attractive opportunities for United States capital investment, both direct and portfolio.

At the same time, a wealthier Europe will mean another source of capital for the underdeveloped areas. Finally, as the European market widens and deepens, there should be enhanced opportunities for United States export sales, although so far there has been little evidence to support the hopeful conclusion that these prospects will materialize or be realized.

While our imports have been moving sharply upwards, our exports in 1959 were considerably less than in 1956, despite prosperous conditions in Europe and further trade liberalization. Granted that some of the decline was due to lower shipments of raw cotton and of coal and coke, U. S. exports of metals and manufactures, machinery and vehicles, and of other items either sagged or failed to respond to the presumed improvement in Western Europe.

There is a good bit that various European countries still could do toward lifting restrictions which operate to discourage U. S. exports, but unless we are ready to abandon a long-cherished notion that a prosperous and growing Europe would be a better customer for our exports, we must find a way to respond to the demands being created in that area.

A distinguished scientist has observed that "the great revolutions in outlook are long in the making and, at last, they change all our ways of thought." This is most assuredly true of what has been going on within Western Europe. A year ago, I noted in closing that one of the most interesting and promising aspects of the progress made had been the pride shown by Europe in its own accomplishments. This view I still hold. But to it I would add the fact that there is a great sense of shared confidence in the future of the European economy.

3

Robert L. Sammons

ASSOCIATE ADVISER
DIVISION OF INTERNATIONAL FINANCE
BOARD OF GOVERNORS OF THE FEDERAL RESERVE
SYSTEM

Latin America

I ASSUME all of you are familiar with an old and not so very funny joke which has to do with the assignment of a task to researchers of various nationalities to write essays on the subject, "The Elephant." I think nowadays you could add a new tag line to that story and say that if you gave the problem to an economist, he probably could come up with an essay on "The Elephant and Its Relation to Economic Growth."

We have left Keynes, it seems to me, and gone back to Adam Smith; for, you remember, Smith was not primarily concerned with the level of employment, but with an inquiry into the nature and causes of the "wealth of nations," which was his name for "economic growth."

Trying to foresee what will be in store for Latin America in the next ten years, our major question indeed must be concerned with the problem: "What will be the rate of growth?" The second question of almost equal, perhaps even greater, importance is: "What changes in the structure of production, consumption and foreign trade are likely to occur?"

Let us begin our attempt to answer these questions with a brief glance, as most of the other speakers have done in this conference, at the past decade. I fully appreciate the dangers and inaccuracies involved in generalizing about 20 countries that are as different from each other as are those of Latin America. Within the limits of the time available, I hope to be able to emphasize a few of these differences.

According to the estimates of the United States Economic Commission for Latin America (ECLA), total gross national product of the area expanded by two fifths in real terms between the years 1950 and 1959. This is an average of about 4% per annum compounded.

In the six-year period 1951-1957, we have individual data for 15 of the countries. In this period the over-all growth of the area was 28% according to the ECLA estimates, but the individual countries varied from around 10% or less in Argentina and Bolivia, up to 90% in Venezuela. An increase of 5% or more per annum, which is a pretty good rate of growth, was registered in Colombia, Ecuador and most of Central America, in addition to Venezuela, during that period.

But there are those—and I number myself among them—who are somewhat skeptical of these gross national product figures, especially for countries where we know that basic data are pretty sketchy. So we might take another measure that is at least partially indicative of growing well-being, namely, the change in the volume of imports from abroad. Here we have data for a somewhat longer part of the decade, 1950-1958.

The increase for all countries in that period amounted to about 50% or $2.9 billion, but eight countries show import rises of more than 100%, eight between 10 and 100% and four of 10% or less. Allowance for rising prices would reduce these figures somewhat, but it appears from the data available that during this decade imports grew more rapidly than domestic production in most countries.

Imports also grew more rapidly than exports and, thus, domestic consumption and investment in Latin America was able to expand more rapidly than production during the period. But the view of some analysts, as I am sure most of you are aware, is that the favorable external conditions which produced this more rapid rate of growth in consumption and investment than in production was the result of especially favorable external conditions, which are a thing of the past. According to this view, the only way that growth can be achieved in the immediate future at a rate corresponding to that of the past is by a large expansion in what the ECLA and others call "import substitution industries."

Another aspect of economic growth that has received much attention, particularly in the studies of Professor Kuznets, is that as countries have developed economically they have expanded their industrial production faster than their total output. I think we can see abundant evidence of this in recent years in the form of new factories in Latin America. Also the statistical data show some increase, although not a very large one, in the percentage of total output arising in manufacturing over the decade. However, only in Brazil and Mexico has the proportion of the national income created in manufacturing reached even the figure of 20%, which is only about two thirds of the percentage we have in the United States and is even smaller in comparison with many of the European countries.

However, perhaps the most significant economic development in Latin America in the past few years—and the one that I, at least, would not have ventured to predict in 1950—has been the relaxation of direct controls over foreign exchange and trade.

In 1950, ten of the 20 countries had exchange control systems of some degree of severity. Most of those countries required specific licenses for all, or almost all, imports. Now, most of these ten—the major exception is still Brazil—have exchange systems that are almost completely free of direct controls and quantitative restrictions and it is fair to say that, as of the moment, Cuba is the only Latin American country which has more restrictions on exchange and trade than in 1950.

(I was interested to note in the *New York Times* for May 19, 1960, that the exchange certificate system in Peru has just been abolished, thus abandoning the dual rate system, and making the Peruvian currency, as the Finance Minister said, "the only completely free currency in South America.")

Admittedly, there are still improvements that can be made. We have prohibited lists and differentiated surcharges and advance deposit requirements in some countries, but you will agree that the progress in the last ten years has been quite impressive. Moreover, these exchange reforms have almost always been accompanied by a reduced degree of dependence on, or elimination of, domestic price controls and rationing and, most important of all, by serious efforts to stop inflation.

On balance in Latin America, as in the rest of the world, the pendulum in recent years has swung back towards economic liberalism of the more old-fashioned variety.

It is still too early to say whether or to what extent these reforms will be completely successful. However, data for recent months are certainly encouraging. The exchange reserves of Argentina, Chile, Peru, Colombia and Mexico, to name just a few of them, rose in 1959. The only major declines in reserves were those of Venezuela, which obviously had some to spare, and of Cuba, which did not. Even more encouraging is the cessation of inflation, at least for the time being; we hope it will last. Prices have been relatively stable now for several months in Argentina, Chile and Peru, and for longer periods of time in Mexico and Colombia and most of the smaller countries of Latin America.

In summary, then, the past ten years have seen a remarkable rate of growth in Latin America, although with great variation among the countries and with some apparent slackening of the rate in the last half of the decade. During most of this period, prices of the principal export products have, it is true, been relatively high; in the last two or three years, however, they have been for the most part well below their peaks.

The extent to which this slowdown in the rate of growth—if it has occurred—is due to these declines in export prices should not be determined on the basis of over-all analysis, but only by looking at each individual country. This slowdown, to the extent it has occurred, may be in part a purely cyclical matter, or it may represent a period of consolidation after earlier rapid advances, which had been accompanied by foreign exchange losses that could not continue indefinitely.

Given this record, what can we say about the outlook for the next ten years? According to the ECLA analysis, the outlook is not very bright. The world demand for traditional Latin American exports is expected to increase at the relatively slow rate of about 3% per anum, which is just barely above the expected rate of population growth in Latin America.

There came to my attention this week a study just published by the National Planning Association, which I commend to your attention, called: "The Future of Latin American Exports to the United States." These projections, if anything, are even more pessimistic than the ECLA projection, but the study does raise some very interesting policy matters which I hope to mention before I finish.

But to come back to the rate of growth of exports, the anticipated slow rate of growth, according to the ECLA analysis, will restrict the capacity to import and thus inhibit the rate of economic development unless a great deal of import-substituting production can be created. With an anticipated 2.6% rate of growth in population, if there is to be a 2% rise in the per capita level of income, there must be an over-all growth rate of 4.6%. Such a relatively high rate of growth over an extended period of time may well prove difficult to achieve, and it points up a very serious political and economic problem.

If one assumes that this 4.6% rate represents a sort of maximum attainable rate of growth for Latin America and if some of these large projections for Europe just mentioned by Mr. Heatherington are achieved, the gap will obviously widen between the levels of living in Latin America and Western Europe, creating perhaps even more serious problems.

However, without being too Pollyanna-ish, I hope we can take a little more optimistic view than ECLA does. Remembering the caveat that each country is different from every other, I would like to point out a few of the broadly favorable factors in the picture. The first is that one is entitled to hope and expect, the Cuban situation to the contrary notwithstanding, that political instability will not have so great an adverse effect on economic progress in Latin America in the next ten years as in the last ten. One's views in this regard are obviously a matter of faith and personal prejudice and I am just stating mine, without attempting to justify them.

Secondly, I think there is a growing realization among the political and economic leaders of Latin America of the necessity for a greater integration into the economy and the social structure of the large masses of workers and peasants, and of the need for making the advantages of at least a primary school education more widely available. If this is true, and to the extent that it is actually implemented in action, it cannot fail to have a beneficial effect on the total output of the country.

In the third place, working for the Federal Reserve System, I cannot help but say this: The recent monetary and economic reforms are laying the financial bases, I think, for a renewed upsurge of economic activity, in spite of some short-run adverse effects on production, especially in construction. Such short-run declines in economic activity almost inevitably follow inflation, which creates demands that by their very nature prove to be unsustainable.

Inflation is the enemy of sound sustainable growth, and when the internal inflation is accompanied by an overvalued exchange rate, the inimical effects are compounded. The Latin American countries, like other underdeveloped areas, have frequently been counseled to diversify their exports. But diversification cannot be achieved without an exchange rate that adequately reflects the real comparative productivity of the labor and capital of the country. Frequently the exchange value of a Latin American currency has been held at too high a level with the use of artificial controls, or because the principal export of the country is produced at a much greater comparative advantage than any other prospective export goods could possibly be produced.

The population-resource ratio is one of the most favorable of any underdeveloped area of the world, in spite of the fact that the rate of population growth is about 2.5%. There is nothing in Latin America—or in but a very few places, at least—that can compare with the overpopulation problem that exists in many parts of Asia.

Over the postwar period there has been a very large amount of investment in social overhead capital, particularly in power and roads. Some of this investment is already bearing fruit; a notable example is the rapidly expanding banana industry in Ecuador, which owes much to the construction of roads in the coastal area of that country.

The effect of this type of investment on productivity tends to be cumulative. Moreover, external sources of funds for public overhead capital expenditures, while not unlimited, seem to be relatively ample. It may be expected, therefore, that this sort of investment will continue, and will continue to affect favorably the rate of economic growth.

The twenty republics contain approximately 10% more people than the United States, but their annual economic output is only about one sixth or one fifth that of ours. Just to mention the disparity is enough to indicate the tremendous possibilities for growth. The extent to which growth will occur depends mainly on the policies followed by the Latin American countries themselves, but I believe that American business faces an opportunity, a challenge and a responsibility in helping Latin America to achieve the rate of growth of which the area is capable.

The opportunities lie in two fields—trade and investment. Our exports to this area in recent years have amounted to about $3.5 billion or $4 billion a year, 20 to 25% of our total exports and 45 to 50% of Latin American imports from all sources. In ten years, their total imports would grow by more than half if they kept pace with a 2% per capita per year rise in total output. Under the more pessimistic ECLA projections, the increase would be on the order of one third in a ten-year period. On the more optimistic basis, and assuming the United States holds its present share in the total, the increase in our exports would be in the neighborhood of $2 billion a year. That is, at the end of ten years, they would be running $2 billion per annum higher than at present.

However, our existing share need not necessarily be considered as the maximum we could attain. Nor do I think that the area's capacity to import is necessarily limited to the slow rate of growth projected by the ECLA staff. The ECLA study, as well as the National Planning Association study, took account only of traditional exports.

As an example of the possibilities in developing new exports from Latin America, we might note that American importers have shown remarkable ingenuity in recent years in developing new sources of supply, notably in Japan, Hong Kong and Europe. Is it not possible that this same sort of entrepreneurship could be productive if it were exercised in the direction of Latin America?

What is probably most needed is technical assistance in design, production methods, quality control and the like; the sort of thing that a prominent retail firm has been doing in Mexico and Brazil and elsewhere, but directed as much toward exports as to the domestic economy. Of course, a development of this type—and this was brought out very clearly by Professor Vernon—requires a trade policy on the part of the developed countries, the United States and Europe, that will be receptive to a growing volume of imports of processed and manufactured goods from the underdeveloped countries.

What I am suggesting is that there is opportunity for American enterprise in Latin American trade, not only by way of increasing our exports to Latin America, but in helping to raise Latin America's exports to the United States and to the rest of the world. This will probably involve the investment of capital, which brings me to the second point.

One third of all United States direct investments abroad, as the Chairman pointed out, is in Latin America. Between 1950 and 1958 the value of these investments rose about 100%—a faster rate of growth than that of the gross national product of the area. Even this figure probably understates the real rate of growth. Since direct investments are usually valued at cost, and given the rise in prices that we have had in the last ten years, the present real value is probably higher than the book value. In 1955, according to a well-known Commerce Department study, American-owned companies spent $4.3 billion in the countries of Latin America for wages, taxes, local materials and services. That is equal to about 7% of the total production of the area.

Needless to say, the real value of these investments to Latin America, to the owners and to the United States economy cannot be measured simply by these over-all statistics, but I think they give some idea of the magnitudes involved.

But recent experience may not be too indicative of the opportunities in the investment field. I am reasonably certain that the next few years are not going to see the stress on petroleum investments, for instance, that we have had in the past. But the rapid rise in population by itself is almost certain to broaden the opportunities for investment in Latin America—that is, foreign investment in industries producing for domestic markets. The opportunities would be even greater, of course, if the goals of increased per capita incomes can be reached.

A major unknown factor in the Latin American picture is the effect of emerging economic integration schemes, common markets as they are usually called, on intra-Latin American trade and hence on the pattern of United States investment in Latin America. The Free Trade Area agreement which was signed in Montevideo in February, 1960, leaves almost all the details of its operation to further negotiation, but I assume that it will open up some new opportunities for manufacturing in Latin America for export to other countries in the Free Trade Area.

I think most of you will recall that after the signing of the Ottawa agreements in the early 1930's, and in spite of a worldwide recession, U. S. investments in Canada and the United Kingdom increased as manufacturers sought to get inside the Commonwealth preference area. It may be deplored that investment for this cause will be at the expense of existing U. S. exports; particularly this might be the case in the European Common Market. However, there is not likely to be any net reduction in U. S. exports to Latin America even when economic integration in that area becomes a reality. For some time to come total Latin American imports are going to be determined mainly by the volume of Latin American exports. Any foreign exchange which they may be able to conserve by producing locally will be spent on some other types of imports. As was said earlier, we might get a change in the composition of our exports to the area. Such a change may create problems for particular firms, but there is no reason to think that total U. S. exports to Latin America will be reduced because of economic integration.

One criticism that is frequently made of the industrialization that has occurred is its heavy reliance on imported raw materials, semifinished products and component parts. Here again is an opportunity for foreign investors, as well as for local capital, to develop production of these commodities in Latin America.

In short, it seems to me that opportunities for profitable private investment in Latin America will continue to grow, both absolutely and relatively to the total economic output of the area. One might even hope that economic and political stability and fiscal responsibility will soon advance far enough in some countries to justify a resumption of portfolio investment.

The opportunities for trade and investment in Latin America can in a sense be measured in quantitative terms as I have just tried to do, however roughly. The challenge and the responsibilities are of less tangible stuff. Although the prejudices against foreign investment seem to diminish in some countries only to increase in others, there is, on balance, less purely nationalistic opposition to foreign investments as such than there was a decade or so ago.

If this is true, it may be attributed to the growing realization in Latin America of the benefits that can be obtained from foreign investment, as well as to a growing appreciation on the part of the foreign investors of their responsibilities in the matter. In any event, actions speak louder than words and the fact is that U. S. direct investments continue to grow.

The successful entry of American firms into the field of retail trade, a field where local opposition is especially vocal, is an illustration. The challenge to American firms is to conduct their operations so as to foster this trend. One major way in which this might be done is by increased use of the joint participation device.

The second and perhaps even greater challenge to American industry is the problem of coming to terms with a spreading reform movement in Latin America. In many cases, abrupt political and social change will have detrimental effects on private business, both foreign and domestic, at least in the short run. However, fundamental economic and social reforms are inevitable in most Latin American countries and, indeed, are even necessary if economic growth is to attain the objective of raising the living standards of the masses.

In the long run, too, a more modern economic and social structure with a less unequal income distribution will provide even more opportunities for American trade and investment than at present. But the successful crossing of the transition period will require a high degree of statesmanship by American business as well as by our government.

As the author of a recent study for the Senate Foreign Relations Committee put it, "the confusions and mistakes through which they [the reform governments] gradually discover the rational limits of effective action can be reduced and the contribution of private foreign investment enhanced if, by greater communications with such groups, the mutual mistrust and hostilities were allayed."

One has only to compare the situation of American business in Mexico today with the attitudes prevailing 20 years ago to see what changes are possible. A long-term perspective is necessary in the foreign relations of private corporations just as it is in the foreign policy of governments. Short-run profit maximization and long-run profit maximization frequently require different courses of action.

I mentioned three things—opportunity, challenge and responsibility. Perhaps the last is already implied in the discussion of the first two.

But it might be made a bit more explicit. Most people would agree that our national interest requires stable, prosperous and economically growing nations to the south of us. Many official United States Government policies are directed toward that objective. But government actions can either be reinforced or offset by the actions of private citizens, both in their personal capacity, especially as tourists, and in their business capacity.

Fortunately we have in Latin America a situation where the enlightened long-term self-interest of American business is fully compatible with the national interest and the decade ahead will, I am sure, present many opportunities for the fuller realization of these joint objectives.

John Davis
DIRECTOR OF RESEARCH AND PLANNING
BRITISH COLUMBIA ELECTRIC COMPANY LIMITED

4

Canada

THE OLD ORDER is changing. This you would gather from the remarks of the Chairman and other members of the panel, and there is plenty of additional evidence of this.

Travelers returning from the Middle East immediately after World War II noticed that the Arab chieftains—sheiks—were being preceded, rather than followed, by their wives. You probably have guessed the reason. The reason was buried land mines.

We are, however, seeing great changes these days and great changes certainly are taking place in my own country, Canada. Looking back 60 or 80 years, Canada was a very forbidding country for the people who lived there and certainly for the new immigrants. Many paused just long enough on their way to make enough money to get to the United States.

World War II proved one thing—that Canadian factories and Canadian labor could turn out goods of a quality and price which were acceptable in the United States. Often priorities were established and defense proposals dovetailed with a knowledge that a little give-and-take on both sides could help maximize our total war effort.

All but a few of these arrangements were disbanded after peace was restored. The manufacturers of fertilizers, farm machinery and equipment were notable exceptions. We have continued to trade freely between Canada and the United States in these commodities, and I am convinced that agricultural and farming communities on both sides of the international boundary have benefited as a result of these open trading arrangements.

Many Canadians would like to have seen tariffs eliminated on other commodities, but this was not to be. We still find ourselves making many of the same things that you make for a market which is one tenth or less of the size of the market in the United States. How much more efficient things would be if we could concentrate on the development of manufactured goods with a broader North American appeal! The consequences for Canada would be far-reaching, while the results for the United States, I suggest, could be equally beneficial.

The most promising field for negotiation is that of industrial raw materials. By industrial materials I mean the minerals and the wood products which the United States has begun to import in increasing volume from Canada and numerous other outside sources in the past ten or 15 years.

This increasing need to import because of a deficit position in raw materials was noted in the late 1940's and became more obvious to people after the Paley report. The President's Materials Policy Commission investigated the situation in the early 1950's. Since then, the conclusion has become widespread that the United States will have to go outside its borders for a substantial amount of industrial materials and, to the extent that these can be found in the Western Hemisphere, so much the better.

Canada's geographical location was a very strong point in its favor. Its vast untapped resources were not too far away to be brought to market over internal lines of supply via rail connections, pipelines and shipping on the Great Lakes. Continuity of service would also be guaranteed by means of long-term contracts with subsidiary companies in Canada.

Various corporations which had never before ventured outside the United States began to set up offices in Montreal, Toronto and other eastern cities. Numerous survey crews spread through Canada's northland and the result for Canada was a resource development boom of unprecedented proportions, which started in the early 1950's and continued until quite recently.

Perhaps this is the time to stress the amount of ownership and control involved. Well over half of "Canadian" industry today is United States owned and controlled. Even higher figures can be quoted for individual resource industries like oil, metal mining and chemicals. These are, along with the capital-goods industries which tend to be predominantly United States owned, the most rapidly growing sector of our economy.

Canadian economy indicators all point in one direction—that the United States and its citizens will be increasingly concerned about the size and rate of growth of the Canadian market. They will be concerned particularly in the case of the resource industries with the growth of markets in the United States for those industries. This means export outlets. I may be belaboring the point, but is it not foolish to lay out hundreds of millions of dollars—I should say perhaps billions of dollars—on the establishment of new reserves and the creation of new processing plants and equipment while at the same time refusing to accept the product of these investments. In so doing a good deal of excess capacity is created and this was not anticipated when the initial investments were made.

Setting up import restrictions under these circumstances is like cutting off your nose to spite your face—a painful procedure and one that cannot easily be patched up afterwards. As a Canadian, I would also like to see us process more of our own resources at home for two reasons. One is that it would provide more well-paid jobs for Canadians. The other is that it would result in a better division of labor between our two countries. The resource processing industries are typically large, well-equipped and extremely efficient operations. Economic studies in Canada have indicated that the value added in these industries per employee is substantially above the North American average. Anyone who has seen a modern newsprint or pulp mill or a large smelter for the refining of metals can attest to this fact. Import tariffs, like those imposed by the United States, which increase sharply with the degree of manufacture, are damaging in that they reduce the advantage inherent in refining and processing or upgrading of these raw materials on site.

Import quotas are even more destructive of good planning in that they may create surplus capacities at times and to an extent which the businessman cannot foresee. In order to play it safe he therefore locates his mill or factory in the importing country. Not only is this practice uneconomic in the international sense but it also sets a ceiling on those very types of industrial activity which are most likely to be productive in resource-rich countries like my own.

In attempting to assess Canada's industrial potential I find myself very much on the horns of a dilemma. Can I assume that the sensible thing will be done and our export activities will be truly economic in character? Or must I be more cautious and assume that the obstacles to Canadian-American trade will persist through the 1960's? The choice, I suggest, is crucial.

Productivity can increase rapidly or suffer as a result of protectionist policies. Unfortunately, it is this productivity factor that is so fundamental to any calculations which I might make as to Canada's gross national product or output of goods and services in the years ahead.

As conditions are now, we can perhaps expect a continuation of our recent history, i.e., a growth in output per man-year of about 2% per annum. But let us think for a moment what would happen if many of the trade barriers between Canada and the United States were removed. Some companies would go to the wall, certainly. Others specializing in certain lines and especially processing resources in a truly efficient manner would, however, be in for an era of prosperity.

On balance, we should be able to produce a greater volume of goods with the same Canadian labor force. Productivity could go up at a rate of as much as 3% per annum. Any of you who have studied the effect of different compound rates of interest on money in a savings bank account will see what I mean. The effect on our Canadian economy in ten or 20 years could be stupendous.

This I consider to be a truer measure of our economic potential.

Closer examination reveals various other growth factors whose momentum augurs well for the future. The first is population. Canada's high birth rate, which rose markedly in the 1940's and has continued through the 1950's, shows few signs of abating. Immigration into Canada has been less predictable and probably will be somewhat slower than in the recent past. But even assuming that it drops to a fraction of its postwar rate, Canada's population should go up, on the average, by 2½% a year. Under these circumstances, our present population would grow from something like 18 million to 23 million in 1970 and 28 million in 1980.

The combined effect of a 2-3% increase in productivity and a 2½% increase in the nation's labor force could bring about a growth in total economy—that is, of all goods and services—of somewhere between 4½ and 5½% a year.

Most projections for the United States fall in the 3½ to 4½% range. I am, therefore, suggesting that Canada may continue to gain slowly on her very much larger neighbor to the south. A somewhat higher rate of population growth is one factor. The other, productivity, may or may not help to close the gap in living standards as it depends so much upon what you are prepared to take from us and when.

Population estimates and forecasts of gross national product are useful in that they provide us with a framework within which the demand for industrial materials may be assessed. We find, for example, that these needs are roughly rising more than twice as fast as the population growth in this continent. We find that they are rising approximately in line with the total output of goods and services.

Broadly speaking, the requirement for energy commodities is rising somewhat less, but only slightly less than gross national product. Metals and other minerals are broadly in line with the total output of all our goods and services. Only in the case of forest products is there a marked difference between the over-all trend and the demand for raw materials on this continent and the difference lies substantially in two obvious areas. One is the decline in fuel wood requirements and the other is in the lumber category.

By and large, the pulp and paper growth is equal to or slightly greater than that of the total economy. For Canadians, it is a matter of considerable interest, looking within this total framework, to see which are the growth commodities—which are the commodities which are not only growing along with other goods and service but growing insofar as market requirements on this continent are concerned, at a great rate.

There are a number of items that are typical of much of our new production, some of them well established. Natural gas is one; nickel, gypsum and potash are others, the last being available in great quantities in Canada. There are others, such as asbestos or aluminum, which we produce from imported ores. These are also growing rapidly.

There are numerous other metals, and some nonmetals about which you heard yesterday whose names are not quite so well known, including titanium. Canada is a large producer of uranium, thorium, lithium, selenium, the platinum group metals and helium. These are commodities in which we have very large reserves established and for which the incentive to develop has only been recent. Therefore I suggest the future growth potential is exceedingly high.

Having ventured so far out into the unknown and for some of these requirements, I hasten to add that these estimates do not really qualify as predictions of the future. They are orders of magnitude only. Also, they are more descriptive of current, long-term trends than of conditions which we may, as a result of good management, actually encounter in the future.

Nor am I ignorant of the fact that most forecasts are outdated by decisions taken after they have served their purpose. It may therefore be appropriate to repeat a little ditty which could be said to have a bearing on forecasts in general:

> Works of others oft remind us
> As we o'er their pages turn,
> That we too have left behind us
> Letters that we ought to burn.

A question which has been bothering Canadians very much can be simply phrased: Are we, in fact, pricing ourselves out of world markets? Certainly our costs are rising. Overseas competition we know is growing keener. Other countries now seem to be capable of producing some of the goods we know were formerly unique to this continent, and they are being offered to us in increasing volume.

What I have been saying now applies more particularly to manufactured goods; raw and semiprocessed materials, because of their relatively low labor content, are not as vulnerable to overseas competition. Some statistics, however, may be worth quoting in this connection.

The Canadian wholesale price index for raw and partially processed materials is no higher today than it was in 1950. Even if the price of Canadian lumber and one or two other exceptions to this are taken into account, it is less than it was eight years ago.

Pulps and certain of our by-product chemicals and nonferrous metals have actually gone down. In only a few export categories have our prices shown a persistent tendency to drift upwards. In a great majority of cases they fell back after the first impact of the Korean war had worn off and have remained relatively stable ever since.

The fact that Canada's resource industries have generally been able to meet these price schedules and, at the same time, make enough money to go on expanding and modernizing their plant and equipment speaks volumes. Rising costs, particularly on the labor front, have been offset by natural resource-type advantages and the adoption of the latest types of plant and equipment. Factories making many of our more highly manufactured goods have not been quite so fortunate. As in the United States, they are now faced with import competition in which wage rates, hours of work and fringe benefits are more decisive factors in determining who will get a larger slice of our own domestic market.

When looking abroad, I must stress, of course, that foreign competitors have similar problems of inflation to contend with. Generally speaking, prices abroad have been rising faster than on this continent. Between 1950 and 1958, the wholesale price index in France and Australia went up by more than 50%. In Japan it rose by about 40%; West Germany has reported a 25% rise when North American countries fell into the 15 to 20% range. Wholesale prices in the United States over the period from 1950 to 1958 rose by about 15%. The corresponding figure for Canada was more likely 8%.

No one knows whether prices in other industrial countries will continue to rise faster than they will in Canada and the United States. But since we will have to compete more with each other, and since we are all subject to common influences such as trade union movements and popular demands for social services, it seems likely that the other industrial countries, too, will experience some measure of inflation over the next decade or so.

I would like, in closing, to say something about our flexible exchange rate in Canada. Should it happen that Canada begins to seriously price itself out of her export markets, then the demand for our Canadian dollar will begin to decline. Fewer people will want it in order to buy those export commodities which they wish to import.

Canadians meanwhile will be offering more Canadian dollars elsewhere in order to buy goods in other countries which appear cheaper and which Canadians wish to import. In other words, Canadians will be trying to unload more Canadian dollars than other people are prepared to take. The result in all likelihood would be a decline in the exchange rate of the Canadian dollar itself. It could fall relative to other countries' currencies; relative to U. S. dollars; relative to the pound sterling; relative to the franc. As it fell, the price of our Canadian exports, measured in these other currencies, would look more attractive to importers in other countries.

At some point they would begin to buy and the prices they would be prepared to pay would, under these newly established rates of exchange, look good to Canadian exporters as well. In other words, a flexible exchange rate can provide Canadians with the useful mechanism whereby an awkward cost inflation at home could be tolerated abroad. Other countries, I am convinced, will still want to buy our goods. We, for our part, may find ourselves less able to afford their imports and take less of their production in return.

These rambling comments may not be sufficient to convince you that our Canadian economy will go on growing as rapidly as it has done in recent years. We Canadians have little to worry about when it comes to a matter of costs and prices.

But I do hope that I have made one point. It is that Canada's future prosperity is intimately bound up with that of the United States. A freer exchange of goods and especially of resource materials can be to our mutual advantage. The policies which your country adopts in this connection will have an important influence on both the character and the productivity of Canadian industry and labor. In recent years we have seen various European countries combining with a view to attaining similar objectives. I see no good reason why, with a little understanding and imagination and good will on both sides, Canadians will not find their world a more tolerable place to live in and Americans themselves a thoroughly reliable source of supply.

5

Discussion

CHAIRMAN DIXSON: We have one question directed to Mr. Davis: Does Mr. Coyne (Bank of Canada) have the support of the business community in his choice of slower rate of growth in preference to increasing U. S. capital import?

MR. DAVIS: I would say, broadly speaking, no; but among the public at large in Canada, that is excluding industry, Mr. Coyne is perhaps a little more popular when expressing his economic and political sentiments about rates of growth and foreign investment. The business community almost to a man would prefer to see a much higher rate of growth, to a restriction of credit.

CHAIRMAN DIXSON: Thank you. This question is directed to Mr. Heatherington: Please comment on the trend of labor costs in Europe vs. the U. S. A. Will the gap tend to close.

MR. HEATHERINGTON: As I indicated in my earlier comments, the labor supply in Europe is certainly getting tighter. The German manpower situation, for example, as you undoubtedly know, has been fairly easy, largely because of immigration from the east during the postwar period. That is closing down and there is a much reduced inflow.

The German economy as a whole is now fairly well stretched out and that is true in most of the other countries of Western Europe. The birth rate is not rising rapidly, certainly not to the extent it is in Canada and some other areas, so that you are not going to have that expansive influence. Looking ahead, I think the one main limiting factor in Europe as far as future economic growth is concerned will be the labor supply. As a second factor, there has also been a sort of inspired patriotism, if you want to put it that way; a determination that "we have to recover, we have to get back" which has been a stimulating force.

As a result, there has been a fairly limited amount of demand on the part of the labor unions throughout most of Western Europe for higher pay, for easier working conditions. That day is over. The time has already arrived when European labor is going to be pressing more and more for decreased hours, for higher wages, higher salaries, and that you are going to have a sharp upturn on that side.

I don't see how this measure can be avoided with the great prosperity that Europe has had, nor how it can possibly be held down. Europe's productivity, on the other hand, has been going up fairly well and is likely to keep on rising. So there isn't going to be any runaway increase on the labor cost side, but there is certainly going to be a perceptible and possibly fairly large increase in the next few years.

Now, how does this compare with the likely trend in the United States? I would suspect that the European rate might certainly be greater in the next few years than in the United States. But there is still a wide disparity between the two areas. It will take a great deal of increase on the European side to catch up in absolute terms with the United States. I don't see a closing of the gap or elimination of the disparity in the immediate foreseeable future.

CHAIRMAN DIXSON: This question is directed to Mr. Sammons: Is it not true that there are more import restrictions in Mexico today than in 1950?

MR. SAMMONS: I just am not able to answer that question. But such import restrictions as do exist in Mexico are primarily for protectionist reasons rather than for foreign exchange reasons.

CHAIRMAN DIXSON: I can state from personal experience that import restrictions via the tariff route are much more serious to contend with today than they were in 1950. The tariff program of

Mexico has resulted in the achievement of the purpose for which the tariff program has been designed, namely, if you want to put it gently, the encouragement of entrance of overseas capital and the development of local industry.

This has unquestionably been accelerated as a result of these pressures resultant from the tariff program. I realize that it is dangerous to make this statement generally, but I do feel that, with minor exceptions, the policy of Mexico in this direction has, in fact, paid off and rendered more secure the economy of Mexico and, in turn, advanced our mutual interests in the long run, particularly as regards those who have had the courage and the foresight and the enterprise to move into Mexico with necessary capital to support adequate operations. Would you agree with that, Mr. Sammons?

MR. SAMMONS: In the first place, my remarks were directed toward quantitative restrictions rather than tariffs. There is some validity in the old infant industry argument for protection.

Although Mexico has had this success, they are now in a position of finding that they have oversucceeded in some respects. They have surplus capacity. This is probably one reason why Mexico is the only northern country that has signed the Montevideo agreement. They are looking for an expanded protected market.

CHAIRMAN DIXSON: There is a growing consciousness in a number of industries in Mexico of the need for export out of Mexico. This, again, I can state from experience in dealing with a number of American and other firms in Mexico and in discussing this very subject.

I think you will find that a great many Mexican companies supported by overseas capital are planning, as Mr. Sammons indicates, utilization of Mexico as an export base. Mr. Sammons, what will be the trend of Common Market developments?

MR. SAMMONS: That is a pretty tough one to answer. I assume you refer to the Montevideo agreement on the one hand, and the Central American integration scheme on the other.

I gather that in the case of the Central American plan, and particularly this new one that has now developed, these countries more nearly contemplate a common market in the sense of the Six, that is, the development of a common tariff against outside countries, and completely free trade internally.

The Montevideo agreement provides for a free trade area which would mean, of course, that the tariff against outside countries of each of the participants could be different and would presumably remain at the existing level.

I am not sure myself how long this could last, because many of those countries have relatively low tariffs or none at all on some of the same products which the more advanced countries in the group want to export to them, and which they cannot do without some tariff protection. So if the thing succeeds at all, it is going to develop more along the lines of the Six than of the Seven; we will find tariffs raised against us in countries where they are now relatively low. Obviously you cannot have economic integration without discrimination.

CHAIRMAN DIXSON: This question is directed to Mr. Davis. Is there much activity from Canada in private investment in underdeveloped countries in other areas of the world?

MR. DAVIS: There is not too much private Canadian capital being invested outside of Canada. There are some notable exceptions, as in the farm machinery and equipment industry which I mentioned, in which there is tremendous Canadian-United States trade at the moment. The Massey-Harris Company, for example, has made investments, particularly in Europe and, to a lesser extent, in other parts of the world. Some of our Canadian-owned distilleries are fairly aggressive. They have investments in Western Europe and, I think, in other parts of the world. But the main investment is through, say, the Colombo plan, or Canadian federal government-sponsored type of investment, in which Canadian engineering equipment firms may attach themselves to monies raised by taxes in Canada through projects in India, Pakistan, Ceylon, Malay, etc.

QUESTION: Is this part of the United Kingdom program?

MR. DAVIS: Well, it is not so much the United Kingdom program in this instance. The Colombo plan is also Canada's plan. The

Canadian Government decides to raise more tax money, or less, for foreign investment of this kind. It is largely government money, tax money, that is going to underdeveloped countries—not private capital raised in Canada specifically for this purpose.

CHAIRMAN DIXSON: This question is addressed to Mr. Heatherington: To what extent do you feel that atomic energy will contribute to Europe's expanding industrial production in the next 25 years in distinction to conventional fuels?

MR. HEATHERINGTON: There are others here, I am sure, much better informed on this particular subject than I. The one thing that I can comment on is that the recent oil developments in Libya and in the Sahara are apparently reducing fuel costs in Europe. This has been one factor which, so far as Europeans are concerned, has tended to hold back their own ambitious atomic energy program which was a fairly large one and one they were pressing.

There is certainly less of an energy problem than there was a few years ago, particularly at the time of the Suez crisis.

The other factor is that, so far as European growth is concerned, energy has been thought of as a limiting factor. That feeling is disappearing; there is less concern that they can achieve their goals without being so worried about energy.

MR. DAVIS: Coming from a power company, I might add a note. Nuclear power is, substantially, a government-type enterprise, largely because of the tremendous amount of capital required, first to develop it and secondly to build the plant. Low interest rates, among other things, are very important and are necessary to make nuclear power competitive.

In countries like the United Kingdom and, to a lesser extent, others like France and West Germany, the desire to be self-sufficient in energy, in the old days, was based on coal. Lately, it has been based on nuclear power. A country might bring in a few hundred tons of uranium a year and fuel many of its power plants. This political-type drive still exists to some extent in Europe. It has been blunted by the slow progress made in reducing the capital cost of nuclear power plants and slowed by the abundance of oil now available from offshore sources.

CHAIRMAN DIXSON: Mr. Davis, what is the background for the present drop in the Canadian dollar?

MR. DAVIS: I am afraid that I am not sufficiently expert on balance of payments to answer this fully. As our export volume is up recently, it cannot be from a diminution in the demand for our exports. There conceivably can be a falling off in the amount of new funds going into Canada, which are unrequited; they are unsolicited, in a sense. The new investment going into Canada demands Canadian dollars, so that equipment and labor can be bought there. If there is a falling off, certainly this would be one factor affecting the exchange rate, in allowing it to slump somewhat.

CHAIRMAN DIXSON: The next question is for Mr. Sammons: What is the United States competitive position in Latin America relative to Japan, Western Europe and Soviet Russia; and a related question: Are we likely to lose ground in the next ten years and, if so, why?

MR. SAMMONS: Well, a question of that sort is difficult to answer in those very broad terms. There must be hundreds of commodities, individual situations, where the competition has been getting tougher in Latin America just as it has in our own domestic markets. In the last five years, at least, there has been no change in the percentage of total Latin American imports coming from the United States and Canada; that is for all commodities in all countries. I would say that if we do lose ground in the next ten years it would be only as part of an over-all deterioration in our international competitive position, and I don't see why that should occur if we follow sound monetary and financial policies in this country.

There will be, obviously, individual situations, as I started out by saying, and as was brought out yesterday morning. The technical gap or the lead time of the transfer of technology from the United States to the rest of the world has been greatly reduced in recent times. It is not going to be easy, but I don't see any reason for tremendous pessimism.

CHAIRMAN DIXSON: Here is one for Mr. Heatherington: American investment decisions in Europe seem to be based, in large part, on the assumption that the European consumer will adopt all the characteristics of the American consumer and end up with an electric can-opener in every kitchen. Is this a valid assumption?

MR. HEATHERINGTON: I think so, except perhaps for the electric can-opener part. The European market has to move a long way toward the American examples. In the first place, the whole economic concept of the Common Market—I am leaving out the political—is based on the idea of mass consumption and not just mass production. We have preached it from this country to the Europeans a long while, particularly since the war. Every delegation that has gone over there, government and otherwise, has told them: "You have got to get mass consumption; that is the way." I think we convinced them of the importance of mass consumption.

This, moreover, relates back to the earlier discussion on labor costs. If you are going to get mass consumption, there will have to be a raising of mass incomes, of disposable incomes. The two go together. The direction Europe has taken is toward the mass consumption concept; the whole idea of the big market. Somebody has described it as a "big market" mentality and everything that I have seen on the European side confirms this as the approach being taken. How many years it will take, and how deep it will go in terms of convincing the small farmer, the peasant in the rural areas, that he has to have an electric can-opener or every sort of household gadget, I don't know. I think that it is going to take a much longer time than is sometimes suggested, but there is going to be a quite rapid spread of the idea of the consumer using more and more manufactured goods. He is going to use Band-Aids rather than just wrapping a little piece of cloth around his finger.

CHAIRMAN DIXSON: I should certainly confirm Mr. Heatherington's view. If we can dismiss the notion of the electric can-opener being an interpretation of the events that are occurring in Europe, and think in terms of, shall we say, over-the-counter packaged-goods type of merchandise appealing to a mass market, the transition during the past ten years is something almost unbelievable. You will be well aware of this change if you visit Italy, Holland, Belgium and Germany—and now, interestingly, England, where selling techniques and merchandising techniques have gone through a complete and total revision—I suppose in response to the admonition of former Prime Minister Eden in 1955, who warned his countrymen that they were a little bit retrogressive in applying modern means of selling and merchandising.

My friends and I in commerce in Europe find there is a tremendous growth in this whole mass-marketing concept. I am not sure that our investment decisions are premised on that fact alone, but upon the simple fact (and I wonder whether Mr. Heatherington would confirm this view) that our export opportunities in Europe will lessen as the European market progresses in its consolidation and demand. Therefore, American industry—American business—should establish a proper bridgehead and proper capital investment in reasonable dimensions, smartly located and intelligently thought through, if they are going to receive the full advantages which are theirs, not through the export route but more through a direct servicing route within the countries themselves.

MR. HEATHERINGTON: I would agree with that, up to a point. As I had in mind in my earlier comments, the presumption always is that investment promotes an expanding economy. This means that the whole demand structure lifts and changes, opening up new fields that we have not been in before. From there the presumption always goes on to anticipate that part of the enhanced demand will be met by the growing domestic industry, part by buying from other countries which have moved into this field earlier.

I would hope that we are going to be able to develop on both scores; both in terms of our plants and our operations there, and in terms of exports from this country. At the same time we can expect the composition of our exports is going to change. For example, we will be pressing Europe more and more to open their markets to American agriculture which, surprisingly enough, is probably one of the most productive parts of our whole economy, and that as a result we may go back to what we did in our early days—to being a supplier of agricultural products to Europe. But I do hope that we will be increasing our exports to the area as well as our sales of products from American-owned plants abroad.

CHAIRMAN DIXSON: Do you think this would be consistent with the necessary tariff implementation as against manufactured goods coming in?

MR. HEATHERINGTON: That is one of the problems we are going to be faced with; we are going to have to convince them and press them, as they have pressed us, to lower their trade restrictions. We have been largely on the receiving end, constantly being accused of having a very high tariff. The European tariffs are not low. Even some of the low ones are not "low."

CHAIRMAN DIXSON: This is the big gamble, though, isn't it?

MR. HEATHERINGTON: That is right.

CHAIRMAN DIXSON: This question is directed to Mr. Davis by one of his countrymen: How can growth rate be as high as you suggest (over 2½% labor productivity) in face of severe manufacturing cost disadvantages in Canada vs. United States and European manufacturers, since three out of four employees are in other than resource-based industries?

MR. DAVIS: This is a matter of personal opinion in Canada. A large proportion of Canadian population is employed in manufacturing and is now very much concerned about import competition from Western Europe. However, we don't have the full complement of manufacturing industries, nothing like the United States has. We have been losing out in some fields, particularly in the last three or four years, in industries like electrical apparatus or chemicals; we have much the same type of problem as American industry —relatively high wage rates, and, on top of that, a smaller market in many cases. The main growth recently has been in our service industries and in resource allied industries like pulp and paper and mining.

CHAIRMAN DIXSON: I have a question which preoccupies a great many American businessmen: Are Communist economic policies likely to adversely affect the economic development of Western Europe for consumer products? That is, will it cause the market to become preoccupied with heavy industry as against producing consumer products, therefore, either opening up the way for importation or for United States investment for consumer goods?

MR. HEATHERINGTON: No, I don't think so; not immediately. First, the tendency has been so markedly toward the consumer line; it seems the future is there; I don't think there will be a reversal. Second is the fact that the two are going along together. There is the development of heavy industry along with light or consumer goods industry. Western Europe is recognizing that it is caught between the two pressures, and is determined to develop itself and at the same time to increase the production of consumer goods.

CHAIRMAN DIXSON: Mr. Sammons would like to add a comment on this problem of exporting agricultural versus manufactured goods into the Common Market or elsewhere.

MR. SAMMONS: The question came up yesterday, and Mr. Despres pointed out the strong comparative advantages we apparently have in agricultural goods in this country. I heard a man from the staff of GATT this winter who had made a comparison of prices to the farmer in all countries of the world. In spite of our very high government supports in this country, he found that there were only two countries, Australia and Canada, where prices to the farmer were generally lower than in the United States. This would imply that if European agricultural protection was reduced—and some tendency in this direction can be expected if urban populations continue to grow and manufacturing continues to expand in importance—then we could export a very large amount of agricultural goods to Europe. This, it seems to me, might have an advantageous effect on American industry as follows: If, as a result of the abolition of agricultural protectionism around the world, the prices of agricultural products fell both abroad and in the United States, there would be a vast amount of consumer purchasing power released which would then be available to purchase manufactured goods.

CHAIRMAN DIXSON: We have one last question directed to Mr. Heatherington. I think we have covered this in part, but you may like to add a further comment: What United States industries are likely to feel greater impact of European competition over the next decade?

MR. HEATHERINGTON: Well, as I again go back to what I said earlier, the only thing you can safely say about the future is that it will be full of surprises. I am not so sure that in 1950 we would have predicted that probably the greatest impact in this matter of imported European products would have been in the automotive industry. Not even automotive people themselves suspected or expected that sort of development. So that in the coming ten years the impact may very well be on things that we haven't the slightest notion are going to be hit. I still think it is going to be in consumer goods, particularly since that is where many of the inroads already have been made. But it is also going to be in the capital goods line. In fact, the whole effort on the part of a great many firms—European industries, the electrical industry is a case in point—has been to develop the market for electrical machinery, generators, etc.—to develop and get into this market. And they have made considerable inroads. I think in this field that you will continue to get pressure. I won't attempt to single out any other particular line.

But one factor to be kept in mind is that these imports still supply only a small part of the United States market. We sometimes tend to think in terms of the big total of imports—upward of $15 billion—that are coming in. But then look at the total in terms of its relationship to United States production and it is still in many cases only 1 to 3% of the total U. S. output. Even if we get a substantial increase of European sales in various items of consumer goods or heavy equipment in this market, we aren't going to be standing still all this time. Our production is going to be increasing. I don't think imports are going to represent any higher percentage ratio to U. S. production than they have been in the past.

QUESTION: Mr. Sammons, you spoke of the reforms expected in Latin America. Do you expect any dynamic change in the agricultural sectors of the economy in the next decade?

MR. SAMMONS: That is another difficult one, especially when you try to think of it in terms of all of Latin America. I would say generally no, although I think that sooner or later we are going to have land reforms along the Cuban lines in some of the other countries too. To what extent this will affect the commodity structure of production, I don't know.

One thing that is important in all this is the fact that, for the most part, Latin American agriculture is not competitive with Temperate Zone products.

Part Two

OUR | DOMESTIC | MARKETS:
The | Demands | Ahead

CAPITAL GOODS MARKETS

R. Arthur Williams
CHAIRMAN

1

R. Arthur Williams
PRESIDENT
STANRAY CORPORATION

Introduction

THE THREE SESSIONS devoted to "Domestic Markets: The Demands Ahead" paint a portrait of an economy in the process of normal growth. A recurring theme of the meetings is that the nation's business system at the start of the 1960's has finally shed the abnormalities apparent in the decade following the end of World War II. The descriptions of energetic growth ahead to be found here make little reference to backlogs, recoupments or unusual stresses of demand. Instead they foresee a vigorous, balanced expansion, maintained and accelerated by population growth, by research and development, by improving productivity and by further advances in living standards.

Around this major note many minor themes are woven. Speakers in the first session on "Capital Goods Markets" stress a need to accelerate the nation's rate of investment in productive facilities. Our requirements for power will continue to grow, and substantial investment will be required to meet the demands of the 1960's; the transportation system is approaching a point where reappraisal and heavy new investment for modernization seems to lie ahead, not just for the railroads, but for water shipment and, toward the close of the 1960's, for air transportation as well. With regard to manufacturing industries, our attention is invited urgently to the need for a sustained higher rate of investment, to modernize facilities and match rates of growth in output and efficiency being achieved by Western Europe, Japan and the Soviet Union today, and perhaps by China tomorrow. For construction, we foresee a building rate reaching $70 billion a year by the end of the decade and perhaps totaling $650 billion in the 1960's as a whole; this projection is cast in terms of satisfying a continuously generated demand rather than of eliminating existing backlogs. Throughout this first session, stress is placed on the relationship between national growth and rising living standards on the one hand, and the rate of increase in the capital stock of structures and equipment on the other.

The second of the three sessions, devoted to "Consumer Markets of the Future," emphasizes the acceleration of growth in population, labor force and household formation that appears to lie ahead for the 1960's and the promise they hold for consumer goods industries. Notable in this session is a tendency on the part of several speakers to distrust past consumption patterns as a guide to the future. The 1950's were dominated by a surburbanization of population which altered the mix of outlays in certain directions. The mix of the 1950's may not hold for the 1960's; new products, directed at new markets, can hope to capture some of the growth potential released as the major industries involved in suburbanization reach their maturity. Supporting and expanding the consumer goods industries in general will be a strongly rising trend in income, and a new broadening of the U. S. standard of living.

The "Presidents' Panel" with which this series of three sessions concludes, invites attention to a number of essential problems and promises of the next decade. Among the promises is the burgeoning of a new electronics and space technology. By 1970 the total electronics industry is likely to double its present volume of $14 billion. This is true even if purely defense requirements for electronics, included in the total, should happily enter on a decline; the opportunities in nondefense work, and most notably in space, would readily take up the slack. And among industries that are often thought of as mature—steel, textiles, agriculture—the speakers point to new technological vistas and new avenues of vigorous growth.

As foreseen by the speakers in these panels, the future is not without its problems. No speaker argues that the demands to which he addresses himself have been permanently immunized against the business cycle; the reader will find many references to the probability of moderate recessions occurring in the Sixties. In all three sessions, there are unmistakable references to the possibility that growth rates will be somewhat slower in the first half of the decade than in the last half as a result of population trends and other influences. Finally, the note is struck insistently that the American price level is already high in relation to that of the rest of the world, and that among the paramount problems facing the American economy are the gradual erosion of our export markets and the rising tide of imports. Several speakers find the essence of this problem in American labor costs, and its solution in more rational labor-management relations leading to increased efficiency and more competitive costs.

James W. Knowles

STAFF ECONOMIST
JOINT ECONOMIC COMMITTEE
CONGRESS OF THE UNITED STATES

2

The Rate of Capital Investment: A Range of Probabilities

My REMARKS are directed to developing a range of probabilities as to the rate of capital investment over the next decade. I shall be dealing entirely with investment in business plant and equipment, excluding residential construction and inventory.

My presentation is, in a way, a by-product of the study I prepared for the Joint Economic Committee last year, "Potential Economic Growth in the United States," a technical paper which developed an analysis of the factors underlying the nation's economic growth and a method of preparing quantitative estimates of future output, taking into consideration changes in both labor and capital.

I assume at the outset that we will avoid any prolonged and deep depressions. I assume that recessions, if they occur, will be similar, though not necessarily identical, to the recessions we have had since World War II—that is, relatively brief, running from 12 to 20 months, and relatively shallow. Finally, these rates are calculated in constant 1959 prices; no allowance is made for changes in the price level, or in the structure of prices.

Before treating investment itself, a few words are in order about the growth rates assumed here for the total economy. I have used three sets of assumptions—high, medium and low. All the assumptions for each model are consistent one with the other. Where it is assumed that the forces will be such as to encourage a high growth rate, for example, a rate of growth in total labor force of about 1.9% per year is used. Since the rate of unemployment is held constant in the model, this means a similar increase in total employment, including armed forces. For the more conservative, this growth rate was reduced by approximately two tenths of 1% per year, or to 1.7% and 1.5%. The same pattern is followed in each of the underlying factors. Assuming that conditions are conducive to somewhat slower growth in general, the same conditions will also generate somewhat slower growth in capital investment, and a faster decline in hours of work.

Using the highest set of assumptions, the rate of increase in the capital stock would be 3.2 % per year; with the medium assumptions, about 2.7% per year; and with the lowest assumptions, about 2.2% per year. With these and other assumptions, the general growth rate of the national economy turns out to be 3.5, 4.0, and 4.5% per annum for the low, middle and high sets of assumptions.

From the growth rates in the total capital stock it is possible to derive some information about how much investment would be required in order to produce this growth; that is, the net requirement for expansion and replacement.

Just as a matter of locating magnitudes, the economy in 1960 could produce about $532 billion of goods and services, on the basis of our current labor force and capital stock. By 1970 it would be capable of producing, depending on which growth rate you assume, between $756 billion on the low-end assumptions, $830 billion on the high assumptions, and about $791 billion on the medium assumptions. On this basis, a few years beyond 1970 we would readily pass the trillion dollar mark in output.

At the slowest rate of growth of 3.5% per year, noted a moment ago, the capital stock of plant and equipment would have to go up 2.2% per year. By 1970 this would mean that the annual amount of investment per year, at 1959 prices, would be about $62.5 billion, of which about $26 billion would be for expansion and the other $36.5 billion would be for replacement.

A middle growth rate in total output of about 4% per year would be accompanied by an expansion in capital stock at about 2.7% per year. This would mean an annual rate of investment of about $66.5 billion per year by 1970, of which about $29 billion would be for expansion and $37.5 billion for replacement.

On the highest assumed growth rate in total output of about 4.5% per year, the private capital stock would increase about 3.2% per year. This would mean that by 1970 private investment in plant and equipment would be at a gross rate of $70.5 billion per year, of which $32 billion would represent expansion and $38.5 billion would represent replacement.

A more rapid rate of growth in the economy and in the capital stock raises replacement requirements by only very small amounts— about a billion out of four or five billion increment in the annual rate of investment, in each case. The increment in investment is largely in the requirements for expansion.

These rates of investment by 1970 would amount to about 8.3% of output on the low assumption, about 8.4% on the medium assumption, and about 8.5% on the high assumption—almost insignificant differences to make such substantial differences in the rate of growth. The reason should be obvious; since output rises, too, the percentage changes only by a small amount. Incidentally, if we were growing at about a 4% rate this year on our trend of full employment, the comparable rate of investment would be about 9.3% of gross national product, or, in 1959 prices, about $49.5 billion out of a total output of $532 billion. This means, to put it a little differently, that the gross rate of private investment in new plant and equipment would go up over the decade by from 26 to 42%, but each of these projections implies that the ratio of gross plant and equipment expenditures to gross national product will decline over the next decade.

What would happen if the ratio doesn't fall? In recent boom years we have experienced a rate of investment varying between about 10 and 11 or 12% of gross national product.

If 10% of gross national product is invested in new plant and equipment over the next decade, the resulting rate of growth in the capital stock would be sufficient to raise the rate of growth of gross national product in real terms to about 5.5% per year, with no change in the assumptions about hours of work or growth in the labor force. However, this would require that the growth in the labor force be toward the upper end of the range of what seems now to be possible.

But a rate of investment this high would run some risk of inflationary consequences. In years when the ratio of investment in plant and equipment to gross national product approaches 10% or more, the prices of investment goods have risen more rapidly than the general price level, or have risen while the prices of other goods and services were stable. In other words, we had a relative upward shift in prices of capital goods under conditions of high investment rates.

If, therefore, we succeed in achieving stable prices as well as reasonably full employment and an adequate rate of growth over the next decade, it seems likely that economic policies will result in a somewhat lower ratio of investment to gross national product a decade hence than has prevailed in the more prosperous years of the last decade, and it seems unlikely that we can avoid this unless new sets of policies can be found which will make it possible to channel such rates of investment into plant and equipment without inflationary consequences, and also to encourage an appropriate increase in demand to prevent the development of excess capacity.

The rates of growth in capital stock that I have indicated are ones in which, in my judgment, this problem would not be serious, in the sense that policies which receive general support would be likely to be able to deal with them and maintain relatively high rates of utilization. But if we decide for any reason to encourage a much higher rate of investment, it would require that the ratio of private plant and equipment to gross national product remain high —in the vicinity of 10% or higher. The historical record suggests that we will then have to deal with the problem of balancing economic policies so as to produce a rise in demand so that the incentives for investment will continue and at the same time prevent inflation.

Stability of investment, therefore, over the longer run at the higher rates would be related to the solution of these two problems. Such policy problems will be much easier to solve at the three more modest rates which I have presented than if we try to drive investment up to the highest rate experienced in the past decade.

3

Robert M. Weidenhammer

PROFESSOR OF FINANCE
SCHOOL OF BUSINESS ADMINISTRATION
UNIVERSITY OF PITTSBURGH

Capital Needs in Manufacturing, 1960–1970

PLANT AND EQUIPMENT OUTLAYS are the keys to the achievement of both cyclical stability and the desired rate of long-term growth. This definition stands even if we fully realize the relative importance of the two other segments of investment, namely the cyclical swings of inventories and the longer cycle in residential housing. To make a ten-year projection of capital needs of manufacturers it seems proper to begin by analyzing the historical role of this segment of our economy.

HISTORICAL ANALYSIS

Going back to 1880, we find that the capital-output ratio—that is, the investment in plant and equipment needed to produce one dollar of annual sales by manufacturers—rose from 1880-1920 as machinery, steam, and later electricity, were applied to large-scale operations and replaced labor. But since about 1925 this ratio has been falling because new machinery was designed not only to save labor but also capital, especially in plant-space occupied.

The modern steel rolling mill, the first of which was installed in 1926 and retired only last year, increased the output of rolled sheet to such an extent that not only most of the back-breaking and dangerous jobs in the old hand rolling mills were eliminated but also now a single modern continuous mill turns out more sheet at a lower investment cost for plant and equipment than had the dozens of old hand rolling mills housed in dozens of separate buildings now replaced.

Or a more recent example: The tonnage of steel required in the construction and equipment of the Fairless Works (Fairless Hills, Pa.) plant of the U. S. Steel Corporation was less than half the tonnage in relation to output capacity than the construction of such a plant would have required in the Thirties. But a new grass-roots plant like Fairless which is incidentally the only new fully integrated steel plant built privately since the late 1920's, did cost $191 per annual ton of ingot capacity while the average cost of the 50% increase in steel ingot capacity between January 1, 1950, and January 1, 1960 was considerably less because the rest was achieved by adding to existing facilities. (The government built the Geneva, Utah plant during World War II; it cost about $135 per annual ingot ton of capacity, but it was sold after the war for 25% of its cost.)

These examples may illustrate the reason why since 1925 investment in equipment has risen more than twice as fast as investment in plants. This very fact has caused some observers to predict or at least not to rule out an early reversal of this trend. To take again the steel industry as an example: Many of our best steel plant locations have, for decades, been fenced in by rivers, lakes, highways and residential districts, making horizontal expansion impossible. Still the process of capacity increase per square foot has continued year by year. The questions have been raised as to when such investment increases per square foot might reach a limit, and how the need for new grass-roots plants would then increase both the relative role of plant and of total investment in relation to output gains. Other factors which might accelerate this trend are the geographical shifts in population as sources of demand and of labor, as well as the exhaustion of old resources and the use of new sources of raw materials. As a limited observation, we might mention that the rapid expansion of the electronics industry seems to require a very low capital-output ratio, and that one of its major location factors appears to be the propinquity of good universities. But this whole question of the future trend of the capital-output ratio is full of cross currents, and while I lean toward the assumption of a further decline, frankly I have not yet come to any clear-cut conclusions.

A second fact of significance is that in the middle 1920's equipment accounted for only 33% of total facilities while at present it is about 50%. Since 1925 annual equipment investment has risen at twice the rate of plant investment, and this trend has accelerated in recent years.

Third, plant and equipment outlays for manufacturers should average about 3% of gross national product.

More detailed information has become available only since 1946. About 75% of total business is done today by corporations for which we have data on the sources and uses of funds. In the postwar period some 73% of all funds went into plant and equipment and 27% into additional working capital. Of the about $450 billion spent, 28% was raised in the capital market, of which 6% was equity financing and 22% debt financing. The other 72% came from retained earnings and depreciation, the latter's contribution rising in recent years. Of the funds spent, two thirds went for modernization and only one third for expansion.

Of total plant and equipment outlays of business, manufacturers in the postwar period have accounted for as high a percentage as 45.7% in 1946 and as low as 36.4% in 1958, with an average of about 41%. By contrast, the public utilities and the communications industry (mostly AT&T) have shown a strongly defined upward trend, while other segments such as railroads have shown a relative decline.

Manufacturers have proved more susceptible to the impact of the three postwar recessions, and in the last few years also to foreign competition. Obviously our public utilities, trade, services, finance, communication, construction and inland transportation are not exposed to the degree of foreign competition that recently has been felt by the steel, automobile, typewriter, sewing machines, cameras and certain segments of the machinery, chemical, and textile industries.

FACTORS DETERMINING THE PROBABLE INVESTMENT IN MANUFACTURING IN THE 1960's

(1) The present and projected rate of capacity utilization. The ingot capacity of the steel industry on January 1, 1960 was 148.5 million tons. Output has been as follows:

Year	Millions of Tons	Year	Millions of Tons
1955	117.0	1958	85.3
1956	115.2	1959	93.5
1957	112.7	1960 (est.)	100.0

For the end of the next decade output estimates vary between 130 and 150 million tons. The lower figure assumes significant increases in competition from net imports of steel and manufactured products, such as cars, and also from further domestic invasion of steel markets from nonferrous metals, plastics, glass and concrete. Increases of present capacity in the next decade will further depend on what safety margin to meet temporary peak demands the industry wants to have, the constant effort of corporations to keep at least their percentage of the available market and the unavoidable capacity increases inherent in the replacement and modernization of equipment.

(2) The age composition of plant and equipment and their ability to meet domestic and foreign competition on a cost basis.

(3) Cost savings from technological innovation. The basic oxygen converter saves about 60% of the investment and some 15% of the operating costs of steelmaking as compared with the open hearth furnace. This saving is so pronounced that some expect by the end of the decade the oxygen converter will account for 25% of carbon steel output instead of the 4% now produced.

(4) Development of new products, especially if they protect present markets from competition by other industries or open new markets. As an example, the steel industry is now preparing to offer thin tin plate in competition with aluminum, and colored stainless steel in competition with anodized aluminum.

(5) The cost of new plant and equipment vs. the cost of labor.

John L. Lewis in his heyday of pushing up miners' wages was regarded as the best salesman of the companies making coal mining equipment; Lewis, incidentally, was never opposed to the resulting shrinkage in miners' jobs. The fact that research and development outlays of American business were $8.6 billion in 1957 and hit $10.7 billion in 1959 is most promising, but it takes from 3 to 10 years before money spent on research leads to plant and equipment outlays traceable to such research.

(6) The burden of a corporate profit tax of 52% which cannot be passed on to customers if foreign competitors pay only, say, a 30% tax and enjoy the benefit of more liberal depreciation allowances.

(7) The rise of the internal cash flow from depreciation allowances and retained profits; 98% of the plant and 60% of the equipment to be depreciated in the next decade is already in use today.

(8) The availability and cost of borrowed funds and of equity financing.

In the past decade, especially in the years 1955-1957, plant and equipment outlays have been in the upper range of their historical role in our economy. Some of the stimulants which provided a favorable climate for capital outlays in the Fifties will still be at work in the 1960's—such as the predictable sharp increase in net new family formation in the second half of the decade and the probable continued high level of expenditures for research and development. But other stimulants, such as the sharp increase in defense expenditures in 1951 and the government grants of five-year amortization certificates, were only temporary factors.

Factors that Will Significantly Affect the Outlook for Plant and Equipment Outlays in the 1960's

(1) As to the high cost of borrowing, experience has shown that while residential building, public utility expansion, and the financ-

ing of state and municipal projects may contract severely, high interest rates have not inhibited manufacturers as long as their profit expectations were favorable.

(2) The high postwar birth rate will, for the late Sixties, create substantially expanded markets for housing, house furnishings, and cars when the postwar baby crops begin to march to the altar. Even if the recent fall in the birth rate should prove to be a permanent development, it would have its effect on business in the Seventies rather than the Sixties.

(3) Inflation, it is hoped, is no longer a factor. This would provide a higher percentage of the funds needed from depreciation allowances but it would eliminate the drive to invest cash before prices rise further. The net effect may, therefore, be inconsequential.

(4) One of the important new factors reducing the demand for capital needs of manufacturers is the certainty that in the next decade the world will have an overabundant supply of low-cost natural gas and oil products, not only from the rich wells of the Near East but also from North Africa and from Russia and its satellites. This development will cut down the exploration activity in this country which now requires the drilling of many more and much deeper wells to produce an equal quantity of hydrocarbons. A further consequence will be the reduction in profitability of new investments designed to increase the thermal efficiency of energy generation in all forms.

(5) This brings us again to what I consider a most important point, namely, the enhanced competitive capacity of foreign manufacturers who for the first time in history will enjoy fuel costs closer to ours.

(6) Foreign manufacturers will become steadily more competitive with ours as they reap the cost advantages from large-scale production and marketing in common markets. Furthermore, as they conclude the present job of rebuilding the ravages of World War II and progress in their various phases of industrialization, a larger proportion of their labor forces and facilities will become available for enhanced export drives.

CONCLUSIONS

If we want to avoid depressions and stagnation, to minimize recessions and promote the steady long-term sustainable growth of our economy, we need steadily rising plant and equipment outlays for two purposes: for the expansion of our capacities and for the cost-reducing results gained from modern facilities.

We have in the past gone through periods when expansion of capacity of certain industries went ahead too fast, and this faulty investment caused bankruptcies and a sharp drop in investment and thereby contributed to a subsequent depression. There is no guarantee that this might not happen again. But a much more likely danger of the next decade is that under the impact of reduced profits caused by foreign competition our manufacturers might at the same time lower their sights and lack the means to modernize their facilities. Furthermore, if we should face a continued deficit in our balance of payments, our monetary and fiscal authorities might be so afraid of an outflow of gold during the next recession as to fight it with a hard money policy, just as was done in 1931. To practice steady investment, manufacturers need both the cash flow and the reassurance that government will fight future recessions as effectively as it fought the three since World War II.

Advocates of long-term capital budgeting have promised that such practice by itself would help to minimize recessions. But with more rapid obsolescence of their facilities through research and development our manufacturers often cannot afford to contribute to a stable economy by investment during recessions before the facilities are really needed. Technical innovations may make them outmoded before they are even put to use. Our government should assure them by an unflagging resolve to fight recessions with prompt monetary and fiscal measures.

A new threat to the profitability, if not the life, of some of our manufacturing industries has appeared on the stage. This threat is the competition from friendly Europe and Japan today and from the U.S.S.R., its satellites, and Red China tomorrow. We hear a lot about the low wages in these countries, but we will not and we cannot ever compete with them on that basis. Instead we should focus our attention on another aspect of this present and future foreign competition, namely that their annual plant and equipment outlays as a percentage of their existing equipment are much higher than ours. The U.S.S.R., with a manufacturing output of some 40% of ours, produces more than four times as many machine tools as we do. It follows that our foreign competitors will have not only a faster growth of manufacturing capacity but a much lower average age composition of their facilities. Their plants will be more modern than ours and their costs, even aside from wages, will be lower.

Corporate profit taxes and depreciation allowances greatly favor manufacturers in the Common Market countries as compared to our own situation. The six-nation Common Market has agreed not only to mutual tariff reductions but also that the burden of all direct taxes, personal and corporate, should not exceed 50% of all government revenues, while we rely on direct taxes for about 90% of federal income.

If our manufacturers, faced with shrinking exports and rising imports, ask for tariff protection, except in selective cases they will have to guard against destroying our remaining export markets. But our manufacturers have a perfectly sound case to demand of their government a liberalization of depreciation allowances and a cut in the corporate profit tax from the 52% now in force.

As long as our manufacturers compete only among themselves, the corporate profit tax is a convenient method of raising federal revenues and as a rule it is not absorbed by the manufacturers but by their customers. In the world markets, however, our manufacturers cannot compete on even terms with foreign producers paying corporate profit taxes at rates which in some countries appear to average less than half that of ours, quite aside from being entitled to more liberal depreciation allowances. Naturally, a cut in the corporate profits tax and liberalization of depreciation allowances would cause a temporary revenue loss to the Treasury until the economic growth of the country wipes it out. To maintain a budget surplus, we may have to close some loopholes or use a temporary indirect tax, such as a general sales tax exempting all

EXPENDITURES ON NEW PLANT AND EQUIPMENT BY UNITED STATES INDUSTRY, 1946-1963 *

(Millions of Dollars)

TYPE OF INDUSTRY	1946	1947	1948	1949	1950	1951	1952	1953	1954
Manufacturing	6,790	8,703	9,134	7,149	7,491	10,852	11,632	11,908	11,038
Durable Goods Industries	3,112	3,407	3,483	2,593	3,135	5,168	5,614	5,648	5,091
Primary iron and steel	500	638	772	596	599	1,198	1,511	1,210	754
Primary nonferrous metals	93	178	193	151	134	310	512	412	246
Electrical machinery and equipment	282	304	289	216	245	373	386	475	439
Machinery, except electrical	511	519	527	383	411	683	701	797	694
Motor vehicles and equipment	591	504	474	348	510	851	855	989	1,295
Transportation equipment excluding motor vehicles	109	95	106	87	82	219	211	180	191
Stone, clay, and glass products	241	326	269	181	280	397	330	346	361
Other durable goods	785	843	853	631	874	1,136	1,107	1,239	1,110
Nondurable-goods Industries	3,678	5,296	5,651	4,555	4,356	5,684	6,018	6,260	5,948
Food and beverages	670	946	1,053	875	760	853	769	812	765
Textile-mill products	342	510	618	471	450	531	434	378	331
Paper and allied products	232	371	383	298	327	420	364	409	455
Chemicals and allied products	800	1,060	941	670	771	1,247	1,386	1,428	1,130
Petroleum and coal products	1,087	1,736	2,100	1,789	1,587	2,102	2,535	2,668	2,684
Rubber products	139	143	102	81	102	150	154	161	131
Other nondurable goods	408	530	454	371	359	382	377	404	451
Mining	427	691	882	792	707	929	985	986	975
Railroads	583	889	1,319	1,352	1,111	1,474	1,396	1,311	854
Transportation, other than rail and communications	1,740	2,697	3,027	2,207	2,316	2,809	3,037	3,255	3,229
Transportation, other than rail	923	1,298	1,285	887	1,212	1,490	1,500	1,565	1,512
Communications	817	1,399	1,742	1,320	1,104	1,319	1,537	1,690	1,717
Public Utilities	792	1,539	2,543	3,125	3,309	3,664	3,887	4,552	4,219
Commercial and Others	4,516	6,093	5,154	4,660	5,671	5,916	5,557	6,310	6,513
Total United States Business	14,848	20,612	22,059	19,285	20,605	25,644	26,493	28,322	26,827

TYPE OF INDUSTRY	1955	1956	1957	1958	1959	1960	1961	1962	1963
Manufacturing	11,439	14,954	15,959	11,433	12,067	15,132	14,161	13,330	13,618
Durable Goods Industries	5,436	7,623	8,022	5,469	5,773	7,662	na	na	na
Primary iron and steel	863	1,268	1,722	1,192	1,036	1,728	1,522	1,142	1,039
Primary nonferrous metals	214	412	814	441	313	372	347	357	346
Electrical machinery and equipment	436	603	599	459	519	742	809	712	648
Machinery, except electrical	809	1,078	1,275	915	909	1,185	1,068	1,055	1,108
Motor vehicles and equipment	1,128	1,689	1,058	558	641	1,020	872	802	898
Transportation equipment excluding motor vehicles	274	440	544	370	390	465	374	333	346
Stone, clay, and glass products	498	686	572	399	529	684	585	577	552
Other durable goods	1,214	1,447	1,438	1,135	1,436	1,466	na	na	na
Nondurable-goods Industries	6,003	7,331	7,937	5,964	6,294	7,470	na	na	na
Food and beverages	718	799	850	742	825	838	837	833	828
Textile-mill products	366	465	408	288	412	470	465	436	433
Paper and allied products	518	801	811	578	630	696	678	556	578
Chemicals and allied products	1,016	1,455	1,724	1,320	1,235	1,642	1,721	1,687	1,738
Petroleum and coal products	2,798	3,135	3,453	2,431	2,491	2,930	2,783	2,811	3,064
Rubber products	150	201	200	134	190	254	245	198	188
Other nondurable goods	437	475	491	471	511	640	na	na	na
Mining	957	1,241	1,243	941	987	1,004	1,015	864	895
Railroads	923	1,231	1,396	754	923	1,015	975	946	908
Transportation, other than rail and communications	3,585	4,396	4,803	4,115	4,689	na	4,657	4,337	4,355
Transportation, other than rail	1,602	1,712	1,771	1,500	2,022	2,144	na	na	na
Communications	1,983	2,684	3,032	2,615	2,667	na	na	na	na
Public Utilities	4,309	4,895	6,195	6,088	5,667	6,066	5,545	5,469	5,631
Commercial and Others	7,488	8,364	7,366	7,195	8,210	na	8,410	7,882	7,923
Total United States Business	28,701	35,081	36,962	30,526	32,543	37,016	34,763	32,828	33,330

* 1946–1959 Actual and 1960 Estimates are based on anticipated capital expenditures reported by business in late January and February 1960. *Sources:* for United States Department of Commerce, Office of Business Economics, and Securities and Exchange Commission. Estimates for 1961, 1962 and 1963 from 13th Annual McGraw-Hill Survey, Business Plans for New Plants and Equipment. (na = not available)

food and necessities. But in competition with friendly countries today and with the U.S.S.R. and China tomorrow we have to accept their economic challenge and give our manufacturers the weapons, that is, the incentives and the cash flow, to fight back. This peril may be only a cloud on the horizon today but in the coming decade it may sweep over some of our manufacturers like a hurricane unless they are equipped with the most modern equipment their cash flow can buy.

Opponents to the liberalization of depreciation allowances granted as of January 1, 1954 have blamed the recession of 1957-1958 and the disappointing pace of business recovery since on the fact that the flow of cash to corporations (after tax profits and depreciation allowances) rose by nearly three fifths while after-tax personal income increased less than one third. The conclusion is drawn that plant and equipment were increased faster than the ability of the consumers to absorb the output of the enlarged facilities. To this contention the following should be considered:

(1) Was the pre-1954 balance between the flow of funds to investment and to consumption more conducive to economic growth *without inflation* than the present balance?

(2) Does not any period of increasing investment draw manpower and goods away from production for consumption *until* the increased output of the modernized and enlarged facilities raises *real* consumption because of lower costs and increased supply and therefore lower prices?

(3) Seeing the handwriting of fiercer foreign competition on the wall, is now not the time to mobilize for it by further modernization of our facilities before domestic unemployment increases and consumption declines?

QUESTION: During the postwar period we had a good deal of investment by American investors in Western Europe, and other nations that were devastated. Now the European nations are becoming more competitive and are building their own industries.

Can we anticipate a shift in emphasis from some of this foreign investment back to some of our domestic economy?

MR. WEIDENHAMMER: The trend is definitely, so far, in the other direction; more and more American corporations try to locate plants throughout Europe either in order to break into the Common Market or even to re-export from Europe or Japan certain goods back into this country. I believe this will go on for a while. It might be stopped by two developments. One is increasing uncertainty of a political nature; in other words, the doubts which might arise about the safety of investment abroad. The other one is that we might have a strong reaction from labor to the fact that American industry is importing goods.

QUESTION: With respect to the increase in investment in Europe in the decade of the 1960's, what will the pattern of this investment be? Will it flow into the areas in the Common Market particularly, which have structural difficulties, such as Belgium, or will it go to West Germany, where full employment prevails?

MR. WEIDENHAMMER: The nature of American investment abroad has changed, as we all know. Until about three years ago it was mostly in raw materials. We went into Saudi Arabia and looked for oil, and into South America for copper. Recently we have gone into manufacturing, and we have so far mostly gone into those countries where the political situation was most stabilized, like Holland or West Germany.

Full employment certainly prevails in West Germany today. Italy probably offers better opportunities for the next decade because there is very serious unemployment in the lower half of Italy and, therefore, definite opportunities to get labor under reasonable conditions.

Paul W. Cherington
PROFESSOR OF BUSINESS ADMINISTRATION
GRADUATE SCHOOL OF BUSINESS ADMINISTRATION
HARVARD UNIVERSITY

4

Expanding the Transportation System

IT IS perhaps paradoxical to talk about expanding our transportation system during the 1960's in view of the fact that one of the basic current problems affecting major segments of that system, whether on land, on sea or in the air, is excess capacity. It is clear that at the present time we have too many ships, too many miles of railroad (and apparently too many airplanes flying around with empty seats). In total, we have a transportation capacity in this country that is pretty clearly in excess of our current, or even our prospective, demand for ton miles or passenger miles.

At the same time, it is also clear that this decade of the 1960's is going to see a very considerable amount of new investment in the transportation system, including a potentially large investment in common carrier transportation. This investment, though, will be of a fairly selective or qualitative nature, designed primarily to improve the system rather than merely expand it. Common carrier expansion I think will occur, but it will occur in specific areas, and anyone interested in marketing goods and services to the transportation industry is going to have to do some fairly careful analysis as to just where the demand for those markets lies.

During the 1960's the largest single investor in our transportation system, taking it as a whole, is going to be government. The multibillion dollar federal highway program alone, when added to secondary and other construction programs, will dwarf all the other transportation investment programs.

Federal, state or local aids to air transport for airports, air navigation and air traffic control will swell the government investment by perhaps another $2½ to $3½ billion, and rivers and harbors add a few billion more.

It is probable that total government investment in our transportation system, considering that system in its broadest sense, and counting all levels of government, will be upwards of $100 billion during the decade. This will be a continuation, but on an expanded scale, of plans that were pretty well started in the last decade.

A lot of investment will be in concrete, earthmoving and heavy equipment, but especially in such fields as the growing air traffic and navigation system. There will be a large demand for highly specialized, technically advanced electronic goods.

In a sense, the private automobile might count as part of our transportation system, and certainly the expenditures for automobiles are pretty sure to constitute a very large sum during the 1960's. During the 1950's this total was somewhere in the vicinity of $145 billion. The trends here again seem to be to somewhat more specialized types of vehicles, to compact cars and to smaller cars.

It is in the common-carrier field, though, and more specifically in rails and marine, where the 1960's could produce some really drastic new investment and marketing opportunities. The words "could produce" I think should be emphasized, because it is by no means clear that these potentials will be realized. The potential investment opportunities in both of these fields stem from technology, and perhaps the 1960's will tell the story of whether these two large transportation industries can be reborn or whether they are really dead.

As you are all no doubt aware, technology has now come to the point where very substantial improvements in both shipping and rail transportation are possible. These improvements lie primarily in the direction of further automatic operation and automatic handling of tonnage. For example, there are no technical reasons why a cargo vessel cannot be made largely automatic in its operation at sea, with only a minimum crew aboard.

There is little reason, from a technical standpoint, why loading and discharging cannot be made largely automatic. This has already come about with respect to bulk cargo. With containers, pallets, other special handling equipment and special ship design, the automatic handling of general cargo is now technically feasible, but whether such developments are economically feasible depends primarily on whether a major portion of the potential reduction in labor costs which will be available both at sea and ashore can be applied to investment.

Last summer a study group known as Project Walrus—the title was taken from "The Walrus and the Carpenter" in *Alice in Wonderland*—under the auspices of the National Academy of Sciences, concluded as follows:

> "The goal of the Maritime Administration's Research and Development Program should be established as the creation of a U. S. merchant fleet which can be self-supporting without subsidy, and the program should be so conducted as to lead rapidly to ships in being which demonstrate this possibility."

Only a fleet which was composed of vessels capable of automated operations at sea and in port could conceivably meet this goal of being self-supporting.

In the railroad field the technical possibilities are more or less similar. The hardware which would make possible essentially automatic train operation is available, or at least is well within the state of the art. Technically there could be a major increase in the mechanization of right-of-way maintenance, in yard and switching operations, and in the automatic processing of the mountain of paperwork which the railroads seem to be able to generate almost at will.

The introduction of this new technology in either the fields of shipping or rail operation would cause a very substantial displacement of seamen, longshoremen, of railway operating and maintenance personnel and railway clerks. The various unions involved—

and they are well entrenched and long established—would certainly resist this trend, unless their membership were protected. By and large, their opposition has materially slowed down the investment in new technology in both of these industries. This is a problem which appears to be at the root of any estimate of what our investment in these two transportation fields will be during the 1960's. If the problem is resolved, investment could jump to several times that which took place during the 1950's and the market opportunities would be substantial, especially in such fields as electronics, handling equipment, railroad equipment, and shipbuilding.

During the 1950's such a revolution took place in the railroad business in the dieselization program, which came about very rapidly. At the end of 1948 there were only about 8,000 diesels in service, and steam still did about 77% of the freight traffic and 54% of the passenger traffic. Ten years later there were 27,500 diesel units and steam had largely disappeared. The impact of this program in labor, however, was indirect. Railway labor declined from 1.3 million in 1948 to about 850,000 in 1958. It is pretty hard to trace this directly to the diesel, although it clearly played a part. A substantial jump in automatic operation either on the road, in the yards, in maintenance of way or in clerical operations would clearly bring about opposition from unions.

Progress made in solving the problem of labor displacement in the past does not encourage the view that industry or labor will be able to work out a satisfactory solution on a timely basis. Industry has tended to take the position that the risk of technological displacement is the same kind of risk and that it should be covered in comparable fashion. Whether the government has to get into this or whether it is conceivable for the unions and management to work this out I am not prepared to say. I would guess, unpopular as it may be, that this is an area where government will intervene, but in the transportation field such insurance might prove to be a cheap price to pay over a period of years for a vastly improved transportation system.

The kinds of benefits which might be gained from a program which met this problem of labor displacement head on can be seen in the shipping field. The operating subsidy alone which we will pay to our ship operators over the next ten years will be around a billion dollars. This subsidy is paid primarily to offset differences in U. S. versus foreign operating costs, primarily labor costs. Even with this subsidy, at the end of ten years under a continuation of present trends we will be essentially a second-class maritime power, sailing an obsolete fleet, and at the competitive mercy of foreign fleets, both those of our allies and those of the growing Soviet fleet. Furthermore, there will be a continuing requirement for subsidy at the same or higher levels.

How do we break out of this kind of vicious circle where we keep pouring money in and yet keep losing ground? As previously indicated, a new, highly automated merchant fleet is now feasible, and the evidence indicates that because of the decreased personnel which such a fleet would require, both afloat and ashore, it could come close to competing with foreign-flag fleets on an unsubsidized basis so far as operating costs are concerned. But now the question we come to is, what do you do with the 50,000 merchant seamen and the 72,000 longshoremen currently employed?

The Project Walrus report points out that even if you took $10,000 a man and retrained or reoriented or retired all the present work force, the cost would be only a billion and a quarter dollars; in other words, just about matching the operating subsidy that we will be paying to the carriers for this cost differential. And, of course, many of the seamen and longshoremen would still be needed under a modernized automated fleet.

Today our merchant fleet consists of about 1,000 active ships, of which about 630, more or less, are in general cargo, and another 370 are under flags of convenience. Most of this fleet is obsolete, or approaching obsolescence, so we have the opportunity now to replace it with some radically new and much more effective and efficient automated ships, automated in operations at sea and operations on shore. If it can be brought to pass, this would open up an enormous market for equipment, control gear and shipbuilding. The real question is whether we possess the imagination and the vigor to put such a program into action.

Thus far we have talked primarily about the shipping and railroad industries. It is in these fields where opportunities seem to exist for major technological revolutions during the decade ahead. Hence it is these fields which might witness the sharpest departure from the established investment and market trends of the past ten years.

In the air, carriers are in the midst of a major investment program in subsonic jet transports, as you all know. This is a $2-3 billion program, a pretty substantial program for an industry the size of the airlines. But this program will be substantially completed by about 1962, and after that the forecast is that new investment in passenger aircraft will decline, at least temporarily. This decline will reflect the extensive capacity of the jet fleet and in part the fact that some carriers will have reached the limits of their ability to finance new equipment.

It is possible, of course, that there will be during the middle 1960's considerable investment in short-haul jets. It is possible, and even probable, that there will be a new cargo plane which the carriers will buy, in view of the fact that the government is actively working toward the development of a suitable commercial cargo aircraft. But it is toward the end of the 1960's that one has to look for the next major investment program for the airlines. At that time the new generation of air transports should be available. Some will be supersonic transports, in all probability, although there are lots of problems still to be solved in connection with these.

In addition to supersonic transports there will also be available an economical short or vertical take-off aircraft especially adapted to short-haul transportation.

In spite of the difficulties which some of the airlines are now experiencing, there is little doubt that air transport is going to continue to grow at a fairly rapid rate. The real question is whether the economics of the industry will yield sufficient profits so that the carriers can invest in the products of a rapidly advancing technology.

In the field of trucks, pipelines and inland waterways, which now account for better than 50% of our domestic freight movement, each of these forms of transportation will also continue to grow during the 1960's, although the rate of growth will be somewhat less steep than that enjoyed in the 1950's. In part, the growth of these industries will depend on the ability of the railroads to make the most of the technological advances available to them and to recapture through better service and more realistic rates, traffic that they have lost to other forms of transport, including private carriers.

In conclusion, the 1960's should see expansion of our transport system, but the real emphasis will be on qualitative improvements rather than on quantitative growth. The level of private investment in the shipping and railroad fields, particularly, will depend largely on the ability of management and labor, with or without government help, to arrive at some accommodation as to the handling of the labor displacement problem arising from technological advances. If this problem can be resolved the market for advanced equipment in both fields should be very large. If it cannot, then both of these industries will represent a slowly declining market for capital goods.

QUESTION: What is the outlook for the trucking industry?

MR. CHERINGTON: I would say that the outlook is for continued growth, but perhaps not quite as rapid as the growth that occurred during the 1950's when it expanded drastically. In part this is dependent on what happens to the railroads. If they move ahead pretty well, I would say this would tend to keep down the growth of trucking. If they do not, then clearly trucking is going to keep on growing.

QUESTION: Do you feel the tendency toward mergers, particularly in the railroads, airlines and trucking companies, will result in more efficient use of facilities, and that elimination of duplication will affect the demand for capital goods?

MR. CHERINGTON: I think consolidation or merger is going to be a major characteristic of the 1960's in all forms of transportation. A merger movement might tend to accelerate the demand for capital goods, partly because, in the railroad field, this would mean a greater concentration of traffic over the most favorable lines and routings, with some requirements for new equipment. In the airline field, the merger movement might very well mean the difference between bankruptcy or disappearance, and the continued survival of the service would call for new equipment over some of the lines. I would certainly agree that mergers and consolidations are coming and, if anything, perhaps they would tend to boost the demand for capital goods.

QUESTION: How long do you think excess capacity is going to persist in the airlines, and how severely do you think this is going to affect them?

MR. CHERINGTON: I don't know that I can date the end of excess capacity specifically. Over the next couple of years we are in for considerable excess capacity, declining load factors, and at least a fair number of carriers in trouble. This obviously depends on the growth of traffic and also on equipment plans. I would hope that traffic, both cargo and passenger, would build up to the point where by 1963, let's say, a good bit of this problem would have been solved. On the other hand, I don't think this is a sure thing. Over the next year to 18 months, we clearly have too many seats for the traffic that seems to be in sight.

5

Edwin Vennard
MANAGING DIRECTOR
EDISON ELECTRIC INSTITUTE

The Power Requirements

ELECTRIC POWER, because it is clean, efficient, quiet, flexible and generally available, is the principal means of running the machinery of production. The power supplier takes the raw material, fuel and water, and makes energy available to the home, office and factory.

Because it takes about three years to design and build a generating plant, a power company of necessity must forecast power requirements for long periods of time in the future. The aim is always to have power enough for all requirements so there will be no shortage anywhere, with ample reserve in the case of the breakdown of one machine, and reserve to take care of increased growth. Reserves are now running between 20 and 30%. Over the long range, it should be possible to reduce reserves to about 15% by 1970 or 1980. Industrial history has demonstrated that building excess reserve does not in itself spur additional industrial production as some people thought it would.

Because of increased production through machinery and mechanization, combined with the desire on the part of the American people for leisure and ease of living, the use of electric power grows more rapidly than the economy as a whole. It grows at the rate of approximately two and a half times the gross national product. In making our forecasts we, therefore, tie in to some basic assumption of growth in the gross national product.

Before going into the forecast of the industry's capital spending in 1970 and 1980, and the associated money requirements, it may be well to note where the industry is as of today.

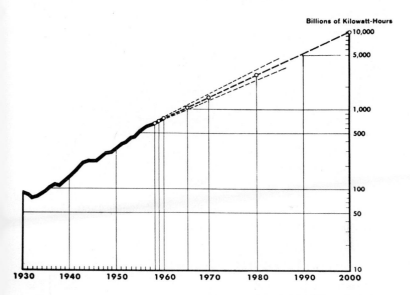

Figure 1. U.S. demand for electrical power, 1930-1960, projected to A.D. 2000.

Figure 1 shows the demand for power from 1930 through 1960, the available reserve, and total capacity, in millions of kilowatts.

Figure 2 shows the transmission-line system of the country. One aim of members of the industry is to pool power facilities, in order to stagger reserves and to enable the building of larger units. This helps to hold down unit investment costs.

The relative demands for power by regions are shown by dots. The fastest-growing regions now, and the ones that we estimate will grow fastest over the next 10 to 20 years, are the Southwest and Southeast.

Figure 3 indicates that we have one sixteenth of all the world's population and one third of all the world's power. We have in

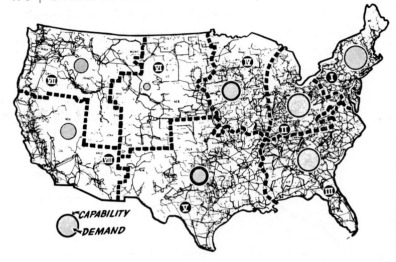

Figure 2. U.S. electrical capability and demand, 1960, showing transmission-line system throughout country.

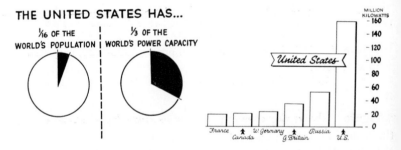

Figure 3. U.S. population and electrical power capacity comparisons.

Figure 4. U.S. electric power capacity versus that of other countries.

America more power capacity than the next five countries combined. Russia is second, Great Britain third, West Germany fourth, Canada fifth, and France sixth (Figure 4). We have three times the power capacity of Soviet Russia. A group of us went to Russia twice to inspect their power facilities and, in turn, had the Russians here to inspect ours. We found them to be good engineers and good scientists. We saw no evidence that they would reach us in electric generating capacity at any time in the foreseeable future. Based on the Russian seven-year plan and our normal forecast, there will be a greater gap in 1965 than there is in 1960.

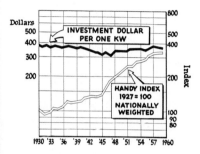

Figure 5. Built-in economies in electric power industry.

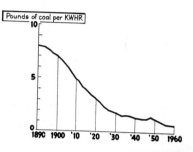

Figure 6. Amount of fuel required per generated kilowatt-hour.

Figure 5 indicates some built-in economies in the power business. Through the building of interconnected systems and larger and larger generating units, it has been possible to hold down unit investment costs. The bottom line shows what is known as "The Handy Whitman Index," which is a commonly accepted index in the utility industry showing the unit prices of equipment and construction costs. Note that it has gone up about 300% since 1930. Despite that, the unit investment cost per kilowatt of capacity in the power business remains at something like $400 per kilowatt. Without the built-in economies the industry's investment would have had to be about three times greater.

Figure 6 shows the amount of fuel required to make a kilowatt-hour, expressed in pounds of coal. It used to require about eight lb. of coal in 1890; the new machines now take something like three quarters of one pound of coal per kilowatt.

Figure 7 shows a forecast for the industry for 1970, 1980 and the year 2000. Each company makes a regular forecast for its own service area for three years, five years, and ten years in the future.

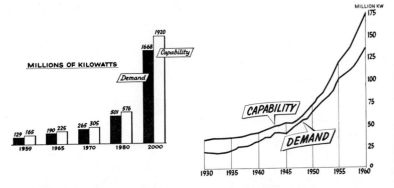

Figure 7. U.S. electrical capability and demand forecast, 1970-2000.

Figure 8. Total U.S. electrical capability and demand, 1930-1960.

It must do that, because it takes three to five years to build the power plants.

Recently one of the committees of Congress asked the Edison Electric Institute to make a forecast of our power loads and capacity and how we expect to supply it for 1970 and 1980. We formed a task force of about a hundred engineers who worked for six months in making a forecast by companies and by areas. Independently, economists on our staff made a similar forecast based on national trends, taking the basic growth rate of gross national product at 3.57% (the actual growth rate since 1945). There is a correlation between gross national product and kilowatt-hour use, a correlation between personal disposable income and kilowatt-hour use, and between kilowatt hours and various other factors—population, for example. Interestingly enough, the sum of all the forecasts of the engineers hit almost exactly the forecast made by the economists based on our estimated growth of the national economy.

The solid line between 1930 and 1960 on Figure 8 is the actual use of electric energy in this country. It is practically a straight line on a semilogarithmic scale. The increase shown is at the rate of 7½% per year, which seems to be the long-term rate of increase in the power business in America.

The center dotted line beyond 1960, going up to 2000, is a line calculated from the correlations with national trends. The little circles at 1970 and 1980 represent the sums of all the forecasts made by the local companies and local engineers. We have some confidence that the forecast fairly well predicts what we can expect in the use of energy in America, assuming we maintain our regular free enterprise system.

Based on the forecast, we have developed plans for serving the load by company, by region, and for the whole country.

Figure 7 shows the capacity that the companies expect to install by 1965, 1970, 1980 and 2000. In 1959 the total capacity was 165 million kilowatts, and the total load was 129 million kilowatts. For 1970 the capacity will be 305 million, and the load 265 million; for 1980 capacity will be 576 million, and load 501 million.

How much private capital will this require? The figures shown so far have been for the whole power industry, which is in two parts. The investor-owned section of the industry serves about 80% of the business; the various levels of government—federal, state, municipal, cooperative—serve 20%.

The investor-owned companies had invested $19 billion in 1950; in 1959 their investment was $43 billion. During World War II the companies could not buy power capacity and didn't have all of the reserves they would like to have had. After the war they could buy more and, therefore, an unusually large amount of capacity was installed in the last ten years. Figure 9 shows that by 1970 their investment will be $95 billion, or $52 billion more than in 1959.

The electric industry generates about 40% of its new investment requirement through depreciation reserves and other reserves. In 1959 the new investment called for $4.3 billion; of that amount $2 billion, or about 60%, was raised in the free market.

By 1980 the industry's total investment will be $186 billion, or $91 billion more than in 1970. The new money required between 1960 and 1970 is thus $52 billion; and the additional investment between 1970 and 1980 will be $91 billion. It is our belief that this can be financed in the free market. There has been no difficulty in financing the difference between $19 billion and $43 billion in the

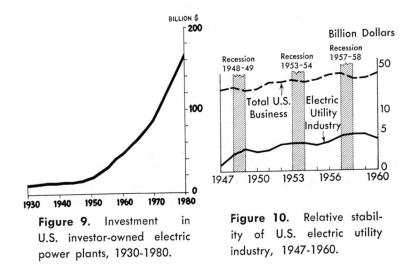

Figure 9. Investment in U.S. investor-owned electric power plants, 1930-1980.

Figure 10. Relative stability of U.S. electric utility industry, 1947-1960.

past ten years. The capital structure is generally 50% bonds, 15% preferred stock and 35% common stock.

If the gross national product continues to grow at 3.57% per annum, it will be about one trillion dollars in 1980 (in terms of 1959 dollars). Our studies indicate that disposable personal income in 1980 should be some $665 billion, and personal saving some $53 billion. Our new money requirements will be some $6 billion per year by 1980, or 11% of estimated personal saving. For the past seven or eight years it has taken around 9% of personal saving to finance the investor-owned electric utility business. We think that the electric companies can attract 11% of personal saving without difficulty.

Economists are interested in the electric utility industry because of its stability. Stability is possible because, even though industrial sales may drop during a recession, residential sales and commercial sales do not drop correspondingly. Figure 10 illustrates this relative stability. During each recession—in 1949, 1954 and 1958—there was a drop in new plant and equipment spending in total industry. Last year the electric industry's spending for new equipment ran 12% of total spending; that is, the investor-owned electric utility industry accounted for 12% of the total capital spending of all industry. During each recession the power industry's investment kept rising; Figure 11 shows the tax on earnings of electric companies, and of all corporations. General business normally suffers a decrease in income during a recession and, therefore, a decrease in federal income taxes. Income in electric utilities has continued to rise through periods of recession.

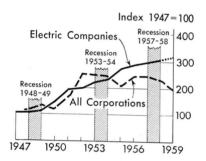

Figure 11. Tax on earnings of U.S. electric power companies, 1947-1959.

Why should 20% of such an industry be in the hands of government? The answer is—it shouldn't be. There is no economic justification at all for government being in the power business. Government is there because of subsidies to government power projects in cost of money and taxes. For example, the power business takes $4 of investment for each $1 of gross. The money costs 6%, and taxes take 5% of the investment. Eleven per cent of $4 is 44 cents; 44 cents of each dollar of revenue goes to the cost of money and taxes. Government power projects generally do not pay these expenses. I close with the hope that some day we may stop wasteful government spending in the power industry, and return to a free market completely.

QUESTION: What is the outlook in the 1960's for electric heating and heat pumps for commercial application in apartment houses and residential single-family units?

MR. VENNARD: Electric heating is coming into prominence, and the power companies are giving it vigorous promotion. They are doing that because of the big demand for air-conditioning which has caused peaks in the summertime; and electric heating can help offset this summer peak. Therefore, many power companies are pricing their service so it is really economical.

There are now about a half million homes electrically heated. That will grow to three or four million homes in ten years, heated either by direct heating or by the heat pump.

6

George Cline Smith
VICE PRESIDENT AND CHIEF ECONOMIST
F. W. DODGE CORPORATION

Construction Demands in Government and Business

IN DISCUSSING the outlook for construction by government and by business, we ought to keep in mind that the construction industry and its statistics do not divide themselves conveniently into these two categories.

The market for building materials and building services is generally measured not in terms of ownership but in terms of building types under three main headings: residential, nonresidential and heavy engineering.

In many individual categories of building there is a good deal of mixing of ownership. For instance, utilities may be private business or they may be government-owned.

Most residential building is under private nonbusiness ownership, but, on the other hand, there are a lot of residential structures, such as hotels and a great many apartments, which do represent commercial enterprises.

Even new hospitals are divided between government and private as to ownership, and some of the private hospitals actually are profitmaking operations.

There are very few major categories of construction that can be lumped together into a single ownership status. It is true that virtually all highways are publicly owned, but generalizations cannot be made for other areas of construction. Even in the group of projects called "public works" a sizable amount of private capital is going into such things as dams and waterfront improvements.

Last year about 40% of all new construction occurred in private residential building. Private housing took about 40% of the entire construction industry. In order to arrive at a base for projections of government and business construction, we have to deal with the remaining 60% of the industry. If you lump together these categories which are clearly business construction—that is, industrial building, commercial building and public utility projects—we are going to find ourselves with a few billion dollars left for such things as private spending for schools, churches, farm buildings and the like. This latter group is about 10% of the construction industry, and it shouldn't be ignored, but, unfortunately, it doesn't fit in under this heading.

Construction is a sort of manufacturing industry. Its products are durable goods, probably, on the whole, the most durable of all durable goods. Estimates of current or future demand for construction are enormously complicated by the existence of a huge inventory of existing structures. The usable life of most of these structures is a matter of opinion, and it is an opinion which may vary from time to time, depending upon short and long-range considerations. The life of any structure can be extended just a little bit longer if conditions seem to warrant, and a series of brief extensions may add up to a long period indeed. I think the World War I temporary buildings in Washington are a good case in point. At least one of them managed to survive well into the 1950's.

Buildings could be divided on the basis of intended use into producer and consumer durables. Some buildings, like houses, schools, hospitals and churches, perform direct services for the public. Others, like stores, offices, factories and so on, are part of the productive process and could be called producer buildings.

But in either case the final demand for new construction depends largely on the number of people, their incomes, and their choices as to the allocation of these incomes. More spending on schools, for instance, could mean less spending on highways. A shift in status symbols from automobiles, say, to houses or to boats might very well produce less of a demand for automobile factories.

We can, of course, make a stab at predicting population and income trends, and we can even try to assess changes in consumer preferences. This is all hazardous forecasting, but it is made even more precarious in the case of construction by the existence of the huge inventory of existing structures of indeterminate life span. In some cases—housing, highways, schools—we can get some measure of the size of the existing inventory, but in other areas, like industrial and commercial building, we not only lack figures on inventory but we don't even have the conceptual basis on which measurements might be made.

Standing, as we do, just inside the threshold of the 1960's, we are absorbed by the prospects that lie ahead in this new decade. The sad fact is, however, that a decade is only ten consecutive years lumped together for the convenience of the calendar-makers. There is no special magic involved in going from one decade to the next. There are at least two important facts that follow from this: First, we should not expect too much too soon from the widely heralded Soaring Sixties. Second, and more important, there are no sharp and radical differences which distinguish the Fabulous Fifties from the Soaring Sixties. The main characteristics of the Fifties were growth and change. The main characteristics of the 1960's are going to be the same, only more so.

The prime indicator of growth is population. It is conservatively estimated that in the next ten years our population will increase by about 34 million people. This is an enormous number of people. It is approximately equal to the combined present population of Canada, Cuba and Australia. This growth of 34 million in ten years means the addition of a population the size of the Chicago metropolitan area every two years.

To take care of this increased population and to provide the rest of us with the continually rising standard of living we have come to expect, our total output of goods and services should rise from its present level of about $500 billion a year to somewhere around $725 billion by 1970.

If that figure seems low to you—because you will hear higher figures here today—I should like to point out that there is a little danger in taking growth projections based on the whole period 1945-1960. We enjoyed very rapid growth in the early part of that period, and much slower growth in the last six or seven years, and if we experience in the 1960's the rate of growth in GNP in the last five years we will come out with a much lower figure. So I put it, and I think conservatively, at what is still a huge total: $725 billion by 1970, in constant 1959 dollars.

Total new construction, now running at about 55 billion dollars a year, probably will rise to nearly $80 billion by 1970. This means that during this decade about $650 billion will go into new construction. Quite possibly, on top of this, another $300 billion will go into maintenance and repair.

It seems clear that the direction of total government outlays for construction will be up over the next decade, and beyond that, as far as the eye can see. Without forecasting the political complexion of the national government after the next few elections, I think we are safe in assuming that spending cuts will exist largely in the minds of the carpenters who put planks in the party platforms. Moreover, state and local expenditures, which are largely for new construction, will continue in their rising trend, quite possibly abetted by new assistance programs from the federal treasury.

About a third of all government construction funds now go into highways. It is somewhat surprising to note that despite all the emphasis that has been placed on the new federal interstate highway program, this proportion is not unusually high. Through most of the postwar period, except during the Korean war, highway spending has accounted for about one third of all public construction. It appears that the interstate program, far from increasing the proportion of government spending going into highways, has merely maintained the status quo, since other types of government construction have also gone up rapidly. However, the next few years should see some increase in the highway share relative to other types of public construction.

Highway construction in 1960 will amount to about $5.7 billion.

This will be a slight decrease from 1959, due partly to the widely published financial difficulties with the interstate program. During the 1960's, however, highway spending is expected to rise each year in succession, with a fairly big jump likely in 1961, and some further increases expected toward the end of the decade, reaching an annual total by 1969 of $8.8 billion. Total outlays for the decade will be about $75 billion, more than $30 billion of which will come from the federal treasury.

The second important category of public construction is schools. Virtually all of the current outlay of about $2.7 million a year represents state and local spending. There is considerable pressure, of course, for the federal government to get into school construction on a much larger scale. Without debating the pros and cons of that issue, there is some possibility that some form of federal aid legislation will be passed during the 1960's. Whether this would, if enacted, greatly increase total school construction outlays, or whether federal money would simply substitute for state and local funds, is highly uncertain.

School construction increased very rapidly in the early part of the postwar period, but in recent years it has tended to level off. Because of continued population growth and increasing emphasis on education, it is apparent that school construction levels will rise again in the 1960's. I think, however, that the construction will tend to concentrate on secondary and higher education facilities more than it has in the past. There are two reasons for this. First, the bumper baby crops of the 1940's are just reaching the higher education levels. Secondly, increased emphasis on education means not that more children will go to elementary school, because they all go there now; it means that more children will stay in school longer. High school diplomas will be a minimum standard and for more and more jobs college and postgraduate degrees will be required, and so we will put more pressure on the upper levels of education and on their facilities than population growth alone would indicate.

Our estimate is that by 1969 school construction will be running a little over $4 billion a year, as compared with $2.7 billion now.

This will mean about $34 billion in school construction during the decade.

Among the other large public construction categories, conservation and development programs will increase substantially, and so, we expect, will sewer and water systems. The two together are running about $2.8 billion a year now, and will grow to perhaps $4.2 billion by 1969. That would be about $35 billion for the entire decade.

Military construction, of course, is an enigma. It has stayed at about the same level, $1½ billion a year, for some years past, and for lack of any reason to do otherwise we have assumed that it will maintain this level throughout the decade.

In total I would expect government outlays to rise from about $16.5 billion this year to $24 billion in 1969. For the decade of the 1960's, then, this would mean total federal, state and local construction outlays of about $200 billion in the ten years.

Turning very briefly to business construction, we find that the most spectacular growth during the postwar period has been in office buildings, with a great concentration of the dollar volume on Manhattan Island. In the past two or three years, spending for office buildings has reached an order of magnitude nearly as great as total outlays for industrial or store buildings.

While this rate of growth will probably slow in the future, we can expect that the 1969 level will reach about $3 billion, as compared with $2.2 billion this year, so that office buildings will total about $26 billion during the decade.

Industrial building is subject to a pronounced cycle. The forecasting of future outlays is complicated by this factor, as well as by problems of inventory of existing buildings and the prospects of technological change and obsolescence of facilities. The 1960 figure is about $2.5 billion, which is well above 1959, but still probably a little on the low side of the cycle. We believe that by 1969 the annual total may well reach $4 billion. It should be understood here that we are talking only about the industrial building portion of capital spending, not including equipment. The total of industrial building for the decade then, would be about $35 billion.

Stores and similar buildings will amount to about $2.2 billion this year. This total should rise, in response to the growth and movement of population, and the new highway program, to about $3.5 billion by 1969, or about $29 billion for the decade as a whole.

Somewhat surprisingly, construction by privately owned utilities has shown no real growth in the past ten years, as measured in annual outlays in constant dollars. This figure includes electric utilities, where there has been some increase, and some other types of utilities where there have been decreases, but the total has been approximately level. This situation should change during the 1960's. We would expect at least a modest increase in annual outlays from the current $5.4 billion to about $6.8 billion by 1969. So the total volume of private utility construction during the decade should be over $60 billion.

Total business construction, which I am defining for this purpose as including industrial building, commercial building and privately owned utilities, currently is about $12.3 billion a year. Our estimates indicate that this will rise to somewhat over $17 billion a year by 1969. Business construction during the decade of the Sixties on this basis could be expected to total about $150 billion.

The 1960's, of course, are not going to be without their problems. Because of the time limitation I cannot discuss them here. On the whole, however, it does appear that the widely heralded Soaring Sixties will truly soar once they get off the ground, and I think the construction industry is going to be both the beneficiary of and an important contributor to this growth.

If residential building is considered, as it should be, we face a prospect of about $650 billion of new construction during the decade. Maintenance and repair, as I said, would add another $300 billion, which would put the industry well within reach of a trillion-dollar total for the decade. This would be by far the largest single market for goods and services that this world has ever seen.

7

Discussion

QUESTION: Would Dr. Smith make some comment on the trend of construction with respect to 1965? Would he expect a different rate between now and 1970 than between now and 1965?

MR. SMITH: I think the growth for the first part of the 1960's in general will be slower than the second half. I think population trends will contribute to that. But we will be in a flatter stage of growth for the first two or three years, at least, of the 1960's. Probably we will have a couple of recessions—mild ones—and that makes it very difficult to forecast specifically for a year like 1965, but in general I would assume the growth curve would be saucer-shaped.

QUESTION: Do you expect any major shifts in types of housing which might affect the figures? I am referring to prefabricated housing.

MR. SMITH: I don't know that they would affect the figures. I am sure we will see technological change in the industry. It has been slow in coming for many reasons, including local building codes, but I am sure we will see definite increases in prefabrication of components, at least, if not prefabricated buildings. There was a time a few years ago when door and window frames were built on the site. These things all come now as preassembled components, and more and more of this will happen.

QUESTION: I understand that housing starts now are around 1.2

million a year. Would you have a projection on starts through 1970?

MR. SMITH: Yes. In terms of the new census series on housing starts, we are estimating this year at about 1,350,000. By 1970 I would say, on this basis, about 1,800,000 a year will be a sustainable annual average.

CONSUMER MARKETS OF THE FUTURE

Milton C. Mumford
CHAIRMAN

1

Milton C. Mumford
PRESIDENT
LEVER BROTHERS COMPANY

Introduction

In my business, what happens in 1961 is much less dependent than it used to be on what we do in 1961, or even in 1960. It is more and more governed by what we did in 1959 and earlier. And the lead time required in planning grows longer each year.

If we do in the next ten years what sober economists believe we will do, we will see a change in our standard of living approaching that which took place during the entire 200 years from Colonial times to 1940. The rate of change is in itself an extremely dynamic factor in our economy. In few places is this factor of greater importance than in consumer marketing.

Consumer markets are dependent in large part on three influences: the number of people, the amount of money people have to spend, and how they think they should spend it.

Probably the most potent factor in the mix is population itself. It appears that we will increase our population over the next ten years by over 20%. Just what these people will want nobody knows for sure, but it is a safe bet that they will want an ever-increasing standard of living. We will continue to educate people at a rate unprecedented in history. There were only 4½ million high school graduates in the country in 1920. Twenty years later, in 1940, there were 23 million. In 1959 there were 49 million. And in a few years there will be 70 million. High school graduates earn something between 50 and 80% more than nonhigh school graduates, depending on whose figures you want to take.

Put these two factors together and you have a fairly important motivator. It would be a rare phenomenon indeed if a better educated population were not to seek—in fact, demand—an increasing standard of living. To be sure, better educated people may want less steel, in the form of smaller cars instead of bigger cars. But then they buy more high schools, more travel, more service, et cetera, and in the end the net pressure is always up.

So there will be much greater numbers of people and they will be seeking more and better things. In what degree they actually consume will depend on what they have to spend. This seems to me to be the central question of the future. Will we have the wit and the skill to provide jobs for this increased number of people, so that they may perform as consumers?

There will likewise be shifts of interest within the group. A greater relative percentage of youngsters and old people will mean many changes. I don't know whether one third of the population can support two thirds, which is about where we are headed. It may be that we will have to find ways to continue our older people in more productive work. Vast numbers of women in the work force are here to stay. Between 1950 and 1958 the number of men employed increased by 2%, the number of women employed increased by 21%, and the number of married women employed increased by 41%. Seventy-eight per cent of the entire growth of the work force between 1950 and 1958 consisted of women. Not only will this mean that women will have a larger voice in the over-all expenditure decisions, it will also mean that while a lot of them are working, men will be doing a great deal more of the shopping. Shifts such as these will have a profound effect on the techniques of the consumer market.

In our forward planning it may be helpful to remember that, with rare exceptions, nobody has ever built the parking lot of a supermarket big enough.

2

Robert W. Burgess
DIRECTOR, BUREAU OF THE CENSUS
U. S. DEPARTMENT OF COMMERCE

The Population Influence

In APPROACHING the problem of surveying the population changes that are likely to occur in the next ten years, I am unable to draw very specifically on the results from the 1960 population census because only preliminary figures are now available. Instead, I turn back to what we found in 1950, and the analyses we have made in subsequent times, especially "Illustrative Projections of the Population of the United States by Age and Sex, 1960 to 1980," a Census Bureau publication issued in November, 1958.

The term "projection" calls for a word or two of comment. A population projection is the mathematical consequence of certain carefully stated assumptions. In this set of projections, as in several previous sets made by the Census Bureau, we stated four projections, on four different sets of assumptions. Projection No. 1 is based on the assumption that fertility rates will be 10% higher than the established rates measured in 1955, 1956 and 1957. We have been fooled once or twice before when we made sets of projections and then found the results actually creeping higher than the highest of the projections. Our projectionists have thus deliberately taken a projection on fertility assumptions which they were pretty sure will be above anything that will happen up until 1980.

The second projection takes the 1955-1957 fertility level, until 1960. The third starts with the 1955-1957 fertility level, declines to the 1949-1951 level by 1965-1970, and continues at the latter level until 1980. The lowest projection starts with the 1955-1957 level, declines to the 1942-1944 level by 1965-1970, and continues at the latter level to 1980.

Some of the characteristics of these projections are noted in Table 1 and Table 2. You will note that projection 1 carries from 181.1 million persons to 219.5 million in ten years, an increase of 38 million. Projection No. 4 yields an increase of only 23 million. The difference between the two extreme projections is substantially due to the difference in the assumed fertility rates.

Only the first three age-group entries show any distinction between the projections. All of the 1970 population in the 15-19 age group and later age groups were born prior to 1958, and therefore the projection is not influenced by future fertility. Among the several

Table 1. CENSUS BUREAU PROJECTIONS OF POPULATION BY AGE GROUPS

ESTIMATES MADE IN 1958 OF MILLIONS OF PERSONS AT JULY 1 OF EACH YEAR

AGE GROUP, YEARS	MILLIONS OF PERSONS		
	1960	1965	1970
All Ages, I	181.1	199.0	219.5
IV	179.4	191.5	202.5
Under 5, I	21.0	23.4	26.7
IV	19.3	17.7	17.1
5– 9, I		21.9	24.3
IV	19.2	20.1	18.6
10–14, I			21.9
IV	17.2	19.2	20.2
15–19	13.4	17.3	19.3
20–24	11.3	13.5	17.3
25–34	22.8	22.5	25.2
35–44	24.0	24.3	23.0
45–54	20.8	22.1	23.3
55–64	15.6	17.1	19.0
65 and over	15.8	17.6	19.5

Projection I—Fertility averages 10% above 1955-57 level throughout
Projection IV—Fertility declines to 1942-44 level by 1965-70.

Table 2. CENSUS BUREAU PROJECTIONS OF MILLIONS OF PERSONS SURVIVING FROM THOSE BORN IN EACH 5-YEAR PERIOD INDICATED

BASED ON PROJECTION I, FERTILITY 1958-1970 AVERAGES 10% ABOVE 1955-1957 LEVEL. NUMBER IN EACH GROUP INCLUDES SOME IMMIGRANTS TO THE UNITED STATES

GROUPS BY YEAR OF BIRTH	MILLIONS OF PERSONS		
	1960	1965	1970
7/1/1965–7/1/1970			26.7
7/1/1960–7/1/1965		23.4	24.3
7/1/1955–7/1/1960	21.0	21.9	21.9
7/1/1950–7/1/1955	19.2	19.2	19.3
7/1/1945–7/1/1950	17.2	17.3	17.3
7/1/1940–7/1/1945	13.4	13.5	25.2
7/1/1935–7/1/1940	11.3		
7/1/1935–7/1/1945	24.7		25.2
7/1/1925–7/1/1935	22.8		23.0
7/1/1915–7/1/1925	24.0		23.3
7/1/1905–7/1/1915	20.8		19.0
7/1/1895–7/1/1905	15.6	Before 7/1/05	19.5
Before 7/1/1895	15.8		

projections with respect to those under five years, those five to nine years old and those 9 to 14, there are significant differences in 1965 and 1970. The 15-to-19 age group rises from 13.4 to 19.3 million in the ten-year interval from 1960 to 1970. Similarly, the 20-to-24 age group rises from 11 to 17 million; the 25-to-34 age group rises from 22.8 to 25.2 million. On the other hand, in the 35-44 age group, very little increase is indicated.

Tables 1 and 2 together illuminate the changes in population distribution resulting from a progressive aging of substantially the same group of people from one year to the next, superimposed upon the pattern of the past and prospective birth rate.

**Table 3.   BIRTHS AND NET CHANGES IN POPULATION,
1940-1959 INCLUSIVE**

YEAR	BIRTHS		NET CHANGE	
	Number, Thousands	Rate	Number, Thousands	Per Cent
1959	4298	24.3	3654 *	2.08 *
1958	4250	24.4	2865	1.66
1957	4308	25.2	2923	1.72
1956	4218	25.1	2984	1.79
1955	4104	24.8	2862	1.75
1954	4078	25.1	2841	1.76
1953	3965	24.8	2681	1.69
1952	3912	24.9	2644	1.70
1951	3826	24.8	2718	1.78
1950	3627	23.9	2520	1.67
1949	3649	24.5	2551	1.72
1948	3637	24.8	2530	1.74
1947	3817	26.5	2638	1.85
1946	3411	24.1	2145	1.52
1945	2858	20.4	1452	1.04
1944	2939	21.2	1581	1.15
1943	3104	22.7	1791	1.32
1942	2989	22.2	1704	1.27
1941	2703	20.3	1367	1.03
1940	2559	19.4	1210	0.92

* Includes effect of addition of Alaska and Hawaii.

The issue is further illuminated by Table 3. The first part of the table shows the number of births from 1940 to 1959. The number has been 4,200,000 or more for four years in a row. The birth rate requires a little attention because of the enthusiastic references to the "population explosion." While there has been a change in birth rates, it has not been of quite such heroic proportions as the term "explosion" might imply.

In 1940 the birth rate, measured over the total population, was 19.4. In the 1930's it was a little lower than that. It began to rise in the late 1930's. It edged up further in the early 1940's and finally the rate in 1947 just shortly after the end of World War II was

26.5. The rate declined for several years after that spurt, but by 1951 it turned up again.

There is usually a spurt in the birth rate after the close of a large war, when soldiers are demobilized and new families started. A bulge, such as we had in 1947, was not unexpected. The effects are just now appearing in the young people entering high school.

There has been some reference to a recent decline in the birth rate. I believe in the early months of 1960 there is just a little further decline. But the decline is in the tenth place in the birth rate; it is a little early to say that a reversal of trend has occurred because the over-all rate is influenced by the age mix of potential mothers—women in their early 20's have the highest fertility rate. In part of the 1960's at least, the over-all rate may rise further because of the large number of young mothers coming in. These are the general facts about the changes in population.

There will be more people moving into the years regularly characterized by college education, professional preparation, and the first stages in an active business, professional and domestic life. The number of candidates and applicants for apprenticeship types of positions has for several years been unusually small, but year by year it has begun to increase. In the years 1965 to 1970 a peak will be reached in actual or would-be college students reflecting the peak birth rate of 1947. It has been suggested that there will be such a large number of young people actively entering the labor market about this time that there should be serious concern about the possibility of finding attractive opportunities for all adults. My own guess would be that if any real stress of this type develops it will come some time after 1970.

QUESTION: What influence is exerted over fertility rates by general economic conditions?

DR. BURGESS: It has been observed that as standards of living rise and as individuals get higher incomes, their fertility rate often decreases. That is, there is an association between high income and a small number of children that seems to hold in certain economic classes in the community. On the other hand, higher income in general should mean more children. This general topic is one that is being investigated further to establish the circumstances under which favorable economic conditions lead to higher fertility rates or lower rates.

3

Dorothy S. Brady
DEPARTMENT OF ECONOMICS
UNIVERSITY OF PENNSYLVANIA

Developing Patterns of Income, Spending and Saving

CENSUS DATA and data from other surveys suggest that married women work for several reasons. First, there are the pin-money workers who earn a little money here and there; they are numerous but not very important for our purposes. Secondly, a major reason why married women work is income step-up. If we classify families by income of husbands or heads and then measure the frequency with which the wife works, we find the frequency is very high indeed at the lowest level of husband's income, and decreases as his income increases.

The group of wives working for what might be called economic necessity is going to become more important in 1970. This is particularly true of the high school and college graduate group of women who marry a young professional man whose income is low simply because he is still going to school. In this population layer, the percentage of working wives fluctuates around 80%.

The forecasters tell us that we are going to have a great many more in the professions and in the semiprofessional callings in 1970. Given an increase in the number of young men from 20 to 35 still going to school, and still working toward professional competence, we are going to have a very large number of wives working to maintain family income and to assure the education of their husbands.

In the last few years the number of women in their middle years, from 45 to 60, who have entered into the labor force and are prepared to stay there, has been dramatic. Most of them are certainly not trained, or their skills are certainly out of date. Most of them go into services in their localities, somewhere near home; checkers in supermarkets, counter-workers in the drug store and soda fountain. They are supplementing income of husbands who are on the downgrade with respect to their lifetime income curve. In certain trades and occupations, the number of semiskilled and unskilled workers over 45 earn progressively lower wages. Married women of 40 to 50 are attempting to fill that income gap by entering the service trades.

The career woman represents still another set of incentives. The woman who trains for a professional calling, or who takes a responsible role in a business enterprise, will be much more numerous in the 1960's. The national stress toward making the best use of our skills makes it almost patriotic for a professionally trained woman to continue work.

Moreover, a woman holding down a well-paid, full-time job adds substantially to her family's income, and tends to raise the whole level of living. At the present time only half of all married couples live on the husbands' income. The others are dependent on a secondary worker—a working wife. In every community some standard of living has been established that implies a definite minimum income. As far as I can determine, in New York State in 1957 that minimum was about $1,000 in cash, per person. The average take-home pay was $80 a week or $4,000 a year, and that would just take care of a four-person family. But prices have gone up since 1957, and probably will go up in 1960. In metropolitan communities generally the lower limit of family income seems now to be closer to $1,200 or $1,300 per person.

The bulk of the recent residential building has been out in the urban fringe, as it is called—in the form of new, rapidly growing villages. Something like half of the real metropolitan population— that is, the people who work in the central city—now live in the suburbs. Of the expenditures reported in the *Life* magazine (1956) survey of consumer expenditures, fully 46% of outlays by families in metropolitan areas went to housing, household operations, and automobiles.

To my mind this proportion is out of line. What the working wife is going to do in the 1960's is bring the family consumption pattern back to what has been a rather stable pattern for the urban community for a good long time.

Within that 46%, over 30% was for running the house itself. I think working wives are going to bring that percentage back down to a normal of about 25%, by adding further to family incomes and by reducing outlays on the automobile.

I think we are going to come back to a spending pattern of about 25% for houses, about 30% for food and, significantly, over 10% for clothing. Medical care is going to go on taking a little more than it has—perhaps around 6% or 7%. The automobile is going to encounter a bit of a problem here. Circumstances of the 1950's raised the automobile expenditures to about 15% of total outlays, and, among the suburbanites, 17%. Henceforth, other things are going to be more important—notably education.

George P. Hitchings
VICE PRESIDENT OF ECONOMIC RESEARCH
AMERICAN AIRLINES, INC.

4

A Close Look at the Hard-Goods Future

THE OUTLOOK for consumer durable goods over the coming decade is, of course, tied in very closely with the prospects for growth in total consumer buying power. Durable goods are a combination of buying out of current income and use of credit, but the primary factor over the long run is the growth of consumer income. For that reason, I propose to discuss for a moment the prospects for growth in the total economy before getting into consumer durable goods and then using the automobile industry as a prime example of consumer goods.

Figure 1 shows the growth in the total national product in billions of dollars. The solid line represents the private nonfarm product and the broken line the total product; the third line represents the private nonfarm man-hours that went into that product.

Over the long term we have been able to go ahead at a rate of about 40% each decade. I don't see any reason for expecting anything much different from 40% in the future. How much growth we actually get will depend, of course, on how efficiently we use our resources, of which man-hours are one component. It may be that in the coming decade we may be able to achieve a rate of increase in efficiency more rapid than in the past. To the extent that we do I suspect we may take the gain in the form of increased leisure, at least, in part. For that reason I would assume that even

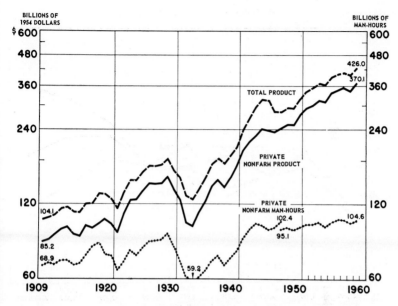

Figure 1. Growth in total U.S. national product, 1909-1960.

if we do get an increase in the rate of productivity gain, we will still get growth in total product at about the same rate that we have had in the past.

What about the impact of this kind of growth in the total economy on the spending power of the consumer? Figure 2 shows the number of spending units in each income group in the year 1957, and a projection to 1965, and 1970. The term "spending unit" embraces a household head, and other members who do not pool their spending with a household head. With that kind of growth in the total economy, and the assumed growth in spending which arises from about a 17% increase in the adult population, we would have a very substantial growth in the number of spending units with incomes over $7,500. This projection would indicate about 22 million spending units in the $7,500 or over bracket, compared with 10 million units in 1957. In addition, there would be some growth in the $6,000 to $7,500 bracket, an increase from about 7½ million spending units to about 9½ million.

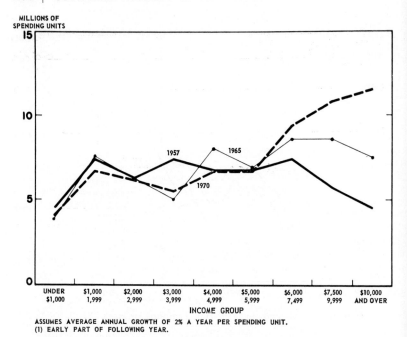

ASSUMES AVERAGE ANNUAL GROWTH OF 2% A YEAR PER SPENDING UNIT.
(1) EARLY PART OF FOLLOWING YEAR.

Figure 2. Spending units by income group, 1957 and projected 1960, 1970 in 1957 dollars.

Virtually no change is expected in the number of spending units in the $4,000 to $6,000 bracket over the coming decade. In the income brackets below $4,000 there will be an actual decrease.

Such an income projection has very important repercussions on the demand for consumer durable goods. Let's look, for example, at autos, which are a prime example of what happens with the growth in income. The top line of Figure 3 shows the proportion in each income group that owns at least one car; the dashed line represents the proportion that owns two or more cars. At the $7,500 bracket, in fact, even as early as the $6,000 bracket, the rate of ownership of at least one car is so high that further growth is not likely. But the ownership of two or more cars increases very rapidly as income rises. The great growth in the number of spending units above $6,000, and particularly above $7,500, thus makes

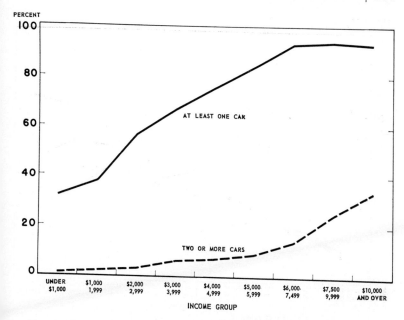

Figure 3. Proportion in each income group owning automobiles, February, 1958.

quite an impact on the ownership of cars, even if ownership rates by income group should remain unchanged.

Figure 4 shows the projection of the number of spending units owning cars, for the moment, assuming that there is no further growth in the ownership percentage at a given income level. The great growth in the number of cars owned comes in the brackets from $6,000 up. Families in these brackets generally own the younger-aged cars. Ownership of cars over seven years of age, for example, is quite low in income brackets from $7,500 up.

The impact on multiple-car ownership is shown in Figure 5. Applying multiple-car ownership rates by income group, a very sharp growth in each ownership appears in the $6,000 and up income brackets.

The important thing to note is not so much the specific figures, but the fact that there is tremendous leverage in the brackets above

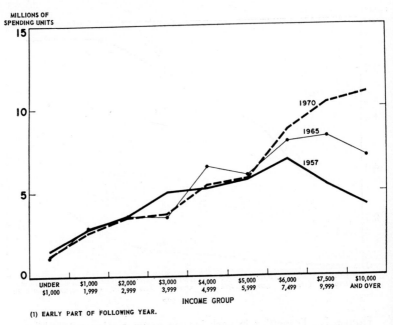

MILLIONS OF
SPENDING UNITS

(1) EARLY PART OF FOLLOWING YEAR.

Figure 4. Spending units owning cars by income group, 1957 and projected 1965, 1970.

$6,000 income and up in terms of expanding multiple-car ownership.

The combined influence on the total ownership of cars would indicate a 26% growth in the decade of the 1960's. Bearing in mind the assumptions involved, the 26% figure seems to be a conservative projection, since it does not assume any further growth in the rate of car ownership within a given income class, but is solely the result of growth in the adult population and in their buying power.

Figure 6 shows the age distribution of cars on the road for recent years. The great bulk of cars on the road in 1970 will be in younger age categories—cars produced in the decade of the 1960's. By 1970 it is reasonable to expect that there would be outstanding about 61½ million cars produced in the decade of the 1960's—namely, the 1960 to 1969 models.

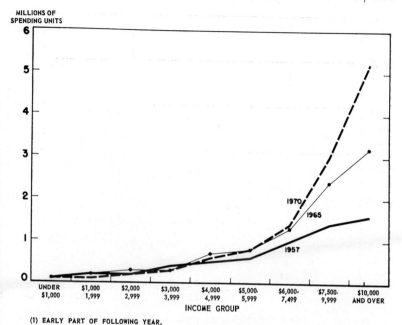

Figure 5. Spending units owning two or more cars, by income group, 1957 and projected 1965, 1970.

Additional cars will have to be produced during this decade to take care of scrapping of the 1960 to 1969 models. As shown in Figure 7, scrapping is not large in the early age of the car's life, but it increases rapidly after about five years of age. The scrappage rate for the years 1955-1957 is probably as good a basis of projection of scrappage that is workable. (The 1958 scrappage rate was lower, but scrappage in that year reflected temporary recession conditions and is not indicative of what is likely to happen in the future.)

In order to take care of the scrappage of cars produced in the 1960-1969 period, an additional 8½ million cars would be required. A total of 70 million cars would, thus, have to be produced for the U. S. market in the decade of the 1960's to provide a level of ownership at the end of the decade which would be consistent with

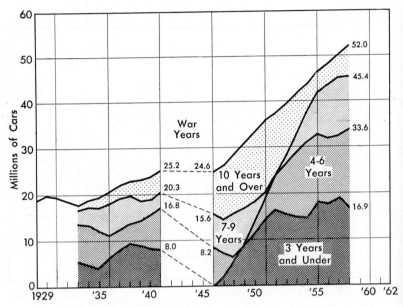

Figure 6. Age distribution of passenger cars in use, 1929-1959.

present desires for car ownership, the growth of the adult population and the perspective increase in buying power.

It will take a very substantial growth in consumer credit to achieve this kind of growth in car ownership. Figure 8 shows the trend of consumer installment credit in recent years. It illustrates the fact that the outstanding amount of consumer credit tends to rise from year to year, and is likely to continue rising. There will be interruptions because of recessions but the important question is whether a given level of consumer credit is reasonable relative to the assets that have accumulated with the use of that credit, and whether they are reasonable relative to the ability to meet installment-payment obligations out of income.

The path upward is not going to be smooth in consumer durable goods, particularly in the case of automobiles. Figure 9 shows the annual fluctuation in new passenger car registrations since 1922. It is a highly sensitive business and will fluctuate with the general

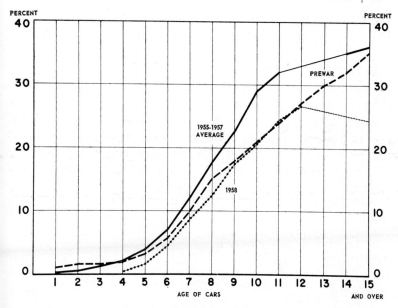

Figure 7. Passenger-car scrappage rates (percentage scrapped annually by age).

business situation. In the depression, for example, new car sales dropped about 75%; in the recession of 1937-38, they dropped 50%. In the postwar period up until 1958, there was no great fluctuation because of the business cycle, but in 1958 a more normal type of reaction or recession set in, in which auto sales dropped about 25%. Consumer durable goods demand can be expected to grow at about the rate of the general economy. The general economy should grow about 40% in real terms over the decade. Of course, particular items of consumer durable goods will not advance at the 40% rate. The more mature consumer durables should be expected to rise more slowly, but consumers will turn frequently to other newer types of durables. There is little danger of so-called saturation of consumer desires for durable goods in general. If saturation is reached on one particular durable, buying interest will switch to another. So I see no reason why the total for consumer durable goods should not advance at least in line with the 40% growth rate expected for the economy as a whole.

QUESTION: In view of your projection of a 26% increase for automobiles, as compared with 40% in the economy as a whole over the next ten years, do you expect a lower price per car? Will other durables have a greater proportionate increase? Or do you look for a more than proportionate increase in services?

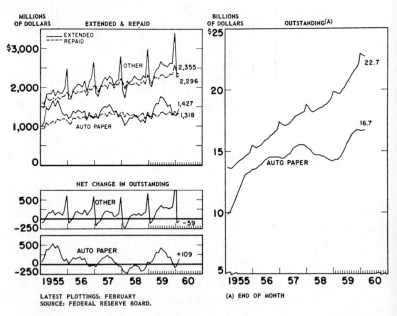

Figure 8. Consumer installment credit (not seasonally adjusted), 1955-1960.

MR. HITCHINGS: I think the difference will be absorbed by other competitive products and services. Consumer durables as a whole may well come close to the projected 40% growth in national product, but it is difficult for a mature product, which has already achieved a very high level of ownership to match the percentage

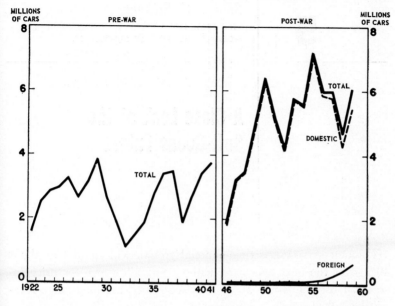

Figure 9. New passenger car registrations in U.S., 1922-1960.

growth of the economy as a whole. I don't think this is an indication that people are going to spend less for durables. I think they are just switching. They are not willing to put money into a car at present, but they are quite willing to put it into other durable goods or services. Look at the tremendous growth, for example, in boats in recent years, years when the automotive industry was having difficulty in selling. In fact, the only way to achieve an over-all rate of growth of 40% for the economy is through new products.

5

Myron S. Silbert
VICE PRESIDENT
FEDERATED DEPARTMENT STORES, INC.

A Close Look at the Soft-Goods Future

My rough estimate is that national growth will amount to about 40% over the next ten years, without any allowance for price increase. I use the word "about" advisedly, because long-range forecasting is far from an exact science.

Of this increase, a little less than half reflects an expected increase in the labor force, and a little more than half an expected increase in productivity, making some allowance for a slowly decreasing work week. The productivity figure used in this projection is 2.1% per man-hour per year. This has been the average for the economy as a whole for the past 45 years. More recent figures might justify a somewhat higher figure for productivity and an indicated gain in total output of as much as 50%. The most recent government estimate suggests a 50% increase in output in the coming decade.

A gain of 40 to 50% would mean that gross national product would increase from about $500 billion now to about $750 billion in 1970. Total personal income will increase from about $400 billion now to $560 or $600 billion for 1970. My own estimate is that output and income will also increase because of rising prices at about 1% a year, or about 10% in ten years. The dollar figures for 1970 would thus be 10% higher than the constant-dollar forecasts.

What is likely to happen to personal spending under conditions of substantial growth in income? Figure 1 shows the number of

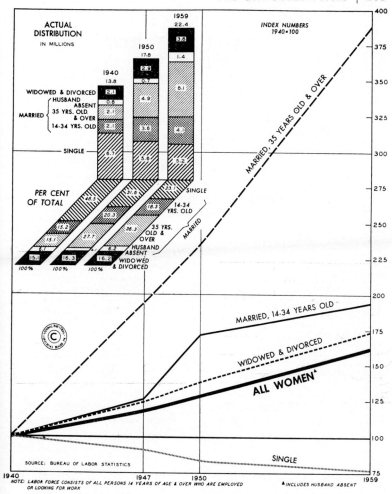

Figure 1. Number of women in U.S. labor force, 1940-1959.

women in the labor force. There will clearly be an increase in the number of working women. Suggested is an important increase in the market for women's items, for more and better items of women's apparel, and greater expenditures for a range of consumer products because of the increase in multiple wage-earner families, and the associated rise in living standards.

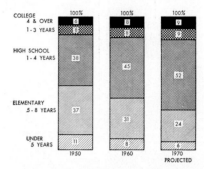

Figure 2. Levels of educational attainment, 1950-1970.

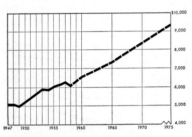

Figure 3. Average personal income per family, 1947-1975.

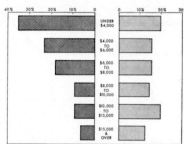

Figure 4. Distribution of family income in percentage of total U.S. families.

Figure 2 shows projected levels of educational attainment. The National Industrial Conference Board's recent chart book, "A Graphic Guide To Consumer Markets," shows that the percentage of persons who will have spent some time in high school will increase from 61% now, to 70% in 1970; those who will have spent some time in college will increase from 16 to 18% of the population. This upsurge in educational attainment will have an important influence on the quality level of consumer expenditures. In addition, people with a broad educational background tend to buy a broader variety of products.

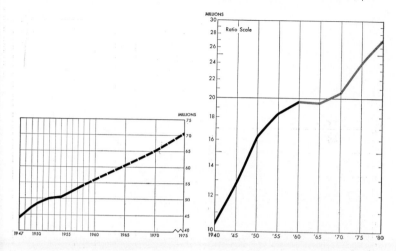

Figure 5. Number of families, including unattached individuals, 1947-1975.

Figure 6. Number of children under age 5 in U.S. population (including families of armed forces overseas); actual 1940-1955, projected 1960-1980.

Figures 3 and 4 show average personal income per family, and the distribution of family income. The total number of families will increase from 55 million in 1959 to 70 million in 1975 (Figure 5). The families with incomes under $8,000 will decrease from 42 million to 37 million; the families with incomes over $8,000 will increase from 13 million to 33 million. This increase in family income will mean an increase in soft goods, and in taste and quality levels.

In the decade from 1960 to 1970, increases in population, by age group, are expected to be of these magnitudes: under ten years, an increase of 30%; ten to 19 years, 33%; 20 to 30 years, 39%; 30 to 50, no change; 50 to 64, an increase of 18%; and over 65, an increase of 25%. The greatest increase is thus in the age groups under 30 (Figures 6, 7 and 8).

Particularly noteworthy in the appended charts is the beginning

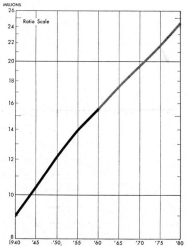

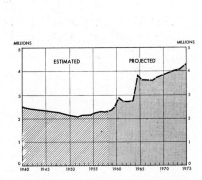

Figure 7. Estimated and projected annual numbers of persons in U.S. reaching age 18, 1940-1975.

Figure 8. Number of persons age 65 and over in U.S. population (including armed forces overseas). Actual 1940-1955, projected 1960-1980.

of a long advance in the birth rate, starting about 1941-1942; a dramatic increase in the population in the 18- to 24-year group after 1960; and a sharp rise in the number of persons becoming 18 years old, which has been climbing in the last two or three years, and will rise sharply starting about 1963.

How will the prospective increase in population and income be distributed in individual metropolitan areas? Our estimate is that most of the nation's metropolitan areas will share in the growth in the 1960's. Very few of the areas are likely to experience an increase of less than 30%. The natural increase in population by excess of birth over death occurs in every community; productivity gains in the utilization of manpower occur in every community. Some areas will have additional gains in income because of in-migration and because of particularly rapid growth in employment opportunities.

My company makes income and sales projections for the next

ten years for individual metropolitan areas, through study of each industry in the area and its potential for growth. With respect to almost all such areas we estimate that sales will increase in both downtown areas and suburban areas. The rate of increase will be much greater on the perimeter, although there will be important urban rebuilding in and adjacent to the downtown section with a consequent improvement in sales facilities and volume.

The department store is in an unusual position to participate in the future sales growth of both downtown and suburban areas. A recent Census Bureau report indicates a total retail sales increase of 17½% between 1954 and 1958. In the same period, department store sales increased 26½%. Between the two years, there was a shift in the accounting of leased concession departments; if that shift is taken into consideration, the increase in department store sales is about 23%.

In 1959 the Census Bureau figures show that department stores again enjoyed larger gains than all retail stores as a whole. Our estimate is that the department store share of the market will continue to improve. The department store will also continue to increase its share of earnings in the 1960's because it will continue to capitalize on opportunities for growth in both downtown and the suburbs.

Along with this growth will come change. Self-service selling will grow in soft goods stores, in department stores, in individual sections of department stores, in suburban outlets, and in new stores arranged like soft goods supermarkets.

THE LONG-TERM BUSINESS OUTLOOK:
Presidents' Panel

Robert E. Wilson
CHAIRMAN

1

Robert E. Wilson

COMMISSIONER
UNITED STATES ATOMIC ENERGY COMMISSION

Petroleum and Atomic Energy

IN PLACE of an introduction, I shall deal briefly with the outlook for two industries with which I have some familiarity: petroleum and atomic energy.

I think the oil industry is in for tough sledding for a year or two because of overcapacity both in this country and abroad, in both production and refining but particularly in production. The refining situation is a little better in hand; with less refinery construction going on, I think demand will catch up with refinery capacity to the extent that in two or three years the industry's refining operations will be back to 92% of capacity, which is considered to be good, economical operation. Until then the situation largely depends upon the restraint of members of the industry, as to whether they will be satisfied with a reasonable share of the market or whether everyone will try to run a little more than their share, with the inevitable result of distress prices.

I will add a brief comment on the supposed competition between atomic energy and the oil industry—or for that matter to the coal industry. Competition between atomic energy and the oil industry is practically nonexistent. The proportion of a barrel of crude which now goes into central powerplant use is about 2.5%, and that is heavy fuel oil, which is the only product which sells for less than the cost of a barrel of crude. If the industry were even to lose all this powerplant business, it would not be any particular hardship. Atomic energy does not constitute any threat to the principal markets of the oil industry in transportation or home heating.

Secondly, I don't expect atomic power to be really competitive in this country, even in stationary powerplants, for approximately another eight years. I believe that by about 1968 atomic power in large units, in high-cost areas such as New England and the West Coast, will be competitive. The condition may come a little earlier or a little later abroad, depending upon fuel costs and other economic conditions in each country.

David L. Luke

2

PRESIDENT
WEST VIRGINIA PULP AND PAPER COMPANY

Pulp and Paper

I WOULD SUMMARIZE the main features of the outlook for the American paper and pulp industry during the 1960's as follows: First, concerning production, we can reasonably look forward to an increase of something more than 40% in physical output and consumption of paper products in the United States during the next ten years. Such a rate of growth, slightly greater than that of the economy as a whole, would only continue a long-established trend.

The economy and versatility of paper products enable them to expand their markets through the growth of population and incomes; through invading markets previously served by other materials such as steel, glass, wood and textiles; and through the creation of brand-new products. The films, the foils and the plastics will doubtless invade paper's markets to some extent, but on net balance, paper will gain new markets.

Second, about capital expenditures, the paper industry, as you know, is a large user of fixed capital. Its expenditures or new plant and equipment in the five years ended in 1959 totaled $3.3 billion, or an average of $⅔ billion per year. I would expect such expenditures to rise during the 1960's to an average not far from $1 billion per year. While the industry has more than adequate productive capacity for the requirements of the next two years, it will need substantial additions in the remainder of the decade. Moreover, a considerable fraction of the existing productive capacity, particularly in the smaller mills, is obsolete, expensive to operate, and in need of replacement.

Third, I would expect the investment, pricing, and profit performance of the industry during the 1960's to be less subject to pronounced irregularities than in the past. There are several reasons for this expectation. The economies of large plants and of integration are so pronounced that we can expect the consolidation and integration movement which has been prominent during the last ten years to continue, and perhaps to accelerate.

Larger units and wider ownership will foster greater discipline in pricing and new investment. The basic requirements for integrated paper production, such as wood, water and easy access to markets, in proper combination, are harder to find; and when they are found they are more costly.

The industry has grown to such size that even substantial amounts of new capacity will add relatively small increments in any short space of time to the industry's total installed capacity. The disruptive influence once exerted by sudden large imports of foreign pulp is unlikely to recur—except possibly from Communist Russia—because foreign pulp is no longer cheap. The disrupting influence once exerted by small mills in their efforts to obtain temporary markets regardless of cost is likely to become weaker as they account for a shrinking proportion of total output. In consequence, while I expect competition to remain vigorous, more powerful natural economic forces will be operating to promote more stable prices and profits than at any other time in our history.

Fourth, I expect substantial progress during the 1960's in the industry's exploitation of its opportunities in chemistry, chemical engineering and forestry. We now make useful products out of only one half of each stick of wood we grow or buy. Most of the rest is burned. The unused half of the stick is made up of complex organic chemicals which present our industry with the same kind of opportunities that were realized by the coal-tar people 40 years ago, and which the petrochemical people are realizing today. When we learn to exploit the other half of the stick, our industry may well be able to double its sales from its present level to perhaps $25 billion, plus whatever increase is added by growth from here on out.

In the area of forest management, we have the same opportunities for prodigious increases in productivity that have already been realized by our wheat and corn farmers and through substantially the same tried-and-true methods. The paper industry is awakening to these opportunities and to others. During the past ten years the industry has spent about $100 million in research. At the rate at which these expenditures are being stepped up, I should not be surprised if they amounted to as much as $1 billion during the decade of the 1960's.

Substantially all the main points that I have made respecting the outlook for the American pulp and paper industry as a whole during the next decade can be made about our own company. We expect to grow at a greater rate than the average of the industry, just as we have been growing at a greater rate than the average of the industry during the past decade.

Our annual expenditures for new plant and equipment, which were running at a little over $30 million by the end of the 1950's, should be running well in excess of $50 million by the end of the 1960's. Our company has undertaken a considerable degree of integration toward end products during the past decade, and I would expect this movement to continue during the decade ahead. If you will forgive me for appearing immodest, I will say that we have led the industry during the past decade in our emphasis upon research, and expect to maintain this position in the decade ahead. We have invested approximately $20 million in real research activities during the past ten years, and expect to invest more nearly $100 million in such efforts during the next ten years.

Underlying all my remarks have been some unstated assumptions. I shall mention only two of them; first, that the decade ahead is one of peace; and second, that it is one in which our economy will fluctuate upward and downward, but fluctuate around a climbing trend line.

While I believe that everything that I have said here is reasonable on the basis of experience and the information available to me, there is one thing of which I am surer than of anything that I have yet mentioned, and that is that in the decade ahead a great many things will come to pass that none can now foresee.

QUESTION: I am wondering if the increased productivity in forestry will come from the increased growth of wood. Will you be able to use solar energy more effectively, or will the gain come from such factors as increased mechanization in handling the wood?

MR. LUKE: It will come from better forest management, just as increased productivity on the farms has come from better farm management. It will come from forest research, which we all do quite extensively. Yet we have only scratched the surface of what we can do in the way of forest research. We find that genetics is important. We have learned that we can grow trees faster, just as a farmer can raise hogs that will grow faster and get fatter. We can do the same thing by selecting superior seed from superior trees. And then we find such simple things as drainage control is very important. If the water table is kept fairly level we are going to have a much more rapidly growing forest than if we have dry years and wet years.

CHAIRMAN WILSON: Genetics is just as important in your industry as in the farm industry, and I think we can look forward to a lot of improvements, but I suppose you are handicapped by the fact that it takes ten years to get results of experiments whereas you can get them in a year in a farm crop.

MR. LUKE: It used to take 40 years to get results, but we are learning how to accelerate. We can get results today in ten, and I have a hunch within a few years it will be possible to get results in three by grafting on to stock that is already in the ground and thus shortening the growth cycle.

QUESTION: Would you expand a little on your remark that foreign pulp is not now as inexpensive as it was? Most people have a fear of foreign imports being cheaper.

MR. LUKE: Pulp is a world commodity. It moves all through the world with no duty. The only restrictions are those of foreign exchange. We have been in world competition for quite some time. Formerly Scandinavia and Canada had lower costs than we. Today we have much lower costs than any of them, and the reason is that we harvest our wood on a daily basis, whereas in Scandinavia and Canada wood is harvested on a seasonal basis. That means you have to carry large inventories; you have to have all the harvest labor in a short space of time. For that basic reason we have lower wood costs.

In addition to that, we have bigger markets, and that means we can have larger plants and more economic units. We have those basic advantages, and they do give us costs that are really considerably below those of any portion of the world today.

QUESTION: Would you give us an estimate on the outlook for opportunities in foreign markets in the paper industry, through export and through participation with foreign manufacturers?

MR. LUKE: We believe that the opportunities are going to be considerable. This country consumes about 450 lb. of paper per capita per year. In Scandinavia and Western Europe the consumption is less than 100 lb. per capita per year.

The people over there are learning the advantages of distribution as practiced over here, and we already are seeing the growth of paper consumption. Scandinavia and Western Europe haven't got the wood to match the increase in demand. The only competitive factors that we see ahead are those from Soviet Russia or from South America. They will take some long time to come. So we see real opportunities in the world.

CHAIRMAN WILSON: Many years ago, people were very much concerned that we were exhausting our forests; we were chopping down all the virgin timber, with no replacement in sight. Even then the paper industry took only a very small percentage of the crop. In spite of the greatly increased demand, it has been found that proper forest management and proper breeding have reduced fears about any shortage at the present time.

QUESTION: Do you foresee a shortage in the near future?

MR. LUKE: The shortage is a long time off. Right now, we are growing many more cords of wood than we are consuming in this

country. The great opportunity we have in the forest is the elimination of forest fires, which over our history have consumed many
more cords of wood than all of us put together have used. Forest
fires are now pretty well under control. In the deep South and
Southeast they still have forest fires, but for the most part this problem has been solved. I think we are safe for the foreseeable future.

3

Fred Maytag, II
CHAIRMAN OF THE BOARD
MAYTAG COMPANY

Major Appliances

MY ASSIGNED SUBJECT is the major appliance industry, but I have taken the liberty of limiting my remarks to one appliance; more specifically, the home laundry industry. I have two reasons for doing this. First, I am most familiar with the home laundry industry because my company is a short-line appliance manufacturing company which specializes in home laundries; and second, I think analogies with home laundry products can be found with many other major appliances.

In general, home laundry appliances include the following: clothes washers (both wringer and automatic type), automatic clothes dryers (both gas and electric), combination washer-dryers (both gas and electric) and ironers.

At the risk of being elementary, I would like to introduce the discussion of market possibilities for these products by describing briefly the sources of sales for them. There are really two basic sources; new owners, and sales to replace existing equipment in households. Sales to new owners arise from newly formed households, or, more precisely, from net increase in total households, and from sales to a larger proportion of the existing households. Replacement sales are generated first by the wear-out of old equipment; and second, by obsolescence of the product even though it may still have a useful life. There has been in recent years a great deal of the latter; that is, obsolescence of existing equipment which still has a useful life.

Obviously, considerations of saturation and replacement due to obsolescence and wear-out have a dominant effect on a market where saturation is already very high. We estimate that as of January 1, 1960 we had about 40 million washers in use in the United States, of which about half were the wringer type and half were the automatic type. Probably not more than one per cent were combination washer-dryers. (A combination washer-dryer is a machine which combines the complete functions of a washer and a dryer in a single unit.) Our estimate of dryer saturation was that slightly less than one fourth of those households owning a washer also owned a dryer.

There is, of course, a practical ceiling for the ownership of washing machines. Unlike the automobile manufacturer, we have not been able to persuade our customers to have two or three washing machines in the laundry room.

Available space for facilities for using the product, and alternate methods very readily available for solving the problem, are all factors that affect saturation. Thus the rate of increase in ownership of washing machines has today a much smaller effect on the total market than it did ten years ago.

Because the saturation of dryers is considerably less than of washers, the increase in ownership of dryers still represents a substantial opportunity for the marketing of this product. However, one alternative method of solving the problem of drying clothes—namely, the clothesline—makes the practical saturation ceiling for dryers somewhat lower than it is on washers.

In 1960 about 70% of industry sales of washing machines will be replacement sales, while only 30% will be sales to new owners. With dryers the situation is different, of course. Only about 10% of sales in 1960 will be replacement sales. The balance will be sales to new owners.

From this discussion you can see that a forecast of a substantial increase in population and in income in the next decade does not necessarily mean a proportionate increase in the market for home laundry appliances.

In looking forward to what is in store for us in the next ten years, we might take a look at the laundry industry during the past decade. Factory shipments of home laundry appliances in 1949 amounted to a total of 3,364,000 units. In 1950, aided by consumer reaction to the Korean war, sales jumped to a whopping 5 million units. Then in 1951 they went back to 4 million. Thus in a three-year period we had a rather violent fluctuation around an average of approximately 4,100,000 units a year.

Ten years later, in 1959, industry sales were 5,441,000 units. (In between, sales were 6 million units in the year 1956, which still remains the largest year in the history of our industry.) The change over this ten-year period represents a 62% increase from 1949 to 1959. But if you look at the 1959 sales in relationship to the 1949-1951 average, the increase is only about 33%.

Another interesting thing is the change in product mix. In 1949 about 63% of factory shipments of home laundry appliances were wringer-washers; in 1959 this type accounted for only 16.5% of the market. In the same period automatic washers rose from 26% to 54% of the total, and dryers from 3% to 25.5%. Combination washer-dryers, which were not on the market in 1949, achieved about a 4% share by 1959. Ironer sales declined very sharply, from 8% in 1949 to less than 1% in 1959. The combination washer, which is a relatively new product, having first been introduced in 1953, has a somewhat uncertain potential. Ironer sales can be written off as of no significance, unless somebody can invent an ironer which will not only iron the clothes but do it automatically and fold them and put them in the drawer.

In the next ten years, we expect the market for home laundry appliances to follow growth patterns not too dissimilar from those of the past ten years. We expect industry sales to increase in the neighborhood of 35% over this ten-year period. We think the long-term downtrend of the wringer-washer will continue, and that there will be corresponding increases in sales of automatic washers and dryers. The future course of the combination washer-dryer still is uncertain. Certainly we can anticipate a substantial increase from the approximately 200,000 combinations which were sold in 1959, but I personally do not believe that this product will dominate the business and take over substantial portions of washer and dryer sales in the next decade.

The ironer market I think we can write off.

To summarize then, it is my feeling that there is an opportunity for very substantial, though not explosive, growth in our industry in the next decade.

There will be some increase in employment in our industry, but it probably will not be in proportion to sales increases, as manufacturers will seek to offset the ever-rising cost of wages. They will achieve labor-saving results both by greater mechanization of their plants and by design changes, and I think the growth in employment will be less than the growth in output of goods. Wages I assume will rise, probably more than productivity, as they have been doing in the past.

Capital expenditures of our industry will be substantial in the next ten years, but they will be less than they were during the last decade. In the 1950's and, in fact, since the war there have been very substantial capital expenditures in our industry, both for modernization of facilities and increased capacity. At the present time we have quite a bit of excess capacity. I do not anticipate that in the next decade the expenditures will be higher for additional capacity, but many manufacturers will make substantial outlays for further modernization of their facilities.

So far as the outlook is concerned, I think it is good. In saying this, I am making two assumptions. One of them is that we will continue to operate on a reasonably favorable level, and in a favorable economic climate; and secondly, that we will not experience a disastrous battle of the giants to increase share of market without regard to profits.

I would point out that our industry is a highly competitive one. During the period since the war it has seen a number of mergers, a number of sales of smaller companies, and the elimination of quite a number of smaller, less efficient producing companies. I think that this process of shakedown is just about complete, and I do not now anticipate there will be further significant changes of this kind, but we do have a situation in which competition between producers is intense. In the past we have, on occasion, had marketing practices in our industry which have at least temporarily depressed profit opportunities.

I should also point out the purchase of major appliances, home laundry equipment specifically, are to a certain extent discretionary with the purchaser, so we are in competition not only among ourselves but also the other producers of consumer goods. Profit opportunities for any particular company in the industry are thus dependent upon how well that company meets the challenge of the marketplace.

QUESTION: Is there a trend away from deluxe equipment to more standardized equipment, and can you anticipate what this will be in the next ten years?

MR. MAYTAG: This, I think, is more a matter of market conditions of the moment than of any long-term trend. Actually, a substantial part of sales in the industry are of the higher-priced units, but when business gets a little difficult there is a tendency for manufacturers to bring out what they sometimes call stripped models in order to get in the marketplace with lower prices. I don't see any particular trend here that is significant, and I am inclined to think that the product mix as between the higher-price and lower-price units will continue to depend upon short-term market conditions.

CHAIRMAN WILSON: We heard a good deal two years ago about the necessity, in the appliance business, of having a full line of major appliances. Is that trend still pronounced or has it run its course?

MR. MAYTAG: That depends upon to whom you talk. My company is a short-line manufacturer. We specialize in home laundry equipment and we have done rather well in the last decade. Personally I feel that we can do a better job by specializing and being a master of a particular trade than we can by running the risk of becoming a jack-of-all-trades.

On the other hand, it must be recognized that there has been a tendency toward the elimination of the short-line manufacturer either by his going out of business or by his merging with another company.

QUESTION: Do you anticipate that ten years from now we will be having appliances of the type and covering areas that today we don't foresee at all? In other words, before the war we weren't anticipating the automatic washer. It came through very fast. Do you see anything like that for the next ten years?

Mr. Maytag: I do not now anticipate major or dramatic changes in types of appliances. I am talking particularly about the home laundry industry now. There are areas where there may be some really important opportunities for development in products where there is rather low saturation at the present time. Some people believe that the combination washer-dryer will eventually largely replace the separate units. I am a little skeptical about this. We have had combinations on the market now for almost seven years and as of last year they represented only about 4% of total sales. I think that this will be the pattern. There will be growth, but I don't anticipate a total replacement of one for the other.

Question: What is the outlook for your industry in foreign markets?

Mr. Maytag: I think the outlook for export of laundry equipment from the United States to foreign markets is rather poor. There is growth in major appliances and laundry equipment in certain foreign markets, but it has taken place mostly in products manufactured in those countries. I do not feel that export of appliances from the United States will be a very significant factor in the foreseeable future. Household habits vary from country to country, and the American product is not necessarily suited to the foreign market.

Question: What about imports?

Mr. Maytag: Up to this time there have been no significant imports. I don't know what the future may hold. Some of the factors which discourage exports from this country also tend to discourage imports, but we must recognize that foreign labor rates are significantly lower than ours. There is a possibility that we might have an invasion of foreign products in this country, but at the present time I do not see any real threat of that kind.

4

William J. Erwin

PRESIDENT
DAN RIVER MILLS, INCORPORATED

Textiles

LET ME BEGIN with a brief and candid observation. Having witnessed in a rather intimate way the vagaries and vicissitudes of the textile industry in the past decade, I concluded it must be a brave man who would venture to forecast the next decade. Nevertheless, I approach the venture with enthusiasm because I am optimistic that our industry is on the threshold of real progress, and is likely to acquire a more respected status in the years ahead.

The scope of our industry extends from Maine down to Texas, but is now concentrated in the Piedmont Section of North Carolina, South Carolina, Georgia and Alabama. Last year 2,202,000 people were employed in the textile industry, including apparel. That, according to what some of the economists tell me, is one out of eight in all manufacturing!

During the 1960's dollar sales volume of textiles will trend upward with both rising price levels and higher demand contributing to the improvement. While the rate of growth will not be spectacular, the exploding population and the trend toward higher consumer incomes assures a larger textile market. The sales of the textile industry last year totaled $13,762,000,000. More numbers of people in our increasing population are important, but much more important is the way in which they satisfy their desires for apparel. Here lies a significant factor. That great big wonderful crop of postwar babies is moving into those delightful teen-age years when clothes become so critically important. This is a tremendous market and likely to be a better one with the apparent demise of the blue-jean and sweatshirt fad of dress—or undress, if you prefer.

In a few more years the teen-agers will marry, start their own households and become excellent customers for fabrics for home furnishings. The makeup of our population in the 1960's, along with its size thus seems to favor increased demand for textiles.

With increased incomes people are living better and this has gradually been extended into a greater clothes consciousness. With more attractive fabrics and a bigger variety available, people will be able to buy more suitable attire, and there will be less tendency to wear garments threadbare. More and better clothes, even with today's percentage of the consumer dollar spent for clothing, will mean more yards of lighter-wear, neater-wear, and easier-care fabrics.

It is my judgment that profits of the textile industry in the next decade will enjoy a growth trend. The anticipated increase in sales volume should help our profit picture. So, too, should higher and more realistic prices and improved productivity.

In the past ten years there have been two highly significant trends in the textile industry. One has been an aggressive effort by the leading companies to diversify their product lines. With greater diversification there will not be the same dependency on a given segment of the market. With increased diversification there is a better opportunity to level out the more violent swings of fabric demand.

The other trend—and this has gone hand in hand with and cannot be separated from the first one—has been the rapid growth, by way of acquisition and merger, of a number of large, publicly owned companies. These companies, with their strong financial position and resources, can and do support extensive research programs to develop new products. This is a recent development; there was a woeful lack of research in the textile industry up until about ten years ago. The larger units now present in the industry spend substantial sums on advertising and sales promotion. They plan and carry out long-range programs of plant improvement. In this they are joined by some excellent but still privately held textile companies. This group of companies, big as they are individually, still represent a relatively small proportion of the industry's productive capacity, but they are beginning to contribute the kind of responsible leadership that has been lacking in the past, and that is essential to a more stable, profitable future.

Another special situation merits comment. For years, barring emergency of war or postwar conditions, the curse of the industry has been overproduction and grossly unbalanced inventories. This situation has changed for the better. In the past ten years attrition among marginal mills has been heavy, with a consequent reduction in total productive capacity. Moreover, the stronger companies with better management are doing more market research. This will give them a better knowledge of what the market requires, and will permit better planning for production and marketing. With better trained specialists to do the job there should be less accumulation of fabrics for which the demand is dying, and, because of this, less need to force the sale of unwanted goods. This, in turn, should help to stabilize our prices.

Now, a brief comment about the new products. The products of the textile industry are vastly different today from what they were ten years ago. This is largely the result of a chemical revolution in textiles, which has produced on the one hand a succession of new man-made fibers, and on the other remarkable new finishes for cotton, blended, and other fabrics.

A substantial portion of the fabrics produced now simply did not exist ten years ago. One startling illustration is the sweeping trend to wash-and-wear fabrics. Such fabrics are manufactured at the rate of billions of yards each year; a decade ago they were more a vision than a reality.

Far more will be spent in the next ten years to study and develop the many new fibers. Consider that we have been studying cotton, silk, linen and wool for hundreds of years to get to the level of efficiency we now have. Multiply these four by ten, and then you can conceive of the problems and opportunities that lie before us in the many new fibers that are now available. The road to increased sales and better profits is paved with new product development. I expect to see substantial progress in this respect in the years ahead.

Capital investment will reflect a growth trend in the next decade, and as in the past an overwhelming proportion of capital expenditures will be directed toward new machinery and equipment and not to new plants.

During the past decade, textile productivity moved ahead rapidly, increasing by about 40%. There are sound reasons for believing that this trend will accelerate in the coming years. New machinery already in existence, such as shuttleless looms, and equipment now on the drawing boards which will soon be available, offer a real possibility of stepping up productivity.

There is no question that the textile industry has the know-how to make the most of any technological improvement. The question is, will it have the resources to finance them? An improving profit picture will help. So, too, would a more realistic policy on depreciation by the U. S. Treasury Department.

In 1959 capital expenditures in the textile industry amounted to $412 million. Most of that outlay was for improved machinery, and not for expansion or new plants It is estimated that capital commitments for 1960 will total $570 million.

For a number of years the textile industry has been severely injured by the persistent problem of declining exports and increasing imports. Vigorous efforts to combat this problem have met with little success. It seems to me that the trend of recent years will continue in the coming decade, with exports continuing to decline and imports continuing to increase, but the rate at which these changes take place will taper off. The problem will still remain a troublesome one. Our best hope of correction lies in the expectation that other strong and powerful industries which are now beginning to feel the full impact of this problem will add their voices to ours in an effort to develop a sound foreign trade policy that takes proper cognizance of the interests of American manufacturing.

QUESTION: I gather that Mr. Erwin expects increased sales in textiles resulting from more spending units in the 1960's. I am wondering whether he expects a greater percentage of the income of these spending units to be expended on textiles and clothing in the 1960's; that is, do you anticipate a change in the consumer budget in your direction?

MR. ERWIN: We are hopeful that will take place. The increase in population and the increase in the standard of living has given us a better market. As a matter of fact, last year, for the first time in about four or five years, we had an increase in per capita consumption of cotton in the United States. We consumed 24.5 lb. per capita last year. In England the per capita consumption is about 12 lb., in France it is a little bit less than that, and in Japan it is about nine pounds. There seems to be an overabundance of textiles throughout the world. At some of the international conferences I have attended, I have made the statement that a lot of the problems confronting us will be solved if we can increase the consumption of cotton goods and of textiles generally in other countries to somewhere near the level we have here. We would then not have overcapacity throughout the world.

QUESTION: Would you care to comment on the future of non-woven textiles?

MR. ERWIN: Nonwoven fabrics have a great future; they will invade quite a few of the normal uses of woven goods at the present time. The future for nonwovens is particularly bright in industrial fabrics.

5

Donald C. Power
CHAIRMAN OF THE BOARD
GENERAL TELEPHONE & ELECTRONICS CORPORATION

Electronics

THE ELECTRONICS INDUSTRY is the fastest growing major industry in the country today—if not the world—and the potential for continued future growth is substantially beyond most other large industries. Aside from the quantitative aspects of the industry's past development and its potential for the future, electronics represents one of the most far-reaching technological developments of the past 25 years. Four or five years ago, someone described electronics as "the world's most promising technological revolution." And I would guess that anyone who wasn't convinced back then certainly is by now.

As recently as the 1930's and the years immediately before the war, there was no electronics industry as we use that term today. There was the radio manufacturing and broadcasting industry, but the word "electronics" hadn't even entered the vocabulary. This business represented sales of some $500 million, with employment of around 70,000 back in 1940.

Then, during the early years of the war, before America was drawn directly into it, the scientists and engineers in this country and in Europe began to find entirely new and broader applications for the vacuum tube and other types of tubes whose function is based upon the generation of electrons in a vacuum. The new applications of this principle and the new devices became so numerous that in the early 1940's we began to hear the word "electronics."

Out of the war effort came so many technical advances and so much new know-how that the end of World War II found us with a new major industry that very few people had heard much about. But then television was taken down off the shelf, and electronics took off in high gear. The entire industry gained momentum in all of its major fields, which include defense electronics, entertainment electronics, industrial and commercial electronics, broadcasting, and distribution and service.

By 1950 sales and revenues had increased tenfold to a total of nearly $5 billion, against, as you will recall, $500 million in 1939 and 1940. More than 60% of the total in 1950 represented TV and radio sets, service, and distribution. Defense electronics was only about $560 million, and was just beginning to move into the entirely new era of supersonic aircraft, guided missiles and space technology.

In the ten years between 1950 and 1959 defense electronics moved up to a total of nearly $4.8 billion, because of such developments as new high-speed, highly reliable communications systems, electronic navigation, electronic countermeasures and counter-countermeasures—jamming of radar, and jamming of the other fellow's jamming, missile-guidance systems, early warning systems, and many other developments. Because national defense is becoming so increasingly electronified, and because of the enormous effort directed toward satellites and space travel, total expenditures for defense electronics this year should be up around $5.2 billion, around $7.8 billion by 1965, and $10.5 billion by 1970. In my estimation these figures are the best projection we can make today, but I wouldn't be surprised to find them revised steadily upward as we move into the 1960's—and closer and closer to the moon, incidentally.

Turning now to entertainment electronics, which includes, of course, television, radio, and hi-fi, this segment of the industry reached an annual volume of more than $3.1 billion in 1950, including the service and distribution businesses. The total passed $5 billion last year, which represents an increase of nearly 70%. It should climb another $350 million this year, reach $6.7 billion by 1965, and $7.5 billion by 1970. This growth will come from new concepts in television set design, more second-set homes and continued increases in hi-fi and radio. Three or four years ago, some people thought that entertainment electronics might be levelling off, but once again the industry has confounded the conservative thinkers.

The third largest segment of the industry is commercial and industrial electronics. Here is a field that was virtually nonexistent 15 years ago, and totaled only some $680 million in 1950. Last year it reached $2.5 billion, and the total this year should be about $2.8 billion. Because of the broader use of electronic devices and equipment in commercial communications, especially electronic data processing and telephony, as well as in manufacturing processes, annual sales should climb to $4.6 billion by 1965 and $6.3 billion by 1970.

As is true of defense electronics, these projections will probably be revised upward as the many opportunities unfold—especially in data processing, which of course is built around the computer and all of its associated equipment. I would be greatly remiss if I were not to point out that a field with an especially interesting potential is the telephone business, because of the development of many new types of devices and so-called "interconnected services" which use many different types of electronic components, and which also are making more and more use of microwave radio systems.

Turning now to the broadcasting business, revenues rose 300% from about $550 million in 1950 to $1.6 billion last year. This year the total will increase by about $100 million, and by 1965 the annual figure is projected at nearly $2.4 billion. By 1970, the projection is $3 billion.

Now let's add up the various totals and see where the electronics industry as a whole is going. From sales and revenues of about $5 billion in 1950, the total rose to $14 billion last year, an increase of 280%. A doubling of business volume in ten years is considered pretty phenomenal in any industry, but this year, sales and revenues, according to present indications, should exceed $15 billion—

which would be a threefold increase in eleven years. By 1965, the industry should attain $21.5 billion annually, and more than $27.4 billion by 1970.

These figures are based on a realistic projection of past trends, and on the application of logic to known historical and current facts.

The potential for growth in electronics appears to be unprecedented from the standpoint of: (1) the introduction of new products and services; (2) the growth potentials in sales and revenues; (3) the expansion of companies already in the industry, and the entrance of new companies; (4) the vast number of new applications in commerce, industry and the home that will be found for electronic equipment and devices; (5) the increased strength electronics will bring to national defense; and (6) the increased opportunities for employment and investment.

E. B. Germany

PRESIDENT
LONE STAR STEEL COMPANY

Steel

Much of the steel industry's growth over the past 15 years has been catch-up in character. The industry's physical plant had been undermaintained because of inadequate incentives to invest throughout the 1930's. Then it was overstrained by the demands placed upon it during World War II.

At the start of the first postwar decade, steel faced an overwhelming tide of demand for the rebuilding of living standards here and abroad. It met this challenge in unparalleled fashion. Since the end of World War II, the steel industry's total capacity has been increased by nearly 60 million tons. Its plant today is vastly more efficient, as a result of something like $12 billion it has invested in new structures and equipment.

So much for the growth since World War II. What about the decade ahead? The industry now faces a new and completely different set of challenges. Steel capacity throughout the world has been expanded sharply. Supplies of competing materials—aluminum, plastics and glass—are, in general, abundant. As a result, the steel market itself is now intensively competitive. I believe this competition will grow even hotter.

Steel demand over the next decade ought to grow as rapidly as the economy as a whole. That's how it has grown in the past. Economists seem more or less agreed that total national output will rise by about 50% between now and 1970. I would be surprised if the total value of steel shipments did not at least match this rate of increase.

Now that doesn't mean that such growth in steel can be taken for granted. Among the great challenges that the industry already faces is the expanded flow of imported steel into the United States. This expansion is evident in the figures, even after adjustment for special influences of the past few years. Its cause is not hard to seek. Although the steel industry has revolutionized its technology since World War II, it remains a high labor cost industry. Foreign producers of steel have always had an important cost advantage over American producers because of steel's high labor content. But as American wage costs have mushroomed over the past 15 years, this cost gap in labor costs widened until it now threatens the industry's very existence.

Foreign steel now competes with American output for an increasingly wide range of products. Fortunately, steel demand abroad is still extremely high. Capacity abroad, while rising, is thus very busily engaged in filling local demand. Foreign capacity will grow still further in the 1960's. As it does, an increasing margin of this capacity will become available for export demand. And the wide cost advantage they have in lower labor costs will further aggravate the problems of our domestic industry in the decade ahead.

So, in my judgment, the fundamental problem of the future for the U. S. steel industry is control of costs. This control can be achieved in two interrelated ways. First, labor as well as management must recognize that the health of the domestic steel industry will be gravely impaired by any further widening of the cost gap. Higher wage costs can only result in an even larger flow of imports or loss of markets abroad. That means we'll be exporting jobs as well as profits to foreign steel producers. Secondly, the industry must stay out front technologically. To do so it must earn enough to reinvest heavily in research and development. That's the way to get even better steel and more efficient steelmaking processes. The need to reinvest in additional capacity in the years ahead may be much less than it has been in the recent past. The need to reinvest in engineering improvements will be ever more pressing, if we are to continue as the world's largest steel producer.

This industry will share fully in the national growth that lies ahead, if these two essential conditions are met: steel wage increases must begin to bear a more reasonable relationship to productivity, and steel earnings must provide the funds and the incentive for a high rate of reinvestment.

7

Richard J. Babcock
PRESIDENT
FARM JOURNAL, INC.

Agriculture and Food

FOOD TODAY is a prime factor of international economic and political policy.

The headlines in the daily press keep our minds on the possibility of atomic war. While we cannot ignore that possibility, one must realize that no one can "win" in a modern atomic war; therefore, only an accident or a madman will start one. On the other hand, there is no question that the fight for world leadership—the cold war—will go on and on.

The Soviet Union and the world both know that no nation can lead other nations upward so long as that nation can provide only a low standard of living for its own people. And the Soviet Union's capacity to lead will continue to lag so long as she must employ 50% of her population on her farms to produce less food than her people need. America's capacity to lead, on the other hand, will remain in the ascendancy so long as we need only 10% or fewer of our population to produce more food than we consume.

Obviously, then, food, and the manner in which we produce it, are vital parts of our arsenal as we fight the cold war to maintain our position of world leadership.

So, the difference in the industrial might of the Soviet Union and the United States cannot be measured only in the number of blast furnaces and the capacity of our electric generators.

It becomes increasingly clear that one of the most significant differences between the Soviet Union and the United States lies in the far greater efficiency and development of our agriculture.

More precisely, that difference lies in the fact that we are able to employ a much larger share of our total working force in industry, distribution, and business because we need a much smaller share on our more efficient and more productive farms.

Thus, America's food supply and farm efficiency are vital to our world leadership.

But the American people do not know this. And therein lies a serious gap in the people's understanding so necessary as a basis for the successful conduct of public affairs.

Consumers see agriculture only in the shape and size of their supermarket baskets. They are distressed about farm subsidies, the high taxes they believe they pay to support farmers, and what they regard as high food costs generally. They evidence a fine and total disregard for the fact that they now spend a smaller percentage of their families' income for more and better food than 10 years ago. It seems axiomatic that any necessity, no matter how cheap, costs too much.

Businessmen, too, are largely lacking in an over-all understanding of agriculture's achievements, its dynamic promise, and its contribution to the preservation of our way of life.

It is a tragic and costly fact that although the physical distance between the farmer and most of us today is still small, the mental distance that separates us is almost infinite.

The result is that public policy toward agriculture is being shaped to no small degree on the basis of indifference, ignorance and prejudice, instead of with proper regard for the total political significance of our productive capacity, and with proper regard for the economic significance of the farm business.

It is, of course, wishful and unrealistic thinking to expect the public to be happy about surpluses, so long as we levy taxes to keep them off the market, even though it can be demonstrated that they make for cheaper, rather than more costly, food. And at the same time, realism tells us that we cannot at once and forthwith abandon the supports that create the surpluses without ruinous effect on large segments of agriculture and, in the long run, on the economy as a whole.

But realism also dictates that we must continue to search for substitutes for the laws which created those surpluses through promises to pay prices higher than demand will support.

What we must do is to taper off on such price supports, reduce the surplus, and then return to a closer relationship with the fundamental and irrevocable laws of supply and demand.

While the search goes on for a mature public policy toward agriculture, however, farmers themselves have been dramatically reorganizing their own industry.

Within my lifetime, the number of farm units has dropped by more than two million; farm family labor has dropped from nearly 11 million people to about 5½ million; hired farm labor has dropped from 3½ million to less than two million. Land under cultivation has decreased 5% in the last 10 years.

Yet in this same period farmers have more than doubled their output.

How? They have done it through a veritable industrial revolution. This was dramatically described by Karl Brandt, a member of the President's Council of Economic Advisers, when he said: "This reduction in manpower was made possible chiefly by the shift from animal to mechanical draftpower, with the replacement of 23 million horses and mules by a fleet of nearly 5 million tractors and 8 million trucks and automobiles."

Dr. Brandt points out that farmers also made vast investments in improvements to their land, and that electricity came to 96% of the nation's farms. Then he makes this big point: "The sharp increase in purchased inputs has done the main part of the job boosting the joint productivity of manpower, land, and capital." And this is still going on. The ratio of output to input has increased at the rate of 2% per year for the past 10 years.

As agriculture has grown, not only in its output, but in the volume of purchased inputs it uses, and as the eating habits of the consuming population have changed, agriculture's position in the economy has been transformed.

The products of American agriculture today are the most important raw materials of our total economy, and not just because we must eat to live. A very large share of our industry, and millions and millions of jobs, are built around the processing and distribution of food.

Agriculture is the biggest customer of many of America's biggest industries. Farm families spend billions for the products of industry in agricultural production, and billions more for the conveniences and luxuries of a good life as well as a good living.

In view of agriculture's importance in the economy, therefore, it is imperative that we know the facts about agriculture, its capacity, its worth, and the direction in which it is headed. Only thus will we be able to arrive at a soundly conceived public policy toward agriculture.

Let us look, then, at some of these facts. And let us start with

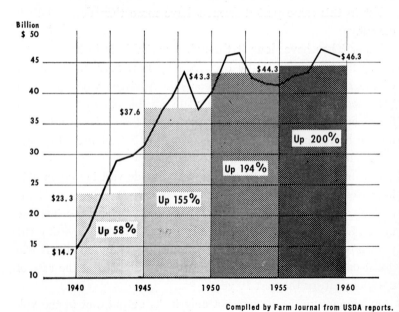

Compiled by Farm Journal from USDA reports.

Figure 1. Gross income, all U.S. farms, all sources. 1940-1960.

Figure 1. Last year U. S. farmers' gross income from all sources was $46.3 billion—the second highest on record. That $46.3 billion compares with $14.7 billion in 1940, and the steady upward march is demonstrated by the five-year average bars, despite the ups and downs of the annual line.

In Figure 2 we see the dramatic effect of the reduction in the

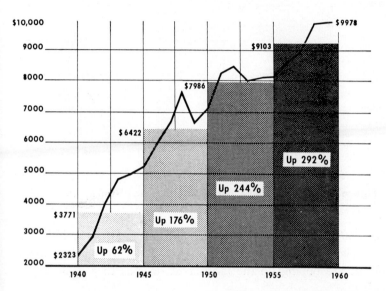

Compiled by Farm Journal from USDA reports.

Figure 2. Gross income per farm, all sources, 1940-1960.

number of farms. Note once more that while the income per farm per year wiggles even as it rises, when studied in the more meaningful time-span of five-year averages, the progress is most significant and steady.

As income per farm rises higher and higher, farmers become better customers for a wide range of consumer goods and services, as well as capital goods for both farm and home. Whereas last year's gross was the second highest for all farms, when we convert it to an individual farm basis, 1959 set a new all-time record.

Now, let us compare the 3 million commercial farms with all U. S. farms (Figure 3). The movement toward farm consolidation con-

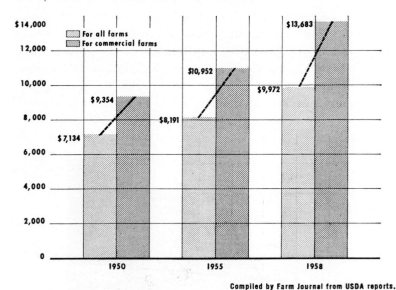

Compiled by Farm Journal from USDA reports.

Figure 3. Gross income per farm, commercial family farms, all sources, 1950-1958.

tinues, not because corporate factories in the fields are gobbling up defenseless little farmers, but because the more efficient family farmers are buying up the farms next door as they come on the market.

Here you'll see that these modern, efficient family farms—the 3,000,000 commercial farms that produce 90-odd per cent of all farm products sold in the United States—are doing 40% better than the average of all farms.

For business, this means more than simply a concentration of buying power, or a target of sales effort. It means that as the discretionary spending power of these higher-income farm families continues to widen, a whole new mass-class market is developing in rural America. To the degree that the ability to consume a wider range of goods and services shapes social and cultural patterns, the significance of what is happening here can be profound and far-reaching.

Unlike most industries which hire labor and use raw materials to

produce finished goods, farmers are using less labor and more
finished goods to produce raw materials. And as these purchased
inputs have risen—agricultural output has gone up. Figure 4 shows
how much agricultural input purchases have increased. This gain of
427% has brought production costs for all farms to a total of $26
billion per year. The outlay for inputs last year amounted to an
average of $5,604 per farm.

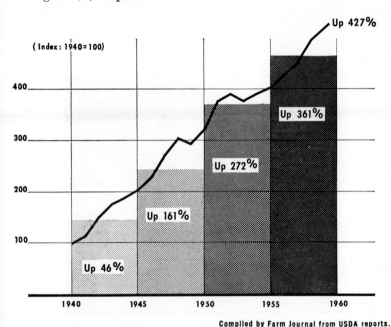

Compiled by Farm Journal from USDA reports.

Figure 4. Total expenditures for production, per U.S. farm, 1940-
1960.

Farmers bought their feed, seed and fertilizer; their gasoline,
fuel, oil, tires and batteries for their trucks, tractors and implements
and paid for part of the family car out of this $26 billion. This vast
sum also includes millions spent for new trucks, tractors and machinery to replace worn-out equipment.

An important measure of the farmer's own attitude toward the
future of farming is his willingness to invest his own capital in

long-term development. Figure 5 shows that farmers are willing to do so. One of the reasons farmers make these inputs, says Dr. Brandt, is because they have managerial freedom, which puts a high premium on experimentation, innovation, and more efficient arrangements. In this free enterprising climate, they plowed back $1,050 into the capitalization of the average farm last year—and the rate of capital investment per farm has gone up 666% since 1940.

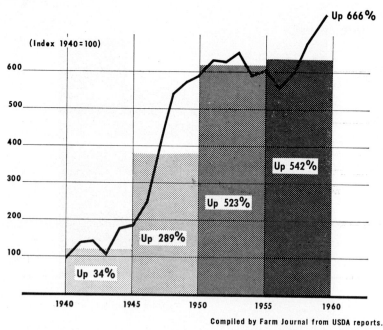

Compiled by Farm Journal from USDA reports.

Figure 5. U.S. farm families' expenditures on capital goods, 1940-1960.

The net income shown in Figure 6 is from both farm and non-farm sources. While the annual net income shows some ups and downs, as you will see from the jiggles on the single line, the more meaningful five-year averages show a steady rise.

Last year we had a serious cost-price squeeze in agriculture that severely hurt many families. Yet it is worth noting that despite that squeeze the average net income from all sources per family was the second highest on record. It averaged $4,374 per farm.

Perhaps the real measure of the economic importance of agriculture, however, is its total asset value—a whopping $208.2 billion, of which $184.2 billion was debt-free on January 1 (Figure 7). Just to give you an idea of relative size—this figure is greater than the assets of the transportation, automobile, petroleum, iron and steel and chemicals industries combined!

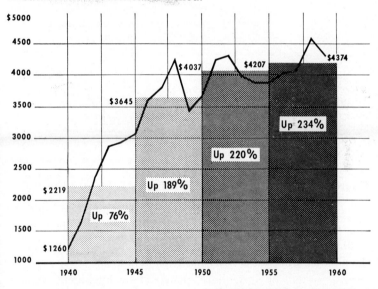

Compiled by Farm Journal from USDA reports.

Figure 6. Net income per U.S. farm, all sources, 1940-1960.

When we convert farm assets to a per-family basis, we find the average farm family has $43,724 invested in its land, buildings, equipment, livestock and savings (Figure 8).

It's easy to understand, now, why the total capital investment per job in agriculture exceeds $20,000. And it's easy to understand, also, that the farmer's basic attitudes and philosophy will be those of the proprietor class, of which he is most certainly a member.

But most significant of all is this look at the simple facts of life about the market for the farmers' goods. By steadily increasing his

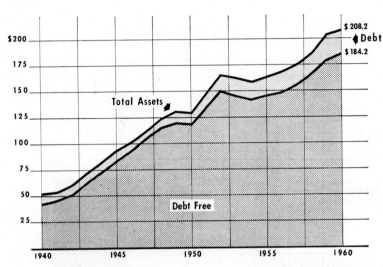

Figure 7. Growth in total farm assets, all U.S. farms, 1940-1960.

efficiency he has kept pace with the rising population. And his market continues to grow. How much? This chart says 44% in the next 20 years, based on Bureau of Census estimates (Figure 9).

Up to now farm productivity has expanded as the result of a free enterprise system of agriculture, managed by intelligent, capable people who have made huge capital investments in equipment and improvements, who have spent heavily for inputs to get the production for a profit.

There is no question that today agriculture is feeling the squeeze between the cost of what it buys and the prices that it receives. Farmers are seeking the answer in several ways. They are organizing their own marketing to get the best prices possible. They are becoming more and more specialized, more and more mechanized, more efficient, and still larger users of inputs provided by industry.

Every thinking person recognizes that the American economy cannot survive without an agricultural industry capable of producing a high quantity of products efficiently. But can we expect to continue to attract the kind of man, and the capital, that such an

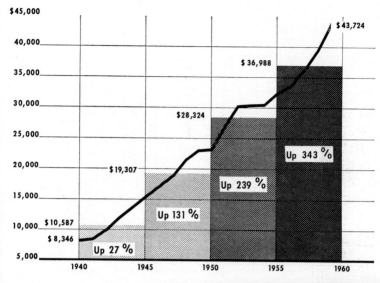

Compiled by Farm Journal from USDA reports.

Figure 8. Growth in individual U.S. farm assets, per farm, 1940-1960.

agriculture needs? Unless it can operate at a profit on a basis that is fair to producer and consumer alike, obviously we cannot.

I believe responsible business, industrial and political leaders cannot fail to recognize that America's food supply and farm efficiency are vital to our way of life. They must and will see to it that we do have the kind of farm program which will ensure the American people a profitable, productive and ever more efficient agriculture. Such a program, however, can be achieved only when grave misapprehensions are removed. The greatest of these is the belief, widely held by the general public, and by some businessmen as well, that farm programs operate only for the benefit of farmers. As we have seen, it is rather the nation as a whole that is the greatest beneficiary.

An almost equally serious misapprehension is that farm programs are a unique type of class legislation that should be abolished. It is an unhappy fact of life that scarcely a segment of our economy is not now artificially supported in some fashion by special-interest

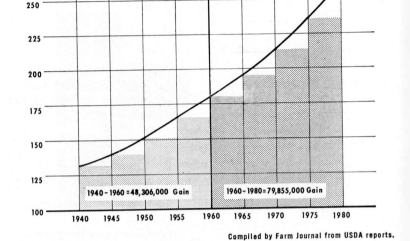

Compiled by Farm Journal from USDA reports.

Figure 9. Growth in U.S. population, 1940-1960, projected 1960-1980.

legislation. To the extent that such programs adversely affect agriculture, and many of them do, it will be essential that there be compensating special-interest legislation with regard to our agriculture—not just for the sake of the people in agriculture, but for the sake of the well-being of our nation as a whole.

When these facts are known and understood we will have a climate of understanding and appreciation in which this great and dynamic growth industry we call agriculture will be secure in its rightful place—economically and politically—in the minds of all our people, and in our national life. Then, when some 260 million hungry Americans sit down to their dinner tables in 1980, the food will be there, ready and waiting. Then we can continue to base our domestic and our foreign policies on the solid assurance that America's industrial strength will be supported by the world's most productive and efficient agriculture.

8

William B. Bergen
PRESIDENT
THE MARTIN COMPANY

Defense

IT IS NO SECRET, military or otherwise, that defense business is big business. Our national defense budget is now, has been for some time and probably will be—for the foreseeable future—in the neighborhood of $40 billion a year. Not all of this, of course, is for military hardware. The military budget now before Congress includes $12 billion for the personnel necessary to man and operate the weapons and other machinery of defense that the United States must maintain to deter her potential enemies from plunging the world into another war.

But the other $28.7 billion of that budget is earmarked for the procurement of new weaponry, for its operation and maintenance, for the construction of adequate bases—and for the development, testing and evaluation of the still newer weapons we must constantly be devising.

This may seem to be an endless cycle. As a matter of fact it is— and a highly competitive one. Basically changeless in its over-all nature, it is everchanging in the details of its individual components, as technological break-throughs render today's most promising weapon systems obsolete for tomorrow's defense needs.

The stakes in this competitive cycle are high—the highest, in fact, for which men and nations ever match their skills and strength. This is because—quite simply and starkly—they spell survival. Defense contractors survive only if their products continue to be better, or at least as good as those of their brightest business rivals. Nations historically survive only if their defenses are maintained at a level of effectiveness which discourages aggression.

Indeed, second-best weapons can be worse than no weapons at all in a showdown. First-rate weaponry is dependent for its development on first-rate industrial talent constantly kept on its toes by aggressive, first-rate competition. Notice has been served on us many times since World War II, that the United States has no monopoly on the kind of talent that makes possible today's highly complex and effective weapons of war. It is my firm conviction that the significance of this fact has not been missed either by our government or by our defense industry.

But, you may be saying to yourselves, as many before have said to us, what will happen to the defense industry if peace suddenly breaks out in the world and a workable disarmament agreement is reached? Our responsible government leaders and a lot of us ordinary citizens think this involves a big "if," without disputing how wonderful a goal it would be to achieve. But it is still a good question and I think, maybe, I have a good answer, assuming that real disarmament is possible and the present talk of it is not merely bait for another international booby trap.

Obviously, defense contractors such as The Martin Company, whose total present business is the development and production of weapon systems, would lose a great deal of business in the event of world disarmament. But there is more to my answer than that. The rest is that they would not lose as much as you might think.

The reason for this is that Martin and companies like it in the defense industry, who saw the handwriting on the wall a decade or more ago and got off to an early start on the transition from manned combat aircraft to missiles, already are probing the frontiers of space with their intercontinental ballistic missiles and scientific exploration rockets.

They already have their feet firmly planted on the threshold of the earth's virtually unknown celestial environment and are in an enviable position to play a leading role in man's inevitable quests into space. They have launched both intercontinental missiles and scientific satellites, whose rocket boosters are very much alike—and they already have the skills and the know-how to exploit still further these achievements in space.

I firmly believe that when and if the United States lays down the heavy financial burden of its present weaponry insurance policy against war, it will make the same investment—and more—in the peaceful exploration of space. As you know, it already has taken substantial steps in this direction through the National Aeronautics and Space Administration (NASA).

This agency, incidentally, aside from its achievements in space, already has established something of a financial reputation for itself in budgetary circles by coming out of the annual hassle over next year's funds with more money than had been requested for it when the budget went to Capitol Hill. Perhaps this augurs well for its future.

At any rate, I venture to predict: If man's centuries-old dream of world disarmament should come true, you will see our space exploration budget expand by at least as much as our defense budget declines. It will do so, not because the so-called "Munitions Lobby" will transform itself into a "Space Lobby," but because our communist competition also has begun probing into space. This is a race no nation that hopes to retain its leadership in world affairs dares abandon.

All of us who are interested in keeping the world out of another war can and should work to keep what our national leaders call the "Peaceful Exploration of Space" truly peaceful. But wishful thinking will neither make it peaceful nor keep it peaceful. The only thing that will do this is to assure ourselves a future stance in space, as good as or better than that of other nations about whose sincerely peaceful intentions the peace-loving part of the world still has honest doubts.

America's stake in space is as real and as vital to the free world's survival as our present-day arsenal is to shield our current way of life from the very real threat of aggression under which we live. Militarily, space is the "High Ground" of tactical advantage sought by combat leaders since the first cliff-dwellers dropped rocks on their enemies. It is the vantage point later sought by the artillery commander, by the airman and now by the ballistic missiler. The conquest of space is not only inevitable and desirable scientifically, it is militarily imperative.

Not all of the present defense industry can be expected to survive such a transition to the space age as I have outlined as a possibility in the next ten years. Part of it has fallen or probably will fall by the wayside in the transition now going on from the old-time aircraft industry to our presently emerging, missile-oriented defense industry. Only those who have forecast and continue to forecast correctly the changing order of things can hope to survive and prosper.

One last word as to predictions. As long ago as 1946, The Martin Company undertook a detailed study contract for the Navy on the feasibility of launching a man-made satellite around the earth, using a multiple-stage rocket with the alternate capability of delivering an intercontinental ballistic missile. At the end of a year, we arrived at the conclusion that such a project not only was feasible, but that we could have it in operation by early 1950. The idea was dropped because it could not be funded under our then very austere defense budget.

Our scientific capability and the state of the art was basically as good then as it was ten years later when we undertook to do essentially the same thing in Project Vanguard and later on, too, in a program with which you are probably even more familiar, Martin's intercontinental ballistic missile, Titan. Fundamentally, the only difference between these projects and our 1946-47 proposal was the existence of the national will to get them done—the very same will that is now vitally needed to insure America's future stature in space.

Technologically and experimentally, our industry has the capability of maintaining this nation's position of world leadership in both military and civil aviation, and in the current era of aerospace activities by which they have been succeeded. The one and only additional ingredient it needs to continue this performance record and preserve America's international prestige is public determination that the United States must continue to refuse to take second place behind any other nation.

Part Three

TECHNOLOGY AND ITS IMPACT:
The Promise and the Problems

THE TECHNOLOGICAL HORIZON

Gilbert W. Chapman
CHAIRMAN

Gilbert W. Chapman

PRESIDENT

THE YALE & TOWNE MANUFACTURING COMPANY

1

Introduction

THE 1950's were a decade of rapid technological advances in many industries dramatized, towards the end of the period, by major achievements in space exploration. Rising international competition and a new attitude towards growth as a major economic objective provided the impetus for these activities which were supported by large and rapidly increasing expenditures of research organizations, the government, and private industry.

During the next decade expenditures for research and development are likely to increase at an even faster rate accompanied by a rapid rise in employment of scientists and engineers. Major advances already appear on the technological horizons which are bound to have a profound impact on the economy during the next ten years.

Important developments can be expected particularly in the broad areas of metals technology, chemical technology and automation. The resultant products and processes will serve to satisfy new and expanding needs and wants. At the same time, problems of economic change and dislocation will have to be solved. The task of controlling the new technical processes and of subordinating them to human needs and aspirations will be greater than ever.

Technological change is the fountainhead of productivity advances which, in turn, result in higher levels of economic well-being. Here the promise is great indeed. Conceivably, the technological gains of the next 10 years could boost the growth of productivity above its long-run average rate of 2.1% per annum.

The distribution of these economic gains between capital and labor will be an important issue during this period, determined mainly by the relative increase of capital and the labor force, and by processes of collective bargaining. These processes themselves may be affected by our greater knowledge and better measurement of productivity gains. Productivity may enter into collective bargaining in various ways which are not yet resolved. On the one hand, it may serve as a semiobjective measuring rod in wage negotiations; on the other hand, it may merely provide a tool for evaluation of the impact of future wage agreements on output and prices.

The technological advances of the 1960's carry with them not only the promise of increased productivity and economic well-being, but also the problems of regional and occupational shifts and dislocations. Some well-established centers of economic activity will face relative, or even absolute, decline. The contraction of the agricultural labor force is likely to continue and the role of the unskilled worker will be further curtailed. This calls for new and improved methods of retraining and relocation.

The demand for the professional worker, the scientist and the engineer will expand rapidly leading to a further up-grading of education and placing an ever increasing strain on our educational institutions. A high premium will be placed on the "generalist," a person of broad education who is not merely a technician finding specific solutions to limited problems. The generalist will be called upon to view problems *in toto*, to coordinate and to integrate the technical and human elements in the highly complex production processes.

2

C. Guy Suits
VICE PRESIDENT AND DIRECTOR OF RESEARCH
GENERAL ELECTRIC COMPANY

An Appraisal of Technological Progress

THE FACE of American civilization in our time is distinguished by a number of social and economic features interwoven in a complex growth curve with a definite upward swing. Among these features are the increasing worth of our urban-industrial economy and our rising level of education and of working skills. We could point also to the growing mechanization and efficiency by which we draw energy from our mineral fuels and transform our ores and other primary resources into useful products, and to the expanding and increasingly efficient communication and transportation networks through which we disseminate information and distribute goods. The increasing rate at which we combine research, development, engineering, manufacturing and marketing to effect technological progress is perhaps the unifying feature of our society. The face of American civilization, seen in these terms, is certainly looking up.

THE STATISTICAL BASE OF TECHNOLOGICAL ADVANCE

Consider first the starting point of technological progress. In this germinal area, which is the area of scientific research, development, and engineering, we are making an increasing effort to foster growth. The curve which describes our support of research, development, and engineering (RD & E) illustrates a typical growth phenomenon, which will be no surprise to those who are associated with this activity (Figure 1). The rate at which human effort has been drawn to research, development, and engineering corresponds, as we would expect, to the upward trend of support in this area. (A word of explanation of the term RD & E may be in order. The most complete industry information which has been collected purporting to show research and development expenditures explicitly includes engineering expenditures—hence the term RD & E.)

To show RD & E growth rates in perspective, we should display these curves in relation to some basic reference points. This is done in Figure 2. It is clear that *expenditures for technology* are growing much more rapidly—25% per year, recently—than is gross national product at 3% per year; and that the *growth rate of technical employment*, at 12% per year is surpassing that of total employment of 2% per year.

How Much Technology Is Too Much?

Obviously, these trends cannot continue indefinitely. If the growth rate of the RD & E function could continue to outstrip that of the gross national product, it would eventually constitute the entire economy—an anomaly that even the most partisan supporters of RD & E would view with dismay. It is apparent that, in the present differential between the related growth trends of RD & E and gross national product, we are still appraising and exploring the technological component of our economy, and are seeking the proper balance between RD & E and the other industrial functions.

What this balance will be and when it will be reached is a complex question. The problem of determining the balance between the various industrial functions derives from their essential interdependence. If we spend more money for RD & E, we will generate more business enterprise, which will require more RD & E to support its growth, and so forth. RD & E is itself one of the major determinants of the gross national product, as are such other functions of manufacturing, marketing, and manpower. Clearly, the optimum combination of these interdependent activities is not a

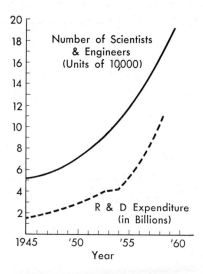

Figure 1. Growth of research, development and engineering.

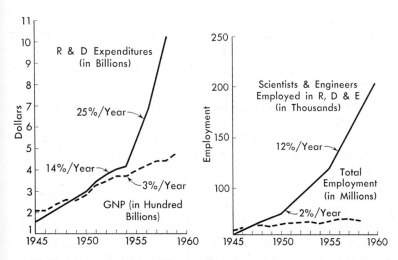

Figure 2. Growth of research, development and engineering expenditures (left) and employment (right).

constant, but a variable that must reflect such changes in the economy as are brought about by its growing complexity.

In spite of this complexity, one is tempted, when examining the abrupt growth curve of RD & E, to ask when this curve will flatten —when the saturation point will be reached. For nothing increases without limit. At some point the rate of increase starts to decrease in response to one or more limiting factors.

The Manpower Limit

The availability of technical manpower has been suggested as one such factor. It has been observed, for example, that if the present trend of technical employment continues, we shall need one scientist or engineer to every 90 persons by 1980, and one to every 40 persons by the year 2000*. Only by greatly increasing the rate at which scientists and engineers are presently produced, could this trend be sustained.

However, it is by no means clear that the rate of production of technical manpower will *not* rise in response to need. In addition to increased output, a traditional effect of advancing technology has been an upgrading of working skills. As mechanization has assumed the functions of routine physical labor, the working force has been freed to gain the higher skills needed in the expanding mechanized industries. So also, as automated systems assume routine mental labor, the working force will be freed to fill the demand for still higher skills in the expanding and more complex automated economy.

But this advance from the bench to the lathe, and from the lathe to the computer console, does more than raise the level of working skills. It also enables increasing numbers of capable youth to be diverted into specialized and highly advanced educational programs, upon which progress of the RD & E effort depends.

Among the important benefits of technological progress are increased opportunity and increased reward for the highest development of scientific and technical proficiency. Thus the advance of the

* Brown, Bonner & Weis, *The Next Hundred Years,* N. Y., 1957, p. 120*ff.*

RD & E function tends automatically to foster the increase of technical skills upon which its continuing progress depends.

THE CAPITAL INVESTMENT LIMIT

If manpower does *not* limit technological advance, will the availability of capital do so? This is certainly far from the case at present.

I hesitate to offend my RD & E associates with an unflattering analogy, but one of the classic illustrations of the saturation effect in growth phenomena is that of bacteria in a controlled culture. With the input of nutrient held at a constant rate, growth of the bacteria rises rapidly to a saturation point that represents equilibrium between the consumption of the nutrient and its supply. This is, of course, not only an unflattering analogy; it is also an inexact one, for the RD & E function does not rely passively upon contributed capital for its support. Rather, it adds to capital by creating new markets, new businesses, new jobs, and increased output. Thus also does the RD & E function tend automatically to add to the supply of capital necessary for its continuing advance. Nevertheless, the growth of new technology at present rates *may* strain our future capital resources; and I hope it does, for this is pleasant trouble to contemplate.

THE MANAGEMENT LIMIT

A further limitation on the growth rate of new technology is our ability to manage it, either in an individual industrial unit, or for the country as a whole. The development of atomic energy as a power source is an example of an advance in technology that has strained our aggregate international, national, and industrial management capabilities to the utmost. The technical problems of atomic energy power production have been unusually complex. But in addition it has been necessary to solve or contain equally difficult problems of health and safety, public liability and insurance, public versus private enterprise, as well as the relationships to the military applications of atomic energy. In spite of intensive effort, large question marks remain in many of these areas.

Increasingly, companies in growth industries are hard pressed to acquire or train enough capable managers at all levels who can successfully "get their arms around" a high rate-of-growth technical business. Increasingly, new technology is so new and different from current practice that its application to products and services draws far more heavily upon the rare human resources of imagination and ingenuity, than upon the safer and more dependable refuge of experience. Thus the management of our technological opportunities is becoming ever more challenging, and it is a question whether our skill can and will keep pace with our future bounty of discovery.

The extent of the RD & E function is determined, in the final economic analysis, by its ability to provide return on investment. Indications, based on the past economic contributions of this function, are that it will continue to grow at its present rate for some time. Although a lessening of the growth of RD & E is inevitable at some future point, it will never completely saturate so long as a rising gross national product and the resultant advance of living standards and upgrading of working skills remain primary objectives of our society.

Industry Growth Patterns

Let us now consider certain industries in which the RD & E function plays a prominent role. The rapidly growing sales of these industries, as compared with the growth of the gross national product, makes it plausible that the emphasis of RD & E has favored the high growth rate. It can be safely assumed that this particular emphasis of RD & E will continue (Figure 3).

It is no secret that industry growth rates vary widely, and that they are spectacular in some cases, as in the semiconductor products industry, where sales have virtually doubled every year in the past decade. This is an example of a growing number of industries whose life blood is technological innovation.

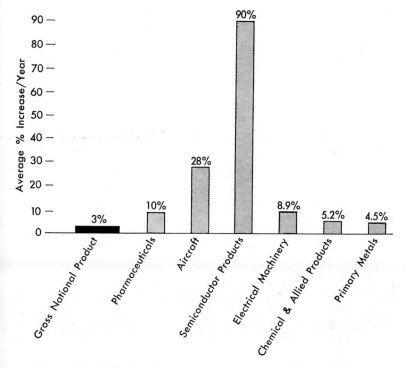

Figure 3. Average annual increase in sales, selected U.S. industries, 1948-1958.

We may conclude that research, development, and engineering are not equally appropriate—or perhaps we have not yet learned how to make them equally applicable—to the various industrial categories. Much of the technical advance, however, that is directly enjoyed by the RD & E-oriented industries passes eventually to those industries in which the technical function is less active and less germane. Thus, for example, the advances in electrical machinery, in data processing and industrial control equipment, in communications systems, and in new and improved materials provide for a general rise in the level of technology throughout all industry.

Man-made diamonds, magnified in Figure 4, and silicone products, shown in Figure 5, are illustrative of research products whose improved characteristics benefit industry generally. *Note that the supplying of technological innovation to industry is itself a business, and is the means by which all industry partakes in technological progress.*

TECHNOLOGY AND PRODUCTIVITY

One important consequence of the ability of a society to generate and apply new technology is increased productivity, defined as the efficiency with which resources are converted into useful output. When properly calculated, it measures the output of goods and services in relation to the total inputs of management, labor, in-

Figure 4. General Electric man-made diamonds.

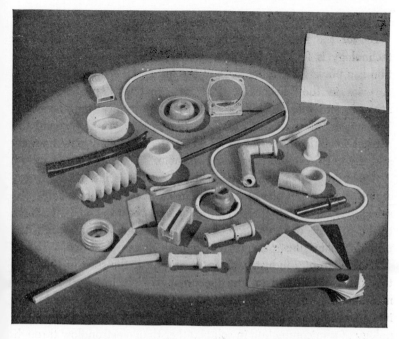

Figure 5. General Electric silicone products.

vested capital represented by plant and equipment, fuel and raw materials. When all of the inputs are considered, we find that productivity in the U. S. is rising at the modest rate of about 2% per year.

Clearly, technological innovation is a key factor in this rise, for the contributions of the other inputs remain comparatively static. The contributions of raw materials tend actually to decline, as greater value added is achieved; and although we strive mightily to maintain the level of human energy input, it probably decreases also. Only the inputs derived from technological advance—new investment opportunities, steadily improving production techniques, increasing mechanization, more efficient exploitation of energy reserves, and the like—reveal an upward trend sufficient to account for the rise in productivity.

Innovation and Obsolescence

By far the most glamorous, as well as important, use of new technology is for innovation in products and services, for innovation is a powerful driving force in the industrial economy. New discoveries in the sciences lead to new materials, processes, phenomena, and ideas which provide the opportunity for innovation. The successful application of these results may greatly expand the market for old products, or may generate completely new markets and the business enterprise to serve them.

A corollary of innovation is obsolescence. It is interesting to examine in some detail just how an "innovated" product creates obsolescence, and how the old product and the total market reacts to the pressure of innovation. The fast moving electronics industry provides many illustrative cases, from which we select one.

The electronics industry, since its origins at the start of this century, has been based on the technology of electron tubes. A tremendous perturbation was created in electronics technology by the invention of the transistor in 1948, providing a basically new technology of semiconduction in solids rather than electron flow through vacuum or rarefied gas. When this discovery was made, it was commonly predicted that electron tubes would experience a rapid decline in favor of the transistor and related solid state devices. For various sound reasons this did not take place, and on the contrary the electron tube business has been growing ever since.

This is not to say that the transistor and other semiconductor devices did not make good on their promise of success. They have performed handsomely, both electrically and economically, and the semiconductor product business, with a doubling period of one year, is regarded by many as an authentic growth business. Only a small part of this growth, however, has been at the expense of electron tubes that have been made obsolete. The semiconductors created important large *new* markets, most of which could *not be* served effectively by electron tubes. For example, the miniature portable radio first appeared on the market as an electron tube set, but because of marginal performance and extremely short battery life, it never achieved acceptance. The transistor portable radio, with good performance and long battery life, has created a large market for this product and the component semiconductor devices. The same case history, with but few changes in detail, could be related for many other applications of semiconductors, such as the transistor hearing aid, the semiconductor computer, semiconductor communication equipment, and the multiple applications of semiconductors to military technology.

Meanwhile, the technical competition of semiconductor devices has greatly stimulated research in electron tube phenomena. At the time of the discovery of the transistor, large R & D capabilities were in place to provide the technological base for the growth of the electron tube business, and these laboratories rose to the challenge.

As a result, impressive electron tube progress has been made, as shown in Figure 6 leading to types which are smaller than transistors, although not lower in power requirements, and with greatly improved signal-to-noise and very high frequency performance. The progress in electron tubes and circuit elements is even more impressive, as shown in Figure 7. The tiny unit on the extreme right

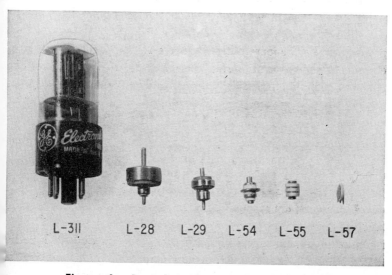

L-3ll L-28 L-29 L-54 L-55 L-57

Figure 6. Progress in electron tubes since 1948.

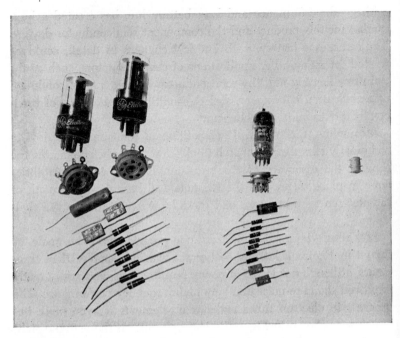

Figure 7. Progress in electron tubes and circuit elements—an impressive example of miniaturization.

performs the functions which formerly required the handfuls of equipment shown on the left. *It is important to observe that the R & D capability required to support a high rate-of-growth technical business is itself a hedge against obsolescence in that business.*

In the case described, the net result of the technological shuffle has been completely new markets for semiconductor devices, some obsolescence in some types of electron tubes, but with net growth in the electron tube business as a result of technological innovation in this older field. So in this typical example of a technological race *nearly everyone wins*. Most importantly, the consumer wins, for he receives the bounty of improved goods and services.

With the announcement of the tunnel diode by General Electric in 1959, we now contemplate a new contender for honors in the electronics race (Figure 8). In this case the new component is a

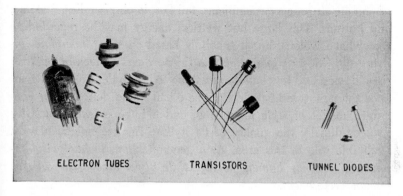

Figure 8. Progress in circuit elements, from electron tubes to transistors to tunnel diodes.

semiconductor device which will in many areas compete with the now old semiconductor device—the transistor. Although it's too early to say how the race will run, I think it's safe to say that in this case also, *everyone will win.*

Already the tunnel diode is showing that it has some unique capabilities that are certain to lead to unusual new products. For one thing, the tunnel diode is peculiarly adapted to FM circuitry. For the first time one can make a real Dick Tracy wrist watch radio, and I think it inevitable that we shall use them for hundreds of short-range communication tasks in the home and in industry. In any event, the tunnel diode is certain to open new markets where none exist today.

VARIETIES OF INNOVATION

At this point in the discussion of innovation a distinction should be made between varieties of innovation. When a couturier innovates by rearranging the geometry and trigonometry of feminine apparel, his economic objective is to create obsolescence by styling. The same motive—styling innovation—is applicable to many consumer products. It accounts for a sizable industrial design activity characterized by a frantic annual arrangement and rearrangement of chrome strips, accent emblems, tail fins, knobs, handles, feathers, and buttons. This large but wattless energy may be regarded as somewhat frivolous, but it *is* solidly based on some *invariable human traits*. Most people agree that the new cars *do* look better than the old ones; and few ladies are willing to retain their old headgear, once the new trend is evident. There can be no doubt of the economic impact of style innovation, and a huge industrial activity lives or dies by the quality of its styling. But technology plays a negligible role in this area. *As a generalization, technological innovation satisfies human needs, while style innovation satisfies human preferences.*

INDUSTRY'S PLACE IN BASIC RESEARCH

One final aspect of the relationship between the advance of the RD & E function and the rise of the economy—an aspect that will have profound effect upon future progress—is the shifting of the "center of gravity" of basic research. This type of research is no longer *exactly* centered in the universities where it has had a traditional home. Prior to World War II very little basic research originated in industrial laboratories, and it was a matter of constant amazement to scientists in the university that any "pure" research was done in *any* industrial laboratory. In some quarters it was believed that preoccupation with the practical usefulness for basic research efforts was essentially sinful. Sad to relate, that archaic idea still persists in some segments of our society.

Since World War II the weight of much evidence has shown that basic research is an eminently practical and economic investment for industrial growth. Constant progress is being made on the achievement of the climate, managerial environment, and facilities for basic research in industry. The outcome has been that the industrial participation in basic research is now widespread, and the results are significant in many fields. Literature studies soon to be published by some of my associates show that the industrially contributed fraction of basic science publication in the field of physics (including all subdivisions) is 19%, in chemistry 22%,

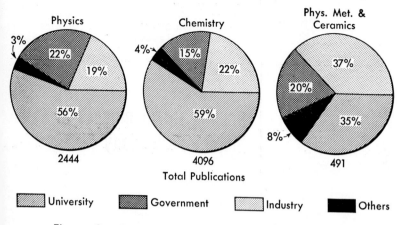

Figure 9. Research publications, 1958 (learning only).

and in metallurgy and ceramics (combined) it is 37% (Figure 9). Government laboratories also have been making impressive additions to the output of basic research. The study I have mentioned reveals the following contributions of government laboratories: physics 22%, chemistry 15%, and metallurgy and ceramics (combined) 20%. University contributions were found to be 56% for physics, 59% for chemistry, and 35% for metallurgy and ceramics (combined).

In many of these areas of basic research, industry participates in a leadership capacity; and the number of such areas is destined to increase in the future. This is a satisfaction to scientists in industry, for *to an increasing extent industry is now "paying its way" in science—by contributing new basic knowledge and understanding of nature to replenish the storehouse from which heavy withdrawals have been made in the past.* Clearly, this contribution will add to the foundations from which dramatic new technological progress of the future will rise.

3

J. H. Scaff
METALLURGICAL DIRECTOR
BELL TELEPHONE LABORATORIES, INC.

Coming Developments in Metals Technology

THIS DISCUSSION will lay special stress on those developments in metals technology in the next ten years which might cause a shift in the demand for products and labor skills. However, despite the title of the paper, to some extent it will deal with nonmetals since in many cases they impinge directly on important uses of metals. From a technological viewpoint, a subdivision of these two fields is no longer possible. This comes about because all of our technological developments are based upon common scientific disciplines. One of the significant developments of the last decade was the emergence of a science of materials applicable to metals, nonmetals and chemical substances alike. To illustrate this point, understanding of the behavior of metals as they are shaped by cold rolling or understanding of their strength properties (that is, why are they not stronger) has been significantly advanced by a study of atomic faults in crystals known as dislocations, and much of this work has been done with nonmetallic substances—lithium fluoride, for example. It seems fitting to include nonmetals in this discussion also.

The fields I have selected to discuss have been based on one criterion—they are fields (currently being investigated in our research laboratories) in which scientific achievement, invention and discovery may produce major technological changes. I have not attempted to forecast engineering advances in existing and well-established products, important as they are, since these developments are just around the corner, and are therefore well known to the leaders in the different fields. Improvements in existing processes to produce raw materials and products more efficiently and economically will continue according to the expected and well-established pattern.

Research expenditures have more than doubled in the last decade. During this same period the number of metallurgical papers more than tripled, so it may be said that metallurgical research more than held its own during this period of expansion. Expenditures for research in the United States in 1959 amounted to some $12 billion, according to recent figures from the National Academy of Sciences and other sources summarized in *Business Week*. Since the ways in which this money was spent depend upon the combined judgments of creative scientists and research managers in government and industry alike, it seems entirely reasonable to predict that many of these programs will have a substantial technological impact in the next decade. I do not think it is at all visionary to say that any one of them may have a revolutionary impact on our economy.

Should any of these fields so selected bear economical fruit, so to speak, what kind of industrial response might be produced? Let's see what happened in a recent case.

When the transistor was discovered, most of us felt that the new infant had an assured future, but the impact on our economy was broader than any of us would have predicted. The semiconductor industry grew at an explosive rate. In 1959 the volume of business exceeded $500 million annually. It required and received support from the chemical and metallurgical industry for materials of unprecedented purity, as well as new crystals of nearly perfect structure.

In addition to new markets for new purity grades of germanium and silicon, new markets were developed by this industry for a host of other materials. To mention a few, semiconductor electronics created new markets for highly pure grades of gallium, indium, arsenic and antimony; for new kinds of solders; alloy wires for terminals; and new grades of chemical reagents. The increased demand for hydrofluoric acid must have indeed been welcomed by its suppliers.

I have estimated the value of silicon used as a raw material by the semiconductor industry in 1959 to be between $15 and $20 million. This is approximately 25% of the total value of silicon produced for standard metallurgical uses.

We thus see that new discoveries and inventions created markets for special grades of material and new products of substantial economic value compared to prior uses.

Eight fields of current research which, in my opinion, will pose a technological challenge to the metals industry and to metallurgical technology are listed in Table 1.

Table 1.   SOME FIELDS OF CURRENT RESEARCH INTEREST

(1) Cryogenics and superconductivity
(2) New forms of energy conversion
(3) High-temperature materials
(4) Materials for nuclear power application
(5) New alloys and devices based on rare-earth alloys
(6) Metallurgy of beryllium, columbium, molybdenum, rhenium, titanium, tantalum, vanadium, tungsten and zirconium
(7) New dielectric and magnetic substances
(8) Imperfections in solids

Studies in the first field, cryogenics and superconductivity, are concerned with the behavior of metals at extremely low temperatures. Such studies were formerly of interest in only a few laboratories and, in these, in connection with very basic research. We now find these very low temperatures attained and used in most laboratories undertaking fundamental programs to the point where cryogenic techniques have become essential research tools. Significant theories to explain the phenomenon of superconductivity are developing, and imaginative and practical technical uses of low-temperature phenomenon are now being proposed and studied.

For purposes of illustration, let's look at a proposed use of a low-temperature effect. In the superconducting state, the resistance to the flow of electrical current abruptly disappears, and in this state the material is perfectly diamagnetic—that is, it is repelled rather than attracted by a magnetic field. Such unusual properties offer many possibilities for the design of imaginative new devices. Figure 1 illustrates a frictionless bearing based upon the use of a

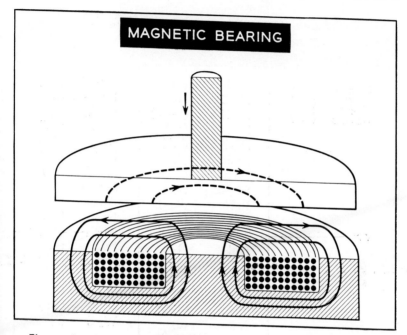

Figure 1. Frictionless bearing using diamagnetic superconductor.

diamagnetic superconductor. In the lower part of the figure is a conventional electromagnet. When current is passed through the windings, shown as solid dots in the cross section of the figure, a magnetic field is produced which would attract a magnetic substance to it. Shown schematically above the electromagnet is a disk of superconducting material. This would be repelled by the field of the electromagnet due to its diamagnetic properties. Such a device, suspended as described, could be used to support a rotating load without friction. This example serves to call attention to one of the unusual ways in which low-temperature phenomenon might be used, but it is only one example of many that might have been used (e.g., computer elements).

Exploitation of the many possibilities of utilizing superconducting effects depends strongly on developments in the materials field. Figure 2 will give some concept of the breadth of research in super-

Both Elements Superconductors		One Element a Superconductor		Neither Element a Superconductor	
Nb_3 Sn	(18)	Nb B	(6)	Au_2 Bi	(1.7)
Pb Tl_2	(3.8)	Nb C	(10)	Ba Bi_3	(6)
Tl_2 Hg_5	(3.8)	Nb H	(7–13)	Ca Bi_3	(2)
		Nb N	(15)	Cu S	(1.6)
		Pb_5 Na_2	(7.2)	K Bi_2	(3.6)
		Pb Se	(5)	Li Bi	(2.5)
		Sm Sb	(3.9)	Mo N	(12)
		Sm_3 Sb_2	(4)	Mo_2 N	(5)
		Ta H	(2–4)	Na Bi	(2.2)
		Ta Si	(4.4)	Ni Bi	(4.2)
		Ti C	(1.1)	Ni Bi_3	(3.6)
		Ti N	(1–5)	Pd Bi_2	(1.7)
		Tl Mg	(2.7)	Rh Bi	(2.1)
		Tl_3 Bi_5	(6.4)	Rh Bi_2	(2.8)
		Tl_7 Sb_2	(5.2)	Rh Bi_4	(2.2)
		V N	(1–3)	Sr Bi_3	(5.5)
		Zr B	(3)	W_2 C	(3)
		Zr N	(9.5)		

Figure 2.

conducting materials. This work looks toward basic understanding of the nature of superconductivity as well as toward the attainment of higher superconducting transition temperatures in useful substances. A number of pure metals exhibit superconductivity. The figure, however, lists some of the known superconducting compounds with their transition temperatures in degrees absolute given in parentheses. This list is not at all comprehensive but will call attention to the fact that a large number of compounds exhibit superconductivity and that superconducting compounds may be composed of elements which are themselves superconducting, or of elements which in the pure state do not show these effects. There seems to be little question that device developments will proceed hand in hand with developments in the materials field and that practical use will soon be made of these interesting and unusual properties.

The second field listed in Table 1, new forms of energy conversion, is concerned with power generation or refrigeration with no moving parts. It is concerned with fuel cells, thermoelectric effects, thermionic converters, solar cells and magnetohydrodynamics. Developments in the thermoelectric field will be discussed briefly as representative of activity in this field. To illustrate the breadth of interest in this topic, the May 1960 issue of *Electrical Engineering* was devoted entirely to this subject. The development of 1-watt, 100-watt, 500-watt and 5000-watt power generators is known to be under way, based upon materials with efficiencies in the range of 10-20%. Improvements in efficiency to about 35% are foreseen by leaders in the field, and should these improvements be achieved, such devices would compare favorably with the standard forms of power generation.

Uses of thermoelectricity are by no means new, familiar applications being in thermocouples and thermopiles for the measurement of temperature. However, with metallic alloys, the voltage differences developed due to temperature differences between the junctions or, conversely, the heating and cooling effects due to application of a voltage across the junction are so small as to be impractical for power generation or refrigeration. However, in semiconductors these effects are sufficiently large to permit practical utilization. The improvement in materials, expressed as the maximum temperature difference attainable in an elementary thermoelectric refrigerator, is illustrated in Figure 3.

A typical application of thermoelectric cooling for the spot cooling of small electronic components is shown in the left-hand part of Figure 4. By passing current through this two-stage device, the top surface can be cooled down to −70°C, and the device has the advantage of small size, no moving parts, and a life expectancy limited only by mechanical features of the design. The electrical

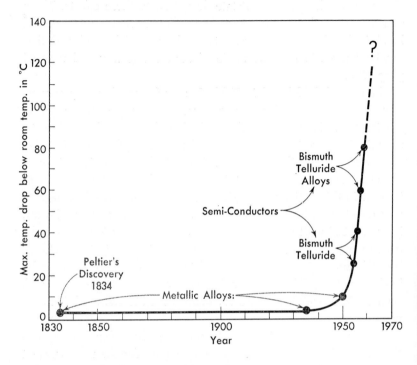

Figure 3. Maximum temperature difference attainable in thermo-electric refrigeration.

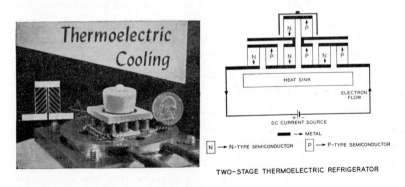

Figure 4.

interconnection of the various blocks of semiconductors in this device is shown schematically in the right-hand part of Figure 4.

Developments in this field are again directly dependent upon the attainment of improved materials. Figure 5 depicts the broaden-

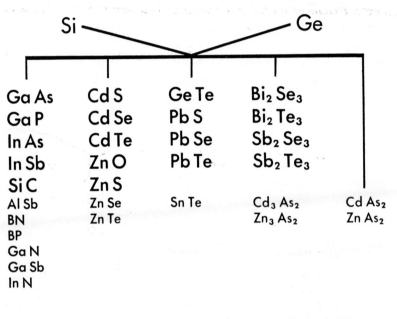

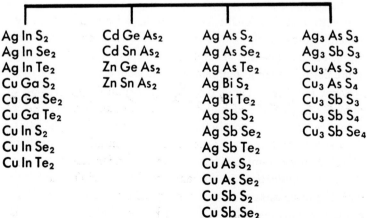

Figure 5. Broadening of research interest in new semiconductors.

ing of research interest in semiconductor materials. For transistors and transistorlike devices, silicon and germanium are the principal materials used commercially. Listed below these elements are semiconducting compounds composed of two elements, with those of present commercial interest shown in boldface type and those of laboratory interest in smaller type. Utilization of these binary compounds, especially the III-V compounds (such as gallium arsenide), so called from the position their constituents occupy in the Periodic System of elements, is increasing. Below these are listed some semiconducting compounds composed of three elements. This list is by no means comprehensive, but perhaps it will illustrate the wealth of possibilities in new materials emerging from research. In the thermoelectric field especially, the requirements the materials must meet are well understood from fundamental physical principles, and it would indeed be shortsighted not to expect major advances to accrue from materials research in this area. With the performance of devices utilizing these materials so directly dependent on material parameters, significant advances in this field seem assured.

The third item of Table 1 is the field of high-temperature materials, certainly a topic of vital interest in the Space Age. Products emerging from the intensive work in this field will not, however, be limited in their application to space hardware but may be expected to have an impact as well in more prosaic applications. One can appreciate the challenge of this field by noting recently published figures of the extreme temperatures encountered in space flight. Nose cones, for example, may be expected to encounter for short periods of time temperatures of 3500°F and higher.

Some facts concerning the element columbium illustrate developments in the field of high-temperature materials. While this element was rather scarce before 1959, new ore deposits have been discovered, and the element is now potentially as available as nickel. Many columbium base alloys are under study, and by 1970 structural applications in the range of 1900 to 2600°F are foreseen, with the utilization of this element possibly to the extent of several million pounds annually. It is well known that stainless steels and the so-called superalloys are now widely used as high-temperature materials, but uses of titanium-base alloys to 1600°F, cobalt-base alloys to 2500°F, molybdenum-base alloys to 2600°F, and tungsten-base alloys to 3400°F are possibilities under study and development. Nor do we need to confine our thinking here to metallic alloys; high-temperature applications of ceramics, alloys with various protective coatings, and graphite compositions present interesting possibilities and challenges.

There are some interesting statistics on the importance of the achievement of weight saved in airframes by the use of titanium-base alloys. A supplier has stated that 945 lb. were saved, for example, in the design of the DC-8 airframe by the use of titanium. This permits an equivalent increment in pay load.

As the fourth item of Table 1, I have listed materials for nuclear power application, where unusual requirements must be met to provide immunity to radiation damage, resistance to erosion, and a number of other requirements specifically related to this new field. Had not notable advances been achieved in this new field, nuclear powered submarines would not have been able to demonstrate the vast possibilities in this field.

As a fifth topic, there are listed alloys based upon the rare earth elements. Until recently these elements were chemical curiosities, known in detail to only a few chemists. Due to developments in extractive processes based upon ion exchange reaction, they are now available in technically useful quantities. Many of them have most unusual properties, and the expectation of the attainment of alloys with new and useful properties is high.

The sixth field of Table 1 embraces the metallurgy of beryllium, columbium, molybdenum, rhenium, titanium, tantalum, vanadium, tungsten and zirconium. These are the so-called exotic metals, many of them applicable to categories 3 and 4 in which the role of purification and special technological processes are of particular importance. Work in this field has interacted in a very strong way with older metallurgical technology. In fact, the development of the unusual melting and fabrication processes, such as vacuum metallurgy, consumable arc and electron beam melting procedures, deriving from the study of these metals has had a strong impact on many other facets of metallurgical research and on the metallurgical industry in general.

New magnetic and dielectric substances comprise Item 7 of Table 1. Formerly this field was dominated by metallic alloys, inorganic chemicals and natural minerals. However, new nonmetallic substances synthesized with specific properties in mind from consideration of atomic structures, internal fields and the like, have invaded this field. Examples are the magnetic ferrites, materials based upon the structure of the oldest known magnetic material, loadstone, or magnetite; magnetic garnets synthesized from the knowledge of the crystal structure of the well-known gem stone; barium titanate ceramics for electrical capacitors; and solid electrolytic capacitors based on oxide layers deposited on the element tantalum. Many new properties have been achieved in electronic devices based upon the properties of such new substances.

Figure 6 illustrates a few typical devices of interest in the computer field which in turn underlie progress in the field of automation, a subject treated later on in this panel. These illustrate in a very general way the kinds of materials and structures entering into this expanding area of technology, which again benefits from improvements coming from materials research.

A wealth of other possibilities might be discussed, but only one more example will be cited. A new type of amplifier for very high-frequency radio waves, known as the maser, has recently emerged from the laboratory. The term maser is a contraction of the words "microwave amplification by the stimulated emission of radiation." This amplifier makes use of electronic transitions in the small concentrations of paramagnetic "impurities" which are dispersed in the atomic structure of the crystal. These extraordinary effects were first achieved only a few years ago with crystals of lanthanum ethyl sulfate containing gadolinium and cerium. At the present time corundum crystals containing chromium are utilized. In a technical sense, these crystals are related to the gem ruby as they are single crystals of aluminum oxide with low concentrations of chromium. Such crystals are grown synthetically, and the very impurities which give ruby its attractive color now perform a new

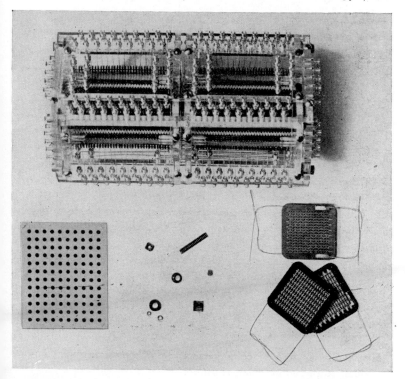

Figure 6. Computer elements: Lower right, three square plates of magnetic ferrites for use in "memory" assembly in upper part of illustration. Lower right, experimental elements for computer studies based on thin, evaporated magnetic alloy. Center, small ferrite devices of experimental interest.

function in the new high-frequency amplifier. Figure 7 shows a number of single crystals, in this case crystals of calcium tungstate, into which can be dispersed various impurities of the kinds needed in new devices. Research of this kind will have an impact on the field of luminescence as well as in the field of maser amplifiers.

The eighth and final field is that of imperfections in solids. This is a very broad term including chemical and physical impurities. For example, the very impurities responsible for transistor action in silicon or germanium may be thought of as a chemical imper-

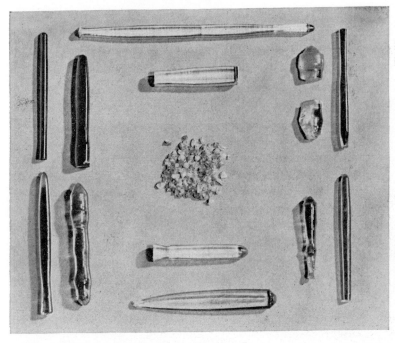

Figure 7. Crystals of calcium tungstate with paramagnetic "impurities" dispersed in atomic structure.

fection in a nearly perfect crystal, and study of the nature of such imperfections has been rewarding in transistor electronics. Study of a kind of physical imperfection in substances known as dislocations has explained why metals are not so strong as atomic considerations would suggest and have given a new insight into many features of the deformation of solids. The impact of work in this field is already felt in increased understanding of the behavior of solids and hardly can fail to have a significant impact on the achievement of materials with unusual properties.

To summarize, large expenditures for research and development have provided a wealth of new ideas, concepts and new technological horizons challenging to the metals industry and to metallurgical technology. Several fields of current research have been selected as areas which, because of the extent of the interest and the breadth of the activity, are likely to lead to development of new products which might cause a shift in the demands for product and labor skills. The impact of the discovery of the transistor and the ensuing economic development is suggested as a typical pattern which might be followed by discovery and development which may emerge from several of the fields of activity discussed.

4

R. W. Cairns
DIRECTOR OF RESEARCH
HERCULES POWDER COMPANY, INC.

Coming Developments in Chemical Technology

To TALK about what lies ahead is to risk trying to be a soothsayer, or else to oversimplify the situation and merely extrapolate the statistics. In an effort to escape this dilemma, I choose rather to speak in more general terms about the pattern of growth we can now observe in chemical technology.

The classical position of the chemical industry has been in the chemical conversion of raw materials into other forms that more suitably fill our basic needs. In the prechemical age the raw materials which we used for our food, to clothe us, to shelter us, and to provide for our other needs were derived rather directly from natural sources. The processes of conversion were so simple that modern technical skills were not required for their accomplishment. In the past several decades, however, the application of technical skills has led to more elaborate processes involving chemical change whereby natural raw materials have been converted into products much more suited to our particular needs than were the natural products themselves.

When this impact of chemical technology first made itself felt, the products of these conversion processes were generally branded as "artificial" materials that at best were substitutes to extend the supply of limited or expensive natural materials. Thus, 30 years ago we had the concept of artificial silk, a poor man's product failing in some ways to fulfill the true values of the thing it replaced. In more recent years, the term "artificial" has been supplanted by the term "synthetic." The connotation of this term has substantially changed in the past decade. For example, synthetic rubber is now regarded as a product in its own right, fulfilling needs which the natural product itself cannot fulfill. In fact, it is perhaps only in the field of luxury goods that the term "synthetic" is now regarded in any sense as associated with an indication of inferior quality, and even there the proponents of the superiority of natural products may have to rely on intangible factors.

In attempting to appraise the present position and future prospects of the chemical industry in its development of synthetic materials, I might remark on the typical way in which a new product grows in usefulness. In Figure 1 we can examine a representative case—the domestic production of rayon up to the present time. This is a typical growth curve characterized by very slow growth at first, followed by a period of accelerated expansion.

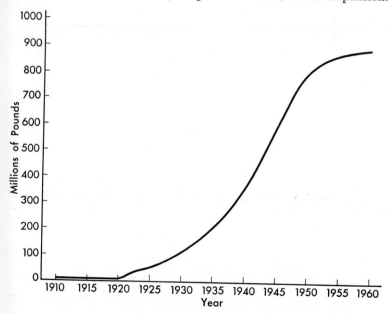

Figure 1.

After a steep rise, the growth curve tapers off toward a slowly rising asymptote characteristic of an established product. Such a curve may be followed by a wide variety of new products, and it is interesting to speculate just how far the chemical industry as a whole has progressed along this pattern. Hopefully, we may surmise that this industry, having shown a rate of growth of approximately 9% per year for the past 10 or 20 years, is still somewhere in the central part of the figure. Some segments of chemical industry are well down on the curve and are in for considerable periods of accelerated growth; others may already have hit their period of maximum increase and may be tapering off to a lower growth rate. Figure 2 indicates the growth of the U. S. chemical industry through 1958, taking 1923 as a base year, and compares it with total industrial production and with population.

The field of chemical technology is so broad that it defies any concise description. What is true of one part, may not be true of another. Development of synthetic products is far advanced in some areas and very limited in others. Perhaps the furthest advance has been in the field of pharmaceutical products where, beginning with the application of chemotherapeutic drugs in the

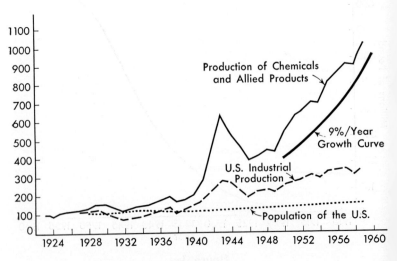

Figure 2.

1930's, we have witnessed a revolution in our concept of the medical treatment of disease. Another spectacular chemical development has been in the manufacture and use of synthetic resins and plastics. Although the first nitrocellulose plastics were discovered almost 100 years ago, and phenolic resins were well developed commercially early in this century, the most rapid economic growth of plastics has occurred since 1939, as shown in Figure 3. Poly-

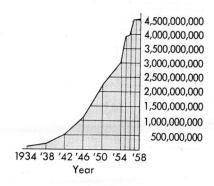

Figure 3.

ethylene and the leading vinyl resins such as polyvinylchloride and polystyrene are in the billion-pound-per-year category. In the aggregate, the production of plastics has now reached 5 billion lb. a year.

The usefulness and easy application of plastics materials has been well demonstrated in many fields with which we are all familiar, particularly in molded and extruded forms and in films and protective coatings. Not only have significant intrusions been made into the replacement of older materials such as metals and wood, but new types of articles have been prepared that were hitherto unavailable in quantity production. The discovery and development of new polymers for application as plastics has been one of the major objectives of the chemical industry during the period since World War II.

The rubber industry (Figure 4) is another segment of the chemical field in which replacement of the natural product by synthetic materials has already progressed to a considerable degree. Already about two thirds of the total rubber consumed is of synthetic origin (Figure 4) and we can expect some continuation of this trend in

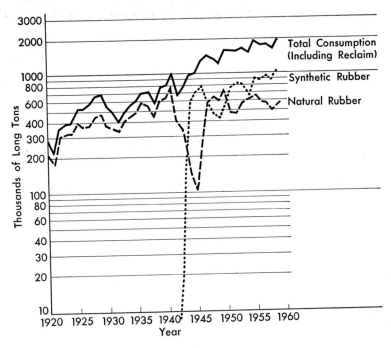

Figure 4.

the future, with the introduction of "synthetic natural" rubber. We have also witnessed revolutionary developments in the field of man-made fibers (Figure 5) which display qualities that cannot be met by any natural product. The growing impact of the synthetics is shown in Figure 5, which also clearly shows the enormous replacement possibilities still ahead.

In addition to the supply of these basic synthetic products filling our fundamental human needs, chemistry has also supplied specialized requirements which we might group under the general heading of auxiliary materials or processing aids. Some of these products, such as detergents, floor polishes and cosmetics can be

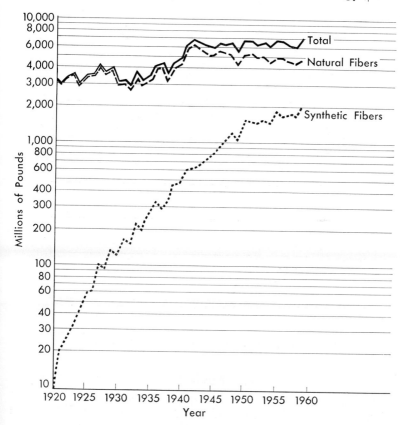

Figure 5.

used quite simply in the household. Others may involve more complex industrial applications, such as lube oil additives, wet-strength resins for paper, and agricultural chemicals such as plant growth aids and pesticides. For example, the surfactant industry (Figure 6) has seen a revolution in just the last ten years when the original product—namely soap from natural fat (one of the first large-volume chemicals)—has been very substantially supplanted by synthetic detergents based for the most part on petrochemical raw materials.

Although such fields as synthetic rubber, synthetic fibers, plas-

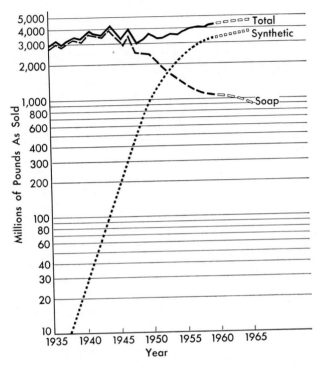

Figure 6.

tics, agricultural chemicals and pharmaceuticals have shown great advances based on chemical developments of the last 20 years, there is every reason to believe that equivalent advances will be made in the coming decade in these same fields. A realization of the significant economic advantages to be gained from research and development is firmly entrenched in these parts of the chemical industry. Aggressive and effective research organizations have been built up and are now stimulated to make their greatest contributions through the incentive of competition. I would therefore expect these fields to continue to grow vigorously as the result of further innovations discovered and developed during the 1960's.

As examples, we can expect pharmaceutical products applicable to a population of increasing age and more complicated living conditions. Drugs which can be decisive in the battle against cancer and against mental illness are in the offing. We are finding new polymers with unusual physical properties that suggest their usefulness in new forms and for new types of applications. Some of these polymers may replace metals or other materials to a much greater degree than in the past. The entrance of polyethylene into the bottle market is a current case in point. Others may contribute key properties in our search for the new Space Age materials. Glass-filament plastic laminates of the highest strength-to-weight ratio yet known have encased a solid propellant to make a rocket motor used successfully as the final stage in putting up 13 space vehicles. We can expect even stronger and more temperature-resistant compositions in the 1960's. New types of synthetic rubber will outstrip natural rubber in those applications for which it is still preferred. New and improved synthetic fibers and blends, and new techniques for their utilization, as in nonwoven fabrics, will accelerate the growth of the synthetic fiber industry.

One can further predict with confidence that several areas of the industry which have thus far been little affected by the chemical revolution will make appreciable progress along the synthetic pathway during the next 10 years. For example, the fields of food and construction show comparatively little effect of modern technology in chemistry. The products supplied in these latter industries represent for the most part the application of natural raw materials with only superficial modifications.

There are good reasons for this lag. In the case of food, strong inhibitory influences toward the application of synthetic products exist; this situation has been aggravated by recent legislative developments governing food additives. Nevertheless, in areas where specific chemical characterization can be made, as in vitamins and amino acids, it is possible to make a synthetic approach, and significant progress is being made.

The construction industry represents a tremendous potential for chemical products but little has been done, primarily because of the peculiar limitations of building operations in the field and the resistance, by unions and politically inspired building codes, to modern methods of uniform mass production with standardized techniques. However, in no part of the chemical industry does the future look more intriguing for growth of volume markets than in the development of synthetic materials for this field. I am well aware that predictions have been made for many years that plastics will make major inroads on established construction materials such as wood, glass and metal. I am also aware that certain limitations imposed by basic physical properties have stood in the way of the full realization of the predicted goals. Nevertheless, through vigorous research, new and improved polymeric substances have been developed which today show great promise for the achievement of these vast potential markets.

The development of rigid polyvinylchloride, high-impact polystyrenes, reinforced polyesters, linear polyethylenes and polypropylene are examples of modern plastic materials which are finding increased applications in markets previously denied to plastics because of their limitations in strength characteristics and weather resistance. Specifically, we can anticipate increasing applications of these and other synthetic polymers in pipes and fixtures, in adhesives, in laminated panels, as binders in wood fiber boards, in flooring and in sealants, in protective films and coatings and in insulating foams. Not only are the physical properties of plastics being substantially improved, but at the same time costs are being steadily reduced. As a consequence, it seems reasonable to predict a doubling in the size of the plastics industry during the next decade with no clear end in sight for the growth potentialities of these new materials.

The inroads which plastics are now making into applications hitherto limited to metals and glass are nowhere more evident than in the automobile industry, where lower costs, lighter weight and ease of application of plastic materials have led to more than a doubling of volume during the past five years, with likelihood of an accelerated increase in usage in the 1960's.

In my references to replacement of metals and other inorganic chemical materials with synthetic polymers, I do not intend to imply any obsolescence of this important part of chemical industry.

There are forces at work which will keep inorganic chemistry a dynamic branch of the science. The needs of the electronics industry are being filled by new and improved inorganic components, as recently dramatized in the field of semiconductors. New and revolutionary advances are being made in the field of ceramics— for example, the translucent polycrystalline ceramic from high-purity alumina and a new form of glass with improved resistance to thermal shock. Untapped possibilities in the organometallic field may well constitute another vitalizing factor.

By and large, the present state of affairs in the chemical industry is quite remarkable. We are witnessing a series of profound changes stimulated primarily by the success of some outstanding chemical discoveries in the first half century. The chemical revolution is heightened by the successful establishment of research and development teams working in well-organized and well-equipped facilities. Research is a very active force in the chemical industry. It contributes vigorously to a high rate of technological change and thrives on the economic benefits gained thereby. There is no reason to suppose that this situation will not continue with increasing vigor in the ensuing decade. In fact, everything points to an acceleration of the pace.

Another very important contributing factor is the growth in human needs that apparently can only be satisfied for the long pull by further chemical discoveries and developments. I refer to the effect of our present so-called population explosion and to the ensuing contraction of natural resources. The resolution of the resultant problems must fall largely on chemical technology, although much of this evolutionary development will extend well beyond the next decade.

Many people have deplored the lack of basic research activity in the United States. I do not believe that such criticisms are valid for the field of chemistry. Industry and academic institutions alike are supporting an ever-widening program of basic research in fundamental chemistry and in many of the interdisciplinary areas adjoining the field of chemistry. I believe that it is not in this area that a shortage of effort has occurred, but rather at the other end of the spectrum in what we might refer to as applications research. Here it has been a relatively recent trend in the chemical manufacturing industry to amplify and refine its efforts on the application of chemical products to new fields of usefulness.

As one visits the newer industrial research locations of major chemical manufacturers, one is impressed by the great strides being taken in applications work. Whereas the emphasis in past years has been on the technology of synthesis, today's keynote is the technology of the application of synthetic chemical materials. This branch of science is now being developed in great new buildings, well staffed with engineers and scientists specially experienced in this work.

Generally speaking, the chemical manufacturer must acquire a very deep understanding of customer problems and practices, in order to see best how to apply his products. Innovations must be made not only in the product to be sold, but in the techniques of application and use. Creative combinations must be sought wherein the product of optimum type and quality is selected to fit a given use, and then the most effective techniques worked out for its application.

The 1960's will be a decade of great progress in chemical applications technology. Much has already been demonstrated of the fertility of research and development of this kind. As outstanding examples, we have already developed particular types of polymers and special know-how for their use in textiles, coatings and other forms. Success in such cases has come as much from advances in applications technology as from inventions relating to the polymer manufacturing process. We still have far to go in working out the best ways to adapt the inherent properties of polymers to practical use, through more effective materials engineering.

Perhaps the best way we can describe this kind of chemical advance is by analogy. We all know of the remarkable progress achieved in the use of metals during the past century. Much of this progress was made possible by the advent and development of metallurgy, the science and technology of applications of metals to practical use. In the field of polymers, almost a century later, we have made the very beginnings toward development of a new science of synthetic polymer applications, which may well have as important an effect on our lives as has metallurgy. This new technological area has not even a name, but might be called "polymurgy." Whatever one calls it, polymurgy or the technology of applications of polymers is fast developing from an art into a science, and the fruits of these labors are beginning to appear in many new and useful articles. Herein lies the genius of the next decade in chemical technology.

5

Robert C. Langford
DIRECTOR OF ENGINEERING
DAYSTROM'S WESTON INSTRUMENTS DIVISION
DAYSTROM, INCORPORATED

Automating the Factory: A Progress Report

IN THE INTEREST of a common definition I suggest we view industrial automation as the substitution of mechanical, hydraulic, pneumatic, electrical and electronic devices for human functions of observation, decision and effort. It is a means of achieving higher productivity and lower costs, the indispensable elements of an expanding economy. The purpose is to lessen human labor. Certainly it is not a new technique or a new art.

By way of historical review we might observe that the industrial revolution has been marked by three phases. The first phase was characterized by the substitution of mechanical power for human effort. It was launched by the automatic weaving machine in the 19th century and from thence it proceeded slowly—steam engines, steam boats, locomotives. They were all elementary but important steps.

The second phase of this revolution is the replacement of human observation by various components for industrial use. These include the translation of the various senses—touch, sight, hearing, taste, smell—and are also applicable to various substances, volume, weight, speed, tension, temperature, etc.

A good current example is the control systems for the machines developed in phase one and already operating. Such a control system, based on tape information feeding to the machine, "tells" the latter what it has to do; in this particular case the machine mills, bores and performs other operations in line with the instructions given to it. The machine senses additionally whether it has done these operations correctly and separates good from bad parts and is self-correcting.

The magazine *Control Engineering* recently conducted a survey of the market for control systems and came up with some interesting figures. Although only 635 control systems (incidentally worth about $7.5 million) had been sold in all the years through 1959, a total of 948 (worth about $12 million) will be sold in 1960 alone.

The third phase involves the decision-making element, and perhaps this is the most rewarding part of the automation revolution. In this phase we will see the application of brainpower or its equivalent to the thinking or decision-making process.

Although we don't currently know how the human brain itself thinks, this type of automation is popularly known as the "thinking machine." For good or evil, this is the phase of automation that we are entering and it will be with us for perhaps all of the foreseeable future.

Examples already exist in the present day. When you make a long-distance telephone call, an application of automation searches the whole country for open routes. You just don't go directly from New York to Los Angeles unless a route happens to be open. The system builds upon the system which had been previously set up for sensing an open route, adding to it instructions to make decisions when an open route has been found.

When you use the system many other things come about. It records the origin, duration and destination of the call, calculates the time against the toll, computes the charges and taxes and, when you are finished, totals the bill and automatically types it, ready for mailing.

This thinking and decision-making element is really a computer in the rather large and yet very narrow sense of the word. You will note it is not a free thinker, but has been given the attributes of a basic intelligence and performs a thinking and decision-making process.

Where will these decision-making and thinking machines be bought? This can be discussed in both the short-term and long-term combinations. In a short-term view, the great development of the 1960's will be the increasing use of computers in industry, either for information or control. Notice the two branches: information or control. A computer system, for an industrial plant, can be achieved by designing and engineering a group of components into an integrated system. If the system is required just to deliver information the components will sense, signal, analyze and do some computations in such a way that decision-making information is supplied quickly, accurately and completely to the human operators of the process.

If, on the other hand, the system is designed for control, it does all these things and something else in addition. Some time previously a set of instructions has been programmed into the computer. When it has all the necessary information, it will cause certain things to act. Thus, it can start up, shut down and operate a complete plant or some section of a plant in accordance with given instructions.

Like all forms of automation, electronic computer control minimizes or eliminates the human element with its proneness to tiring, to err, and above all to fall behind the potentialities of the machine to which it is applied. It differs from earlier methods that were mostly concerned with the physical handling of materials and products. The electronic computer controls other aspects of industrial activities which have hitherto devolved upon the mental faculties of man—such as observing, manipulating and calculating.

An electronic computer control system utilizes a great many other instruments than the computer itself. In fact, the computer generally accounts for only one third of the total costs of the average installation. Most of these components have been in operation for a fair amount of time. What is really new in this process of industrial automation is the linking together of all this peripheral equipment into one self-contained system that provides a communication route from start to finish. The system digests the information, performs computations, and with the results of these computations corrects errors in the operation of the plant. Major computer systems can operate most efficiently in continuous-process type of industries, such as the chemicals, petroleum refining, steel and electrical power production.

When the Great Lakes Steel Corporation finishes its fully automated mill, it will have the fastest and most powerful system in this country. It will roll out steel at the rate of 3000 feet per minute, which is much faster than any human operator can do. Naturally the company executives have demanded the highest possible return on their investment as measured, frankly, by production of superior quality steel.

Engineers made a long study to determine how they could achieve this objective and recommended that the plant be operated and controlled by a solid-state computer system—in other words, automation. Once the plant goes into operation the computer will monitor and control every function from the time the steel leaves the furnace until it winds up as a completely coiled package ready for shipment, accompanied by the bill.

What the system will do will be determined by at least two types of information. The first will come from the customer. It will constitute specifications for the type of steel requirement, dimensions, etc. The second will be determined by what the engineers say the process should be—for example, the temperatures at various stages in manufacturing process. All this has to be given to the computer and stored in its memory.

Another type of information to be given to the computer will be the data supplied by the senses around the roughing and finishing stands. This will give information on the metallurgy of the steel while it is being made, and these points will be monitored many times a second, the computer seeing that this is done correctly. It will do nearly 50,000 computations a minute and will constantly refer this information to the requirements as stored in the computer memory.

Once having done this, it will then make decisions and send instructions. It will control temperatures and alter pressures on the mills, so that the slab finally comes out at predetermined requirements.

The computer will also perform many other functions. It will give an alarm if the operation fails to do what it is supposed to do in accordance with the directions and instructions contained therein. It will compute the bill and give information in the form of an identifying label, thus preventing errors in the shipping process.

Summing up, the characteristics of the short-term view of the future is mainly that of the computer control system which will sense, decide and power a complete set of operations in accordance with a preset plan. The preset plan is the principal distinguishing characteristic of this short-term system. At the present moment the best estimate from our present state of knowledge as to the structure of the brain gives a minimum estimate of the number of effective elements of about 10^{54}, whereas some of the largest computers are working around about 10^6. This is in such a small size and with such reliability almost staggers the imagination.

Now what as to the future? Fortunately the brain does tend to set a pattern and researchers are experimenting on these lines with a device called a "receptra." This device can be compared to a very backward child in its earlier stage of the learning process. The receptra tries to find out how a large computer with a memory of 10^6 elements can be taught to think for itself.

It is interesting to note that if you compare the receptra with a very backward child you find it following exactly the same sort of pattern as the child. You can tell a backward child that he will be burned if he places his hand in the fire, but the only way he seems to learn is to do exactly that, and thus learns the hard way. The receptra is starting to learn by this precondition process which sets up a conditional reflex in the memory elements.

A good deal of study is going on in these lines. When part of it is solved, perhaps we can face the start of the real information. However, there is no date set for this beginning. Too much has yet to be learned.

Management faces two critical challenges before it can expect to enjoy fully the advantages and the possibilities of automation.

For one thing, management must recognize the situations in industry that offer great opportunity for the applications of these techniques to the company's own very diverse manufacturing processes with satisfaction and profit to both management and employees.

Management must join with others in industry, including labor, to determine how automation can be worked into our industrial and economic systems painlessly and without turmoil. It is not news to anyone that automation has become a bogeyman for labor leaders and an issue for politicians. Everyone seems to have his own ideas about it and a program of plans of action. Management must face up to the job of deciding on ways and means of handling the system in the best interests of the national welfare.

PRODUCTIVITY AND WAGES:
The Outlook and the Implications

Donald F. Valley
CHAIRMAN

1

Donald F. Valley

CHAIRMAN OF THE BOARD
NATIONAL BANK OF DETROIT

Introduction

OF ALL the factors that will affect growth and development of the American economy over the next ten years, none exceeds in importance those of productivity and wages. Our ability to increase the standard of living, to compete in world markets and to maintain the purchasing power of the dollar largely depends on achieving further gains in productivity and an equitable distribution of the benefits of such increased productivity.

Government authorities have estimated that by 1970 the gross national product can be increased by 50% to $750 billion and that this will provide our expanding population with a 25% gain in the standard of living.

These same sources estimate that the labor force will be increased by 20%, which means that productivity per worker will have to increase by more than the rise in the labor force in order to make possible a 50% gain in gross national product.

Such a gain in productivity seems possible of accomplishment provided we make full and effective use of our expanding technical knowledge and provided that the necessary capital equipment can be placed at the disposal of the labor force.

We must remember, however, that incentives to savings and investment are essential to capital formation, that capital as well as labor must be rewarded in proportion to its contribution to the national product. The successive speakers will discuss the range of possibilities, the historical record and the views of labor and management concerning the future role of productivity and collective bargaining.

John W. Kendrick
PROFESSOR OF ECONOMICS
GEORGE WASHINGTON UNIVERSITY

2

Productivity Gains:
A Range of Possibilities

THE MOST IMPORTANT FORCE determining the future rate of increase in the national output of the United States, and thus the increase in our planes of living and potential national security, is the rate of productivity advance. Over the past 40 years (1919-1959) total factor productivity—the ratio of output to the associated tangible inputs of labor and capital, in real terms—has risen at an average annual rate of 2.1% in the private domestic economy. Since real private product increased at an average rate of 3.1% a year, productivity gains have accounted for roughly two thirds of the economic growth of this period; the increases in man-hours worked, and in the associated real stocks of capital, including land, have accounted for the other one third of our growth.

Widespread concern about the adequacy of the economic growth of the United States in relation to that of the Communist bloc has inevitably focused attention on productivity. In this panel, we are particularly concerned with the outlook for productivity advance as a major determinant of possible increases in real average hourly labor compensation. The other determinants are the rate of growth in the real capital stock and the movement of the rate of return on capital.

Application of a "productivity formula" to arrive at increases in wage rates in labor contracts that are consistent with price stability in the economy as a whole encounters a variety of difficulties, which are discussed by others in this series. Some of the difficulties center around problems of projecting productivity change, the probable movement of nonlabor income, the dispersion of industry and occupational wage-rate changes about the economy average, and short-term fluctuations as distinguished from secular trends. This paper treats one of the problems—projection of the productivity trend.[1]

In order to project productivity, it is necessary to be clear about the particular concept of productivity that is being used, and to know the past behavior of the several productivity ratios that are most commonly referred to. The table on p. 313 shows four interrelated productivity measures, and their rates of change over the 40-year period 1919-1959 and the postwar period 1948-1959, broken down into several shorter periods between business-cycle peaks, 1948-1953, 1953-1957, and 1957-1959, which is the last year for which estimates are available.

The key measure in terms of which the outlook may best be discussed is "total factor productivity." It is the ratio of real gross national product (private economy) to the sum of labor and capital inputs. It shows the *net* saving in tangible factor inputs per unit of output and thus the gains in efficiency in use of our basic labor and nonhuman resources. Over the business cycle, changes in productivity are affected by changes in rates of utilization of the stocks of human and nonhuman resources. But the *trend* in productivity over two or more cycles reflects mainly advances in the technology and organization of production, including those induced by increasing scale of output as well as those which are the result of autonomous innovations.

The 2.1% average annual rate of increase in total factor productivity since 1919 is somewhat higher than the rate recorded for the decades prior to World War I. Since 1948, the rate of advance has been 2.2% a year on average, but this is not convincing evidence of a further acceleration in productivity advance because decadal rates of change have varied within plus or minus 0.3 per-

---

[1] The author has discussed the full range of problems in his article "The Wage-Price-Productivity Issue," *California Management Review*, Spring, 1960.

centage point of the longer-run average rate. The variations from one cycle peak to another are apt to be even greater (see table below).

U. S. PRIVATE ECONOMY PRODUCTIVITY RATIOS

AVERAGE ANNUAL PERCENTAGE RATES OF CHANGE * 1919–1959, WITH RECENT SUBPERIODS, AND PROJECTED RANGE, 1959–1969

Productivity Type	1919-1959	1948-1959	1948-1953	1953-1957	1957-1959 p	Projection 1959-1969
Output per man-hour						
N.B.E.R.*	2.6	3.2	4.0	2.6	2.6	2.5 – 3.0
B.L.S.						
(A) Based on B.L.S. MH		3.1	3.7	2.5	3.2	
(B) Based on Census MH		3.4	4.3	2.7	2.6	
Output per weighted man-hour	2.3	3.0	3.4	2.7	2.7	2.3 – 2.8
Output per unit of real capital	1.3	–0.2	0.1	–0.5	0	0.5 – 1.5
Total factor productivity	2.1	2.2	2.7	1.9	1.9	1.9 – 2.5
Addendum:						
Man-hours	0.5	0.2	0.3	0	–0.3	1.0 – 1.5
Real gross private product	3.1	3.4	4.4	2.6	2.3	3.5 – 4.5

* All calculations are based on the author's estimates for the National Bureau of Economic Research, except those designated as based on estimates of the Bureau of Labor Statistics.
p Preliminary.

My best guess as to the future is that total factor productivity will rise by at least the same rate as in the past—around 2.1% a year, on average, and possibly at a slightly higher rate. Projection of a past trend implies that the net effect of causal forces will be the same in the future as in the past. Let us look at the chief causes of productivity advance, and consider briefly the evidence bearing on their probable impact in the future.

The main cause of the technological progress that underlies productivity advance is intangible investment in activities designed to produce inventions and innovations that reduce production costs. Such investment can roughly be measured by outlays for research and development. Basic to this is investment in education and training which produces an increasing quantity and quality of the scientists, engineers, technicians, and business administrators who create inventions and innovations, and of all the other professional, clerical, and production workers necessary to operate an increasingly complex productive apparatus. Still more fundamental are the values of a people that motivate them to seek material progress, and the institutions that channel their energies.

With respect to investment in research and development, the latest McGraw-Hill survey shows that all private industry plans to increase these expenditures from $9 billion in 1959 to almost $12 billion in 1963—a faster rate of increase than is probable in the national product. Some people point to this relative gain as an indication that the rate of productivity increase will accelerate. But research and development outlays have grown substantially faster than GNP at least since the 1920's.

Between 1953 and 1959, for example, total outlays for research and development rose by about 140%, far more than the increase in gross national product.[2] Relative gains must continue just in order to maintain the past rate of productivity advance.

With respect to education, the Census Bureau projects that the median number of school years completed by persons 25 years old and above will rise from 10.8 in 1960 to 12.0 in 1970. But this, too, is a continuation of past trends towards more education that have prevailed for at least a century. Between 1950 and 1960, for example, median school years completed rose from 9.3 to 10.8.[3]

It is in the area of basic values and institutions that the expectation of a possible acceleration in productivity advance is grounded. There has been increased conviction among informed people generally, and in Congress, that our rate of economic growth should be increased. This has found expression in the 1960 platforms of both political parties. It seems probable that during the 1960's there will be increased relative emphasis by Congress on research and development, aid to education, and other intangible and tangible investment programs; also, revisions in the tax system, and

[2] See "Funds for Research and Development in the United States, 1953-59," National Science Foundation, December, 1959.

[3] Bureau of the Census *Current Population Reports,* Series P-20, No. 91.

other institutional changes designed to encourage private innovation, investment, and expansion. It is true that many of the possible measures will take effect only after considerable time-lag. But their effect should be noticeable before the end of the 1960's. This is made more probable by the fact that periods of less-than-average productivity advance, such as characterized the 1953-1959 period (see table, p. 313), are generally succeeded by periods of more rapid advance. It is not unlikely that the rate of productivity advance will accelerate modestly—up to 2.5% a year over the next decade.

Next, consider the more conventional productivity measure—output per man-hour—for the private economy. It is unlikely that the rate of advance in real product per man-hour will be as great as the average rate of 3.2% a year from 1948 to 1959. This rate was well above the 1919-1959 average annual rate of 2.6% due importantly to a much faster growth of real capital stocks per worker since World War II than before.

It is a crucial fact that the growth of the labor force and of man-hours employed will accelerate significantly in the 1960's compared with the 1950's.[4] Even if people save the same proportion of income in the 1960's as earlier, the growth of real stocks of productive capital will proceed at a *slower* rate in relation to labor force and man-hours than was true from 1948 to 1959. So the possible acceleration in total factor productivity will tend to be offset in its impact on output per man-hour by a slower rate of growth in capital per man-hour. During the past 6 years, output per man-hour has been increasing at its long-term rate of 2.6% a year. The rate of increase over the next decade is unlikely to be substantially in excess of this percentage.

When man-hours worked in the various occupations and/or industries are weighted by average hourly earnings in each, the resulting weighted aggregate rises more than unweighted man-hours, owing to the shift of workers from lower to higher-paying industries. Thus, output per weighted man-hour has risen somewhat less than output per unweighted man-hour in the past, and

[4] *Ibid.*, Series P-50, No. 69.

may be expected to continue to do so in the future, owing to continued upgrading of the labor force.

Finally, since real capital stocks cannot be expected to rise as much as real product during the coming decade—as the rate of output growth is accelerated by a higher rate of growth in the labor force—output per unit of real capital may well rise by one percent or so a year, on average. This is in line with longer-term trends, but above the rate of the postwar period. Note that total factor productivity is a weighted average of the labor and capital productivity ratios—with output per weighted man-hour receiving about four times the weight of the output-capital ratio, in line with the relative shares of the national income.

In conclusion, if the rate of return on capital remains constant, or rises by less than the output-capital ratio, it will be possible for real average hourly labor compensation to rise a bit more than output per weighted man-hour. This has been the case in the past. But the slower growth of capital per worker in the decade ahead, i.e., the increasing relative abundance of labor, will probably mean that both money and real average hourly earnings will increase at a somewhat slower rate than in the postwar period to date. If so, the general price level will rise less in the 1960's than in the 1950's, assuming that monetary and fiscal policies do not permit an inflation in aggregate demand and profit rates.

3

Marvin Frankel

RESEARCH ASSOCIATE PROFESSOR
BUREAU OF ECONOMIC AND BUSINESS RESEARCH
UNIVERSITY OF ILLINOIS

Distributing Productivity Gains: The Historical Record

IN ANALYZING the distribution of productivity gains, it seems desirable to try to do three things: first, indicate approximately the magnitude of these gains; second, show (necessarily very roughly) how these gains have been distributed; third, note the principal factors that appear to account for the historical record and, relatedly, identify the mechanism by which productivity gains get distributed. My discussion of these matters will be oriented to the intermediate and long term, and to real as distinct from money changes in output and earnings.

PRODUCTIVITY FACTORS

Let us begin by asking how large have the gains in output and productivity been over the past five or six decades. The data in the table on page 318 (Section A-1) indicate that in 1957 real output in the American economy stood at about six times its 1900 level. This rise reflects the operation of two main forces: an increase in the quantity of resources—labor, capital, raw material—used by enterprises, and an increase in the productivity of these resources. Coordinate with the increase in output, output per man-hour rose to approximately three times its 1900 level. Thus, per hour of labor expended there were about three times as many goods and services available at the end of the period as at the beginning. Break-

DISTRIBUTING PRODUCTIVITY GAINS

A. GLOBAL DATA

(1) Some trends in the private domestic economy (index numbers, with earlier year as 100)

	1957-1900	1929-1900	1957-1929
Output	634	282	225
Output per man-hour	312	162	193
Real hourly earnings	392	166	237
Output per unit of tangible capital	185	130	142

(2) Indicators of returns to property:

(a) Average rate of return on reproducible assets

Period	Per Cent
1900-09	8.8
1915-24	8.8
1925-34	6.7
1939-48	9.2
1949-57	8.9

(b) Industrial bond and stock yields, selected averages

Year	Bonds	Stocks
1920	6.9%	5.8%
1929	5.3	3.8
1939	3.3	3.8
1948	2.9	5.9
1956	3.5	3.9

B. SECTOR AND INDUSTRY DATA

(1) Output, earnings and profits in manufacturing, 1947-56

Output per man-hour, 1956/1947: 140
Real hourly earnings, 1956/1947: 132
Profits after taxes as percent of stockholders equity:

1947	15.1
1950	15.0
1953	10.4
1956	12.0

(2) Output, productivity and earnings in selected industries, 1899-1953 (index numbers, 1899 = 100)

Industry	Output	Output per Man-hour	Real Hourly Earnings
Anthracite coal	51	148	362
Oil and gas	2434	607	409
Foods	554	252	308
Lumber products	128	192	334

Industry	Output	Output per Man-hour	Real Hourly Earnings
Chemicals	2335	583	377
Primary metals	910	341	366
Machinery, nonelectric	1046	272	333
Tobacco	661	1442	276
Average for 25 mining and manufacturing industries (unweighted)	1397	436	336
Relative dispersion for 25 industries (unweighted)	83.3%	45.0%	16.1%

Sources:

A,1. John Kendrick, *Productivity Trends in the United States.*
A,2a. I. Kravis, *American Economic Review* (Dec., 1959).
A,2b. Joint Economic Committee, *Productivity, Prices and Incomes* (1957), Table 47.
B,1. Same as A,2b, Tables 57 and 33.
B,2. Same as A,1.

ing the 57-year period into roughly two equal parts, we observe that substantially larger productivity gains occurred following 1929 than prior to it.

What has become of these productivity gains? There are various ways in which we might try to account for their distribution. We might, for example, attempt to allocate the increase in output per man-hour by various occupations, e.g., lawyers, doctors, merchants, chiefs or some variant on that theme. There have been substantial disparities in the way in which occupations have shared in productivity gains. Figures for just a few occupations will illustrate the point. Medical, legal and engineering employees experienced an 83% increase in real income between the years 1935 and 1957. For federal civilian workers, the figure was 38%; for manufacturing employees, 90%; for physicians, about 125%; and, I am sorry to add, for University teachers, a meager 7%.

Another way in which we might break down our data is by industry classification. For the traditional industry groupings, to what extent have profits received and earnings received risen as compared with increases in productivity? In this connection a fragmentary picture may be seen in Section B-2 of the table on p. 318 which shows how earnings in a few selected industries have varied.

One might also try to allocate productivity gains by income size classes, seeking to determine, for example, the extent to which the highest 10% of income recipients, or the lowest 10%, shared in the gains. A final way of trying to allocate the gains, is by the functional groupings of classical economics—wages, profits, interest and rent, or some variant like labor income and property income.

It is the last category that we usually have in mind when we ask about the distribution of productivity gains. Not only do the breakdowns of this category have a special functional significance for the economist, but they are of historical and doctrinal significance as well. They lead us to think of social classes—of capitalists, rentiers, workers. It is this last, functional category that I shall be mainly concerned with.

I must caution that the data to be referred to in this connection are fragmentary and do not, on their face, bear any close relation to social classes in the traditional sense. Perhaps it should be added that to some extent I shall be using them for things that perhaps they shouldn't be used for. However, they should suffice for the limited purposes of this discussion.

In terms of a functional breakdown of this kind, what has happened? Accompanying the approximately three-fold increase in productivity has been something under a four-fold increase in real hourly earnings. (See Section A-1 of table, p. 318.) Let us not worry too much about the discrepancy between the one rising approximately four times its original level and the other three times its original level. Other types of measures somewhat differently constructed, and including government might bring the rise in the two measures closer together. In the 1900-1929 interval, productivity and earnings moved pretty much in line. Since 1929, earnings have advanced more rapidly.

The data in the table under A and again under B show another part of the picture. One's interpretation of it may vary depending on the particular set of data used. We know that profits, to take one type of property return, may vary widely from firm to firm, industry to industry, and year to year. But one conclusion certainly stands out: returns to property are not "going anywhere."

The long and intermediate-term trends show steadily rising returns per unit for labor, but stable or oscillatory returns per unit for capital. Putting it a little differently, an average investment today earns about the same as an average investment would have earned 40 or 50 years ago, but an hour of labor today earns very substantially more than an hour of labor would have earned 40 or 50 years ago.

What forces have operated to produce this outcome? One relates to supply trends in the two classes of inputs, labor and capital. Growth in the labor supply is ultimately dependent on population growth. It is dependent also on the willingness of the population to participate in the labor force, that is to enter gainful employment, and also on the length of the working week. Growth in the supply of capital is dependent, among other things, on the willingness of the people to save. The supply of capital over the 57-year period has grown a good deal more rapidly than the supply of labor. (The figures in the table under Section A-1, on output per man-hour and output per unit of capital, indicate this.) This fact accounts for growth in capital per worker, which is a principal circumstance making for high productivity. It also means that capital has become increasingly abundant, hence cheap relative to labor.

A second force contributing to the disparate movements between wages and profits is technology, which underlies the productivity of both classes of factors and, together with their supplies, determines the proportion in which each will be used. Other things being equal, had our changing technology in the past half century been more labor-saving or more capital-using, returns to capital would have fared relatively better. Other outcomes are conceivable, though the facts are as one sees them in the table.

A third conditioning but less specific influence is the economic environment with its institutions, including business and labor organizations and government. The significance of this factor and its components are exceedingly difficult to measure. With respect to the long term, I am inclined to regard the first two forces— factor supplies and technology as fundamental.

Extent of Productivity Changes

Over-all averages and long-term averages frequently conceal great diversity in the components that underly them. Thus we know that profit and interest rates may vary greatly from industry to industry, enterprise to enterprise, and year to year. And over both the short- and long-term, rates of productivity growth may vary widely among industries.

Section B-2 of the table, on p. 318 illustrates the case for some individual industries. The period differs from that under Section B-1, but that is not important for the point I wish to make. Note that in a period of more than half a century, output and productivity gains differed widely among industries, yet there was relatively little dispersion in the trends in real hourly earnings. That is, in individual industries earnings moved quite independently of productivity. Thus in the tobacco industry, output per man-hour advanced to over 1400% of its initial level, whereas the comparable figure for real hourly earnings was a bit under 300%. The measures of deviation summarize the picture for 25 mining and manufacturing industries. Profit data are not given. However, I suspect that, in addition to showing considerable dispersion, they would exhibit two characteristics: a tendency to correlate with productivity increases, i.e., high levels of profit being associated with high productivity increase; and no long-term tendency to rise or fall.

Apparently, productivity increases are not alone sufficient to assure an increase in labor earnings in individual industries. As noted, such earnings in major degree move independently of productivity. To explain this, let us ask, and try to answer, the question, When does an increase in labor productivity "allow" an increase in wage rates in a particular enterprise? The answer may help us to see the relation between global and industry data and the forces acting in each.

The answer depends on several factors—one of these being the amount of the productivity increase. Presumably productivity increases are implemented by management when they afford a net cost saving or net revenue gain to the firm—a saving or a gain out of which a wage increase might be paid. It depends also on the requirements generated by the productivity change for additional quantities of complementary factors, i.e., whether much new capital or additional raw material is needed to carry it out. We can visualize a situation in which, after all expenses have been provided for, there is little left over for wage increases. We can also visualize a situation where other factors as well as labor are saved, so that more is available for wage increases than labor savings alone suggest. Finally, it depends on the state of competition, together with the extent to which the productivity improvement is generalized to other enterprises. A firm which is obliged to pass on productivity increases to consumers in the form of lower prices may have little or nothing remaining for wage increases. In sum, what is available for wage increases may in individual cases be less than, equal to, or more than the amount suggested by the productivity gain.

Productivity change is not limited to a single firm or industry. It goes on continuously throughout the economy. Individual firms adapt to this change—of more or less unique dimensions for each—in diverse ways. Employment opportunities for factors expand or contract; output expands by varying amounts; factor prices may rise or, with labor displacement, fall; product prices may rise or fall relative to other product prices.

Given the maintenance of reasonably full employment—whether by accident or design—the over-all result is an increase in demand. That is, on balance, individual demand functions shift to the right, for aggregate output and income are rising in response to the economy's expanding productive potential. This is the essence of a growing economy. Concurrent with this process of productivity advance and economic expansion, factor supplies—capital and labor—also grow, but at dissimilar rates. We also have noted that dissimilarity in these rates, along with the nature of the technological changes that occur, are primary determinants of the disparate global trends we have observed in labor earnings and profit rates.

How does all this help to explain the relatively uniform advance in earnings in individual industries, compared with highly diverse productivity movements? In the intermediate and long run, it is approximately true that firms and industries draw their labor (and capital) from a common, economy-wide market. Labor is mobile— between firms and industries and also occupationally. Hence, earnings in firms and industries tend to move more or less in response to economy-wide or global pressures—that is, in response to basic trends in factor supplies and technological change. By contrast, technology affects individual industries in quite different and sometimes extreme ways, resulting in productivity trends among them that tend to be highly dispersed.

Technological Changes and Global Forces

To recapitulate briefly, over the intermediate and long term, and for the economy as a whole, returns to labor have surged ahead, as rapidly as or more than labor productivity. By contrast, returns to property, and to profits as the chief constituent of this class of return, have remained relatively constant. This record is to be explained in terms of two basic forces: the slower rate of growth in the supply of labor than in the supply of capital (with these rates in turn dependent on still more basic forces); and the labor-saving, capital-saving nature of changing technology.

In individual industries, productivity gains have varied widely, and bear little relation to increases in earnings. By contrast, earnings in different industries, while showing significant differences in their rates of increase, exhibit a relatively small dispersion. The productivity record is attributable to the differing, specific ways in which technological change acts on individual industries. Some benefit much more than others. The earnings record is primarily attributable to the fact that, very roughly speaking, all firms and industries seek their productive factors in the same broad market —in a global market affected by global forces. Productive factors, being comparatively mobile, seek employment that yields the highest pay, thereby generating wage-rate equilibrating forces among industries.

Nothing has thus far been said of price inflation as a factor affecting the distribution of productivity gains; our discussion has been in real terms. The omission does not indicate that this factor has no relevance to the problem. But in the approach we have taken, its role may fairly be said to be an indirect and secondary one.

Neither has anything been said of labor-management rivalry as a determinant of how productivity gains are shared. I do not mean to exclude it from the picture, nor would I exclude other factors—e.g., immobilities in certain industries and occupations. But in the context in which I have been speaking, such rivalry is a secondary force. It might fairly be said to embellish the trends we have been discussing, but not to condition them in any fundamental way. If one is concerned, on the other hand, to explain the earnings dispersion—I have stressed how small it is, but we might ask, why does it exist at all? Then one may well want to accord labor-management rivalry an influential role.

4

George G. Hagedorn *

DIRECTOR OF RESEARCH
NATIONAL ASSOCIATION OF MANUFACTURERS

The Future Role of Productivity in Collective Bargaining: A Management View

OUR POINT OF DEPARTURE is a brief review of the role of productivity in collective bargaining in the past in order to establish a basis from which to discuss its role in the future.

Certainly productivity has been talked about at length. We see it mentioned and discussed in full-page ads that both sides take in some of our national collective-bargaining controversies. But when the chips are really down and the decisions are hammered out, how much of a role has productivity actually played in determining the outcome of those decisions?

I do not suppose that we who observe from the outside can answer that question. And I doubt that even those who are actually making those decisions could tell you how much of a role productivity played in determining just how they arrived at their settlements. It would probably take a psycholanalysis of the participants to determine how much the concept of productivity had entered into their minds and how much it had actually guided their final conduct in what they agreed to.

One area in which I think productivity has played a substantial role is in the hopes of many sincere people who have been both-

* The opinions expressed herein are those of the speaker, and do not necessarily reflect the views of the National Association of Manufacturers.

ered by the way collective bargaining has been conducted over recent years. It has been a painful process, both for those engaged in it and for those who observe it from the outside and the results have not been such that, in general, any of us can feel very happy about them.

The main reason for the painfulness of the collective bargaining process and the dissatisfaction with the results is that there seems to be no objective criterion, no way of really settling the arguments, no principle on which everyone agrees that can form the basis for the settlement.

In this state of affairs, many very honest people have turned to productivity as the answer to the problem. Is productivity not the objective criterion that should guide the conduct of collective bargaining they ask? And, if we all accept that criterion, then does it not furnish a way of settling these painful problems, or at least of greatly reducing their scope?

Now, the many people who have had that hope may more or less be divided into two schools. One group has felt that productivity can enter into collective bargaining settlements in some sort of precise mathematical way, a formula for deciding the courses of wages and fringe benefits. The other group has felt that productivity should be a general guide, but has been unwilling to say that it should necessarily be in the form of a precise mathematical formula. Rather, they would take the rate of gain in productivity as the guiding factor in determining the rate of gain in employment costs per hour, recognizing you might have to shade it upward or downward in particular instances.

The main thing I want to say about the future role of productivity is that it is my belief that the hope that I have just outlined is going to be abandoned and that, *as a working tool of the conduct of collective bargaining,* productivity will be de-emphasized in the future.

I have a number of reasons for reaching that conclusion. I am going to give you the reasons in inverse order of the weight that they have in leading me to that conclusion. In other words, I will start with what I think is the least weighty reason for coming to that conclusion about the de-emphasis of productivity in the future, and conclude with what I think is the most important reason.

My first reason is that we have such a wide variety of conflicting and varying concepts and statistical methodologies in measuring productivity that the acceptance of the productivity criterion, even in principle, simply shifts the ground of the argument without settling it.

We have seen this happen in the recent study of the Bureau of Labor Statistics on output per man-hour. This study contains a summary table of various measurements covering various time periods and with various types of curves fitted to them. The calculation of the increase in output per man-hour per year derived by those various methods varied from about 1½% per year to something like 5% a year.

That greatly understates the variability of different concepts and measurements you can use, because the Bureau of Labor Statistics table cited was very far from covering the whole gamut of possible concepts.

In analyzing this problem, you have to decide whether you are going to use as your guide output per man-hour, output per unit of capital input, or output per unit of labor and capital combined. Then you have to decide on your weighting system, whether you are going to use base-year weights or current-year weights or some combination.

You have to decide whether the effects of internal shifts on the final outcome is going to be included or is going to be eliminated by some sort of mathematical technique. Then, finally, you have to decide what kind of a curve you are going to fit; that is, the technique you are going to use; whether you are going to fit a straight line, or a parabola, or a hyperbola, or a broken straight line, or one of the many other alternatives you have. You have so many different choices that actually, as we have seen, merely agreeing that productivity should be the guide does not really settle very much.

It leaves you almost as much ground for argument as you had before. Of course, if there were agreement on the principle that productivity ought to be the guide and, if people sincerely wanted to use it, they probably could iron out many of these statistical difficulties.

This brings me to my second reason for believing that productivity will be de-emphasized in the future—is it the right thing to do in principle? Is it the right guide to turn to in settling individual cases of collective bargaining?

As I recall, in an earlier stage of discussion of productivity and what role it should play in collective bargaining, one thought was that the guiding factor in each settlement should be the productivity of the particular industry, or, perhaps, of the particular company or the particular plant that was involved in the collective bargaining. This is a naive approach, and, as Mr. Frankel has already stated, wage trends have not conformed with any such principle in the past. There has not been a close relationship, industry by industry or plant by plant, between productivity and wages or employment costs. And there would be no reason to expect, in any kind of a logical, rational economy, that there should be such a relationship.

A second approach, and the one that has been generally applied where productivity has been used as a guide in collective bargaining, has been to base each individual settlement on the productivity of the economy generally.

According to this principle, everybody's wages and other forms of compensation would go up along with the productivity of the economy as a whole.

That is a little bit more logical, because, as Mr. Frankel pointed out, to some extent our labor market is one market. People do move around from one area to another, and to the extent that it is one market, you have to expect supply and demand to equate the wages and other forms of compensation paid in one area with those paid in another.

But I think we have to recall, too, that in many important respects, the labor market is not one market. It is very far from being one market. So that my second reason for believing that productivity will be de-emphasized in the future as a factor in collective bargaining is that it is not really right in principle to try to apply one universal criterion to every particular case.

That is the sort of statement that requires some qualifications, and the qualifications in turn require some reservations. It certainly would be illogical to say that the companies that are in a better competitive position and that have done better than other companies, perhaps through having a greater productivity rise, should therefore pay higher wages, and that companies who are in a bad position competitively should somehow get away with paying lower wages.

We cannot simply say that every company should pay whatever level of wages will keep it in business. On the other hand, in a particular area of the country where jobs are not plentiful a company may be faced with the alternative of either closing up or offering its people a rate of wage increase that does not go up along with the national average. If the workers in that area, recognizing that they have the choice between taking these lower wages and seeking a new career in some other part of the country, prefer to remain where they are and settle for less, there is again no reason for preventing them from doing so.

This is getting very complicated, but the whole problem boils down to the fact that you cannot establish productivity as any universal guide to particular cases of settlement of collective bargaining questions.

Now, my third reason—and I am getting into the reasons that I think are most important in my prediction that, as a working tool in collective bargaining, productivity will play a smaller role in the future—is that the impact of foreign competition in the future will be such that everybody, both on the labor and on the management side, is going to have to think of distributing the productivity gains in the form of lower prices rather than in the form of higher wages.

In many cases, industry is improving its plant and equipment at great expense in order to improve its productivity and cut its costs, so as to be able to compete with foreign competitors both in home markets and in foreign markets. It would certainly be very unfortunate if those lower costs were then simply cancelled out by labor claiming the productivity gain in the form of a proportionate increase in hourly wages.

Another reason for predicting a de-emphasis on productivity in the future is that technological developments are going to lead to quite an extensive reallocation of the labor force among different industries, different types of occupations, different geographical areas of the country.

In bringing about that type of reallocation, of course, wages and wage levels and other forms of compensation have a role to play in the economy, guiding the reallocation of our manpower resources. Wages are not simply an outcome of the economic process. They are a very important part of the machinery, and if such reallocation is to go on, wage rates and fringe benefits have to be adapted to the supply and demand conditions in the particular localized labor markets and, hence, cannot be tied to any formula. It would greatly impede the process of reallocation if we did try to tie them to any rigid sort of formula involving productivity.

I come now to my final reason for believing that there will be a de-emphasis on productivity in the future as a working tool in conducting collective bargaining. This, I believe, is the most important overriding consideration.

There is an inner contradiction in the belief that somehow we can find some objective guide to the conduct of collective bargaining, some formula or some rule of thumb that will divide up the benefits of future progress in a way that will be satisfactory to everybody. The reason for that inner contradiction lies in the politics of collective bargaining.

Those politics compel the unions to ask for something more each time the contract is opened up—each time they come to the collective bargaining table. Suppose, somehow, all these other objections that I have mentioned to the use of a productivity guide in collective bargaining had been solved, or, if they had not been solved, that they had been brushed aside, and that we did have a formula that everybody agreed was the right way of dividing up the future benefits of productivity in the country.

If it divided up all the future benefits of productivity, then what would the labor unions ask for the next time they came to the collective bargaining table—because they have to ask for something more? If the formula already embodies all those future benefits, then what can you give on top of that?

That sort of an inner contradiction, I think, is the chief impeding factor in the development of any type of formula, whether it involves productivity or any other rule of thumb, in guiding what collective bargaining settlements ought to be.

When "improvement-factor" clauses first became fashionable, about a decade ago, we heard statements like the following: "This is it; this is the end; from now on we have the solution to the problem of collective bargaining. If only we had thought of this idea 30 years earlier and if it had been universally adopted, wages would have gone up just about the way they did go up, and we would have spared ourselves all the infinite turmoil and pain of those years of collective bargaining."

The thought in the minds of some optimists was: "Well, now we finally have reached the happy land. We have the answer. From here on, collective bargaining need be concerned merely with minor administrative problems in putting this agreed-upon principle into effect."

The trouble with that sort of a conclusion was that it would have left the labor unions involved with nothing much to do from there on—nothing further to gain for their people. Labor leaders would have been left with merely an administrative job rather than a crusading job.

Well, nobody can believe that labor leaders were ever going to adopt that attitude and, of course, they didn't. Now we realize that it was rather foolish to expect them to. But this is the main difficulty. It is the central problem involved in any type of systematic use of productivity as a guide in collective bargaining. The disillusionment with productivity as the answer to collective bargaining that I think has already set in stems from this awareness.

At this point, I want to read to you two very interesting

sentences from President Eisenhower's Economic Report of January, 1960:

"Labor-management negotiations in all industries offer opportunities to help promote sound growth by avoiding settlements that contribute to inflation. Settlements should not be such as to cause the national average of wage rate increases to exceed sustainable rates of improvement in national productivity."

I have read that statement at least 20 times since January and I am still not sure just what it is meant to imply. Note that it did not say that individual settlements should be in line with national productivity. All it said—at least what I got out of it—is that things ought to happen in such a way that, at the end of the year, you will find the average of all the wage settlements has turned out to be the same as the average of all the productivity gains.

That is the neat trick if you can do it. How can either side in an individual collective bargaining settlement determine on what the effect of that settlement will be on the national average?

An average, of course, always has some components that are above it and some that are below it. I do not imagine anybody would like to accept the fact that he is the one who is chosen to be below the average so as to counterbalance somebody who has been chosen to be on the high side of the average.

The conclusion that I have drawn from this statement in the President's Economic Report is that productivity is not very practical as a working tool in collective bargaining, in hammering out individual settlements. But as an analytical tool for appraising what has happened after it has happened, it is a very useful device.

In other words, it is a device of the economists rather than of industrial relations people. I think it can be very important and very useful in that respect and I believe that in the future we will have a clarification and refinement of the concepts and of the statistics. That will help us further in using this as an analytical tool.

Productivity will be one of the concepts that will help the public judge—as they observe what is happening—whether collective bargaining is being conducted on a generally sound basis from the point of view of the whole national economy.

Thus I come back to where I started: collective bargaining is still a very painful process, both to those who participate in it and those who observe the results at the end of it. We still don't have any clear objective guide that would help in establishing some more reasonable state of affairs in that area.

It is a will-of-the-wisp to look for any such economic guide. This is a market economy and we have to depend on our markets to be the guide in keeping things in order, and keeping them going in a reasonably desirable direction. But we want them to be free markets, and collective bargaining can result in settlements that are in the interests of the whole country, only if it is true collective bargaining. It must be purged of all monopoly elements. I think that is the solution to the painful process that we have observed in the past.

Nathaniel Goldfinger

ASSISTANT DIRECTOR OF RESEARCH
AFL-CIO

5

The Future Role of Productivity in Collective Bargaining: A Labor View

PRODUCTIVITY will obviously be a factor in collective bargaining in the period ahead and it may be a factor of growing importance.

Organized labor's views on this subject go back to the last century. In 1897, for example, Samuel Gompers wrote that it was important for "the consumptive power of workers to keep better pace with their productive ability," if the economy is to maintain balanced growth. In 1925, the AFL's declaration on wage policy called for continuing increases in real wages, coupled with a continuing reduction of working hours, "in proportion to man's increasing power of production."

Formal recognition of this principle by a major company came in 1948, in the UAW-GM agreement, which provided for quarterly cost-of-living adjustments to protect the purchasing power of worker's hourly wages and for an annual improvement factor wage increase "to provide for improvement in the standard of living of employees."

Whether the goal of rising real wages in relation to rising productivity is achieved through long-term agreements of the UAW-GM type, with formal arrangements for the contract period, or through more frequent bargaining, the goal itself remains.

For us, the general productivity yardstick is the average annual rise in output per man-hour in the total private economy for the recent period of time. At present, this would mean the average yearly rise of output per man-hour in the postwar period.

The rise in output per man-hour produces economic gains. When output per unit of capital rises, it produces additional gains. These gains are shared among various groups in the population. In terms of these gains, if the employee share of national income is not to decline, and if markets are to expand sufficiently for maximum production and employment levels, average real hourly employee compensation should rise in proportion to the rise in output per man-hour of the total private economy, or somewhat more.

But in an economy of hundreds of thousands of different enterprises, with hundreds of different product and labor markets and varying degrees of price competition and price administration among the scores of different industries—in such a pluralistic economy, national averages can at best provide only broad and flexible guidelines for trade union collective bargaining policies in specific firms.

If the percentage rise in output per man-hour in the private economy, for example, were the sole determinant for all employee compensation determinations, all wage and salary earners would simply receive the same percentage increase in hourly compensation and the national economy would lose some of its flexibility. If output per man-hour in specific industries were the only determinant, differences in the pace of productivity advance among industries would produce great and widening differentials in hourly earnings among wage and salary earners in the various industries.

Furthermore, an increase in hourly compensation at any particular time is not simply a sharing of the benefits of current productivity gains. It may also include some catch-up with the past, when employee compensation lagged. It may also represent an attempt to increase the employee share in the distribution of income among the factors of production.

American trade unions do not necessarily accept the distribution of income among the factors of production, at any particular point in time, as ethically good, socially and economically desirable or inviolable. The American economy is a flexible and dynamic one, in which continuing and varying changes in productivity and employee compensation in hundreds of thousands of enterprises are all part of a continuing process.

As a result, productivity, from the union's viewpoint, is a factor, but only one factor in any particular collective bargaining negotiations. There are other pertinent and important factors—such as the profits of the employer and industry, wages and fringe benefits for the same or comparable work in the industry or area, any rise in the cost of living, the union's desire to eliminate substandard wages and working conditions and the economic situation in the product market.

Nevertheless, productivity is a factor of some relative importance. And underlying one's views on the relationship between productivity and real hourly employee compensation is the kind of economy and society one prefers.

Organized labor does not prefer the kind of economic and social developments that occurred in the 1920's, when real hourly employee compensation lagged considerably behind the rise of output per man-hour. To observers such as myself, the aroma of economic trends of the past few years has become uncomfortably similar to that of the 1920's, although the growing imbalances seem to have developed this time primarily from federal tax, monetary and budget policies and the pricing and investment policies of key industries.

A problem concerning real wages has been developing, however. In the past three to four years real earnings have risen at a rate that is much slower than in the previous postwar period. The rise of real hourly earnings of factory workers, including the real value of fringe benefits, has been at an average yearly rate of approximately 1½ to 2%—a pace that is approximately slower by one third or more than in the postwar period prior to 1956, and slower than the average yearly rise of output per man-hour in the entire postwar period since 1947.

With considerably lower levels of capacity and manpower utilization since the low point of the last recession than in 1955-1957— as well as the slowdown in the rise of real hourly earnings—the average yearly increase in the purchasing power of factory workers' weekly earnings, after taxes, has been only one per cent in the past four years. A somewhat similar slowdown can be found in the trend of the purchasing power of per capita after-tax personal income and in the purchasing power of average family income.

With such a slowdown in the rise of consumer purchasing power, accompanied by relatively stable federal government expenditures, is it any wonder that economic growth has slowed down to a state of near-stagnation and that the economy exhibits a persistent underutilization of productive capacity and manpower? The slow rise of output and low levels of capacity utilization, in turn, have contributed to some slowing down in the rise of output per man-hour from the very rapid pace of 1947-1956. How can the economy get out of this seeming cul-de-sac, except through substantial increases of real wages and salaries, a substantial rise of federal expenditures for improved national defense and public services, or a combination of both—policies which business spokesmen usually battle as unrelieved evils.

Under the leadership of business and administration spokesmen, the nation in recent years has concentrated much of its attention in the decadent effort to defeat a nonexistent runaway inflation, instead of concentrating on economic growth to meet our national needs in this second half of the 20th century—more adequate national defense and public services, adjustments to radical technological change, elimination of poverty at home, technical and economic aid for the less developed areas of the world.

As a nation, therefore, we have concentrated our attention, efforts and policies in recent years on the wrong economic and social issues, ignored or shunted aside the major economic and social issues of our time, and failed even to deal with the actual problem of a slow, creeping rise in the price level. This creeping rise of the price level has been falsely diagnosed as runaway inflation, based on the fiction of excessive general demands and widespread shortages, and it has been blown up for propaganda purposes into an overriding national economic issue, to be combated at all cost by depressing the rise of demand for goods and services from both the private sector of the economy and the federal government.

While major industries and corporations are protected against the kind of underutilization we have experienced—protected by low break-even points, large profit margins, administered prices and substantial depreciation allowances—many businesses and the vast majority of wage and salary earners have little or no such protection.

This brings me to another area, in which productivity and collective bargaining are involved. It is the important area of jobs.

Output per man-hour has risen at a rapid rate since 1947, more rapidly than in earlier periods. Between 1947 and 1953, the swift rise of output per man-hour was accompanied by a rapid increase of the real volume of production and sales. Full-time job opportunities also rose. The economic, social and human adjustments to ever-increasing productivity, in most cases, were relatively easy in an environment in which job opportunities expanded rapidly.

Since 1953, however, the real volume of output has risen very slowly, not much faster than the growth of the population. This condition of near-stagnation has somewhat depressed the rise of output per man-hour. In a period of radical technological change, however, the rise of output per man-hour has continued at a fairly fast pace, although a bit slower than in the earlier postwar years. The rapid rate of advancing output per man-hour, in an economy whose production levels have been rising slowly, has meant layoffs for many workers, short work-week schedules for others, an inadequate number of job opportunities for a growing labor force and an increasing number of economically distressed communities.

A considerable portion of the economy's potential for growth in recent years—its rising productivity and growing labor force—has been translated, not into increased output, but into joblessness and part-time work.

From the first quarter of 1953 to the first quarter of 1960:

Factory production and maintenance jobs have fallen one and one-half million;
Mining jobs have declined 200,000;
Railroad employment has dropped over 400,000.

Most of this job loss has been for unskilled and semiskilled workers, although some skilled jobs, as well, have been displaced.

It may sound rational to some business or government executives to tell factory and railroad workers and miners to seek jobs elsewhere. The realistic problem faced by American workers, however, is: Where are these new job opportunities and at what kind of wages and working conditions?

In that same period of the past seven years, between the first quarter of 1953 and the first quarter of 1960:

The labor force has grown by five million persons;
But employment has increased only 2.9 million;
And, as a result, the number of unemployed has doubled—increased 2.1 million.

But the actual situation is even worse. Most of the inadequate rise in employment has been in part-time work. While farm employment has dropped in the past 7 years, the rise of full-time non-farm employment has been less than a million.

And where are these 2.9 million additional job opportunities? Laid-off factory and railroad workers and miners cannot overnight become engineers, technicians, school teachers or clerical employees. Are they to be joyous about the rise of employment—much of it part-time—in retail and wholesale trade and the services, usually at low wages? The only other significant alternative has been government employment, for which most factory workers, railroaders and miners probably do not qualify. The number of man-hours worked in the total private economy has actually declined.

It is ironic in this period of business domination of economic policies and American life that there has been only a small net increase in private employment—much of it in part-time work—and that most of the increase in employment is accounted for by the rise of state and local government jobs. In this environment it is no wonder that workers and unions are concerned with jobs, job displacement, work-schedules and the danger of layoffs. A variety of issues connected with adjustments to rising productivity and radical technological change, therefore, are becoming of increasing importance in collective bargaining. I suspect that they are becoming of increasing political importance as well.

In conclusion, let me say that the trade union movement hopes that the economic and social environment will be considerably different in the period ahead from what it has been in recent years —a faster rate of economic growth, a greater degree of utilization of productive capacity and manpower, an easier adjustment to radical technological change, a better atmosphere for labor-management relations, and above all, a much greater sense of national purpose.

6

Discussion

Mr. Hagedorn: The central question here seems to be the insufficient number of job opportunities in the economy and the problem that Mr. Goldfinger is worried about is the preservation of job opportunities. But I never could see how you preserve somebody's job by making it more expensive to hire that person. Certainly, if you are trying to retain the market for your product, no matter what it is, or trying to expand the market for your product, the last thing you do is raise the cost to the purchasers of that product. So I cannot understand the argument on the labor side that, if there are not enough job opportunities in the economy—in other words, if labor is not able to sell as much of its products as it would like to—that the solution lies in raising the price of that product to those who buy it.

It is true if somehow labor prices itself out of the market and there aren't enough job opportunities around that you can use the government to get yourself out of that fix temporarily by adding an additional demand for labor or, arbitrarily, taking the supply off the market. Of course, the long-run effects of depending on the government to keep our economy going rather than depending on maintaining wages at a reasonable economic level, is inflation.

If you have granted uneconomic wage increases and then turn to the government to bail you out, inevitably you are going to have inflation. I don't think you are going to solve the problem that way, because as soon as we accept government action as our only solution to the problem of joblessness created by uneconomic wage increases, the economy will depend on that medicine and, to the degree it depends on it, the medicine will be ineffective.

MR. GOLDFINGER: When Mr. Hagedorn speaks of uneconomic wage increases, he forgets the very subject we are discussing. Wage increases in relation to what? I mean in relation to productivity. The price is the cost per unit and that is the combination of the labor payment as a total, including the wage increase and the number of units produced, which, in the American economy in general, has been increasing at a fairly rapid rate.

If you take the example of steel, on the basis of Secretary Mitchell's report, which was issued in the early days of the steel strike, you would see that the total employment cost—that is the total cost of wage and salaries of the production and maintenance workers represented by the union, plus all the supervisory employees, the management officials, etc.—that the employment cost per ton of steel in the first half of 1959 prior to the strike, was less than it was in 1957, despite the increases in wages. Why? Because of rapid increases in productivity. Therefore, if we are talking about costs, let us talk about the real cost, which is unit cost.

MR. HAGEDORN: May I make another comment? Mr. Goldfinger said the question is wages in relation to what, and then answered his own question by saying the right way of answering that is wages in relation to productivity. I would say no—that is the wrong way of answering it. I think perhaps the burden of my previous talk was to emphasize that fact.

The right way of answering the question is wages in relation to the thing wages are supposed to do in our economy. Wages are supposed to balance supply and demand in the labor market, or the labor markets, to be more accurate. If you are complaining that there aren't enough job opportunities around, why then it seems to me you are simply citing evidence that wages have not been at a level that would do their job properly—to balance supply and demand in those labor markets.

QUESTION: Mr. Goldfinger, you dismissed the foreign automobile competition. How about foreign competition in general, not just in the automobile industry?

MR. GOLDFINGER: I did not altogether dismiss foreign competition in autos. I said it was not a major, nor any kind of significant problem in autos.

Now, in some particular industries there is a problem of competition, but it is primarily not an issue in metal-producing industries such as steel, autos and other similar industries, despite the industry propaganda. There may be some shocked faces around here, but facts are facts. The industries that have been affected by foreign competition, in terms of prices, are such industries as textiles, or certain types of textiles, and selected other soft goods.

There have been problems of competition from Japan, problems of competition to some extent from Hong Kong and the trade union movement is seriously concerned about this.

But, mind you, we have not rushed into the protectionist area— an area which is self-defeating, not only for the trade union movement and for American industry generally, but for the country as a whole.

We are seeking ways and means of preserving a generally liberal trade policy while, at the same time, protecting the jobs and the businesses in those specific industries and specific areas that have been affected.

Now, we have come forward and supported the Trade Adjustment Act. The Trade Adjustment Act would be a program that would give government financial assistance to businesses and to workers who are directly affected by foreign competition. That would be one thing.

Another thing is that, in recent months, we have urged our State Department to raise the issue of fair labor standards in exporting countries because, to some extent, this foreign competition is based upon very low and exploited wage levels.

QUESTION: We have been talking about foreign competition, and I wonder, Mr. Hagedorn, if you couldn't sort of transpose the point you made about foreign competition being a reason for not using productivity measurements in labor negotiations, and say instead that it actually *is* a reason—for if productivity abroad is rising more rapidly than wages, and if productivity in America is rising less rapidly, then what is facing us is increased competition; and this very fact may force us to pay a great deal more attention to the relative rise of productivity and wages in the United States. Would you care to comment on that?

MR. HAGEDORN: I think, certainly, considerations of productivity help us to understand what is going on, and help us to decide on the course of action we ought to take. But to use them as a specific guide in deciding our wage settlements, I think, may be fallacious. Let me explain.

I think labor gets its share of the technological progress of the country, the increase in efficiency of the country, whether they get proportional dollar wage increases or not. We had a long period of our history, some 20 years, I think, from about 1870 to 1890, during which dollar wages stayed roughly level. Labor got its share of the productivity gains over these 20 years in the form of lower prices, as we had a continual down trend in prices during that period.

Now, I don't know whether that is the ideal solution or not, but nobody had to think about it. Nobody measured productivity in those days and decided how much to reduce prices so as to give labor its fair share. It just happened through the free operation of our markets. I think we ought to let that happen today. Let us feel the full impact of foreign competition and let it influence our price level the way it has to and then fit our wages to that sort of framework.

QUESTION: Mr. Goldfinger, government data show that average weekly earnings after deductions in the current dollars were $82 and, in 1947-1949 prices, something like $65. Now there is a spread of $17. You referred to it as imaginary inflation. If it is imaginary inflation, what has happened to the production worker's seventeen dollars?

MR. GOLDFINGER: Well, first, I didn't say imaginary inflation. I said that there has been a phony bogeyman of runaway inflation, which has been nonexistent and we have not had anything like runaway inflation. There has been a creeping rise of the price level in the past number of years.

The big increase in the price level, and the last period of sharp inflation that we have had in the United States, occurred between the middle of 1950 and the middle of 1951. It resulted from the Korean war. This was clearly a picture of classical inflation that fits all the textbook variety of shortages, speculation, anticipation of shortages, etc.

More recently, what we have had is not that kind of sharp inflation at all. We have had a slowly creeping rise of the price level. But what did the business community—at least most of the business community—and also what did the administration do about it?

The business community started to shout, and shouted even before it happened, about wage inflation. "You have to push down wages." That is fine, except that the result has been you have also pushed down the rise of consumption. The other thing that happened was that the Administration, following in the footsteps and in the ideology of the business community, immediately began to fight runaway inflation when it was nonexistent.

The Administration fought the wartime inflation and the inflation of the Korean war in the period from 1953 to 1959. How did it do this? For one thing by tight money. We have had a tight money policy consistently ever since about April of 1953. That was one of the first acts taken by the Eisenhower Administration. What is a function of a tight money policy? Essentially it is to dampen down, to depress the rise in the demand in the private economy. It is to dampen down the demand for goods and the demand for services.

The second thing it did was to follow a restrictive budget policy, so that federal government expenditures during this period have been relatively stable. The government said it had to produce surpluses or to balance the budget at all points. But what actually happened? The budget has not been balanced during most of these years, and in the fiscal year 1959 we had the largest peacetime deficit in history. Why? Because of the recession. Why also did we not achieve these budget surpluses, or balances? Because the state of economic stagnation has meant a slow growth in income, a slow growth in production and this has meant a slowdown in the rise of tax revenue.

What I am saying is that this whole myth of runaway inflation since 1953 has been a poisonous one. It has poisoned American economy and it has poisoned American society because the wrong tools were used to fight what existed.

We did not have runaway inflation. We had a creeping rise of the price level of about 1½ to 2% a year. Surely, it was a problem but it was not a major one.

The major problems that we face and that we have faced haven't been the creeping rise of the price level. They have been the problems of adequate defense, of adequate public services, the adjustments to technological change and the whole world situation with the demand for technical and economic aid from the underdeveloped countries.

What we did in terms of business policy and in terms of government policy was to suppress demand and not to meet our national needs while, at the same time, we did not hit the actual problem of creeping rise of the price level.

QUESTION: Dr. Frankel, you made the point that returns to capital have stagnated while returns to labor have increased over the long-run period. You attributed this to the large supply of capital. Could it not rather be that investors are satisfied with an adequate return, that they don't fit this image of the rational man seeking as much as he can get, but are satisfied with an adequate return of six or eight per cent?

DR. FRANKEL: I think we are not very much in disagreement. The answer to your question turns, I suppose, on what motives you ascribe to savers and investors. Over the long term, people who are investors and savers have received, roughly, a stable return on their investment commitments.

Presumably, since they made these commitments, they were satisfied with that return. Otherwise, they would have cut back, I suppose, the amount which they were willing to commit and the supply of capital would have grown more slowly. If this had happened, I think it would follow that the rate of return, instead of remaining stable over the long term, would have risen.

What is involved here, underlying the rate at which saving and investment takes place, are the terms on which savers and investors are willing to engage in their respective economic functions. I think that the sort of explanation I gave and your observation are both entirely consistent with one another, but one is at the level of motivation, if you like, and the other is pitched at a different level, or in a different direction.

QUESTION: Funds available for investment in the hands of pension trusts, insurance companies and the like have grown. Is this not indicative of an increased supply of capital or a reflection of the volume of savings available for investment?

DR. FRANKEL: To the extent that this is so, and this is the point that troubles me here, I would expect this to show in the data we have on the volume or rate of savings and investment in the economy. If your hypothesis here were correct, the data should show over the last decade that the rate of savings and investment in this country has risen.

Now, it may be that the figures are too gross; that is, insufficiently sensitive to show this movement. However, I think it can be said that the figures do not show any such rise.

What may well have happened here is not so much an increase in the volume of savings in the economy or, more accurately, rate of saving, but rather a transfer of funds from other sources or different institutional arrangements for handling the savings which the economy annually generates.

CHAIRMAN VALLEY: I would like to ask Mr. Goldfinger this question. This foreign competition is perhaps a little broader than the inroads that you mentioned in the two fields of textiles and the other fields. I refer specifically to the copper fabrication industry. Now, this competition is not from Japan. It is from England and Germany. Mills in England and Germany now can lay down copper rod in the Middle West at a price that an effectively managed company in the United States can barely meet. If a company here were to meet this price, it would make perhaps 1% on sales—which, of course, under any conception is completely inadequate.

Another round of wage increases will be forthcoming. What will the union's attitude be in this situation? Will the union member's wages be somewhat comparable to wages in other industries, or will they accept a settlement that would preserve their jobs? The companies are not going to go broke. They simply go out of those lines, which means there would be some unemployment created. Would you meet this problem by an increase in the tariff rates?

MR. GOLDFINGER: Before I answer, let me say that I would not meet it by increasing the tariff rate because, as far as I am concerned, this is a self-defeating measure. We went through this kind of thing at previous times in American history with sad results. I am no foreign trade expert and I know nothing about copper rod, but let me just make a few comments:

In the first place, there has been an increase in imports of various kinds of things. This does not come as a surprise. In fact, we should be proud that the shattered European economy has been rehabilitated to a very great extent by American economic assistance. In addition, we pushed the development of economic integration in Europe, of the Common Market, and of OEEC. These are things which we wanted and I think that, in general, they are good things.

To some extent, they are causing us problems, but they are causing a number of different problems in different specific industries. I claim that there is no general over-all problem because, on an over-all basis, our exports are still greater than our imports.

I think that the Trade Adjustment Act that I described before should be adopted. I think that the United States Government, through the ILO and through the GATT International Tariff Conferences should raise and push this idea of fair labor standards in exporting countries.

What does the local union in the copper pipe company do? I don't know the precise circumstances. There are quite a number of things they could do but let us not omit one of the problems—that is, real fat profit margins in a lot of industries and for a lot of specific products, which could be reduced. In some industries we also have to raise productivity.

CHAIRMAN VALLEY: I would just like to say this: I am the Chairman and I am not taking sides, but the plant is efficient and the profit margin is 1%, so what should the union do in the next negotiations? Should they go along with their present wages or should they cut them so that the company can compete? Or perhaps they would prefer unemployment, because you can't get these legislative acts done overnight, as we all appreciate.

Mr. GOLDFINGER: As I said, Mr. Valley, I don't know the specific circumstances. The local union and the people they call on to advise them will have to face up to the facts as they exist at the time they go into the negotiations.

QUESTION: Since we have had a political afternoon, I think it may pay us to cut through some of the smoke screen we have seen here. It seems that tariffs are to be abhorred and we are to resist them and I think the people in the trade union movement have learned that this is not a useful tack, so now they hold up the fair labor standards tack.

If you should subscribe to this, I would venture to say that to-morrow you wouldn't have any coffee in the pot, you wouldn't have any bananas for breakfast, or what have you.

This fair labor standards tack will do away with trade in the same way that any tariff law would do away with trade. You are, in effect, going to equalize working conditions, standards of living and the like, in different countries whether you use tariffs or some type of standard that you dig up. I think that the net result is the same.

Secondly, we speak at various points of administered prices. I had hoped we would include wages in those prices too, since administered prices tend to have an emotional connotation that get people aroused in thinking in terms of monopoly power and the like. In this context, it seems we are facing a situation in the nation where we see the unusual phenomenon of rising unemployment, de-creasing production and wages going up.

Mr. GOLDFINGER: The kind of suggestion that we have discussed with the people in the State Department and elsewhere does not involve doing away with trade as the questioner implied. It does not do that in any manner whatsoever.

What we have suggested is the introduction of some kind of fair labor standards applicable to the individual country in question and not the extension of our own fair labor standards act. It can be brought about practicably by using the ILO and the GATT International Tariff Conferences.

We have one example that has had some degree of success. The GATT Conference a couple of years ago brought about a gentlemen's agreement with the Japanese Government that they would establish their own fair labor standards act in order to provide some kind of floor for wages in Japan.

We are not trying to do away with trade and we are not viewing this in theoretical terms, as the questioner seems to view it. We are viewing this in terms of a practical problem that we have to face within the general context of a liberal trade policy. This is a general principle of the trade union movement.

QUESTION: I do think that Mr. Goldfinger painted with a rather broad brush when he said that about the only industry seriously affected by foreign competition was the textile industry.

It is a matter of ascertainable fact that over a period of about ten years we lost enough of the watch industry in the United States that 60% of those previously employed in watchmaking are now not working; yet the people who make watches in Switzerland are not paid a substandard wage by Swiss standards—they are among the highest paid workers in Switzerland.

It seems to me that in the first place we are refusing to face the problem, and in the second place we are pointing to a solution which is obviously one that will not solve the problem. It is not the way to approach a problem which is real.

Mr. Goldfinger remarked that, in the case of steel, competition from abroad was hardly worth talking about. But, just compare the change in the balance of trade in steel for the years 1953 to 1957 with the year 1959 and the first quarter of 1960. While part of this change may have been due to the strike, you will find that instead of being a net steel export nation, as it has been ever since the turn of the century, the United States during the past year and a quarter has been a net steel importer. The change in trade balance affects approximately 8% of steel shipments in the United States, and 8% of the steel industry employment means approximately 50,000 jobs.

It is rather shocking to hear a labor spokesman sweep under the rug something that may involve unemployment of that type.

MR. GOLDFINGER: We don't sweep it under the rug and, as I said at the outset, I am not a foreign trade expert. But when you speak of the rise in steel imports last year, part of the reason, of course, was the strike.

Another part of the reason is also obvious. We don't expect currently the same kind of steel trade balance that we experienced in the late 1940's and early 1950's and for a very simple reason. The European companies have been rehabilitated and there has been a resurgence of economic strength in those countries. This is something that the United States Government and all of us, or at least most of us, supported and this is all part of the result.

Now, when you speak of steel imports and steel exports, another thing that we would have to look into would be what types of steel have been imported to any great extent, and where has the effect of competition of imports been?

Is it not possible—I am just asking the question—is it possible that certain branches of the American steel industry are grossly inefficient?

Is it not also possible that the American steel industry has not wanted to compete, for various reasons, with the Belgians and the Germans on nails and barbed wire? These are things that have to be looked into.

What about the profit margins in the steel industry and the low break-even point of under forty per cent?

VOICE: Since you attempted to answer the question by asking questions, I think it is only fair to comment with respect to the desire to compete, that there are companies whose sole business has been in the items which have been hardest hit and which have, of course, been anxious to sell these items.

Furthermore, I am talking not about the export market, but about the home market in the United States, which has been thus affected primarily.

As to the question of profits, I can simply say this: That over the period of the past 20 years, the average profits in the steel industry have been lower than the profits in all manufacturing.

ABSORBING TECHNOLOGICAL CHANGE:
The Employment Problems Ahead

J. E. Jonsson
CHAIRMAN

1

Seymour L. Wolfbein
DEPUTY ASSISTANT SECRETARY OF LABOR
U. S. DEPARTMENT OF LABOR

Prospective Shifts in the Occupational Structure in the Next Decade

A MONTH OR SO AGO we at the Department of Labor issued a document called "Manpower Challenge of the 1960's," in which we tried to take a look ahead. Among the topics explored in this pamphlet are the changes in the occupational structure expected to take place between now and 1970. It is our finding in this particular area which I shall summarize.

That the United States has manpower resources for a much higher standard of living during the 1960's is shown in Figure 1. When we made these charts, we decided to take a look ahead on a more or less conservative basis to what our gross national product might do over the next ten years. As you might well guess, this chart gave us the most trouble. Apparently there are differences of opinion on the future rates of economic growth of the United States, especially when compared with some other countries. Nevertheless, the chart of Figure 1 indicates the basic assumptions which we used. We start off the 1960's with $500 billion of gross national product.

We made three assumptions in projecting gross national product. One, that we will not have a severe depression, although we will have the ups and downs of business cycles, as shown on the chart; we projected on the annual rate of about 3½%. Secondly, we projected with the international scene in mind—that is, we assumed

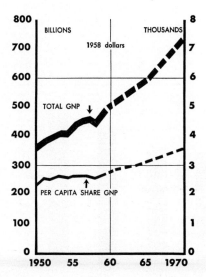

Figure 1. Gross National Product, 1950-1970, showing $500 billion GNP for 1960.

there will be no war. Thirdly, we projected a continuation of the same rate of productivity increase that prevailed in the dozen-odd years since World War II. The bottom line of this chart tells us that total GNP in constant dollars will grow from about $500 billion to $750 billion. This means a 50% increase in the aggregate over the decade. On a per capita base, the increase would be about 25%.

Population will increase by 15% over the decade, increasing from 180 million to 208 million by 1970 (Figure 2). From the year 1946 —that is, the first full peacetime year after World War II—to 1959, a dozen-odd years, 55 million babies have been born. Something like one out of every three people alive today in the United States was not born until after the end of World War II. This is a whole new world with new attitudes and new expectations. A couple of months ago I was giving a lecture on the impact of World War II which obviously was not getting across to the audience. I soon realized that those who were sitting in front of me—a graduating class of an American university—were people who were at most

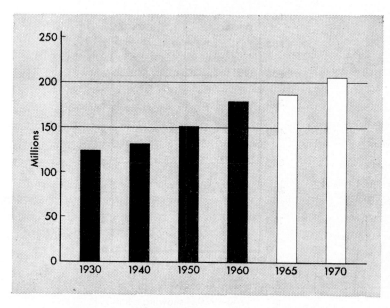

Figure 2. U.S. population growth, 1930-1970.

three to five years of age during World War II. World War II seems to them as remote as the Spanish American War seems to me. When I told them the meaningful experience of the United States during the 1930's, I found the same thing.

A lot of speeches have been made to young graduates about the world of work. A short time ago I gave a talk down at Arlington, Virginia, in a high school describing the coming world, the changes in industrial trends, and so forth. After my talk the chairman of the meeting asked if there were any questions. At first there was the usual embarrassed silence, but then five youngsters had questions. A young lady of 17 was the first to raise her hand. She wanted to know how much of a pension she could expect to receive when she retired! Needless to say it is a forward-looking generation. You might keep that in mind.

Population growth will be especially rapid among the youths reaching working age (see Figure 3). The number of people reaching 18 is close to 3 million a year now, and will rise to 3.8 million

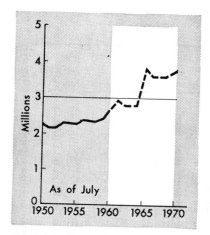

Figure 3. Young persons in U.S. reaching age 18 annually, 1950-1970.

in the year 1965. Since the average age of graduation from high school is 18, and since the average age of entry into the American labor force on the part of males in the United States is also 18, the growing number reaching this age each year has many interesting implications—whether you are considering what is going to happen to the colleges in the United States or the new entrants into the labor force.

Of course, the labor force of the United States will also go up. In the next decade, the number of workers will increase faster than the population. The work force will grow by nearly 20%. As already mentioned, population will grow about 15% over the same period. In Figure 4, which shows the labor force growth from 1930 to 1970, the 1960-1970 increase is the biggest ten-year jump in the history of the American labor force.

Young workers will account for a major share of the changes in the working population, as shown in Figure 5. There will be more workers under 25, a relatively small increase among workers 25-34, and actually fewer workers in the ages 35-44. The number of workers 45 years and over is going up. These are the older workers.

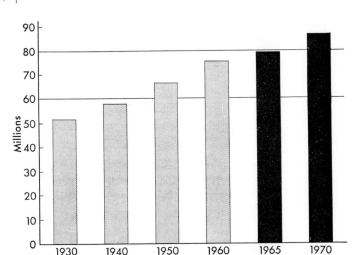

Figure 4. Growth of U.S. labor force, 1930-1970.

Once the starting age for older workers was 65 years, then it became 55 years, and now it is 45 years!

By 1970 we will have 33.4 million older workers. There will be 26 million new young workers coming into the labor force during the 1960's. That is an absolute tidal wave in sheer numbers of new labor force entrants and I suspect they are one of the major challenges of the 1960's. How we guide those people, counsel them, and recruit and train them is truly going to be one of the major problems of the 1960's.

Incidentally, the age group 35-44 is a very interesting one. It shows a decline of 200,000 men and women. In our projection we assumed that immigration will continue at the rate prevailing during the 1950's. If this assumption was not included in the projection, there would have been a decline of 1.2 million for the age group 35-44 instead of the 200,000 drop we anticipate.

Figure 6 also shows the difference in our manpower posture—1950's to the 1960's. Let's take the age group under 25. In the 1950's we were just able to squeeze out a half-million increase. Look at the story now. The number of workers under 25 is expected to

1960 (Millions)	1970 (Millions)	Numbers (Millions)	Per Cent
13.8	20.2	6.4	46
15.3	17.1	1.8	12
16.6	16.4	−.2	−1
27.9	33.4	5.5	20

Figure 5. Changes in U.S. working population, 1960-1970.

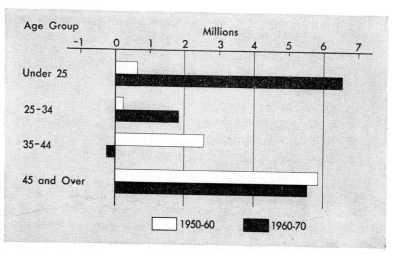

Figure 6. Changes in number of U.S. workers in each age group, 1950-1960 and 1960-1970.

increase by nearly 6½ million during the 1960's. Note the changes in the number of workers in each age group between 1950-1960 and 1960-1970. This coming decade is going to be quite different from the decade we have just finished.

A larger proportion of women, especially older women, will work. Figure 7 shows the per cent of women in each age group who will

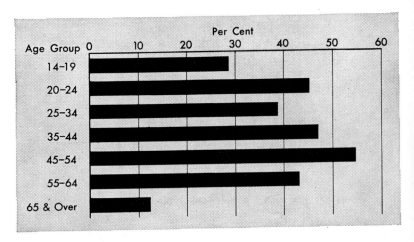

Figure 7. Percentage of women in each age group who will be in U.S. labor force in 1970.

be in the labor force in 1970. As you all know, women are a significant factor in the labor force. They outlive the men. They produced 55 million children in the past dozen years and at the same time they flooded the American labor market. Almost one out of every three workers in the United States is a woman; given the population profile just described, you don't have to be a high-class prophet to see that this ratio is on the increase.

Have we developed a pattern? The young lady gets her education and training and comes into the labor force. Then she gets married, and goes out for a while, but back she comes. So look at the projection in 1970 of the percentage of women 45 to 54 years of age in the labor force. During the first three months of this year the figure already was 51%, and our projection for 1970 of 55%

may already be too low. Apparently there is nothing in the offing which is going to change this pattern of working women.

Employment will continue to grow faster in service industries than in production. The trends in employment from 1930 to 1970 are shown in Figure 8. You have all heard by now that the United

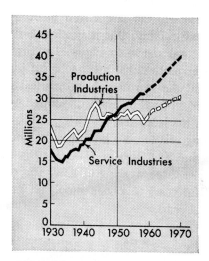

Figure 8. Trends in employment, 1930-1970.

States, for better or for worse, has more people employed in the production of services than in the production of all the goods that we make in this country.

Perhaps the major reason we can afford this kind of industrial distribution of our work force is that we have had tremendous increases in productivity, especially in the goods sectors. Agriculture is an excellent example. This is not a completely black-and-white situation, but at any rate we again see nothing in the offing, even with the technological developments we expect in the 1960's, which would reverse that trend. So we see, relatively speaking at least, a faster growth in employment for the service sector than for the goods producing sector.

The kinds of jobs industry will need workers for will continue to change (Figure 9). In the 1950's for the first time—and this has happened in an evolutionary way—there were more persons employed in white-collar occupations (clerical, managerial and sales personnel) than in blue-collar occupations (the skilled, semiskilled and unskilled). Again, so far as we can see into the future, these will be some of the overriding occupation trends.

Job opportunities will increase fastest in occupations requiring most education and training. Our projections for the Sixties on an occupational basis are shown in Figure 10. There will be a substantial increase in professional and technical jobs, in the skilled craftsman jobs and the managerial and clerical group. Note that no change is projected for the unskilled group, thus continuing their relative decline in the labor force.

There is a strong relationship between the kinds of jobs people hold and their education. Figure 11 shows the average years of school completed of those working in 1959. The clerical group, for example, shows 12.5 years of school completed and the proprietors and managers, 12.4 years.

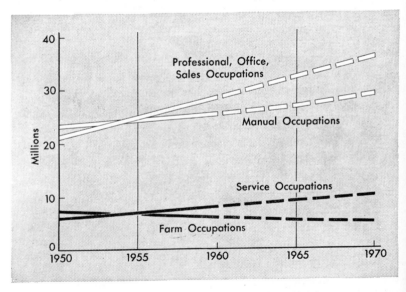

Figure 9. Employment by occupation, 1950-1970.

Millions of the new workers in the years ahead will still lack a high school education. Despite all the advances in educational attainment that we look forward to—incidentally, the Office of Education tells us we can expect roughly 50% increase in high school enrollments and a 70% increase in college enrollments—there will obviously be many without a high school diploma. (Figure 12).

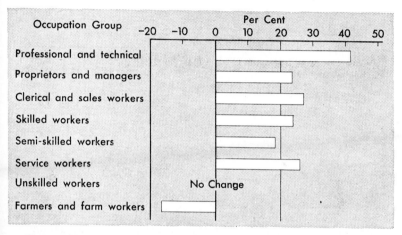

Figure 10. Percentage change in U.S. employment, 1960-1970.

People who Work in These Occupations	Have This Kind of Education:		
	Less than high school graduation, %	High school graduation, %	Some college education, %
Professional and technical workers	6	19	75
Proprietors and managers	38	33	29
Clerical or sales workers	25	53	22
Skilled workers	59	33	8
Semi-skilled workers	70	26	4
Service workers	69	25	6
Unskilled workers	80	17	3
Farmers and farm workers	76	19	5

Figure 11. Kind and amount of education young persons receive affect their lifetime careers.

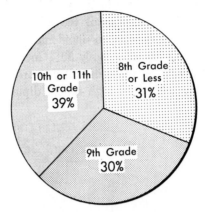

Figure 12. School grades of youth leaving before high school graduation.

We are still going to have 7.5 million of our new young workers leaving school before they get a high school diploma. These people are known by the insidious term of drop-outs.

These are our projections of drop-outs for 1970. The actual figures are higher for 1950 and still higher for 1960. We are projecting a declining drop-out rate and an increase in educational attainment. We have just finished making a study of what happened to about 12,000 of these folks in the four or five years after they dropped out of school. Four of them had incomes of $1 million or more a year! This underscores the point that the relationship between education and earning power is not absolutely rigid. But the prognosis is rather negative because the drop-outs do tend to get jobs in the unskilled sector of the American economy. In the sector of drop-outs, the girls do better than the boys.

Finally, let me mention a few of the problems that stem from this type of labor supply and demand. There obviously is going to be a major problem in terms of the positions suitable for young people.

I think from a management point of view there is something that can be done about it. There will be a shortage in the central age groups. This points up the fact that the older worker, for better or for worse, is going to be an increasingly important manpower resource. True, when both a young lady of 26 and a lady of 52 come to an office for an interview for a job as secretary, for some reason or other, the 26-year-old always gets the job. But, believe me, after a while it is the 50-year-old that you are going to be fighting for. Similarly, I think a great deal can be done to meet our manpower requirements by more and better on-the-job training of our young workers.

DISCUSSION

MR. DRUCKER: I have a statistical question for Mr. Wolfbein. If you take the number of new entrants into the labor force each year and deduct from them the number of people who reach 65, my impression is that the number left, the net new jobs, isn't very much larger than it was in the 1940's and 1950's.

MR. WOLFBEIN: There are two comments on that. First, you will find that in this decade the withdrawals from the labor force are hardly the same as the number of new young workers.

MR. DRUCKER: Not the same, but if you can deduct the people who reach 65 from the new ones, don't you come out with a total of new entrants that isn't very much higher than it was in the 1940's?

MR. WOLFBEIN: I am sorry I have to remind myself about the 1940's. I think you will find it different from the 1950's, but the other comment is this. I think we have agreed that the problem isn't a statistical one but from what type of job the worker of 65 retires. It isn't necessarily the type a young person of 21 is trying for.

2

Solomon Barkin

DIRECTOR OF RESEARCH
TEXTILE WORKERS UNION OF AMERICA, AFL-CIO

The Changing Workforce: Labor's Problems

THE PURPOSE of looking ahead is to define the broad outlines of the future to be better prepared for what is ahead. One conclusion which our current insight suggests is that we shall face far-reaching occupational, industrial, and geographical changes in the nature and location of jobs. Another is that the job seekers will be concentrated more nearly than ever before among the younger and older-age groups; and vast numbers of nonwhites and women will become part of the active labor force.

The very practice of projection is founded on a great confidence in our creative potential to bring new employments into being. The arts of expanding production have been mastered. But we still have to prove our ability to create a sufficiency of jobs for the employable and to adjust successfully to the ever-changing nature of the employments.

Will we be able to design jobs to fit the new workforce? Will we help individuals, industries and communities adapt themselves to the rush of change, or will we sit by complacently as the tribulations, sacrifices and failures in adjustment bring ever-increasing human and social wreckage? Will we strain the patience and tolerance of the American people to a high rate of economic change by maintaining a large volume of unemployment?

American society has hitherto inspired confidence in the beneficence of our economy. The wide distribution of its benefits and the ready availability of new jobs to replace older ones has served to support the constructive image. But we have experienced periods of high unemployment when the human scrap heap of the old and the minority groups grow higher and higher, and the protests mounted louder and louder, demanding more and more restraints on economic change. The determination of the prevailing attitudes to economic innovation will depend upon our success in providing employment opportunities and facilitating the adjustments of people to the new circumstances.

Our economic society will determine the general mood, whether it will favor or resist change. What lies ahead of us may be an age of intense social conflict designed to enforce security and determine the division of the meager fruits of industry or an age of easy adjustment, with all groups fully enjoying employment and some of the abundance of a highly productive economy.

The answer will be spelled out primarily in terms of the level of unemployment in our nation and the degree to which we provide individuals, industries, and communities dislocated by economic change with technical advice and counsel, financial aids, and incentives to accelerate their individual adjustment by redevelopment, rehabilitation, retraining, and relocation.

This is the story of the older worker, the older community, the older areas of our country. We have to concern ourselves with these problems in the future. It is the burden of my remarks that we are learning a new method of economic growth in this world. It is our responsibility in this country to develop the intellectual meaning of this growth, and the tools for achieving it. And we can achieve it by taking the older man, the old capital, the older community, and adapting them to the new trends.

This procedure, I believe, is more economic and cheaper in the long run than one that tries to build wholly new cultures—scrapping older people and older communities. Redevelopment will be proven to be the most economic course.

The projected shifts in the jobs in our society spell out the magnitude of the changes. The work force in agriculture will be squeezed out still further. By 1975, 1½ million fewer people will be employed on the farm. As these breadwinners seek other employments, millions more will have to move off the farm. Mining and manufacturing and transportation employment will lag in their rate of growth. Some segments within the industrial group will actually contract.

Even within the groups with high growth rates, enjoying more than average rates of expansion, individual industries will shrink or be stable. Within all industries, some plants will be liquidated and others will move from one area to another.

These industrial currents will force large numbers of people out of established employments. Labor turnover will not be sufficient in many places to take care of the contraction. People will have to change their jobs, and the transformation of the industrial complex of our economy will also alter the occupational patterns. Some established types of jobs will dwindle in importance; new ones will gain prominence.

The manual worker, both on the farm and in industry is likely to have relatively few opportunities. In fact, the number of farm jobs and industrial laborers will be reduced, despite the population growth.

The relative proportion of factory operatives will decline and that of the skilled workers will remain about stationary. Their futures will, therefore, be more constricted. The occupational growth areas will occur primarily in the professions and technical employments. Our scientific age is producing an impressive new fount of jobs. The use of new technical information requires the hiring of more technicians and professionals competent to deal with and apply the current information as well as to help us extend our own frontiers of knowledge.

The nature of management is itself changing under the impact of the new tools of automation, including both the servomechanisms and electronic computers as well as the more sophisticated tools of analysis introduced by operations research. The enterprise is being integrated, telescoping operations and bringing the executive management directly in contact with the operating units.

The new era of automation is routinizing many clerical, technical and professional jobs in the same manner in which the industrial revolution converted the manual worker into a machine tender.

Whether this summary of the nature of automation and its implications is correct can be tested by the new IBM (Stretch) computer. This is an interesting first major advance in computer technology which shows the possibilities and the practical opportunities for doing that which is implicit in that technology—namely, eliminating the middle management group and concentrating management controls increasingly in the hands of the executive office. This raises very serious questions about the accuracy of the projections by occupations. In the 1960's we are going to see a tremendous revolution in the nature of managerial activity.

In the recasting of the curriculum of our business schools, one of the great drives is to eliminate the specialist, the marketing expert and experts in all fields. This is the drive in business, which is being reflected in the shaping of the curriculum; it is creating a situation wherein the academicians are beginning to call for generalists. Preference now is not for the man who knows a specific area but for the man who has sophisticated insights about the business process and some knowledge of the tools of business decision making. This is implicit in the new technology being provided in business.

Economic change will mean that more and more people will have to be trained for these employments demanding advanced schooling. American industry has depended and will continue to depend on the young to fill these jobs, as witness the annual rush to the universities to recruit its new executives and management elite. But it cannot afford to be indifferent to the mass of older people it leaves behind. There must be jobs for them.

They, too, will have to be trained and retrained to keep abreast and to fit into the developing new employment patterns. Even the young will have to be re-educated for the rate of technical obsolescence is very great. Adult education will become a commonplace, and continuous lifetime schooling will have to be an accepted practice for all.

Private industry has undertaken some responsibilities in these areas, but to allow the broad mass of employees to enjoy the opportunities necessary for adjustment, these schooling facilities will have to be opened to others. We need public educational agencies for adults who want to keep ahead or fit into new areas of expansion. Already we have witnessed shortages of people for the growth occupations because we lack facilities for upgrading and retraining and the finances to support people in this adjustment. The displaced necessarily flounder in their search for self-supporting employments.

With established occupations stagnant or contracting, they must seek new ones. But these are limited, despite the abundance of jobs at the higher level. Many are forced back into the undifferentiated and expanding service trades with their low wages and poor working standards. All estimates point to the relative and absolute growth in these already overcrowded areas. These low wages are holding back increases in productivity in the personal service industries in our country. They have become the refuge of the displaced, the manual workers, the minorities to whom doors are closed by discrimination, and of the older people whose gray hairs stop them at the threshold of the employment offices.

These are the people who are becoming economically disfranchised, and the source of the new wave of social unrest of the future. In most of the projections of the future this problem of the great numbers of people in the personal service industries is completely neglected. I am highlighting it here to provide some insight as to what my concern is for this grave social problem.

This is the area of employment in which unionism is expanding at the present time. These people have been taught that they have rights, that they are entitled to economic opportunity, and that they should be self-supporting. Most of them have, in fact, had productive jobs and advanced skills and capacities. But they will be destined for the scrap heap if society remains indifferent to their needs for assistance to help them adjust and retrain for the new jobs. They will stand as an eloquent challenge to the complacency of the next decade.

Industrial change will accentuate geographical shifts. Newer industries are likely to seek newer locations. Population centers will move. New local industries will sprout in these areas as similar ones close or stagnate in older areas. The industrial crescent extending from the State of Washington on the West Coast running down the Pacific and along the Gulf and to Florida continues to expand, but the Northeast and even some of the Middle Western states may well be lagging behind if not contracting economically.

These declining communities, and states and regions represent colossal personal, commercial, industrial and public investments. They reflect large accumulations of capital, private and public. They cannot be abandoned. People, moreover, won't leave them. They are reservoirs of great human achievement ready to be redeveloped and modernized into new thriving economic areas. They are likely to become new centers in the future.

As with individuals, the question will primarily be whether the process of economic renewal is to be accelerated, or is it to be permitted to languish and flow along at an accidental rate which will destroy human enterprise, repress hopes and wreck past contributions. Will we start the process of economic rebuilding before decay sets in?

Our nation has shown its faith in governmental intervention to promote economic growth in other countries. We have extended aid to ravaged countries to help them rebuild, and we have achieved significant results. We are assisting developing countries in creating their new economies. We know that technical and financial aid can build up the human and capital resources and accelerate the rate of economic recovery in other countries. Yet we have shown only the most preliminary signs of accepting and applying the same principles to our own country.

Aid for area redevelopment of depressed urban communities and regions or underdeveloped rural areas in this country warrants the same attention and support as we have extended to other countries. It is necessary to transfer the chapters on international economics we have written in our foreign aid programs to our book on domestic economic policy for our own plans of growth.

The same help can equally be applicable to many of our "sick" industries. Redevelopment, I believe, is the key to our economic future. Industrial research has shown that the declining economic fortunes of a number of industries have been reversed by the persistent study of their resources, advantages of their products, or processes, and the potentialities of their manpower, both managerial and productive. The declining paper industry of the 1920's has been converted into a growth industry. The "sick" coal industry promises in the future to be a prosperous one. Even the ancient textile industry, with which I am associated, is on the threshold of a renaissance as new individual uses are being developed by enterprising investigators, adventurous practitioners and inquisitive researchers in the consuming markets.

The great changes in our workforce and industrial structure are disarranging the established patterns of jobs, industries and communities. The world is undergoing vast changes. The people, jobs and places will be different. The great challenge is whether we shall aid people, industries and communities to adjust; whether the processes of adaptation will be accelerated to give courage and incentive to advance and to utilize the full potential of human beings; or whether the ancient shibboleths of the virtues of individual self-reliance shall blind us to the realities and inhibit action.

Shall we enter upon an age of smooth change with adequate programs and facilities for adjustment, redevelopment, renewal, rehabilitation, retraining and relocation for effective participation in a more productive and expanding full-employment economy, or shall we sit by, hoping that individuals, industries and communities will find their own salvation as best they can in this highly complicated and advanced technical society—praying that the human cost and the capital loss and social waste are not prodigious or fatal in our contest with Communism?

The trade unionist's position is clear. He will choose and strongly support the positive program of action designed to assist individuals, industries and communities to accelerate their adjustment, so that they can ride through these waves of change smoothly, confidently and enthusiastically—and thereby participate in an efficient, economic and beneficent society which utilizes its resources and distributes broadly the benefits of high productivity.

Such a program will accelerate and make more confident private decisions and action for growth rather than impose external decisions upon the displaced persons or declining or stagnant areas and industries.

Some elements of the program can be implemented within the plant and company through devices initiated by management or negotiated in collective bargaining. But the greatest number of new techniques or provisions and the needs of the greatest number of people, industries and communities will have to be met through public governmental programs.

Discussion

Question: Mr. Barkin mentions the need for education of the individual because of the changes that are coming. Then he mentions the need of additional schooling facilities for training these people, to give them new skills in this changing world. Do the trade unions have some sort of a program for taking on the responsibility to do this or shall we expect management to do this?

Mr. Barkin: I would say that trade unions plan to make contributions in this field, but their contributions are very modest and limited at the present time. As a broad generalization, I would say that the major contributions have been made by older craft unions.

The most significant efforts—and they are all modest—are in the plumbers' and electrical unions. The major interest of the union movement throughout the country has been in promoting the development of adequate vocational educational systems maintained and financed by the public school systems rather than their own facilities.

The two unions I have just referred to use university facilities, largely employing university professors and local community rather than their own resources, for upgrading their own constituency and membership. One of the most interesting projects is that of the Electrical Workers Local No. 3 in New York. They have not only undertaken this job for their own members but also for foremen and superintendents in this field. That program is an extraordinarily ambitious one but it is not typical.

QUESTION: I was very glad to hear the chairman say something nice about the computer industry. I happen to work for the company which manufactures the Stretch computer. Furthermore, I worked in the operations research of the research division of that company. I can't resist challenging your statement that the Stretch computer or other computers are eliminating jobs in middle management, or eliminating middle management.

I assume your authority for this statement is a recent article by Leavitt and Whisler in the *Harvard Business Review* which is entitled "Management in the 1980's." * They had a similar view. These are operations-research people also, and I thoroughly respect the work that they have done. However, I would remind you that in that article they admit that their view is more in the nature of an extrapolation than a derivation. In our company, one of our colleagues made a survey of the management areas and came up with 328 different types of decisions in the management areas. It is very difficult for us to figure out how these can be automated. This illustrates the difference in results when you use the process of derivation rather than extrapolation.

Furthermore, I would say extrapolation of past trends in the operation research or management science area is very dangerous. It is very logical for scientists to work on the easiest problem first, the ones where they can make the most rapid advances. The hardest problems have been left undone. It is highly questionable whether the really difficult problems can be so completely solved by computer procedures so as to eliminate management.

MR. BARKIN: The problem you raise obviously gets at this question of what is decision-making and the degree to which it can be done by machines. We already have seen very distinctive changes in the performance of management and the elimination of many middle-management and low-management decision-making responsibilities.

* Op. cit., Nov.-Dec., 1958, pp. 41-48.

Let's take the problem of concentration of decision-making in companies. One case I have in mind concerns a company with ten plants. They have the task of deciding how long they will run particular machines, where the materials are to be shipped, and how much inventories to be accumulated in a particular plant. All these important decisions formerly made at the local level are now located at the central level. The resolution of these particular problems has been transferred to what we might call upper middle management —the executive office of the central organization, depriving local areas of these decisions. While there are decisions still to be made, the facility of transferring them from a local level to a central level has been greatly accelerated. We see this happening right now and the presumption is that this trend will continue during the 1960's.

3

Peter F. Drucker
MANAGEMENT CONSULTANT

The Changing Workforce: Management's Problems

I AM GOING TO LOOK at the manpower projections, trends, problems and opportunities for the 1960's with this question in mind: What can a business do about them?

I want to start out with the remark that Mr. Jonsson made this morning. He said that in looking at long-range planning—I will paraphrase—one of the things that surprised him was how few companies put "thinking about people" into their planning. This is a very cogent remark, because in those enterprises I have been connected with the planners tend to forget that work is done by people, and that it is not done in the abstract; that people are the central resource and the slowest-growing one, and take the longest to prepare for anything.

Yet it is the one area where we can really do more than try to anticipate, the one area where we can shoot in on the main targets. We don't have to guess about the size of the labor force in the next 20 years. We know the maximum number of available workers and what they will be, if there is no radical shift in immigration policy. We know they are likely to continue to be of two sexes. We know a good many things about them. But we don't know other things.

Our failure to start out with those things we know in our long-range planning which is labor-force structure is an example of our blindness, of our great tendency to do almost everything we can to

376

look for the more difficult way (which we then call industrial engineering) instead of asking: Isn't there a lazy man's way of doing it?

I would like simply to set down some conclusions on major questions that are a primary concern to a business.

The first one is that our problem is not one of numbers. It is one of shifts in composition. Looking ten years ahead, we are very likely to see a labor force that is composed predominantly of young men of high school education or better. In this labor force, however, there will be many older women of very low schooling—the schooling of an earlier generation. Furthermore, most of them will have been out of the labor force, that is at home, in those years when most of us were learning the little we know, from 25 to 40. This will result in a very curious labor force. Within this group of older women there will be large minority groups, whereas the younger men of higher education will be predominantly in metropolitan areas and will be white. I am not very happy about this, but it is too late now to change it for the next 15 years.

Another shift which I think is very important is the generation jump to which Mr. Wolfbein referred, and which I think he understated. While today, one out of three in the American population was born after World War II, they are not in the labor force. By 1970, one out of two in the American population will have been born after the end of World War II and most of them will be in the labor force.

The workforce of 1970 will be very different in experience from the workforce of today. They will have grown up at the latest jump which makes our figures much more important. It frequently makes the things we have said meaningless and causes that glazed-eye look in an audience.

This situation is not confined to the United States. The Soviet Union faces an even greater jump, though theirs will come perhaps five years later than ours. And the situation prevails in the entire Western European area. You will see in every place that leadership is moving from men, who, like Dwight Eisenhower, are essentially pre-World War I in their formative experience, to men who, like President Kennedy, are, at earliest, World War II.

The new leadership will come from people who take educational opportunities for granted. It will come from people who are oriented to using their minds rather than their hands. These are people who have been indoctrinated into long-range planning and who, therefore ask, "What will I get when I retire?" We have told them to look ahead and for once they have learned something, but now we don't like it, of course. Let's not thrust upon these people of the future the education, training and tradition of the past.

The next thing I would like to mention is that increasingly our economy will depend on the knowledge worker. We have heard a discussion of the disappearance of middle management. What is really happening is not that there are fewer people. What is happening, if anything, is that the title is changing. If you think you are getting fewer people by the installation of computers, I am afraid you are going to be sadly disillusioned—because you are probably going to have more people. We have learned the one lesson that the ability to do more, creates jobs. It has never in history done anything else.

True, it changes jobs, but it also creates jobs. The more we can do the more we try to do. That is what accounts for a tremendous increase in employment.

We no longer have plant managers. They are now called senior programming engineers, a distinction probably exceedingly important to the wage and salary administration (but that is about all). If you look at them closely you will find they are one of the big cost items in our labor force, even though they are not the biggest in numbers. However, I am afraid the conclusion is that we don't know how to make the process work. That is important.

We have had this fabulous increase in numbers unmatched with an increase in the rate of productivity. The only conclusion one can draw, is that we don't yet know how to make the "knowledge worker" really productive—with one very important qualification. The qualification is productivity in agriculture, which has shot up like a rocket as the result of 40 years of work. There is a possibility, therefore, that the knowledge worker is more productive than ever, but that the gestation period is longer.

Here is our great challenge. How do you make these knowledge workers really contribute? The very fact that the knowledge worker used to account for one per cent of the workforce 50 years ago and now for 50% means that the old way of using them must be wrong.

Today we have the job of thinking through what are the really important contributions to be made by the knowledge worker, to concentrate on them, to set priorities and not squander our brain-power. Doing just a little more efficiently the jobs that should not be done at all is what is usually achieved with most of these methods. But the really good methods man says, "Do we have to do this nonsense?"

Let's be conscious of the fact that here is a tremendous opportunity of thinking through how to make our productive resources count. For the first time we have a supply of people who at least, by formal schooling, should be capable of doing knowledge work. We are obviously not using them. We are frittering them away in large quantities.

We think that by hiring bodies we get minds. I am afraid that you will get minds only by challenge, not merely by having them around. They require tremendous demands to be productive at all. The threshold of productivity for mind work is very high—the opposite of unskilled labor.

The next thing is the skilled worker. Here is the one area where I would advise a client, "Don't trust Wolfbein's figures because it only seems that way." He is projecting the skilled workers we should have. But here the educational revolution is really having an impact. Not so many years ago the bright boy went into an apprentice training; today that same boy goes to a university and four years later comes out a cost accountant and never does an honest day's work again in his life.

The people who went into apprentice training, our skilled craftsmen, are the oldest group. The figures obscure this, as Mr. Wolfbein has warned you. I am not quarreling with him by describing these classifications as very dubious. I am merely pointing out that they are classifications for what the man should be, not for what he is. These should be all the skilled workers, but they won't be. Our skilled people are the oldest group in our labor group, next to the union leaders, and they are not being replenished.

What is most important is that the concept of skill is changing. It does not take much imagination for me to say that ten years from now the bulk of commercial printing, including book printing (but not newspapers) will be done not by the time-honored method of mechanically putting ink on paper, but by the utilization of photoelectronics. This also requires skill, but it does not require any of the traditional printing-trade skills.

The definition of the skilled man tomorrow is not the man who has learned an old trade but the man who knows how to learn a new one. I doubt whether we can produce the generalists in education Mr. Barkin talked about much under the age of 40. I think when a man reaches 40 he looks at what he has been doing and asks himself if it makes any sense. Then he is ripe to become a generalist in education. But we also urgently need people who are generalists in skill.

One thing is certain: these changes spell trouble with the skilled-labor unions. Such unions are all obsolete. They are all deeply entrenched, conservative, proud and highly respected. And they are all dedicated to the maintenance of a craft as an island unto itself. They are going to be the real storm center of our labor relations—not because they are naughty boys, but because they can't help it.

The concept on which we have built these unions is under atack. It is not the skills that are under attack but the concept of skill as something you have learned as an exclusive area of application with a monopoly on certain tools. This is simply obsolete, even though we cannot yet define the new skilled man.

Incidentally, another problem will concern all of us and that is the problem concerning the only untapped reservoir of skilled labor —the nonwhite minority. Here you have people who have the skill and the ability but who are denied, by and large, the educational opportunities that are given to the white boy with the same characteristics. Here you have a group to whom skill is still a major opportunity and a major avenue of escape and a major avenue of becoming a full citizen.

This, whether you like it or not, will push you into tapping this reservoir. (I hope you will go a little faster than you will get pushed.) This, too, will get you into real trouble with your craft unions. For you find segregationists not only in the governors' mansions of southern states, but above all in craft unions. They are citadels of white supremacy.

I talked about the generation jump, the knowledge worker, the skilled worker. I should add something that is implicit in all of this, and that is the fragmentation of our labor force. The use of broad occupational categories is not particularly helpful in analyzing adjustments to change.

You cannot take a meteorologist and make a sales forecaster out of him. You cannot take a chemist who works on the processing of petrochemical compounds and put him in a fermentation plant. Both are highly educated men but not transferrable from one kind of job to another. Yet they have geographic mobility of a kind that the traditional worker never had past the age of 30 or 35. (Even in our mobile society, older workers cease to have geographic mobility.)

This is particularly important for employee communications. I am appalled at the people who employ as many as 2,500 engineers and yet send out an annual report to their employees written by accountants for accountants.

Let me now talk about two big things outside of business that will affect people. We are going to have very serious trouble as managers, because of the hollowness and weakness of the trade unions, and especially because of the lack of successors to today's leaders. This is largely a result of the educational revolution.

Many years ago one of my friends, president of a large automobile company, said, "If Walter Reuther had been born ten years sooner, he would today be president of General Motors instead of Charlie Wilson; and if he had been born ten years later, he would succeed Wilson as the next president of General Motors. He was born just at the time when the ladder of opportunities out of the shop closed, and the ladder of educational opportunities wasn't open yet."

I don't know whether this is true of Walter Reuther. The ability is there, but whether this would have satisfied him, I do not know. However, the comment is very pertinent. What you have in tomorrow's union is not the people who went into union leadership because they have the ambition, the ability, the drive, but no other opportunities. We have people who go in there because they have neither the ability nor the ambition nor the drive to go after other opportunities. And on top of that they don't really believe in unionism any more. It isn't a cause anymore. It is just a job.

But weak union leaders are the worst kind of troublemakers, as some of us have found out. This is partly because they cannot enforce the contract, and partly because they can see only what is in front of them and not beyond the next move.

The leadership crisis coincides with real crisis in the union movement. The big industrial unions are shrinking because the new job opportunities do not involve mass production workers. I am not saying these newer jobs could not be unionized; I am saying only that they cannot be unionized by way of the UAW, the Steelworkers, the Rubber Workers. These new employee groups, as any white-collar, technical union in any country has shown, have to be organized on the basis of differentiation. For the industrial unions, this violates all their basic concepts, which are concepts of equality.

At the same time, and for the first time in our history, we face the possibility of government regulation both of labor relations and prices. This is very real because we have a new factor in our situation. For the first time in a hundred years the international economy is relevant to our survival. Our competitive strength in the markets of the free world is very precarious, not because of the Russians, but because of the performance and growth of the free world around us.

What does this mean for planning? To be specific here I would have to know your company and its goals. All I can tell you is that if you do not plan a personnel and labor policy, taking advantage of these shifts, you will maximize the dangers and miss out on the opportunities. If you do not think through these things you might as well forget your long-range planning. You are going to be so busy fighting the fires you have started yourself that everybody is going to rush around with fire extinguishers and nobody is going to make the future.

It is, therefore, our job in management to work today on tomorrow's manpower and labor policy. Which of these developments are going to effect us? Which are opportunities and which are threats?

And it is our job today to make the systematic organized efforts in personnel and industrial relations to give us the labor force we need tomorrow.

4

Discussion

QUESTION: One thing in Mr. Drucker's talk impressed me very much. He said "pro-labor" or "pro-management" makes no sense to the new generation. What, then, is the key for us to go by? What does make sense?

MR. DRUCKER: I wish I could tell you. All I can say is whenever you get to any college campus the younger people are profoundly disinterested in this. It just makes no sense for them. Perhaps we have been guilty of trying to teach them that one uses occasionally a little thinking and they have learned to listen and look at our labor relations and say, "Why don't you use it there?"

I think what makes sense to them is a policy that has a focus on results, that has a goal, that has an objective and an international interest and not a partisan interest and that they don't get excited about these other things.

MR. BARKIN: Mr. Drucker's statement highlights the fact that our American school system, American newspapers, public relations people and others, have failed, and unions also have failed, to convey to the American people an understanding of our society and of the nature of the contests of economic interest which constantly exist.

MR. DRUCKER: That's right.

Part Four

FINANCING NATIONAL GROWTH

CONSUMER FINANCE IN THE 1960'S

L. W. Lundell
CHAIRMAN

1

L. W. Lundell

PRESIDENT
C.I.T. FINANCIAL CORPORATION

Introduction

ECONOMIC GROWTH depends upon the appropriate mix and instruments of finance. Intertwined with the private financial potential are governmental and central bank policies which can either promote or hinder proper financial development. Generally speaking, the papers that follow conclude that further gains are in store for the American economy over the coming decade. While their overall view does not indicate further acceleration, the decreased likelihood of depression or inflationary pressures could result in sustainable growth and pave the way to new highs of prosperity.

Among the factors responsible for growth in the use of consumer credit have been increases in the margin of income over the amounts required for the basic budgetary items, wider acceptance of the use of consumer credit by an ever larger group of families, early marriages without a substantial cash nest egg, growing regularity of consumer incomes, and expansion in the supply of consumer credit. For these and other reasons, consumer installment credit could well increase by 60% over the coming decade, with little or no change in the 13% ratio between installment debt to disposable consumer incomes which has been maintained in recent years. Playing an important part in the growth of consumer credit will be the expansion of new types of consumer credit, such as financing vacation travel and educational needs, as well as new methods, including credit cards, check credit, and revolving credit.

Mortgage credit, on the other hand, is expected to double over the decade of the 1960's, greater than the expected rise either in installment debt or consumer incomes. Nevertheless, this 100% gain represents a slower rate of growth than the surge in past postwar years, when it took only five to six years to double the volume of mortgage debt outstanding. The mortgage market may be expected to retain and perhaps even further enhance its position relative to others. In most years of the past decade, more money went into mortgages than into long-term corporate securities.

The growth over the past 15 years in housing and the accompanying mortgage debt was due to an important extent to federal government intervention. The effect of the use of government programs to sustain a given level of construction was to shift decision-making from persons motivated principally by consideration of costs and prices to the legislator. To the extent that this continues it may be increasingly difficult to project market behavior on the basis of usual market forces.

On the business side of financing, retained earnings can be expected to grow as fast as after-tax profits; the growth of depreciation allowances may be slowed. In contrast, the capacity for short-term borrowing over the coming decade has been increased considerably, and long-term borrowing potentials are also higher. Further, financial officers could draw more heavily on the equity markets if desired.

In the 1950's, business finance was aided by a great expansion of bank loans made possible because banks were willing to sell a part of their securities and use these funds in addition to new deposits for the purpose of making loans. The coming increase of bank loans should fall more closely in line with the over-all rise in economic activity, as a further gain in the loan deposit ratio will necessarily have to be much more modest than in the past decade. Banks will exercise greater selectivity in lending, and the trend toward term loans may be eased by shortening the length of the term portfolio and by a somewhat higher proportion of short-term credit.

Life insurance companies, too, will continue to play a major role in financing American business; in the past they have been the largest single source of long-term funds. Nevertheless, the rate of increase in savings through life insurance has steadily declined over the past 15 years. Life insurance savings have also lost ground to other institutions and their relative strength among financial intermediaries was halved within a decade. Still, the gross volume of funds from insurance companies available during the 1960's may be 50% greater than over the previous decade. Thus the decline relative to other financial intermediaries would not be as fast as in the 1950's.

The contribution of business finance in enabling national growth would not be complete without an analysis of the stock market. A great new surge of stock prices in the 1960's is deemed unlikely. However, the fact that readjustments will not be accompanied by depression may contribute toward a 50% increase in stock prices and earnings—a modest gain relative to the advance of the past decade. This expected slower gain suggests heightened investment competition in the coming years.

The analyses of financing national growth are considered in terms of broad monetary and fiscal policies, the strength of the dollar abroad and the adequacy of national saving. Thus, the increase of total new credit in the 1960's is anticipated by one participant to be proportionately smaller than the gain in the gross national product, so that total new credits will impose less severe pressures upon the supply of funds. If credit demand proves less strong, money supply could grow more in step with growth in the GNP than it did in the 1950's. As a result, interest rates could be lower in the coming decade than, say, in 1959, though there was some measure of disagreement among the panel on this crucial point.

Federal government expenditures over the next ten years could possibly increase at a slower rate than the GNP, provided that defense outlays can be kept at a reasonable level. However, continuing deficits are likely on the state and local level because of increasing pressures for additional expenditures.

The competitive superiority of the United States in relation to the rest of the world is not as strong as it was ten years ago and the maintenance of a comfortable gold reserve thus becomes more important. Since it does not appear likely that foreign nations will incur deficits with the United States as in earlier postwar years, gold and dollars acquired by them in recent years would continue to remain outside this country. Thus more restraint will be needed in implementing countercyclical government action. The maintenance of a stable dollar should also be promoted by adequate savings in the 1960's. National savings in the coming decade are expected to bear the same relation to total output as in the 1950's and other periods of normal activity. It would be very difficult to change this relation.

That consumer finance should command equal time and emphasis with monetary policy and industrial financing as the triumvirate of forces which will determine the course of economic growth in the next decade is certainly indicative that consumer finance has come of age and has gained recognition as one of the prime movers of our consumer-oriented economy. Perhaps we should stop and remind ourselves that this was not always so. Certainly, we can be reasonably sure that those attending the first annual meeting of The Conference Board some 44 years ago, in 1916, would have thought it an astounding thing to rate the influence of Mr. Consumer's use of his personal credit on a par with the employment of credit in business and the administration of the Federal Government's monetary and credit policies. Fifty years or so ago it was the general attitude of businessmen that consumers should pay cash for what they wanted to buy or they should go without. Today, however, we realize that the consumer's buying power, as expressed through his use of credit, is a force that sustains great industries, gives employment to millions and can make the difference between national economic growth and a thoroughgoing economic recession.

I doubt that there is any better manager of his credit than the typical American consumer. His record for responsibility, integrity and a shrewd appraisal of his ability to handle his financial obligations sets a standard that many respected and ostensibly hardheaded businessmen do not equal.

Of course, the present stature of consumer credit was not easily earned. In each of the past four decades, it was severely tested at least once. In the late 1920's, there came the test when there was a collapse of security and equity values. Then, of course, in the 1930's consumer credit was tested by a prolonged depression. The 1940's brought war, which virtually suspended the use of credit for the purchase of nonexistent durables in the first half of that decade. Then in the second half came the postwar adjustment period. In the 1950's, particularly 1955 and 1956, we experienced a tremendous expansion in the use of consumer credit, along with an easing of credit terms. This, in turn, brought a new round of problems.

Now we are on the threshold of the 1960's, with all of its promise and all of its potential. What will these years bring? It is certainly safe to say that they will bring continuing growth along with new challenges and tests. Forecasts tell us that by 1970 this nation will have 33 million more citizens, 14 million more wage earners, 10 million more households, and an aggregate 50% increase in personal incomes. What this will all mean to consumer credit as an institution so intimately related to population, paychecks, homes, and consumer incomes, is an interesting question. That is the challenging assignment facing our first speaker.

Ernst A. Dauer

DIRECTOR OF CONSUMER CREDIT STUDIES
HOUSEHOLD FINANCE CORPORATION

2

How Much More Installment Credit?

IN RECENT MONTHS there has been a great deal of attention devoted to consumer credit. There have been comprehensive articles in monthly reports of a number of the Federal Reserve Banks and other financial journals, and less comprehensive comments in newspaper columns. This isn't unusual since the increase in consumer installment debt during 1959 of $5.4 billion was the largest dollar increase on record. At the end of the year consumer installment debt amounted to $39.5 billion, as compared with $2.5 billion at the end of World War II.

The last previous occasion on which we had a similar rash of articles and comments was in late 1955 and early 1956. The widespread interest then was the result of the sharp rise in debt of almost $5.4 billion, amounting to a 23% rise in a single year. It is not surprising, both now and in 1955, that people should ask whether consumer debt was increasing too rapidly for the good of the economy and whether consumers were being unduly burdened with debt.

There have been in the recent period relatively few professional viewers-with-alarm who have expressed concern solely on the grounds of dollar amounts outstanding or changes in dollar volume. Almost everyone recognizes that dollar aggregates have been reaching new highs year after year in all areas of the American economy.

Practically all the recent studies have attempted a careful appraisal in the light of all relevant factors.

One of the most common measures used has been to relate repayments of installment debt to consumer income after taxes (i.e., disposable personal income). Since the middle of 1956 that ratio has been hovering in the neighborhood of 13%, having reached a peak somewhat above that level late in 1957, and being in the process of reapproaching it at the present time.

It would be easy to conclude that, since that ratio reached a peak in 1957 without dire results, a ratio of this magnitude is not burdensome. By implication, it would be just as easy to conclude that any figure in excess of the previous peak should be a subject of some concern. Unfortunately, it is not that easy—it is necessary to go beyond the national aggregates. We must obtain an understanding of the degree to which debt exists among individuals and the degree to which it is, or can be, burdensome.

The Burden of Consumer Installment Debt

As compared with the situation ten years ago, more families today have debt and more have larger amounts of debt. More also have home mortgage debt, but others will discuss that. *The Survey of Consumer Finances,* prepared by the Survey Research Center of the University of Michigan for the Federal Reserve Board, shows that in recent years six out of every ten spending units have had short-term installment debt. The highest concentration exists among families whose heads are between 25 and 34 years of age. Home mortgage debt, on the other hand, finds its highest concentration in a slightly older age group, those from 35 to 44 years of age. However, all families whose heads are between 18 and 44 show a greater concentration of consumer installment debt than the average, whereas the older spending units and the unmarried use it much less frequently. There is also a higher concentration of debt in the income groups between $3,000 and $10,000 a year. The least use occurs among those with incomes of less than $2,000, where we find most students and other part-time workers and those who are retired or otherwise unemployed.

When we combine the 25-to-34 age groups with the middle-income groups, we find that about nine out of every ten such families have installment debt. This brings forcibly to our attention the fact that consumer installment debt has become a way of life for the groups which the sociologists call the "Young Marrieds" and the "Growing Family." At this point in their life cycle they use it almost constantly for the purpose of acquiring the family fixed assets that are so important a part of the American scale of living.

The Survey of Consumer Finances also throws light on the burden of debt among individual families. Early in 1959 installment payments alone absorbed 20% or more of consumer income after taxes, in the case of about 13% of all spending units. A few units had committed 40% or more of their income to installment payments. In the lower-middle-income group with an annual income of $3,000 to $5,000 per family, almost 20% of all spending units were devoting 20% or more of their disposable income to installment payments. This is the group in which there are many younger families whose breadwinner lacks seniority and hence such families are particularly vulnerable to unemployment in recession.

A broader measure of payments would include (in addition to installment payments) mortgage payments and rent, life insurance premiums, and payments for social security and retirement funds. Early in 1957, the latest date for which such information is available, such payments absorbed 20% or more of income in the case of one half or more spending units; and absorbed 40% of income in the case of somewhat less than one fifth of the spending units.

These figures suggest that a significant proportion of the population has committed itself to a fairly heavy burden of regular fixed payments. Yet despite what appear to be burdensome commitments —and the level has not changed much in the last five years—the record shows that delinquency and repossession rates and the rate of charge-off remained moderate even during the 1957-58 recession. The most adequate figures are available with respect to delinquency rates of commercial banks. These remained below 2% of the number of loans on the books, and were significantly lower during 1957-58 than the average for the entire postwar period. Repossession rates covering automobiles and charge-offs rose, but not excessively above the very low level of recent years. Obviously, too, during the steel strike delinquencies and losses rose. That indicates the potential danger which does exist regardless of the amount of debt if severe economic contraction with widespread unemployment were to occur.

ESTIMATED GROWTH IN THE ECONOMY

Any estimate of the growth of consumer credit in the next decade is directly connected with and dependent upon an estimate of the growth of the entire American economy. The time available does not permit going into detail with respect to such an estimate. I am just going to use the results which have been fairly widely publicized as a result of the research of the National Planning Association, and of the staff of the Joint Economic Committee. Both came up with a middle estimate for gross national product of $790 billion for 1970. For my purpose, I am going to round that to $800 billion as of 1970, or an increase of 60%—a little more than the 50% you mentioned, Mr. Chairman.

ESTIMATED CONSUMER INSTALLMENT DEBT, 1970

Let's assume that the relationship between the use of consumer credit in the total economy remains unchanged. The present total of consumer installment short and intermediate-term debt is $40 billion. A 60% increase would bring it to $64 billion. Is such an amount attainable and reasonable ten years from now?

At first it sounds much too low, in view of the $5.4 billion increase in both 1955 and in 1959. However, we must remember that in 1958 the total of consumer installment debt actually declined, and that in 1956 and 1957 the increases were modest. I think the reason for that is clear if we examine briefly the nature of the growth in consumer installment debt.

The years 1954 and 1958 were years of recession with higher than average unemployment. In such a period, those who are unemployed and those who fear that they may become unemployed are reluctant to make major purchases and to assume installment debt. Thus they postpone the purchase of durable goods. However, if the deterrent to purchase is fear of unemployment rather than unemployment itself, they continue to build up liquid assets throughout that period. When recovery is resumed, those families which have postponed purchase of desired durable goods become more acutely aware of these deficiencies. Then their accumulation of liquid assets and their optimism as to future employment prompts them to purchase and go into debt.

However, in the prosperity phase a point is reached when a substantial number of families feel that their debt is such that it is not prudent to add to required monthly payments. As the cycle proceeds, there is a point at which debt is created at a slower pace and, at the same time, the total of monthly repayment obligations has crept upwards and the difference between credit extensions and credit repayments narrows.

Thus the net addition to consumer installment debt proceeds in a somewhat wavelike pattern, occurring at the most rapid rate early in the recovery phase, tapering off after a period of time, and reaching a minimum, becoming nonexistent or even a negative figure during the recession phase of the business cycle.

Recognizing that we are likely to have only a year or perhaps a 15-month period out of each cycle of four years or so in which the rate of increase in consumer debt will be really large, the projection over the next ten-year period of a total increase of $24 billion does not appear unduly low. However, our estimate will be too low if the use of consumer credit in relationship to the economy continues to grow in the future as it has in the period since World War II.

FACTORS INCREASING THE USE OF
CONSUMER CREDIT

What factors have been responsible for the growth in the use of consumer credit? First, and by far the most important, has been a constant increase in the margin of income over the amounts necessary for mere subsistence spending. In 1941, only 15% of American families had an annual money income, before taxes, of more than $3,000. By 1951, 54% and by 1958, 66% had incomes in excess of $3,000. We have already found that the greatest degree of use of consumer credit occurs among families with incomes of from $3,000 to $10,000 a year. This segment of the population will continue to grow as increased productivity permits higher annual wage incomes.

Second, there has been an increased acceptance of the use of consumer credit by an ever-widening group of families. The growth of private and public pension funds, hospital and medical insurance, unemployment compensation and other forms of institutional savings have made families more willing and better able to use credit to acquire family assets.

Third, the tendency toward earlier marriages has prevented young couples from building up substantial cash nest eggs before their marriage. To acquire the family assets which they consider essential, they have utilized consumer credit. They have been able to service such debt readily, thanks to high salaries for beginners, and the customary practice of the wife working until the first child's arrival is apparent. Use of installment credit has been the highest in the first five years of marriage and has continued at a reasonably high level throughout a 15-year period.

A fourth factor has been the growing regularity of consumer income. The proportion of workers in agriculture and manufacturing has been declining and the proportion in government and service establishments of all kinds has been increasing. The latter groups have been characterized by a greater degree of regularity of employment and of income, a condition conducive to a greater willingness to assume installment debt.

Fifth, there has been a continued growth in the supply of installment credit. This has been reflected in the replacement of single-payment bank loans by installment credit, and the recent development of check credit. It has been reflected in the widespread adoption of revolving credit plans by department stores, replacing the traditional charge account and cash purchases. These appear to be long-term trends which will continue and will certainly not be reversed. There has also been a progressive relaxation in the terms required on time payment contracts.

All five of these factors contribute to a growth in the volume of installment debt and have been reflected in the increased ratio of installment debt to the income figures of all kinds, and in particular consumer income after taxes.

I would be remiss if I were to conclude without making reference to the effect of the bulge in birth rates in the postwar period. Population changes from now until 1965 are dominated by a 29% increase in the number of people in the age group from 15 through 19—the "Teenagers." The next five-year period from 1965 to 1970 will show a 28% increase in the age group from 20 through 24—the "Newlyweds." The succeeding five-year period from 1970 to 1975 will show a 28% increase in the age group from 25 through 29—the "Expanding Family."

In the next few years, there will be a fairly low rate of family and household formation. The "Teenagers" will dominate the direction of family spending. In general, living expenses of high school and college students will put a strain on the family budget and less will be spent on furniture and appliances of all kinds. A second car may be necessary, but the cost of running the car and the cost of insurance will go up. Thus in this first period, convenience credit—namely, charge accounts especially for soft goods and services—will show the greatest relative increase.

The second period will be dominated by the "Newlyweds" and the needs which accompany a high rate of family formation—the demand for furniture, certain major appliances, radios, phonographs, television and housing. Thus, from 1965 to 1970 (or a few years earlier), consumer credit representing use of the time payment plan will be particularly stimulated. That stimulation will continue into the third five-year period, as the "Expanding Family" requires additional furniture, certain other types of major appliances, and additional housing space.

Everything considered, the estimate of a 60% increase in consumer installment debt by 1970 seems reasonable. All available evidence seems to indicate that such a relationship of installment debt to consumer income has not resulted, and will not result, in a burdensome debt for any significant percentage of the population. If we take into account the factors leading to a continued expansion in use of consumer credit, and the facts with respect to family formation during the next decade, I think the estimate can be described as conservative.

3

J. Andrew Painter
VICE PRESIDENT
THE FIRST NATIONAL CITY BANK OF NEW YORK

New Uses of Consumer Credit: The Growth Potential

LET ME BEGIN by mentioning briefly the historical record of the development and growth of the consumer credit industry. While other financial and retail institutions have been engaged in the consumer credit business many years longer, the commercial banks of the United States are celebrating this year the 50th anniversary of the introduction of consumer installment credit in the commercial banking system. The initial event was the founding of the Fidelity Bank and Trust Company of Norfolk, Virginia (now the Bank of Virginia) on April 5, 1910. I mention this 1910 beginning because it precedes the origin of the Federal Reserve System in 1914. Both have been time-tested under the same economic conditions. It was established and chartered especially for the purpose of catering to the savings and personal credit needs of wage earners, salaried and professional people, and small businessmen in the community. Savings certificates, to be paid for in installment payments, were issued to both savers and persons obligated on notes for personal loans. The fully paid certificates in the case of borrowers were used to retire their loan indebtedness upon the maturity of the respective notes. Thus a system was established to encourage consumers to become thrifty and self-reliant in personal money affairs.

The system spread to other states with the founding of the Morris Plan type of industrial banks or loan companies, most of which today are doing a general banking business along with consumer credit financing. While from 1910 to 1928 many industrial and small commercial banks engaged in the making of personal loans, the announcement by the National City Bank of New York that it was opening a personal loan department on May 4, 1928 aroused world-wide interest. The fact that a major commercial bank was prepared to provide personal credit facilities for wage earners, salaried and professional people, and small businessmen in a department separately organized for the purpose, elicited general approval. The response of the public was instantaneous. Loan sharks had been operating extensively in New York at the time and the press hailed the innovation as sounding their death knell. Today a news story on a loan-shark incident is a rarity rather than commonplace.

Installment credit departments were started in commercial banks in many cities across the country in the years immediately following, but it was not until the inauguration, in August, 1934, of the Property Improvement Loan Insurance Program by the Federal Housing Administration under the National Housing Act that a large number of commercial banks actively entered into the consumer installment credit business.

In the succeeding years, as the general economy emerged from the depths of the great depression, it was timely that the commercial banks should become more actively engaged in the extension of consumer installment credit. Not only did they assist greatly in providing funds and facilities for financing the mass marketing of the mass production of the new and expanding consumer goods industries, they added stature and maturity to an important phase of American economic life. It no longer was deemed improvident to borrow. Retail banking became an essential banking service to savers and borrowers.

Since the end of World War II, we have witnessed an extraordinary growth in the American economy and in the increased use of consumer credit by the American public. Today, consumer credit is a major factor in the general economy. The figures for all extenders of both installment and noninstallment consumer credit, reported by the Board of Governors of the Federal Reserve System, showed outstandings as of December 31, 1959 at a record high of $52 billion. That amount represented about 11% of the 1959 gross national product of nearly $480 billion, 15½% of total disposable personal income, and 13⅛% of total personal income, before taxes. There is hardly an area of commerce and industry in today's national life that does not place some reliance on the use of consumer credit. The major part of the consumer credit outstandings is found in the various classifications of installment credit which at the end of 1959 totaled about $39½ billion. Single-payment loans, charge accounts and service credit make up the other $12½ billion of consumer credit.

The process of evolution and innovation in the American free-enterprise system has encouraged the development of new consumer credit techniques particularly during the past 15 years. To a degree, they are merely extensions of the basic concepts of credit for the individual, merchandised to accommodate his taste and convenience.

Consumer installment credit increasingly is being used for the purchase of many major household appliances that are essentially labor-saving devices. This is really a transfer in the household budget with a possible savings on the net outlay of family income. The convenient appliances are available. People want them today and are willing to work to pay for them.

However, there are other uses of consumer installment credit besides financing our material needs. The earliest concept of installment credit was for necessitous borrowing for emergencies. Such worthy purposes have continued to play an important part in the extension of installment credit.

In the postwar era, there has come into being a broad and insistent demand for consumer credit to finance vacation and travel expenses. The travel industry has capitalized on the slogan, "Fly Now, Pay Later," which familiarly describes this new use of personal credit. The airlines, steamship companies, railroads and bus lines, on a self-interest basis alone, participate in such travel financing plans. It is better to have a seat occupied by a credit customer—with all of the good experience indicating there is a strong possibility of payment—than to make the trip with an empty seat.

Currently, the Federal Government and the governments of many states, and universities and colleges throughout the land are seeking to induce students to attend institutions of higher education on a "Study Now, Pay Later" plan. Some of the lengthy terms suggested by these various governmental and institutional plans would shock even the more liberal extenders of credit.

It is gratifying, nevertheless, that because of the intrinsic soundness of installment credit, it has become recognized as a tool to use in broadening the base of our educational system. Commercial banks throughout the country now are endeavoring to meet this latest demand for consumer credit with a variety of plans that may solve the problem of financing education privately and soundly, rather than by government subsidy.

During the past generation, consumer credit has become interwoven in the American way of life and integrated with our national economy. It is now taken for granted as an essential financial service by the general public, government officials, legislators, monetary authorities and economists. It is an important adjunct to marketing and industry.

The base for consumer credit has been broadened in recent years at both the single-payment charge account level and the installment credit account level. Additionally, there has been developed in recent years a crossover between the two by means of revolving credit—a "hybrid" out of the laboratories of banking and retail trade.

Consumer credit is brought closer to daily retail purchases and personal expenditures by the use of charge accounts, credit cards, check credit and other forms of revolving credit now gaining popularity, prestige and public acceptance.

Revolving credit outstandings in commercial banks, according to a survey recently conducted by the Instalment Credit Commission of the American Bankers Association, are a great deal less than generally supposed. The survey was directed to 533 banks most active in the field of consumer credit, and considered most likely to have revolving credit plans. The 465 banks which responded to the survey reported a total of $9,750,948, 440 outstanding in all classes of consumer credit, representing about 65% of the total consumer credit outstanding held by all commercial banks in December, 1959. Of these 465 banks, 182 were operating check credit plans with outstandings of $193,145,788, and 42 banks were operating charge account plans with outstandings of $32,111,591. The combined total of $225,262,370 in revolving credit represents just over 2% of the total consumer credit held by the banks surveyed, indicating that banks are moving conservatively in this new endeavor to serve the general public and retail trade.

Revolving credit plans assist in financing consumer expenditures for goods and services at the retail level. Charge account and credit card arrangements are of particular benefit to smaller retail and personal service establishments, which are thus relieved of capital requirements and the operating costs incident to extending credit. Check credit plans, on the other hand, necessitate no formal prior arrangements with retailers and service organizations to accept such checks, which may be taken without cost or obligation in the normal course of business, just as they would any other personal checks.

Commercial banks determine their participation in either or both of these revolving credit plans in accordance with institutional policies and local requirements. Obviously, check credit plans have more universal use and wider appeal. This is borne out by the larger number of banks engaged in that business compared with the number with charge account plans, according to the American Bankers Association's survey. Check credit is used for the entire range of household budgetary needs, including educational, medical and emergency expenses, as well as for the payment of goods and services.

Under the impetus of economic growth and competition among retailers and financial institutions in catering to consumer needs, the use of revolving credit in its various forms will increase rather

than diminish in the coming years. This is not to be viewed criti-
cally. The built-in safety controls now inherent in the consumer
credit industry will assure its ultimate soundness for the prudent
lender.

In the daily operation of consumer installment credit departments in commercial banks and other lending institutions, there
can be observed a number of built-in safety controls which have
assisted in keeping the business sound and within reasonable limits.
True, some safety controls, if ignored or not observed, might work
hardship on certain financial institutions. Reasonable observance
by lenders of the danger signals of rising interest costs, increasing
unemployment or delinquency, or overselling or pyramiding of
debt by individuals, may be ignored only at their peril. If individuals are permitted to overborrow, the lender must risk exposure
to loss, and the borrower assumes protracted, burdensome debt.
But such cases are the exception rather than the rule. Furthermore, in times of money stringency, many banks and lenders tem-
per their promotion of consumer credit, and upon occasion defer
plans for the introduction of new credit facilities, or curtail their
operation.

The thrifty American can and will count the cost of consumer
credit and bear it, if it continues to be beneficial. He likes the convenience of these new consumer credit services and, at the same
time, his nest-egg and rainy-day savings are mounting to unprecedented totals. This presents a paradox for motivation research specialists to unravel. At least the successive surveys of the financial
position of consumers, conducted by the Survey Research Center
of the University of Michigan, indicate a substantial amount of
liquid assets held by those carrying the bulk of personal short-
term and intermediate-term indebtedness. The consumer is now
a capitalist with all the budgetary concern for personal investment
in the plant (in his case, home and consumer durable goods) and
in liquidity (cash, savings and securities) for the rainy-day emergency—or even as the skeptic might say, "Another down payment!"

The excellent behavior of consumer credit—both installment and
noninstallment—over the past two decades, in responding to the

ebb and flow of the economy, would indicate that the velocity of consumer credit extensions and hence the aggregate outstandings will increase, at least apace with expansion of the total economy.

A modest estimate of consumer credit outstandings in 1970, on that safe assumption, would be about $84 billion, including consumer installment credit, charge accounts and single-payment loans. This estimate is predicated on a ratio of 13⅛% of consumer credit outstandings to total personal income in 1970, the same ratio as at the end of 1959.

However, a more likely estimate of $100 billion is projected on the basis that the 1960's will witness an accelerated use of consumer credit comparable to the increase in the 1950's over the five highest peacetime years for the previous decade. Increased wages and hence more discretionary spending power will generate more demand for consumer credit.

Outside estimates for the growth of consumer credit, which I prefer to reject as not sustainable in the light of other aspects of the total economy, would indicate the possibility of consumer credit reaching a total of $115 or even $134 billion by 1970, based on an accelerated growth pattern in the 1960's comparable to experience of growth in earlier decades. Unforeseeable events might well indicate that the economy could sustain such a growth if gradually attained and amply demonstrated to be sound as it proceeded from year to year. Consumer credit is in direct competition with other forms of credit which sustain a vigorously active economy. Business loans and mortgage credit still dominate the credit situation, and a proper balance must be maintained.

We find ourselves well within the extremes and nearer to the lowest figure of $84 billion when we determine upon $100 billion, not as a target but as an area of possibility. The consumer credit industry must assume responsibility for holding credit under manageable control. The ebb and flow of the economy will present many opportunities for the consumer credit industry to contribute to a velocity of commerce and industry that will help full employment and sound economic growth without inflation.

CHAIRMAN LUNDELL: It is safe to make another prediction concerning the use of consumer credit in the 1960's. This is that new methods will develop and that novel applications will emerge in the constant ferment of innovation. Improvement through trial and error, trial and success, will continue in this field just as it has in the past. Of course we cannot be sure that every experiment and innovation will prove to be sound and worthwhile to either borrowers or lenders, when subjected to the test of the market place. We can be sure, however, that business ingenuity will continue to adapt the basic principles of installment credit to the expanding needs and desires of the American people; and that the over-all result will be an expansion of the social usefulness, the convenience, and the amount of consumer credit that our people will use.

Our next two speakers will deal with that all-important sector of our economy having to do with financing housing, the question of our mortgage debt and government's most important role in this area. In size, existing mortgage debt for nonfarm dwellings is many times larger than the outstanding installment debt of all other types. The sheer size of such debt, touching as it does the lives of all of us, cannot help but be an important subject for review in this broad area of consumer finance. The interrelationship between money availability and housing starts is a sensitive one. Of course, the effect of housing starts on our economy reaches into all sectors and plays an important part in determining whether prosperity or recession may be our lot.

Leon T. Kendall

ECONOMIST
UNITED STATES SAVINGS AND LOAN LEAGUE

4

How Much More Mortgage Debt?

LET ME BEGIN by citing my over-all conclusions: Residential mortgage debt at the beginning of 1960 totaled $148 billion. By 1965, the amount American consumers owe on their homes will reach $200 billion; and by 1970, it should touch $300 billion. Thus, before the decade is out, we will double the amount of mortgage debt outstanding. Today, for every American household, there is $2,800 of mortgage debt. By 1970, the debt per a greater number of households will be $4,900 per household. Mortgage payments and expenditures for housing will take a relatively greater share of personal income in 1970 than in 1959.

These numerical estimates are based on a two-year study of the residential financing and housing demands facing the United States and its capital markets during the coming decade.[1] The study was conducted by the School of Business of Indiana University under the direction of Dean Arthur M. Weimer. It was underwritten by the United States Savings and Loan League in order to gain some insight into the potential growth prospects and tasks in home financing facing savings and loan associations and other lenders during the coming decade.

---

[1] School of Business, Indiana University, *The Next Decade and Its Opportunities for the Savings and Loan Business,* Chicago, United States Savings and Loan League, 1959.

HISTORICAL PERSPECTIVE

Let us briefly look backward. The housing stock of the nation was inadequate and depleted. During the depression, few new homes were added. The total number of housing starts between 1930 and 1940 were 2,700,000 units. (Almost an equivalent number were added to our housing stock in the years of 1958 and 1959.) During World War II the only civilian construction allowed was emergency homes. Thus, in 1946, next to the general problem of economic stability, housing was the number one domestic issue facing the American people. Public housing was held out as the number one solution to the problem. Its advocates said we could not trust the task of producing the 12 million new homes we would need in the next ten years to a housing industry which had to rely on the private builder seeking a contract, a construction worker seeking a job, a real estate man seeking a commission, and a financial institution seeking an investment.

In 1946, the mortgage loan as an investment was held in considerable disrepute. Insurance companies, mutual savings banks and other institutional lenders, looking back on the record of the 1930's, simply avoided home mortgages. The machinery through which they might develop a mortgage business—a network of correspondents and brokers—was at a low ebb.

What did happen? Despite these problems, private mortgage lenders were able to finance the houses demanded by the American people to the extent that no backlog of housing demand exists today. Total mortgage debt outstanding at the end of 1946 was $28 billion. In five years, by mid-1951, the amount of such debt outstanding doubled, totaling $56 billion. It doubled again by 1957 reaching $112 billion. This time the process took six years. Moving into the 1960's, by the end of 1965, mortgage debt will once again double and total $225 billion. This time the doubling process will take eight to nine years.

Although the rate of growth in mortgage debt is slowing, certainly the volume of outstanding is not. We can say that a prime characteristic of the postwar capital markets has been the rise in the demand for mortgage debt and the ability of the economy through its financial institutions to provide such funds.

Before attempting to describe the factors which make us feel that such rapid growth can continue, let me attempt to relate the growth in mortgage debt to what has been happening in corporate debt. Between 1946 and the end of 1959 net public and private debt outstanding rose by over $350 billion. Corporate debt and mortgage debt were responsible for most of the increase. Between 1946 and the end of 1958, $110 billion of additional funds flowed into mortgages. If one separates corporate takings of funds into long-term and short-term, mortgages actually grew more than the demands of business in the funds market.

Since most of the competition for mortgages is in the long-term market, this is where corporate treasurers face the greater pressures from mortgage investment. Every year since 1946, except two, 1951 and 1957, more money went into one to four family home debt than into long-term corporate securities. The one fundamental difference between home mortgage debt and corporate financing is that home mortgage financing comes directly from the capital market—the savings stream. Much of corporate financing comes from retained earnings and internal funds of American corporations. Although time will not permit development of this thought, you will hear more and more of the vital character of mortgage debt to institutional investors during the years ahead.

As a postscript, I would draw the following inference regarding the competition in the capital markets between corporates and mortgages. The mortgage market may be expected to retain and perhaps even further enhance its position relative to other markets during the years ahead. The national character of mortgages should be improved further. The tendency for investors to take greater risks in terms of down payments and maturities will probably push upward the outstanding volume of mortgage holdings. Congress, with its eye constantly on housing, will probably see to it that a continuing large flow of funds finds its way into this sector. The economy will offer mortgage debt to investors in goodly volume during the years ahead. Those financial institutions accepting such debt and servicing such debt may be expected to grow.

What about housing demand during the years ahead? New housing must be constructed:

- to house an increasing number of households;
- to permit the continued migration of families from farm to city, from city to suburbs, from north and east to south and west;
- to replace housing unfit for use, or destroyed, whether by accident or for the purpose of converting land to other use;
- to provide second homes for families that wish and can afford them;
- to enable American families to improve the quality of their housing as standards of living continue to rise.

While new houses conceivably might be financed without use of mortgage funds, no trends in that direction yet have developed, nor do they appear to be on the horizon. Home construction in the decade ahead undoubtedly will require mortgage financing just as at present and throughout our history.

Mortgage funds also will be needed to finance the purchase of existing houses and to enable families to use some of their equity in their homes for spending or investment. In the savings and loan business, two out of three dollars lent goes to support resale of existing properties.

HOW MUCH MORTGAGE FUNDS WILL BE NEEDED?

The amount of mortgage funds needed depends on many things, the most important being people, employment and income, and how much they are willing to spend for housing. The population of this country is expected to increase 33 million in the decade of the 1960's, reaching 214,000,000 by 1970. The number of persons employed is expected to increase 13.5 million. This employed force will be more productive and output per employed person is expected to increase approximately 25%. In gross national product terms, this will give us a GNP figure of $750 billion in 1970.

If such expectations come to pass, we can expect an average of between 1,300,000 and 1,400,000 new housing units being started annually. (These figures were determined prior to recent revisions in housing statistics.) Total expenditures of the decade of $247 billion for new dwelling units and for alterations and additions compares with $163 billion for the decade of the 1960's. For every $1.00 spent on home construction in the 1950's, we will spend $1.50 in the 1960's.

The big decade of home construction also is based on an estimated increase of over 10 million in the number of nonfarm households, an increase of approximately 25% in annual income per household and an increasing proportion of family expenditures going into housing. Housing may be going through a cycle similar to automobiles where accessories were added. In homes we add built-ins, added services, air-conditioning, finished basements, automatic lawn sprinklers, built-in vacuum cleaner systems, etc. A look through any builder's magazine will demonstrate the extent of the effort on the part of material suppliers to push the trend along. Acceptance by consumers of any of these ideas will push demands for mortgage dollars upward.

Probably the later years of the 1960's will see higher levels of home building than the earlier years. We might even reach a 2-million-house year before 1970. The average, however, will be closer to 1.3 and 1.4 million units. The number of dollars needed to support such home building will rise more rapidly than the number of units, for Americans have consistently added to the quality of their homes.

The Indiana estimate of residential construction appears to be conservative in the light of some estimates which have already been made. It seems to be a reasonable projection, however, in terms of population growth, gains in income and output and national production.

Between 1961 and 1970 the annual average increase in residential mortgage debt will be $15.3 billion. This will be $5 billion or almost 50% above the 1951-1960 annual average. Furthermore, by 1970, we will be over that average and be adding $18 billion of mortgage funds to debt to satisfy the home building and home financing needs of Americans. Americans will owe over $300 billion on home mortgages, almost twice the 1960 amount.

IMPLICATIONS FOR BUILDERS AND OTHERS

What are the implications of this growing housing market for builders, building materials supply manufacturers, financiers and others working in this field? As a minimum, these projections should help to establish objectives for the development of any commercial enterprise whose future rests in the home building and residential construction field. The projections should help us to make plans and to achieve these objectives. The one big conclusion the Indiana study points out is that a tremendous potential exists in the home building market in terms of consumer spending, product sales, financing opportunities and profits. We have before us a growing market. The number of customers will rise. They will have more income to spend. The quality of the product desired will grow.

Despite the fact that such plus factors exist in this market, there will be much keener competition during the years ahead. This will appear among builders, among material suppliers and among mortgage financiers. The housing market is now an established and recognized growth area. Ten years ago this was not true.

1. Builders have come of age. No longer can we describe the home building industry as a group of relatively small, independent craftsmen. A recent survey by the National Association of Home Builders of its membership showed that in 1959 the largest 10% of the builders constructed 59% of all the homes in this country. Each put up an average of over 350 homes. Builders building over 100 homes per year—volume builders—produced 64% of the housing units in 1959. When you start to get an industry of this type, research, experimentation, adaptation of technology, all become

possible. And the trend does not appear to have reached its peak. Major industrial firms are examining the growth area of home building as an area for new ventures.

2. Materials supply manufacturers are recognizing the importance of the housing market to their success. They now work on all aspects of the market, direct and indirect. I will cite only one illustration. The gypsum companies have been attempting to organize something called a "Down Payment Club." It would be somewhat like a Christmas Club; and its purpose would be to permit individual families to generate down payment sums more quickly. The idea stems from the claim of builders that a lack of down payments is the number one stumbling block to more home sales.

3. For financiers, the more ready acceptance of the mortgage instrument as an investment has been one of the major developments of the 1950's. We will see further steps taken to improve the marketability and national character of the individual home finance contract. Broadly speaking, the competition in the capital markets for residential mortgages should increase. Already the interest spread between the mortgage rate and other rates has narrowed. The mortgage instrument is a considerably more acceptable instrument than it was ten to 12 years ago as measured by the interest rate differential between, say, a Corporate AAA Bond and mortgages. According to some measurements we have made, the spread between Corporate AAA bonds and residential mortgages in 1947 was 2.40%. By the end of 1958, the spread had narrowed considerably to 1.54%. Although the measurements are crude, they illustrate the change well.

Innovations in mortgage finance are equally possible. At the present time, I understand, a firm is being organized entitled the National Trade-In Financial Corporation. Its purpose is to develop a capital fund which will finance trade-in houses much as used cars are financed today.

The problems in the housing area, and some of the stumbling blocks to the fulfillment of my estimates, include: rising home prices, scarcity of land for building in desirable locations, rising real estate taxes, building codes, and other similar problems.

I turn now to one final subject.

Does Too Much Savings Go Into Housing?

Some economists and financial experts maintain that too much of our savings flow goes into housing. Very possibly steps ought to be taken to slow the pace of home building so that the other sectors of the capital market—sectors more closely akin to economic growth and progress—might get a bigger share of our pool of savings. It may be that housing secures "too much credit" relative to other potential uses of savings. The concentration of savings funds in intermediaries—that is, savings and loan associations and others—which support home financing almost exclusively, may keep funds from business investment. Although this concentration may be desirable from the standpoint of supplying much needed funds for residential financing, we must not ignore the question, "Is this the most desirable use of savings funds for economic growth and progress of this country?"

On this issue, I will make two points: The kind of debt that is going to be offered depends on the structure of the economy. If mortgage debt is available, investors are going to buy that kind of debt. Market forces, then, will determine through the interest rate mechanism what kind of debt is to grow most rapidly. My second point is to ask, who is to make the decision as to how a more "appropriate" allocation of funds might be administered? Do we want governmental agencies determining whether Americans should spend their money for housing, steel plants, farm subsidies, schools or sewers?

In a free choice society, individuals are free to work where they choose; dispose of their property as they see fit; and use their incomes as they see fit. They are free to spend for consumer goods or to save; to invest or not to invest. There are better ways to build and finance houses. A free enterprise environment will provide the stimulus for the Americans of today to discover those ways and means.

Conclusion

The growth of home mortgage debt has been accomplished in harmony with the market forces of the economy. It has permitted the working of the free choice of consumers regarding how they desire to spend their funds, aided greatly in the mobility of the population. It has preserved workable competition in the housing industry. These tasks were accomplished with a minimum of governmental aid and support, and they were accomplished under the influence of general monetary controls. If the future permits such forces to work, the estimates made earlier regarding residential mortgage debt ought to come fairly close to realization.

CHAIRMAN LUNDELL: Our federal government, as we all realize, plays a most active role in the housing and construction field through its insuring and financing agencies. In the position of chairman, I wondered what I could say about it, and I concluded the safe thing was to say something like this: It is established national policy, under either Republican or Democratic leadership, that the federal government must assume substantial responsibility for the maintenance of an active housing market. In times of boom this may mean to restrain excessive expansion; at other times it may mean to encourage expansion.

Ernest M. Fisher

PROFESSOR OF URBAN LAND ECONOMICS
GRADUATE SCHOOL OF BUSINESS
COLUMBIA UNIVERSITY

5

The Government's Role in Housing Finance: Developing Trends

MY REMARKS with respect to the government's role in housing finance and developing trends are in the nature of judgments that are not necessarily documented. Many of them probably cannot be documented. They are given, therefore, as a challenge to our thinking. They are judgments which, I hope, will stimulate your thinking. I do not wish you to take my observations or conclusions as being expressions of approval or disapproval. I am not trying to indicate what I consider to be the moral content of the trends to which I wish to refer.

The subject assigned to me does not specify which level of government is to be considered. It is obvious that the federal, state and local governments all play a role in housing markets and consequently in housing finance. But the subject is big enough for the time allotted to it if we confine discussion to the role of the federal government alone.

There are three ways in which this role of the federal government is enacted: first, through the insurance or guarantee of loans made by private lending institutions; second, through the direct or indirect advance of government funds or credit on the security of home mortgages; and third, through the financing or guarantee of loans made for financing in the construction of publicly owned and operated housing.

Perhaps I may mention a few statistics to indicate the order of magnitude of each of these operations. At the end of the year 1959, of the total estimated nonfarm mortgage debt outstanding of approximately $148 billion, nearly $60 billion was insured or guaranteed by the Federal Housing Administration or the Veterans Administration. This is approximately 40% of the total debt outstanding. At the same date, the Federal National Mortgage Association held in its portfolio mortgages on which the outstanding balances totaled $5.5 billion. Balances outstanding on Federal Home Loan Banks to banking institutions amounted to $2.1 billion. The Veterans Administration had made advances of government funds on which $902 million were outstanding. All together, outstanding balances of government funds, directly or indirectly advanced, on housing mortgages amounted to some 60% of the total outstanding indebtedness.

The magnitude is again suggested by some of the annual summaries of operations of these agencies. Purchases of FNMA have exceeded $1 billion in three years—1950, 1957 and 1959. Direct purchases of college housing issues have risen from $160 million in 1955 to $952 million in 1959. Federal Home Loan Bank advances rose from $657 million in 1950 to $1,364 million in 1958, and to the all-time peak of $2 billion in 1959. The combined injection into the market was nearly $5 billion in 1959.

Funds advanced or guaranteed by the federal government in connection with public housing, urban redevelopment and renewal, and military housing are a bit difficult to compute, since they are not allocated solely for housing and are not reported as segregated. Neither do the totals above include funds advanced for nurses' housing nor for the construction of public facilities needed in connection with the building of homes. These would, all together, account for several billion dollars, if future commitments were capitalized.

The significant trend indicated by these figures is to be found in the fact that while home mortgage indebtedness has multiplied some fivefold in the postwar period, the advances, direct and indirect, of federal funds have multiplied some tenfold. Over this postwar period, if the insurance and guarantee functions of FHA and VA are included, the federal government has probably participated, directly or indirectly, in nearly half of the transactions connected with mortgages on nonfarm housing. The other half of the market, of course, has been affected by this active participation of the federal government in the mortgage market.

The second important trend is found in the nature of the government participation in these markets. In the early age of government intervention, the FHA operated solely as an insurer of funds advanced to private lenders on broad conditions of eligibility. The Home Loan Banks advanced funds to member institutions on the security of their usual loans. Gradually, the nature of government intervention has been broadened: in 1937, to include what amounts to a guarantee of advances made to local housing authorities; in 1949, to cover funds advanced to local public agencies engaged in urban renewal; and in subsequent years, to include funds needed for college housing, nurses housing, for loans to veterans, and now for our "senior citizens," or whatever you call us. FNMA was revived and authorized to make advance commitments to purchase FHA and VA guaranteed loans, extended as "special assistance." The height of something was reached in the Capehart program, under which the Defense Department owns the land in fee on which housing for government personnel is built by private builders, assisted by mortgage loans advanced by private lending institutions insured by the FHA.

The effects of this government intervention have been most felt in connection with the liberalization of the terms of mortgage loans. Since the end of World War II, the maximum term of loans insured with the FHA has been lengthened from 20 to 30 years and, in some cases, to 40 years; and the minimum down payment reduced from 10 to 3%. There is no down payment required for the VA loans, for which the maximum term is 30 years. There is now a bill pending in Congress, approved by the House, that would provide for the elimination of the down payment required for FHA insurance and for the extension of the term to 40 years, provided the mortgage is not in excess of $13,500.

There are convincing indications that these provisions of existing legislation and regulations have had an important effect in the whole mortgage market, especially in financing of new home purchases. In 1950, for example, 54% of the VA loans for new homes had no down payment; in 1955, 48%; in 1958, 29%; and in 1959, 66%. Only 16% of the FHA loans exceeded 90% in 1950 on new homes; but it had reached 54% in 1958 and 69% in 1959.

According to figures of the Home Loan Bank Board, the average loan value ratio on conventional loans made by savings and loan associations rose from 58.4% in 1950, to 66.6% in 1959. The average term in years on most of the VA loans insured or guaranteed in 1950 on new homes was 23 years. In 1954, it was 25 years and nine months. In 1959, it was 28 years and nine months. Over the same period, the term of FHA insured loans on new homes increased. The percentage of these having a term of 30 years rose from 27 in 1955, to 52 in 1958, and 78 in 1959.

There are no comprehensive statistics on the term of conventional loans, but there is a consensus that the average term has increased considerably during the postwar period, especially since 1950.

The ostensible purpose of public officials in liberalizing the terms of insurable loans was to make mortgage funds available to those who are unable or unwilling to make larger down payments and who would prefer, or were obliged, to secure agreement to smaller monthly payments on account of debt service.

That the actions of public officials at least partly failed to accomplish this purpose is indicated by the scattered information available on prices, incomes, down payments and monthly debt service of those who purchased new homes, especially under these programs. Consideration of these data raises the question whether these actions benefited builders and sellers of new homes much more than they did purchasers.

The mortgage market phenomenon upon which government action has had least effect appears to be the interest rate. Legislative and administrative control of the interest rate on FHA and VA loans has apparently had the effect of limiting the extent to which these agencies participate in the market. But it seems to have affected the interest rate on conventional loans only slightly, if at all. It has been effective in the market for FHA and VA loans largely because of the direct purchasing activities of FNMA and the direct loans made by the VA.

Actually, allowable interest charges on insured loans have risen almost continuously since 1952, as has the rate on conventional loans—most of the time with a long time-lag, but eventually to the point where the return to the investor is comparable to the return on conventionals. Even the massive purchases of FNMA previously cited did not suffice to sustain the market for the low-yielding insured and guaranteed loans over any long period of time.

One is tempted in this connection to call attention to the actions of the Federal Reserve and Treasury officials in the immediate postwar period in attempting to keep the interest rate on government bonds pegged.

What one may conclude is that, so far, the means used by the federal government to influence the mortgage market have not proved effective in controlling or affecting the interest rate, except for short periods of time and to the extent that the agencies have invested government funds directly. In view of the expansion of these direct operations, however, it would seem reasonable to suppose that the trend toward influencing the mortgage interest rate will continue, and that the means used may not be confined, as they have in the past, to legislative and administrative control of the rate on insured and guaranteed loans and to the direct market operations of FNMA and the limited advances of the VA.

Another market phenomenon upon which the influence of the government intervention is not clearly discernible is price. Here it can only be noted that, from 1950 to 1959, the average price paid for a new home with aid of a VA-guaranteed loan rose from $8,900 to $14,500—an increase of 63%. The median appraised value of the new home on which FHA insured the mortgage rose during the same period from 8,000 to 14,000—an increase of 73%. The average purchase price of the existing home purchased with VA guarantee rose from $8,400 to $12,600, or 40%. The appraised value of FHA existing homes increased about 45%. The average purchase price of a home purchased with the aid of conventional savings and loan mortgage rose from $9,427 to $15,782, or 67%.

In brief, these scanty figures indicate that the average purchase price of new homes increased by nearly 50% more than did that of existing homes over this period. Thus the limited evidence seems to suggest that the liberalization of mortgage terms may have influenced price. And one might think that if future government intervention should take other forms or should only consist of an increase in the extent of the participation characteristic of the past, some means of more directly influencing price may be introduced.

Another pronounced trend in recent years not susceptible to statistical treatment is toward the use of the programs of federal agencies to achieve or sustain a given level of new house construction. Several times in the postwar period Congress has amended the housing legislation or administrative officials have amended regulations with the avowed purpose of increasing the number of new dwelling unit starts. A bill is now pending in the Senate which would, if enacted, require the President to establish each year a "quota" or "goal" of new houses to be constructed, and to recommend to Congress such action as he deems appropriate to assure that the quota or goal will be realized. Said the Subcommittee on Housing of the Senate Committee on Banking and Currency, in introducing the bill: "The Subcommittee believes that a minimum of 16 million permanent housing units should be constructed during a ten-year period beginning January, 1960." In contemplation of these statements and of the action of federal officials, both administrative and legislative, in the very strong sellers' markets which have prevailed in most areas of the last decade and a half, one can only wonder what "perfection and supplementation of existing housing laws" might come about if a widespread buyer's market should develop, with its accompanying phenomena of falling prices, wholesale defaults and delinquencies, mounting vacancies, and disappearing equities.

I am not predicting that. The effect of this trend toward the use of government programs to sustain a given level of new construction is to shift the process of decision-making in connection with the determination of the volume of new construction from the usual market institutions and persons motivated principally by consideration of prices, costs and profits, to the public administrator or legislator.

The criteria by which public officials are to be guided in making these decisions have not yet become clear. Those which have received the most attention and discussion are "social needs" and economic stabilization. It is argued that a given volume of residential construction is "necessary," either to meet the "needs" of the nation, and especially of the lower-income groups, to eliminate substandard housing, or to provide a decent home and suitable living environment for every American family, or to sustain full employment in the building trades or sustain a high-level gross national product, or to assure an adequate volume of capital accumulation.

In this discussion of goals, quotas and national objectives there is little reference to costs and prices and their relation to a proposed volume of construction. It is never quite clear whether the government should provide a market for the home construction and affiliated businesses (and, if so, whether the government should determine the location, size and kind of accommodations to be provided, what materials of construction should be used, or at what prices the products should be taken off the market); nor are there answers to several of the hundreds of questions upon which some decision must be reached before and during the process of production. Barely mentioned in public discussion are the conflicts that may arise when the attainment of these multiple objectives suggests directly opposite actions on the part of public authorities. They will probably receive much more attention in the coming decade.

It is likely that this discussion will clarify the role of the federal government in housing finance. It may eventually define the extent to which any forecast or projection of the behavior of housing markets, especially in the short run, will have to be based upon "what Congress is going to do," or "what action the federal government is going to take." It will, on the contrary, be increasingly difficult or impossible to predict or project market behavior on the basis of analysis of the usual market forces as they are expressed in the thousands or hundreds of thousands of individual decisions made in the market places of the land.

6

Discussion

QUESTION: In New Jersey we are in the process of passing what has been politically called an "honesty-in-advertising" or "honesty-in-banking" bill, where the lender now has to show the true interest rate rather than the simple interest rate. Here are two questions, both related: Will this "honesty in advertising" lessen the interest on the part of the consumer in using installment credit? Will this bill showing the true interest rate cause a pressure on the part of the consumer for lower interest rates on the part of lenders?

DR. DAUER: The industry with which I am associated has been advertising the rate of charge for the last 40 or 50 years depending upon the state. Our company, for example, in its advertisements in the newspapers, in the car cards, has quoted payments and directly below them have been the words, "These charges are at a rate of so-and-so much," as required by state law. We have been doing this for decades, depending upon the individual state, i.e., for as long as small-loan legislation has existed. I am not aware that it has deterred people from borrowing.

MR. PAINTER: The answer to both questions is "No." But the consumer might be confused and hence not helped by a well-intentioned legislative effort in New Jersey. However, the exact wording of the statute would have to be studied to judge its full effect. Certainly there should be full disclosure of the cost of consumer credit financing. The simpler the cost is stated, the better. An exact statement of so-called "simple interest" is virtually impossible on retail installment sales credit transactions and very difficult on loan transactions as well. The commercial banks of New York State for 22 years, from 1935 to 1957, were required to state not only the discount charge, but also the effective simple interest on unpaid principal balances in notes and applications for personal loans in compliance with applicable banking legislation. The consumer was more apt to be confused, rather than informed by this double statement of the rate of charge. And in 1957 the legislation was amended to simply provide for a statement of the charge in notes and applications as a rate in dollars per annum discount per $100 face amount of loan.

Since 1941 the New York Personal Property and Lien laws have required the disclosure of credit service charges in all consumer retail conditional sales contracts and chattel mortgages. In 1956 and in 1957 New York State adopted legislation regulating retail installment sales financing for motor vehicles and other consumer goods and services. While both of those statutes established maximum credit service charges and require full disclosure of all terms, the credit service charges need only be stated as a separate amount in the itemization of the transaction.

These legislative provisions are indicative of the concern of the New York State Legislature for disclosure of charges to consumers on an understandable basis for the type of credit extended.

CHAIRMAN LUNDELL: Perhaps you will permit me to add a supplementary thought. The finance industry, as has already been indicated, has felt for years that the customer should be protected by stating in the contract the amount, either in dollars or at a dollar rate, that the customer pays in connection with installment transactions. As you know, the Douglas bill, pending in Congress, advocates that the common denominator of an interest rate, a per-annum rate, be stated in connection with installment transactions. I think the industry is generally very much opposed to the quoting of a per-annum interest rate because it is felt it will not accomplish the objectives that have been generally outlined for the bill. It will make installment credit transactions very difficult, from the merchant's point of view; and it will unnecessarily complicate the whole process and add additional costs.

I don't think this would have any depressing effect on the volume of installment business but, in some respects, it might drive underground what the installment fraternity have been preaching—namely that the public interest must be protected at all costs; that it can be protected by stating a dollar amount of financial charge, together with a great many other protections that should be instituted in the consumer's interest; and that there is very little point in adding many administrative problems to a very technical situation by trying to equate historically grounded dollar rates with a theoretical per-annum interest calculation.

It might have an unfortunate effect in terms of what merchants can do, for example, in connection with skipped payments, farmer plan payments, school teacher payments and the like, which are on a basis of irregular payments. Here, a simple interest calculation becomes a mathematical exercise of considerable complexity.

QUESTION: This probably reflects some ignorance on my part. When we thought of installment credit in the past, we thought of its effect on durable-goods purchases. With the advent of revolving credit in department stores and check credits in the banks, doesn't this mean installment credit loans include soft goods? I believe the question should go to Mr. Painter.

MR. PAINTER: Yes. The consumer credit figures, reported by the Board of Governors of the Federal Reserve System in the Monthly Bulletin, cover both installment credit and single-payment credit, each of which is broken down by type of credit. It is my understanding that revolving credit and check credit are included in these figures, and respectively classified as "Other Consumer Goods Paper" and "Personal Loans."

With the introduction of Revolving Credit there is a crossover between Charge Account and Installment Credit. The "Federal Reserve Board" has adjusted the consumer credit figures from time to time over the past twenty years to respond to new techniques that have come along. They may break down the Revolving Credit and Check Credit into new classifications one of these days, but since they are relatively a small amount in the total, I think Federal will wait until they are larger factors before you get a separate series of statistics.

DR. DAUER: I think the question was that we have in the past associated time-payment credit largely with the sale of durable goods. Revolving credit in department stores is nothing more or less than a charge account paid off over a period of time, the maximum amount of which could reach a line-of-credit figure; that charge account could be used for any purpose that the purchaser wishes, limited by the merchandise offered by the store. Of course, you will have a higher degree of soft goods included in such transactions than you have had in the traditional time-payment purchase plans.

Similarly, in the case of check credit that can be used for any purpose whatever—services or anything else. That will, likewise, not be limited to durable goods.

QUESTION: In the kind of society where our consumers have acquired the consumer durables they have acquired since the war and they are taking on new debt—basically a psychological motivation more than anything else—do you not think there is developing a very much greater swing over the business cycle, and the amount of consumer credit taken out of this will contribute markedly to the instability caused by consumer credit in the business cycle?

DR. DAUER: The question of using or not using consumer credit isn't the important point. The point is the type of society in which we live. In other words, if we have a high-level economy in which we as consumers have acquired a very substantial amount of family fixed assets—just as our business firms have acquired a large amount of plant and equipment—we are then in a position where if for psychological or other reasons we wish to tighten our belt, we can tighten it and we can cut off our purchases of certain things completely. There is no doubt about such a possibility. If everyone, for some reason, decided not to buy a car during the next 12 months, I don't need to tell you what would happen. In other words, it is the level of the economy and not the existence or non-existence of consumer credit that creates that situation.

We have to arrive at methods, which are general in character to bring about stability in the economy to take care of that. I don't know of any way other than creating a set of conditions which will be conducive to forward planning and optimism on the part of 178 million people, or 58 million spending units, so that they will feel justified in going ahead and living an orderly life.

DR. KENDALL: There is one point I would like to make on that. Following the 1955 expansion of consumer credit, the Federal Reserve undertook a comprehensive study of the subject. The bulk of the evidence in that study demonstrated that we did not need special controls on consumer credit.[1]

One of the points was simply that there is a self-limiting element in consumer debt. The consumer who has zero debt can go on a splurge, to be sure. But a consumer with the amount of debt that Ernst Dauer mentioned—20% of income going into these installment payments, and an additional 30% going into mortgage payments—will soon get together with his wife and stop going further into debt. The credit examiner who looks at your accounts may exercise the check for you. Whether you want to do it this way or do it through controls is another question.

CHAIRMAN LUNDELL: I have felt there is a certain lead time in this development of contraction or expansion of consumer credit. The American people do not turn around on a dime and make simultaneous buying decisions. These decisions are made over a period of time. Therefore the impact is cushioned by the factor of time, based upon expectations, the hope for continuing employment, local conditions and a general feeling for the business situation.

MR. PAINTER: On that point, in the experience of all the commercial banks in New York City handling personal loans, we find that Monday is our biggest business day. Probably 50 or 60% more applications are handled on a Monday than on any other day

[1] Board of Governors of the Federal Reserve System, *Consumer Instalment Credit*, Parts I-IV, Washington, D. C., U. S. Government Printing Office, 1957.

of the week, indicating that personal credit is a household project where many decisions to make purchases or revamp the family budget situation are made on a family basis over the week-end.

QUESTION: Mr. Painter, there has been a lot of talk that commercial bankers are disillusioned with the profitability of the volume of check credit and credit card plans. What are your comments on it?

MR. PAINTER: We are knee-deep in Ready Credit. We have not turned back. We have not promoted it as actively in recent months as we did to get the Plan under way in early 1959. But this has not been because of disillusionment or unprofitability. Revolving charge account credit was started by John Wanamaker in 1938. Credit card banking started in 1953 and check credit started in 1955. These have been experimental years for such plans to be tested under a variety of economic conditions.

In a period of general credit curtailment, or credit stringency, it is proper for commercial banks and other lenders to treat the situation with proper consideration—and they have. Some may defer entering into such plans, others may curtail their operations, while still others, like ourselves, may continue seeking to provide credit equitably to all segments of the economy for the use of business, both large and small, and consumers in the variety of their needs.

QUESTION: I believe Dr. Dauer indicated that family or household growth would be much greater in the 1965-70 period than from 1960-65. Do you expect the 1960-65 period to be a drop-off from what has been experienced in the last five years?

DR. DAUER: I don't think the population figures indicate that. I think the population figures indicate the family formation rate will be about the same in the next few years, but that the big bulge will come thereafter—namely, that it is in that next period that we will have the very sharp pronounced increase in the 20-to-24 year age level at which the bulk of marriages are occurring. Of course, the typical bride's age now is about 18, so it will be a little before that.

The population figures are not published in exactly a manner which leads to exact precision with respect to these conclusions.

Population figures have been forecast for 5-year intervals and for certain age groups, so you can't be completely precise.

QUESTION: Dr. Kendall referred to a housing need of 1.3 million or 1.4 million units over the next ten years, including 1960. Recognizing that housing starts this year are running at about 1,150,000 or approximately 17% behind the same period a year ago, could he pick out some above-average years in the next ten years?

DR. KENDALL: Let's do this year. The course of starts in an individual year depends on two things: one, what happened in the preceding year and, two, the financial machinations that come from government and elsewhere which tend to pack the demand in one year as compared to another.

Why did we start between 1,350,000 or 1,400,000 houses (old series) in 1959? Part of the answer rests in the $1 billion of special assistance housing funds authorized by Congress in 1958. Although the bulk of $1 billion of FNMA money was committed in July and August of 1958, the houses weren't built until 1959. So we bunched some of the demand this way. Also, I think when we make money available on a no-down-payment basis, we steal from the succeeding year.

Taking Ernst Dauer's population figures, I would say that the big-volume, two-million housing-start year is going to be late in the 1960's—in 1967, 1968 and 1969. It wouldn't surprise me if the next couple of years averaged out to 1,250,000 units(old series).

All the housing-start figures are about to be revised. I think we are going to find we had a million-and-a-half starts last year next year!

THE FINANCIAL OUTLOOK

James F. Oates, Jr.
CHAIRMAN

Tilford C. Gaines
ASSISTANT VICE PRESIDENT—RESEARCH
FEDERAL RESERVE BANK OF NEW YORK

1

How Much Money for How Much Growth at What Cost?

IN EACH PERIOD of our recent economic history there has been at least one problem at the center of the stage that has attracted the most intensive appraisal by economic analysts. During the 1930's the problem was "secular stagnation"; during the war it was the "inflationary gap"; then it was "postwar depression"; and more recently it has been "creeping inflation."

The most discussed problem currently is our ability to maintain an adequate rate of economic growth. We may assume that the concentrated attention given to these problems in the past has provided insights that have helped to shape public policies useful in correcting or preventing the problems, although at times some of the discussisons must have caused us to wonder. I believe we may also be confident that the current interest in economic growth will, in time, develop useful insights.

Everyone, of course, is in favor of economic growth, just as everyone is in favor of health, happiness and low taxes. But what do we mean by growth? And what public policies would be best calculated to promote it? Some of the proposals would imply government intervention in the economic process in ways that might choke off the forces of private initiative that have powered the growth process in the past and have made us the wealthiest nation

433

in history. Others remind me of a problem that I understand agrarian scientists are now struggling with.

It seems that the dramatic growth in yield per acre that our farms have achieved in recent years has been accompanied by deterioration in the mineral content and nutritional value of some agricultural products. In other words, the increased productivity and growth in our farm economy apparently has not been all that it seemed to be. Part of it has simply represented puffing up the product without a corresponding increase in the real value of output. Growth in the dollar value of our total economic output that might result from fertilization through inflationary money supply expansion would also represent growth in water and pulp content rather than in real values.

Before taking up the question of "how much money for how much growth," it would be helpful to digress for a moment on the question of what we mean by economic growth and to mention some of the circumstances we might expect to result from or be conducive to an optimum growth rate. There are many useful ways to measure growth, the simplest being in terms of the annual rate of increase in the gross national product at constant prices. Perhaps we would all agree, however, that the most meaningful measure of growth is in terms of real output per worker; that is, in terms of the rate of labor productivity growth. Rapid increase in total output of goods and services would of course constitute growth, even if the labor force were increasing equally rapidly, but this rate of growth would not add to per capita real income. And, needless to say, a rapid increase in the dollar value of output per worker would not be growth in any meaningful sense if it reflected price inflation rather than real output.

Real economic growth per unit of labor input depends principally upon the development of new and richer material resources, upon technological innovations, including managerial, and upon improved skills in our labor force. In our country we should expect economic growth to result principally from the latter two sources—technological innovation and improved labor skills—although shifting of resources to new and more productive uses should perhaps be mentioned as an additional source of growth.

Technological innovation may take many forms, but it may generally be assumed that the profitable employment of innovations over time requires capital outlays, both to replace outmoded equipment and procedures and to expand capacity to produce products that progress has made possible. Similarly, longer-term improvement of labor skills requires constantly more and better training facilities in the form of schools, universities, laboratories and so forth. And to support a growing economy, we must provide an ever-larger supply of such social overhead capital items as improved highway systems.

In short, history teaches us to expect a positive correlation between real economic growth per capita and the rate of capital formation, including in capital both privately owned and public facilities that contribute to the economic process. History also indicates, however, that the growth of capital facilities does not occur at an even rate, year in and year out. There are periods during which capital formation appears to speed up, leading to a rate of spending on capital items that tends to create demands for financial capital funds greater than savers had planned to set aside. In such periods we would expect that the discrepancy between planned investment and planned saving would lead either to strong upward pressures on interest rates as demands for capital funds competed for a limited supply, or to price inflation as total credit expanded at an inflationary pace, or to a mixture of the two.

It is not at all necessary for the most rapid rate of economic growth to occur at the same time that capital assets are being accumulated most rapidly. In fact, for the two to coincide it would be necessary that technological innovations generating greater productivity and growth should be centered in the capital goods and construction industries. Therefore, periods during which the capital foundation is being built for future growth may themselves be periods of apparently moderate economic growth, of upward price pressures, and of heavy credit demands.

The 1950's were such a period. An unprecedented rate of capital accumulation was achieved in the combined outlays for private industry, the highway program, new school construction, the defense establishment, and for scientific knowledge through the outpouring of funds for research.

Let me stress that the capital expansion I refer to here is not confined to capital outlays in private industry for tangible plant and equipment. It includes all of the wide range of demands upon current output that tend to add, in one way or another, to future economic capacity rather than to current satisfactions. While not adding directly to economic growth, it should be mentioned that consumers simultaneously accumulated capital assets—homes, autos and other possessions—at a record pace. Reflecting this heavy loading of capital-type expenditures, the flow-of-funds accounts show that net credit extensions between major sectors of the economy averaged almost 10% of GNP during the decade of the 1950's.

While we do not have similar data for earlier periods, the historical data for total public and private debt outstanding suggest that never before in our history, except during major wars, has credit been used so extensively. This fact clearly is related to the emphasis upon capital items during the decade.

Let me add two more observations about economic circumstances related to the growth process. First, periods of rapid innovation and the formation of growth forces will not necessarily be periods of full employment. There always are numerous influences at work determining the level of our unemployment statistics, but one very important influence in a period of dynamic growth is a process of shifts in the mix of products being turned out and in the types of labor skills required. Both types of shifts, particularly the latter, will generate technological unemployment of a type that is particularly difficult to correct in the short run except through policies that might slow the growth process.

Though everyone favors full employment, there are times when some unemployment may have to be accepted, and its hardships relieved at public expense, rather than resisted by artificial makework restrictions or by flooding new money through the spending stream.

In the longer run, education, retraining and mobility will correct the problem. It is illuminating that in recent years unemployment has been running even higher than usual in the unskilled and semi-skilled groups, but has been negligible in the technical and professional groups.

My second observation is that a precondition for sustained and well-balanced growth is broad price stability or, more precisely, the absence of firm expectations of continuing price changes in a single direction. The introduction of either an inflation or deflation factor in the process by which the myriad plans affecting the economy are shaped will tend to distort the allocation of resources and to stunt real growth.

Now let us turn to the question: "How much money for how much growth?" The first point that should be made is that there is no correlation between the rate of economic growth and the rate of increase in the money supply from one year to the next. In examining this relationship, the simplest measure is to compare changes in the money supply with changes in the gross national product in current dollars.

During the decade of the 1920's, GNP rose at a compound annual rate greater than the percentage rate of increase in the money supply—2½% per year for GNP against 2⅛% per year for the money supply. The slower rate of increase in the money supply during the 1920's was partly a reflection of the fact that the money supply had almost doubled during the preceding World War I years.

The relationship between money supply and gross national product was reversed during the 1930's, as money supply expanded by almost 2½% per year while GNP actually fell. The 1940's saw both money supply and GNP shoot sharply ahead, at average annual rates of roughly 14% and 12% respectively. Even the rapid inflation of the war and postwar years did not fully absorb the tremendous ballooning of the money supply during the decade of the 1940's, with the result that money supply growth during the 1950's could be relatively restrained. While gross national product grew at an annual rate of about 6½% in the 1950's, the money supply grew at an annual rate only slightly greater than 2½%.

Over the full 40 years from 1919 through 1959, the money supply has grown at a compound annual rate of nearly 5%, while gross national product has grown at an annual rate of less than 4½%. Using a constant-dollar measure for GNP would, of course, affect the size of some of these figures, particularly in sharply reducing the apparent rate of growth in the 1940's and 1950's, but the absence of correlation between money supply and GNP would remain.

It is clear that the historical data give us few clues as to the relationship between money supply and economic growth, other than to indicate that there need not be a fixed relationship in any one year or a brief period of years. Developments during 1959 provide an interesting illustration of the complex nature of the relationship. Gross national product increased by almost 9% from the recession-affected 1958 level, while the money supply increased by less than 1%. At the same time, net credit extensions, in the flow-of-funds concept, amounted to more than $60 billion, by all odds the largest credit expansion in a peacetime year in our history.

Thus 1959 was a year in which the money supply grew very little but in which a huge amount of credit was made available to support the swelling expenditures of industry, consumers and government. Part of this credit came from current savings, both by individuals and corporate businesses. Another part took a form very close to money supply expansion, as nonbank corporations and various other institutions and individuals purchased large amounts of highly liquid short-term securities from the federal government and from banks and other financial institutions as a substitute for money balances.

By and large, the funds supplied to the credit markets from the latter source would not have been available for longer-term investment, and the credit instruments purchased by these investors were generally considered by them to be the equivalent of money. The potential for pulling funds into such money substitutes, which has been continuously in evidence in recent years, suggests that in the years ahead as in years past the changing supply of money substitutes will be an important determinant of the amount of money needed in the economy to support any specified rate of economic growth.

The foregoing comments suggest that the answer to our question should be stated in terms that give recognition to the broader concept of total credit rather than in terms of the money supply alone. Optimum economic growth at whatever rate the economy can sustain without generating inflationary forces is facilitated by a total supply of credit available to both the private and public sectors in amounts, types and maturities that will support the broadest opportunities for developing new techniques and new products and for expanding the total of economic output. Contained within this prescription is the unstated assumption that an adequate credit supply would support maximum realizable employment of the labor force consistent with the difficulties of achieving "full employment" mentioned earlier.

In periods of rapid capital accumulation, such as the past few years, the prescription would imply heavy credit usage at high rates of interest, side by side with temporary upward price pressures and relatively high transitional unemployment rates. In other periods, during which the fruits of the preceding burst of capital growth were being enjoyed and the rate of capital expansion was more moderate, the prescription would be more likely to call for less pressure on credit supplies, lower interest rates, more nearly full employment and steady or declining prices.

From the longer view, of course, the total of expenditures supported by net credit extensions must be equal to the total of funds made available to borrowers out of the savings process. Changes in the money supply, in this longer view, should be geared to the increases necessary to provide for transactions requirements as the total of transactions rises. The application of this analysis cannot be too precise in our modern economy, however. Money is held by businesses and consumers in amounts greater than needed strictly for immediate settlement of transactions, and there is a wide range of highly liquid short-term assets that may substitute for money in other than transactions uses.

There has been an almost unbroken process in recent years of substituting these liquid nonmoney assets for money in the balance sheets of business corporations, individuals and other institutions. This process has meant that the additions to credit supply that would otherwise have been provided by additions to the money supply have, in substantial part, been provided by the creation of money substitutes. The money supply, accordingly, has not grown at what one might expect to be its long-term rate of growth.

Let us now apply the preceding analysis to the outlook for the 1960's. On balance, it would appear likely that net credit demands will be proportionately somewhat smaller than in the decade just ended. The word "proportionately" is important. As economic activity and incomes have grown and continue to grow, the total of savings, partly in the form of repayments of the already huge volume of debt outstanding, provide an ever-larger supply of funds for financing further growth. The total of new credit created in the 1960's possibly will be greater than the total created in the 1950's, but it probably will be smaller relative to gross national product, and this suggests it is likely to impose less severe pressures upon the supply of funds.

Looking at the components, we see that the federal budget has been in a basically deficit position since the Korean war, but revenues derived from expanding personal and corporate incomes have now grown up to our defense and foreign assistance burden. Barring other massive new programs not now visible, the federal government should be a smaller user of credit, or even a net source of savings, in the years immediately ahead. The highway program, at all levels of government, will continue to call for large expenditures for an indefinite period of time, but annual expenditures may not increase much from present levels. Great needs remain in building school and college facilities, but continuation of the rates of expenditure achieved in recent years would make steady progress in meeting our requirements, and even a speed-up might not impose as large net credit demands as those to which we appear to have adjusted already.

Consumers may be expected to continue to add to their debt, both in the form of consumer credit and mortgage debt, but the rate of increase in such debt relative to the level of income will probably not match the growth in the 1950's.

In the area of business credit requirements we should, I believe, expect to see steadily large demands. Here again, however, we have recently seen the tendency for a large proportion of gross corporate capital requirements to be met out of internally generated savings, principally depreciation allowances. This tendency may be expected to continue in evidence. Even larger additions to plant and equipment and to inventories than have occurred in recent years may, therefore, require relatively little if any more access to external financing.

Meanwhile, if these other conditions are broadly fulfilled, I would expect the money supply during the years immediately ahead to grow at a rate more nearly in step with growth in gross national product than it has in the 1950's. In the first place, if there should be some reduction in the relative pressure for credit, the monetary authorities will have less need to maintain pressure on the commercial banking system to prevent credit demands from being met through monetary inflation. In the second place, it is likely that there is less room for the substitution of near-moneys for money than there was ten years ago, so that additional money needs may be met, in the net working out of all the balance sheets in the economy, through relatively more money and relatively fewer money substitutes.

Let me stress, however, that what I have said does not imply a one-for-one correspondence between the rate of growth in economic activity and the rate of growth in the money supply. The amount of money growth needed to service any given economic growth rate may, and very likely does, fall short of the economy's growth rate and may in fact bear a changing relationship to economic growth rates as levels of activity move steadily higher.

What does all this mean for interest rates? I have been asked to venture a forecast of the profile of interest rates for the 1960's. I am glad that a long-term forecast was requested. It would have been much more risky to forecast what rates will be next month or even next year. It is obvious, of course, that any statement on interest rates for the next decade must be constructed of the flimsiest material. It is a bit like predicting the winner of a horserace before the horses in question have been born.

With these disclaimers, the guess on interest rates that would seem to follow logically from what I have said (about credit requirements relative to the level of saving from current income) is that they might decline. I should, on the basis of much of what I have said, expect interest rates on obligations of most types to average lower as the 1960's pass than the levels reached in the past year or so. But all of that is to reason only for our own economy without looking outside to the great needs for capital through much of the rest of the world, and the strong pressures that those needs may exert upon the savings and the capital markets of the countries that have already advanced further along the path of growth.

Just where, on balance, all of these forces will come out I frankly cannot venture to predict. There will be a strong blend of international statesmanship as well as domestic economics in any profile that does eventually emerge.

I do believe, however, that strong future growth in the 1960's can now proceed in an orderly way from the broad base for growth we have built in the 1950's. In our home affairs, though credit may still expand in even larger absolute amounts, the proportions to other economic magnitudes may decline. There is, in short, a good possibility for closer correspondence between intended investment and autonomous saving, for lower interest rates, for improved employment opportunities and for reduced inflation pressures. But all that will not simply "happen." At the least it will require, on the side of public policy, a vigilant use of fiscal and monetary measures to help provide the environment in which these conditions of sturdy growth can flourish.

Henry C. Wallich

2

MEMBER, COUNCIL OF ECONOMIC ADVISERS
EXECUTIVE OFFICE OF THE PRESIDENT OF THE
UNITED STATES

Financing the Government: The Outlook for Spending, Taxing and Debt Management

Let me begin with a look backward at the 1950's and see what lessons, if any, those years might hold for us. During the 1950's state and local expenditures, as well as federal, more than doubled. Even allowing a little for price increase, 100% is still a very large increase.

There seems to be no evidence, moreover, that the rate of the GNP in the postwar period has suffered if we compare, say, the 1920's when taxes were low, with the later period when taxes were very burdensome indeed. Perhaps you might say that the economy would have grown faster during the 1950's if we hadn't had this tax load, but a slowdown is pretty hard to demonstrate.

The big increase in federal government expenditures, which, of course, brought on the rise in tax rates, came in the defense sector. Defense expenditures went from about $13 billion in 1950 to over $40 billion today. In addition, there were some other large programs that advanced sharply. Agricultural expenditures, while they had some ups and downs, certainly rose very sharply during the period as a whole.

One of the most dynamic expenditure factors, which however is outside the federal budget, was the social security program. It went from $1 billion to about $10 billion, partly as a result of increases in benefits, mainly, however, because of the maturing of the system owing to the advance of people into age brackets where they become eligible.

A number of smaller programs showed increases: On the federal side, atomic energy and space and, outside the budget, the highway program; on the state and local side, education—which increased far more than 100%—as well as other items.

What does any of this tell us as to what might happen in the 1960's? The defense program is obviously a function of the international political situation. One must hope that it can be kept at its present level, approximately, or if it has to go up, that at least it will not repeat the performance of the 1950's. If defense can be kept to reasonable amounts, it will be quite possible for the total of federal expenditures to go down in relation to GNP, even though a lot of other federal programs might still have to rise.

Outside of defense, there are some areas where either at the federal or at the state and local level one can see substantial increases ahead. One of them is education. Quite likely the federal government will get further into that in the course of the next decade. Primarily, however, education will continue to rest with state and local authorities.

There is urban renewal, for which expenditures made so far are actually quite moderate. This is an area where there is great pressure and where potential expenditures could be very large. At the same time the obstacles are also considerable. It has taken a number of years merely to get under way the local arrangements that are necessary before a major renewal program can go ahead. We have here a potential source of expenditures that continues to be restrained by mechanical and legal obstacles. It is something to watch, however, to make sure that whatever money is spent there is spent sensibly.

The space program quite plainly is on its way to absorbing considerable amounts of money. Atomic energy may experience some increase. The main increases in this area came quite early in the 1950's. Since then there has been a rather gradual rise. Federal Aviation Agency expenditures probably will go up sharply. They are now budgeted in that direction.

How much of an increase is ahead for the social security program —which, of course, is outside the budget—is anybody's guess. Legislation now on the books would not imply very large increases. Our experience shows, however, that every even-numbered year the Congress finds it proper to legislate for an increase. Meanwhile we face the prospect, also, of expenditures for health insurance. As regards the old age, survivors and disability programs I would say that, being independently financed, they have a sort of automatic balancing mechanism. Increases in benefits tend to produce increases in tax rates. It is a great blessing that this program is not in the general budget. The same can be said of the highway program, which is financed out of its own independent trust fund, and I hope it will continue to be financed that way.

Now, on the federal side, it seems quite possible that, when you add up all this, the following picture might emerge: (1) a more slowly moving defense total, or if things went well internationally, some defense reductions, and (2) other programs rising. That combination might give us an aggregate volume of expenditures rising more slowly than GNP. But if defense advances in line with GNP, the sum total of federal expenditures would probably grow faster than GNP.

Let me just say a word on the state and local side. There the situation seems to be the reverse. The pressures at the state and local level for additional expenditures are very strong indeed. The state and local level bears the brunt of the population increase, of the move to the suburbs, of the rise in the number of school children, and of the gains in the degree of schooling. At the same time state and local revenues tend to be less elastic than the federal, although they could readily be made to yield more if rates were increased, since in most instances—except for local property taxes— they are still low relative to the level of federal taxes. One can foresee, therefore, continuing deficits and need to borrow at the state and local levels. That does not mean, however, that the federal government must necessarily come in and bail out states and municipalities, because in many cases, as I said, they have not at all exhausted their own revenue possibilities.

It is perfectly understandable that the residents of any particular state or city would rather be financed by the residents of other states and cities—that is by the federal government—than to tax themselves, and it is perfectly understandable that they exert pressure to that end on the federal government. At the same time it is equally understandable for the taxpayers in general to resist that trend and for the federal government consequently to try to keep much of the burden of these increases on the states and municipalities, where it belongs.

Turning now to the revenue side, we all know that, thanks to the progressive income tax, the federal government may take in proportionately more than a rise in GNP would indicate. If there is a price increase, as, of course, there was during the 1950's, the movement into the upper brackets becomes accelerated. At the same time, the corporate income tax injects some uncertainty. It amounts to almost one fourth—maybe more—of our budgetary tax take, and its productivity depends of course on the share of corporate income in the GNP. There are different theories as to whether profits have held their share in GNP. If they have not, or if in the future they should fail to hold it, the corporate income tax will lag and may even cause federal budget revenues to lag behind GNP.

From this account of the 1950's, particularly as it relates to expenditures, let me draw one other lesson. It isn't a forecast, but it seems to me it is a useful lesson to draw. One hears a great deal about the need for this and that additional expenditure. Often these things are perfectly good, viewed in isolation. I think we are all for education, we are all for having decent cities, and so forth. But the experience of the 1950's shows that it isn't just any one expenditure that goes up, but expenditures all around, and it is a question of how tight or how loose the purse strings are in an overall sense that strongly influences decisions as to how much is going to go to the increase of any one activity.

The people who argue for more money for education or more money for research have to face the fact that if they are going to get more, some other programs will also be expanded. They may be very critical of those programs. They may say those other programs ought to be cut back. But the historical fact is that, by and large, if you give to one, you give to all. In the political log rolling, it is not "the more there is of mine the less there is of yours," but it is "come one, come all." There seems to exist a kind of political surcharge on any one kind of an expenditure. The people who want more education or want more research must recognize that this means more of a great many other things. Every dollar of their program carries this mortgage of added dollars for other programs that they may not like. And in that sense these federal programs that they recommend become very expensive. One might be in favor of a certain amount to be spent for education, say, but when one realizes what it means in terms of the over-all budgetary picture on the other programs, I think it might give one pause. That is how I read recent experience. That is probably what we are going to face again during the 1960's.

Let me turn now to our over-all budgetary position. If we succeed in holding governmental expenditures to no more than the rise in GNP, or actually succeed in pressing them below the present ratio to GNP, then there is a good chance that we will have a built-in structural tendency toward a budgetary surplus. This would be a very pleasant position, and we would have to then ask ourselves what we are going to do with this surplus.

I would suggest that this is partly a question of allocation of resources, but also partly a question of cyclical policy. If the economy is buoyant, then there is a good case to be made for running a surplus and for using it for debt reduction. The effect would be to feed capital into the economy through the budget, which is one of the possible ways in which interest rates might be induced to come down. Of course, the assumption is that the economy is sufficiently buoyant to stand the surplus.

If there are incentives to invest and a strong demand for capital, then savings created through the budget will go into investment. If the economy should not be buoyant and there is no demand for these savings, they will simply deflate the economy. In that case there is no strong case to be made for running a budgetary surplus.

An economy that is not buoyant is an economy in which the savings that accrue are not being fully used by the people who do the investing. Hence it would not be advisable for the government to increase the supply of savings. Under those conditions, which I have no strong reason to expect and which hopefully will not arise, we would have tendencies toward recession, and we would be justified in running a deficit. The government would then absorb some of the savings accruing in the economy. But that imbalance is the less likely situation, and the question to focus on is what we would do in case of a surplus.

There is a tendency as soon as a surplus appears in the budget to say we can cut taxes. That is a problem of resource allocation, and a tax cut may indeed be justified. But before we come to that conclusion I suggest that we ought to ask ourselves as I did a minute ago whether the economy needs the additional capital that a continued surplus would supply. Secondly, we should ask ourselves whether the surplus was needed to restrain inflationary pressure.

If there is no inflationary pressure, it is quite feasible, even at a time of high activity, to use a surplus for tax reduction. If there is inflationary pressure, tax reduction would intensify those pressures. Then the Federal Reserve would have to work all the harder to restrain them. This would mean putting greater pressure on interest rates—they would have to be higher. There is much to be said for using a surplus, if we have one, to restrain existing inflationary pressures. By the same token, to look at the opposite situation, if we have a recession there may be a good case for a tax cut.

But all this would have to depend upon the circumstances. The academic economist would probably say: in an expansionary phase run a surplus and don't cut taxes; in a recession run a deficit and cut taxes. I think that may be an oversimplification. We might face a situation during the Sixties when a mild recession could perfectly well be overcome without a tax cut. A tax cut might well build up trouble for the future, as it would have in 1958. At that time it would have increased the deficit that was already very large and aggravated the problem of public debt management. So I would not want us to establish any hard-and-fast rules as to the treatment of any government surplus that we may encounter. Neither would I want to decide now as regards a possible tax cut, whether that should be done during a period of recession or during a period of expansion. I think we shall have to judge that on its merits.

Finally, let me briefly discuss public debt management. At the present time we suffer from a lack of flexibility in debt management owing to the 4¼% ceiling. If that ceiling isn't removed, I would foresee considerable embarrassment for the managers of the public debt particularly during the early 1960's. They might then face a rather large volume of short-term debt that would have been built up because of the difficulty of long-term financing. For the longer run, however, if our budgetary hopes materialize the problems of public debt management should ease. This would certainly be true if we face a situation of surpluses in the budget and of frequent debt repayment. Even if that should not materialize and if the public debt should rise moderately, it would probably still become a smaller part of total public plus private debt and for that reason would become more manageable. In any case the amount of debt that creates a problem is not, of course, the total debt of about $290 billion, but only an amount of a little more than half that size because, of the rest, some $80 billion is in the public trust funds and in the Federal Reserve, and almost $50 billion is in savings bonds. So the public marketable part of the debt really comes down to $160-odd billion, which is the troublesome part.

As liquidity needs of business rise, an increasing part of this public debt could quite legitimately take a short-term form. It would gradually, to that extent, be absorbed into these liquidity positions, thanks to rising demand of nonfinancial holders. Furthermore, if the money supply is to rise, particularly if it rises at about the same rate as GNP, there may be a rising need for banks to buy government securities. Thus the troublesome part of the debt that we are concerned about today, the long-term part which is so hard to refund, may well shrink as the demand for short-term and medium-term debt increases.

I have given you my "ifs" and "buts" as I went along, and I have not undertaken any very specific forecasts. I would just like to stress once more the qualifications. Obviously anything one can say now about the 1960's may very possibly look very foolish very soon, and it is subject to that hedge that one says anything on the subject at all.

3

Miroslav A. Kriz
ASSOCIATE ECONOMIST
THE FIRST NATIONAL CITY BANK OF NEW YORK

Gold Reserves and the Standing of the Dollar

THE UNITED STATES today finds itself in a world of competition. In day-to-day economic and financial relationships, the Free World is more closely interlocked than at any time since the early 1930's. International trade and payments have grown much freer than many thought possible only a few years ago; and the exchange, money and capital markets of Western Europe have been regenerated and are growing in scope and flexibility. After two decades of controls, this is a deeply significant development. It is like an invalid throwing away his crutches—an unmistakable sign of recovery.

This is, of course, what the United States has sought all along by helping to restore the economic and financial strength of Europe. The rise in output and productivity, the rehabilitation of currencies, the freeing of trade and payments and the replenishment of gold and dollar reserves in Europe are the most dramatic proof of the success of our international economic and financial policies. As a result, planned and controlled economies have given way to free economic systems, and the productive vigor and economic cohesion of the Free World have been greatly enhanced.

At the same time, however, a high degree of mutual sensitivity has been established throughout the Free World. In a world in which market mechanisms—prices, exchange rates and interest rates

—are working once more, the long insulation of the United States from the influences at work through the balance of payments has come to an end. Above all, the United States can no longer conduct its domestic financial affairs without regard to its ability to supply goods and services at competitive prices. To be sure, there is no clear-cut statistical evidence that the United States has priced itself out of world markets, but there are numerous concrete examples of products in which we have become noncompetitive, as well as unmistakable indications of intensified competition in world markets and of a growing world capacity to produce goods for export.

As [Former] Secretary of the Treasury, Robert B. Anderson, noted in his article in the April, 1960 issue of *Foreign Affairs,* "The United States has little margin of competitive superiority. This means that we cannot risk any erosion in the stability of United States prices if American producers are to succeed in expanding their exports."

The international money market has also become more competitive. The United States today is more exposed to drains of funds in response to interest differentials between New York and the principal money markets abroad than has been true for many years. Last but not least, in a world in which capital movements are freer, the United States must preserve a feeling of complete confidence in the dollar by its own people as well as by foreign nations.

In this world of competition, the United States gold position has become a much more important and meaningful guidepost in policy-making, at home as well as in international economic and financial relationships, than at any time in the past quarter of a century.

Even now [May 1960], after substantial transfers of gold to other countries, the United States gold reserve, exceeding $19 billion, is large. The United States still holds almost half of the monetary gold stock of the Free World. Ten years ago, it should be recalled, it held two thirds of the world's stock; in 1928, it held approximately two fifths, and in 1913, one fifth. By any comparison with the past, except at the height of the postwar "dollar shortage," the U. S. gold reserve today is large.

The United States needs a comfortable gold reserve for two fundamental reasons. First, it needs a certain cushion in the event of a recession. Obviously, nobody can foresee how the next cyclical downturn will shape up either here or in other industrial countries, but under such circumstances some loss of gold by the United States is highly probable. Yet, as [Former] Secretary Anderson pointed out, "substantial changes" in our gold reserve "can be viewed with equanimity only if they are likely to be of relatively short duration and not persistently in one direction."

Second, the United States needs a gold reserve large enough to give confidence to foreign holders of dollar assets that dollars can be converted into gold without restriction at a fixed price. If the United States Treasury were to stop selling gold to foreign monetary authorities—or, in other circumstances, buying gold from them—the whole system of trade and payments of the Free World would be thrown into confusion. Our Secretaries of the Treasury have repeatedly stressed that the assured interchangeability of dollars and gold at $35 per ounce is a basic element of strength in the international financial structure.

Far-reaching deductions are sometimes drawn from the fact that, out of a gold stock of $19 billion, gold required as cover for currency stands at about $11.5 billion, and only $7.5 billion is thus left free. On the other hand, our short-term liabilities to foreigners amount to $16 billion. With short-term liabilities to foreigners of $16 billion and free gold of only $7.5 billion, so runs the argument, the United States will have to restrict gold convertibility and devalue the dollar.

Nothing of the sort is, of course, inevitable. Foreign officials, bankers and traders are watching us closely. And, on the whole, they have been enlarging, not reducing, dollar balances. They are aware that the United States is a richly endowed country, with an efficient, productive and flexible economy; that it remains, even after the rehabilitation of other industrial nations, the world's largest exporter of manufactured products; that it is the world's largest capital exporter, and possesses long-term investments abroad that exceed long-term investments of foreigners in our own country by some $40 billion.

So long as the United States manages its affairs properly, other countries will be satisfied with a gold backing of less than 100% for their short-term dollar claims. If they were to lose confidence in the dollar, they would of course seek to transfer funds into more desirable currencies or into gold. Even more important, however, if the idea gained ground that conditions were developing under which a rise in the price of gold would be inevitable, Americans themselves would seek gold. Americans and foreigners, it must be hoped, will not take fright at shadows. More than anything else, however, their willingness to hold dollars is directly and immediately influenced by the monetary, fiscal, and other policies that our government and the Federal Reserve decide to pursue.

Although we are not confronted with an emergency, we must not take our balance-of-payments deficit lightly. For it could not be sustained for many years, nor will it be corrected by the mere passage of time without conscious effort.

Several ideas to help strengthen the U. S. international position have recently captured the imagination of some students of international banking and have received considerable publicity here as well as in Europe. One suggestion is that Congress abolish the 25% legal gold requirement against Federal Reserve note and deposit liabilities. Another is that the U. S. Government guarantee against devaluation all dollar balances in the hands of foreign treasuries and central banks so that dollars held by foreign monetary authorities would become as good as gold.

Still another proposal is that dollars held as reserves by foreign treasuries and central banks be transferred to a reformed International Monetary Fund, an arrangement that would remove once and for all the threat of a run on our gold. Another variant seeks to ease the access to the resources of the International Monetary Fund as presently constituted. This would enable members, including the United States, to regard at least a part of their drawing rights on the Fund as an addition to their own reserves.

Finally there is the perennial recommendation to raise the U. S. gold price, in conjunction with a world-wide gold appreciation— this time specifically designed to write up the U. S. gold reserve and thus re-establish an allegedly more sustainable relationship between our short-term liabilities to foreigners and our gold.

The proponents of these ideas are, of course, fully aware of the overwhelming need for monetary stability in the United States. For my part, however, I strongly doubt whether the policies necessary to maintain monetary stability would be implemented more promptly, more courageously and more effectively if we were to eliminate our legal gold reserve requirement or dispense with the use of the dollar as an international reserve currency.

To deal with our external deficit effectively and responsibly, we must concern ourselves with the substance of difficult and delicate problems. There is genuine danger that changes in our present institutional arrangements and practices might mistakenly be regarded as substitutes for substantive policies. The fundamental task we face is to secure as much economic growth, and as high a standard of living, as is attainable with reasonable monetary stability. We would deceive ourselves by thinking that mere changes in our institutional arrangements and practices would help to solve these fundamental problems for us.

Since our problems cannot thus be disposed of, we must face them squarely. The task of bringing our balance of payments into reasonable equilibrium is truly formidable. For two years in a row, the United States had a balance-of-payments deficit of the order of $3.5 billion. This year [1960] there are signs of improvement as United States exports are benefiting from booming business conditions in Europe and Japan, from the lowering of barriers against dollar goods, and from the increased foreign sales efforts made by American manufacturers disappointed with domestic sales volume.

More fundamental measures undertaken earlier have quieted recurrent rumors that the dollar might be headed for devaluation: the rebalancing of the budget, the Federal Reserve's flexible credit policies, the Treasury's efforts to improve the federal debt structure—although much more remains to be done in this regard—and the steel industry's resistance to wage-price spiraling.

Our efforts are rightly being directed toward strengthening our ability to supply goods and services at competitive prices and to preserve a feeling of complete confidence in the dollar by Americans as well as by bankers, finance ministers and investors abroad. As the leading international trader, the United States would lose by slashing imports, for these enable foreign nations to buy American goods and to service their debts.

To finance ministers and central bankers abroad, there is reassurance in the fact that American opinion so widely recognizes that balance-of-payments deficits of $3 or $4 billion a year cannot be sustained indefinitely.

As our balance of payments is righted, as it must be, our international position will remain sound provided that our defense outlays abroad and our grants and loans to other nations are matched by an export surplus. For the money we send overseas must have a counterpart in goods shipped or services provided. Otherwise, the result is an increase in our short-term indebtedness to foreigners, which represents a claim upon the U. S. gold stock.

Gold and dollars that foreign nations have acquired from the United States have been the largest single factor in the growth of their monetary reserves during the past decade. This source of reserves will necessarily dry up as our international payments are brought into balance. But the reserve position of foreign nations has by now improved so much that the disappearance of the U. S. payments deficit, or at least its reduction to manageable levels, would not leave them pinched. Clearly, gold and dollars that foreign nations have acquired through transactions with the United States will remain outside the United States so long as the rest of the world does not incur deficits with us, as in the earlier postwar years. There are currently no signs of this. Therefore, even after the United States has succeeded in righting up its balance of payments, the rest of the world—and above all, Europe, where most of the gold and dollars supplied by the United States have gone—will be reasonably well off, at least for some time, with regard to its monetary reserves.

An entirely new situation has thus arisen in the world economy and finance. The era of "dollar shortage" has been closed. In the next decade, some of the responsibility for economic and financial leadership—as well as for providing hard cash for defense and development—will fall on Europe, which has remarkably increased its productive strength, internally as well as in relation to the other continents. European currencies are now convertible for most practical purposes. Some of them are convertible completely, while others may well become fully convertible before long. They are thus comparable in strength to the U. S. dollar. By the same token, however, convertibility enhances the need for monetary discipline, since each of the newly convertible countries wants to maintain and further improve the position it has now attained.

Basically, this is a most promising development—provided that our trading partners remove obstacles to trade. Direct quantitative restrictions on dollar goods have now been largely dismantled in countries with ample, if not overflowing, reserves. But it is also important to review tariffs, which in many countries are much higher than in the United States, and to remove the potential discrimination against outsiders, including the United States, implied in the new regional arrangements in Europe. To cope with trade and payments problems of the 1960's, it is essential to restore a sustainable payments balance throughout the whole world by means that enlarge trade and promote economic growth and efficiency.

Yet the substantial advance toward free multilateral trading and payments—and hence competition—may cause us new difficulties. While our gold stock is still abundant, the United States is much more exposed to external influences than until quite recently.

Our policies will therefore have to be adjusted to the changed international environment. From now on we shall have to pay more attention to the levels of labor costs, interest rates and prices here and in other industrially and financially advanced nations. This does not mean that we cannot take reasonable measures, including easier credit conditions, to deal with business recessions. Nations abroad would expect us to undertake such measures, as they would do in similar circumstances. They themselves have a large stake in the maintenance of business activity in this country, which provides the biggest import market in the world.

At the same time, however, it is clear that we will need to exercise more discretion in the use of economic stimulants than at some times in the past. Specifically, we can no longer afford to carry cheap money to extremes or loosen the reins on government spending. As Prof. Arthur F. Burns of Columbia pointed out recently, we need to find fiscal policies, such as tax reforms, which can check recessions and stimulate creative effort and growth without opening the floodgates to inflation.

In a world in which market mechanisms are once again working domestically as well as internationally, the United States, like any other nation, is subject to balance-of-payments discipline. Indeed, in the past year or so the United States has had to take very much the same steps as other countries to halt the decline in its gold reserve, in particular, measures to balance the budget and restrain credit.

A generation ago the late British economic iconoclast, J. M. Keynes, resented the link between the domestic economy and gold on the ground that it took the control of domestic economic and financial affairs out of a country's own hands. He dismissed gold as a "barbarous relic" and advocated "scientific" monetary management. As time passed, however, it became abundantly clear that domestic economic and financial affairs cannot be divorced from a country's international reserve position.

Postwar experience offers many striking examples of the consequences of domestic conditions and developments for the country's international reserves. Indeed, whenever a country loses gold and foreign exchange in large amounts there is reason to believe that it has faulty domestic policies. It may tolerate inflation, which brings about excessive spending on imports or deflects exportable goods into the domestic market; it may fail to check cost increases and thus price its exports out of world markets and make imports unduly cheap; and, because of expectations of further monetary and fiscal disorders, it may suffer from loss of confidence in its currency.

When on the other hand a country restricts domestic demand and prevents or moderates the rise in domestic costs—and thus expands exports, holds down imports, and maintains confidence in its currency—the result has been shown to be an improvement in its balance of payments.

To be sure, the balance-of-payments problem of a given country is not necessarily a mere by-product of inflation; it may also stem from structural problems of production, productivity and foreign trade. But even though these structural problems are important they cannot be dealt with realistically without checking inflation, which greatly aggravates such problems.

This, in a nutshell, is what most Continental European countries began to realize as far back as the early postwar years. England did so during the sterling crises of the 1950's; certain Latin American and Asian countries in the last few years, and the United States in 1959.

In the world of the 1960's in which currencies of the principal trading nations are convertible for most practical purposes and may well become convertible completely, the need for monetary discipline is even more real, and penalties for its disregard even more direct, than has been true for many years. From now on, no country will be able to inflate with impunity, as in the earlier postwar years when the consequences of inflation for the balance of payments were offset by inflation elsewhere. It is true that most of the less-developed countries are consuming and investing more than they are producing. But this state of affairs can continue only so long as there is a kind fairy from without to make good the balance-of-payments deficit. The act of charity hurts the kind fairy in her turn if, like the United States today, she fails to match her economic aid and private capital exports by a trade surplus.

By and large, therefore, the balance of competitive advantage between the United States and other economically and financially advanced countries will depend more and more on the vigilance, skill and courage of those responsible for economic and financial policymaking, and on the popular response to the policies they pursue. Which country will have the more flexible monetary policy? Which will be more alert to the need of managing its public debt in ways that will help maintain monetary stability? Which will conduct its fiscal policies more effectively, and, above all, devise a tax system that will provide for the most effective incentives to savings and productive investment? Which will be more alive to the need of avoiding rigid price and cost structures?

Whether or not the United States will, during the decade ahead, manage its economic and financial affairs better than other economically and financially advanced nations, nobody can tell at this time. One thing is certain, however: If we do not want to let our competitive power deteriorate, success will have to come the hard way, by raising output and productivity, without at the same time allowing the purchasing power of the dollar to be whittled away. This calls, above all, for financial discipline and responsibility.

4

Raymond W. Goldsmith
PROFESSOR OF ECONOMICS
NEW YORK UNIVERSITY

Adequacy of National Saving

IT IS WELL KNOWN that if we view a period's economic transactions after the period has come to an end—that is as an accountant does, or *ex post* as economists say—the nation's investment is always equal to its saving during the same period. This is necessarily so if we define saving as an excess of current income over current expenditure and investment as expenditures on durable goods; and if in the case of a nation we regard a net increase in foreign assets as equivalent to expenditures on durables irrespective of what form the assets involved actually take. Hence any one period's saving is just sufficient unto the same period's investment, no more and no less.

What can the term "adequacy of national saving," which has been set as the subject of these remarks, mean in such a situation? "Adequacy for what?" one immediately is impelled to ask. The question obviously cannot be directed toward the possibility that any one period's investment may be statistically larger or smaller than the same period's saving if we are thinking of nationwide aggregates. There are, however, three problems associated with the subject at hand.

First, will the volume of national saving in the 1960's be large enough to finance a volume of investment that we regard as necessary or desirable, using either historical relationships or some other

461

criterion of need or desirability as the standard? We might, for instance, define that volume of investment as necessary or desirable which is compatible with or leads to a given rate of growth in real national income. If saving were smaller than this standard we would call it inadequate.

Secondly, will the distribution of saving by form be such that saving will fail to match that collection of demands for investment funds that is regarded as necessary or desirable? Here again standards of necessity or desirability will have to be set up extraneously. They may, of course, be the same standards that would be applied to the question of the adequacy of the aggregate volume of saving.

Third, will the matching of saving and investment—now disregarding problems of distribution among forms of saving and investment as well as the aggregate size of the usual national totals—occur at a level of interest rates that may be regarded as high enough, on the basis of historical precedent, to indicate a serious strain on the capital market?

All three of these questions obviously are shot through with value judgments, as, of course, is the formulation of the subject itself. The economist cannot deal with these questions easily. The economic historian or the statistician may be able to do so, but only to the extent that they make the performance of the past the standard for the future.

Let me then start by taking the easy way of speculating whether the volume of saving in the 1960's is likely to be smaller relative to national product than it has been in the past. That may be regarded as one test of the adequacy of national saving, and possibly the simplest and least controversial test. The answer to the problem so posed and so simplified is that there appears no good reason to expect that the ratio of national saving to national product will be much different in the 1960's from what it has been in the past during periods that may be regarded as reasonably normal—say the 1950's, the 1920's, and the decade before World War I.

In those periods the gross national saving ratio (the quotient of gross saving of all sectors to gross national product, both expressed in current prices) has been fairly stable over business-cycle averages, provided we define saving broadly; in particular, provided we include saving through consumer durables. Different statisticians obtain different values for this ratio. The one I prefer to use, which includes civilian capital expenditures by the government as well as consumer durables, puts the ratio at fully one fourth. I see no compelling reason to doubt that the average level in the 1960's will be reasonably close to this long-term average, always excluding our participation in large-scale hostilities.

In view of the relative stability of the ratio in the past, the burden of proof would seem to be on those who contend that the national saving ratio in the 1960's will differ substantially from that of basically comparable periods of the past. This statement implicitly also answers a question which may be prominent in your mind. If for one reason or another—for instance, increased requirements of defense, foreign aid or social capital—we must in the 1960's devote a substantially larger proportion of our total national product to investment in the sense of expenditures on durable goods, including net foreign balance, and if we must, therefore, have a substantially higher gross national saving ratio, it will be very difficult to obtain it under conditions of "business as usual." Specifically, I doubt that a rise in the level of interest rates within historical precedent, say up to a level of 5% or even 6% for high-grade, long-term securities, would lead to a substantial increase in the national saving ratio.

A sharp increase in the national saving and investment ratio, as well as a radical redistribution among forms of saving, will require either a substantial increase in the level of taxes relative to national product (the additional government revenues being devoted predominantly to investment—civilian, military or foreign) or (and I am not even positive about the efficacy of this alternative) a very substantial change in our system of taxation in the direction of less progression or even definite regression in the system, and of the conscious preferences of the saving use of income over the consumption use.

So far I have dealt only with the expected relationship of aggregate national saving to national product. Regarding the possible disparity between individual forms of saving and individual forms of demand for funds, I see no reason why particular difficulties should be expected during the 1960's in meeting the demands for funds that emanate from the main sectors of the economy in so far as aggregate demands keep within the usual proportion of national product. In this case, however, there is not as much specific historical evidence, or it is too complicated to summarize quickly. One must rely here on the proven ability of the capital market to adapt itself effectively and rapidly to the changes in the forms in which saving is supplied and loanable funds are demanded.

There always will be a few types of demand for funds for which no matching supply can be found. The difficulties and the very high cost of arranging equity financing outside of the circle of family, friends and neighbors for small enterprises which do not want to give the suppliers of risk capital a say in management constitute a classic example. And the difficulties the United States government has had in finding permanent lodgement for its long-term debt are not as easy to explain but are equally plain. These difficulties are likely to continue during the 1960's. But apart from these and maybe a few other cases, I do not expect specific difficulties in matching saving flows with demand for funds.

Since it is impossible at this time to discuss systematically each of the major demands for funds and major forms of supply of saving, let me just highlight two: total loanable funds (the total of debt securities, mortgages and other loans, excluding, however, trade credit) and the demand for and supply of equity securities.

During the last full business cycle nonfarm households absorbed approximately one half of total loanable funds; nonfinancial corporations nearly one fourth; state and local governments fully one tenth; the remaining sixth has been divided among financial, unincorporated nonfinancial business enterprises, agriculture and the federal government. What is more interesting, the distribution of the total was very similar in the two cycles 1949-53 and 1954-57.

While we cannot expect the distribution to be exactly the same during the 1960's, I do not see any good reason why it should be much different. This assumes that the federal government will over the decade as a whole increase its marketable debt only moderately and rely for additional financing largely on the accruals in its own funds. This assumption presupposes absence of war or large-scale additional defense expenditures.

The second point concerns the supply and demand for corporate common stock. The small volume of new issues of common stock during the postwar decade is one of the financial characteristics of that period. In the 14 years between the end of World War II and 1959, less than $30 billion of funds were raised by the sale of common stock to old shareholders or to the general public, excluding stock of investment companies and excluding the stock of small corporations that do not go through the investment banking machinery. This total of less than $30 billion compares with net issues of corporate bonds during the same period of about $60 billion; net issues of state and local government securities of about $45 billion; and an increase in mortgage debt of about $150 billion.

More relevant, perhaps, is a comparison of the rates of growth of the stock of these different types of financial instruments, eliminating the influence of fluctuations in security prices. In the postwar period the supply of stock has risen at the rate of not more than 1% a year, compared to increases of about 7% for corporate bonds and state and local government securities, and of more than 10% for mortgages. Common stock issues have shown no definite trend over the postwar period in relation to real national product or national saving, accounting for between ½% and 1% of the GNP and for between 5% and 10% of national saving. It is not likely that offerings of common stock will move outside this range in the 1960's. At the present low level of most stock yields, stocks must be sold mainly on the basis of expected capital gains, or expected price inflation, and capital gains such as we have seen in the last ten years are not likely to recur. Such level shifts in stock prices may happen once in a generation but not more often. We would need to know much more than we do about who bought and who sold stock in the 1950's before going much beyond these generalities.

Certainly institutional purchases of common stock, apart from investment company purchases, will increase, and might increase very much if there was a stampede into variable annuities, but I doubt whether this will lead to a marked increase in the percentage of new common stock issues to GNP or to total savings. Nor is there any reason to assume that the net supply of stock will increase sharply. The factors that have kept the supply low in the 1950's are likely to do so in the 1960's; for example, high internal saving ratios, satisfactory corporate liquidity, high indirect advantage of debt financing, aversion to diluting equity.

I shall now turn to the interpretation of the last question I have to discuss, the level of interest rates during the 1960's. This has already been commented upon by some of the previous speakers and, as you will see, what I have to say is not always completely in line with their views. Here I shall be a little more positive, although my answer may not convince you. My feeling is that we shall have to reckon in the 1960's with a relatively high level of interest rates. I mean at least as high as now, and possibly even a little higher.

The first set of reasons which lead me to this conclusion is the expectation, which I cannot justify here in detail and probably need not because you have heard enough during these sessions about automation, technological breakthroughs, arrears in housing and social capital and the needs of the less-developed countries for funds. The pressure from the demand side for funds will be strong enough through most of the 1960's—recession years, of course, excepted—to give interest and yield rates a generally mild upward trend.

My second argument is more definite, but cruder. Over the last century, interest rates in the United States seem to have moved in long waves of 50 years' duration. In this country the level of interest rates moved upward for several decades until the end of the 1860's. It then tended continuously downward until near the end of the century. This decline was followed by a sharp upward movement lasting until shortly after 1920, about 50 years after the preceding peak.

The pronounced and extended downward movement of interest

rates, which started in the 1920's and came to an end in 1946, again almost exactly half a century after the preceding trough, is well known. During the last 15 years there has been a fairly steady and pronounced upward movement, always allowing for short and quite limited interruptions during recessions.

I do not want to make too much of this apparent regularity. I admit, however, to being impressed by the fact that none of these long-term movements, once started, has reversed direction in less than about 20 years. Both upward movements that we can follow in the past century lasted slightly longer than the two decades. On this crude precedent we therefore should not look for an end of the rising trend in interest rates before the late 1960's.

If you are an optimist you may, however, produce at least two arguments for an earlier termination of the upward trend in interest rates. The first is based on the unusual rapidity of the rise in interest rates during the last decade. From 1899 to 1921 high-grade corporate bond yields increased from 3¼% to 5¼%. It thus took 22 years for bond yields to advance by 2%, or by fully three fifths of their initial level. In the postwar period high-grade corporate bond yields, increasing from 2½% in 1946 to 4½% in 1959, needed only 13 years—practically only 10 years since the level of yields in 1950 was only a little above that of 1946—to advance as much in absolute terms and more in relation to the starting level than during the long upswing early in this century.

The second argument relies on the fact that subsequent long-term peaks have been established at declining absolute levels of interest rates. At the 1870 peak, high-grade corporate bond yields reached 6½%, but the 1921 peak was established at a level of only about 5¼%. So the present upward swing in interest rates has lifted high-grade corporate bond yields to 4½% for outstanding and to 5% for newly offered bonds. There is thus little room for further rise even if the downward movement of successive peaks does not continue.

I hope that notwithstanding their brevity the conclusions to which I come have been sufficiently clear, but I must stress again that they are tentative, and I am well aware that they are controversial. I cannot see a serious problem of a shortage of saving in the aggregate or for important sectors of the market, provided the concept of shortage is reasonably interpreted. I rather expect national and personal saving to account for approximately the same proportions of national product and of personal income as they have in the normal periods of the past. The matching of the supply of with the demand for funds, however, is likely to occur at a level of interest rates at least as high as that which has prevailed during the last few years.

If it is felt that, for one reason or another, more saving is needed in relation to income than we can expect on historical precedent, we are unlikely to get the extra saving by means of increases in interest rates within the range of our experience. We rather will need measures that are new and unconventional, at least in the United States. Prominent among the possibilities is saving by the central government, which practically means large-scale use of federal taxes to finance capital expenditures, public or private.

5

Discussion

CHAIRMAN OATES: Before we open the session to general questions, I think it appropriate for me to call on Mr. Gaines and give him an opportunity to reply to Mr. Goldsmith's prediction for continued high interest rates throughout most of the 1960's. I think I understood these men to be in some kind of conflict on this matter, but differences of opinion between experts are usually likely to lead to a stimulating discussion, and I expect this occasion will not be an exception. Mr. Gaines, will you comment on Mr. Goldsmith's view?

MR. GAINES: I think that a stimulating discussion of differing opinions usually is found in a discussion of what has happened in the past rather than in a forecast of the future. As both Prof. Goldsmith and I have indicated, we have made up our models out of whole cloth. It is a matter of differing judgments that is involved, and I think in this instance the differences in judgment are marginal rather than major.

As I interpret the growth in credit demands during the 1950's and their reflection in interest rates, I would not anticipate the same relative type of pressure ahead as has given us our present level of rates. Now, that does not mean that I am forecasting a steep drop-off to the 2½% rates of the World War II period, or anything of that sort, but rather a diminishing degree of pressure over the decade that would tend to give us a slightly downward trend if we have only the domestic economy to deal with.

I did hedge though, by referring to the foreign sector, where I would anticipate growing demands upon domestic capital markets that could very well offset the relaxation of pressure that I anticipate from the domestic economy. In any event, it is clear that we have a marginal difference of opinion. A relatively small swing in dollar amounts one way or the other could give either the slightly uptilted or level rate trend that Mr. Goldsmith talked about, or the slightly dipping rate trend that I mentioned.

MR. THOMAS: Mr. Goldsmith, would you like to elaborate a little bit on the effects of demand on the development of underdeveloped nations and their demands for credit? I am thinking particularly of the fact that Canada has had occasion to enter the U. S. market substantially because of shortages of capital at home.

MR. GOLDSMITH: I think this has been in a way taken care of by Mr. Gaines. We have to agree on a certain demand for foreign capital. There might even be a possibility that we could accommodate a slightly higher amount proportionately to either total saving or total national income than in the preceding decade because there might be some abatement of domestic demand along the lines Mr. Gaines talked about. But this would immediately run into the balance-of-payments problem. I wouldn't think that there is any hope for really massive capital exports from the United States. Mr. Kriz I think is the right man to take on that question.

MR. KRIZ: Well, this puts me on the spot. As a general judgment about the 1960's, I, for myself, believe that this is going to be a period of shortage of savings and capital; it is going to be a period of protracted pressures on economic resources. We may be better able and more williing to deal with inflation than in the past although I have some doubts about it. I feel therefore that there will be many limitations of financial nature on the prospective economic growth. I am sorry to sound like Cassandra in this august assembly of optimists.

MR. WALLICH: We have all avoided the question of what prices would do during these ten years, and I trust that wasn't deliberate, but whatever they do will, of course, influence the trend of interest rates. If we succeed in holding down inflation, as we have succeeded in the most recent period, I think that obviously will save us the inflation premium that would follow.

CHAIRMAN OATES: Mr. Parks of the General Electric Company has the next question.

MR. PARKS: My question has more to do with the volatility of interest rates than an attempt to look at the trend.

For the last ten years or more, as you all know, interest rates, technical interest rates, on government bonds, have been becoming more volatile, and this has its counterpart in price fluctuation. There have been a number of explanations offered regarding this, but the one which intrigues me a little bit and the one which has gone unnoticed, perhaps, is this double tax option which commercial bankers are afforded.

Just very briefly, when bankers sell their government securities they can do so and treat the loss as on stock in trade and, therefore, can write off the full amount of the loss as a deduction from their revenues, and this applies to all bonds, and I think to most certificates, as well. The same class of securities can be treated as a capital asset for gains purposes, and are taxed at a maximum of 85%. Over the cycle of the postwar years the commercial bankers perceived periods of expansion and sold in the neighborhood of $10 billion, and in periods of recession the commercial bankers bought very large amounts of government securities, again in terms of dollars.

Now, what I am concerned about—and I am just guessing, I don't really know—what I am guessing about is that the peculiar tax option afforded commercial bankers may be a contributing factor to the instability which we have witnessed in the government securities market.

CHAIRMAN OATES: Mr. Parks wants to know if the commercial banks' tax treatment on the loss taken on the sale of government bonds which has been evidenced in the swaps we have all been hearing a good deal about, has in your judgment any effect on the volatility of interest rates.

MR. PARKS: I am not interested in the swaps. I don't think that this may have a net effect on the market. This is an exchange. I am interested in the purchases and the net sales.

MR. GAINES: I am glad you put in that qualification, because obviously the swaps themselves, in logic, have no net effect. In other words, if the bank attempts to take advantage of this tax provision by selling today, planning to repurchase three months from now, it may involve a considerable loss if the market moves. Eliminating the swaps, which constitute the greatest volume of trading growing out of the tax arrangement, the other phenomenon which you have mentioned is related only marginally, if at all, to tax considerations. These changes in commercial bank portfolios have resulted from the fact that Federal Reserve monetary policies have not allowed the banks sufficient reserves both to make all the loans they wished to make and to hold their government securities at times of credit restraint, and on the other side of the cycle the System has pushed reserves into the banks in excess of the reserves they needed to support loan expansions.

The only way in which the influence you mention may be relevant is that the banks may be more willing to take a capital loss at the time interest rates are high and they have to liquidate because they can write this off against current income. I doubt very much, though, in the total considerations affecting the commercial banker at the time he has to sell, that this is in any sense a decisive one. I think this is pretty much a marginal influence.

MR. PARKS: I had the same rough idea. I just wondered.

MR. MITCHELL: I would like to get Mr. Gaines' opinion about the future of the nonbanking financial intermediaries. There has been a great increase in installment credit outside the commercial banks, and I wonder what his views might be regarding a continuation of this increase.

Of course, I am quite interested in this because this is an area over which the Federal Reserve System does not have the same control as over the commercial banks.

MR. GAINES: That is a tough one. The one point that I think we can agree upon is that consumer debt will in all probability continue to increase at about the rate of increase of disposable income. I don't believe consumers are likely to add too much more to the proportion of their disposable income used for debt service.

As to the distribution among types of lenders, my guess—and obviously that is all it can be—is that commercial banks might find themselves carrying a somewhat larger proportion of the net growth than they have in recent years. I would anticipate in the 1960's that a somewhat smaller part of the total growth in this type of consumer credit would be to finance automobiles. I believe the larger proportion would be to finance other types of consumer durables and consumer expenditures.

The bigger finance companies have specialized in automobile loans, so unless there is an institutional or structural shift in the industry, I would think that you would perhaps see more of the consumer paper coming in through retail merchants to the commercial banks. But this is certainly a difficult thing to judge, because if new automobile paper were to become less important relative to the total, then there would be nothing to prevent the nonbank intermediaries from developing their activities in that direction further than they have.

CHAIRMAN OATES: Mr. Wallich, I would be very interested personally if you would extend your comments about the "come one, come all" experience; if you appropriate for one good cause, it necessarily means that you have to appropriate for all good causes. Hasn't there been some experience of discrimination in that regard?

MR. WALLICH: Well, I wouldn't want what I said taken completely literally, of course. You have seen that there are some programs that have gone down actually, like the mutual security program, during the 1950's and others have gone up ten times, but what one can envisage is the sort of climate in which the Congress and the Administration make these decisions. If there is a strong push to cut down expenditures, then inevitably everybody is affected.

Now, there may be some programs that grow sharply, nevertheless, but they grow less than they would if there weren't this atmosphere of economy, and, by the same token, if ever there were to be a rather relaxed economy you would have the same feeling about things that ought to be cut back sharply but don't get cut quite so much.

FINANCING BUSINESS IN THE 1960'S

Murray Shields
CHAIRMAN

Roger F. Murray

S. SLOAN COLT PROFESSOR OF BANKING
AND FINANCE
GRADUATE SCHOOL OF BUSINESS
COLUMBIA UNIVERSITY

1

Funds for Business: A Broad Look at the Prospective Sources

IN TAKING a broad look at the prospective sources of funds to finance business in the 1960's we are heavily conditioned by the decade through which we have just passed. We think of this past decade of the 1950's as one of great growth in the sources of funds for business. Yet we can all recall that during that decade there were recurrent shortages in the money and capital markets with each wave of economic expansion. Should we expect similar experiences in the 1960's?

Most of us are naturally inclined to answer these questions in the affirmative and we may be correct in doing so. But before reaching such a conclusion, we ought to take a closer look at the factors which will influence the sources of funds in the decade ahead.

During the 1950's, nonfinancial corporations had some $380 billion of additional funds at their disposal for the purpose of expanding productive capacity, modernizing plant and equipment, and meeting enlarged working capital requirements. You might take a look at the breakdown of these sources of funds, even though it is fairly familiar to all of us.

Of this $380 billion, 24% came from retained profits and depletion allowances; 38% came from depreciation; a little over 13% came from the increase in current and other liabilities; short-term bank credit provided 3.3%; net new bond issues provided under 12%; increases in other long-term debt—this would include bank term loans and mortgage financing, among other sources—provided 3.6%; and, finally, new stock issues provided 6% of the total.

Corporate business, then, came to the money and capital markets for just under 35% of its funds, while internally generating or borrowing elsewhere than from the capital market provided about 65% of its funds in the decade of the 1950's. Whether financial intermediaries face a serious problem in supplying the needs of an expanding business system during the 1960's, therefore, depends to a substantial extent on what happens to internally generated funds. So it is appropriate for us to take a look at them first.

Starting with retained corporate profits, we all know that during the past decade they showed only a modest upward trend. This was in large part because the payment of dividends increased more rapidly than profits increased, so that retained profits provided a progressively smaller share of total funds throughout the decade. I presume we are now closer to a normal payout ratio for business firms, and that from here on out earnings retention may be expected to grow just about in pace with the growth in profits after taxes. This is a mighty small plus for the 1960's.

Also, we have to realize that current profits are more real. They are in harder dollars, in the sense that there is less overstatement of earnings because of the inadequate allowances for depreciation derived from the historical costs of fixed assets.

Quite unlike retained profits and depletion allowances, which have shown a flat trend in recent years, the annual depreciation item grew from less than $8 billion a year at the beginning of the 1950's to a current rate of $21 billion. Truly, this has been the most rapidly increasing source of funds. Basically this is a reflection of almost $250 billion of new plant and equipment outlays during the past decade, but there is also the influence of the accelerated amortization of some $23 billion of defense-related facilities following the Korean war. The impact of this program, of course, on depreciation charges is substantially behind us since the last certificates were issued in 1955 for accelerated amortization. However, the provisions of the 1954 Internal Revenue Code permitting more rapid depreciation are still very much in the picture. It has been estimated that possibly one sixth or about $3.5 billion a year of depreciation charges is attributable to the current provisions of the Internal Revenue Code.

But even here it appears that a large part of the impact of these changes in the tax laws has already been felt. We cannot simply project into the 1960's this upward trend in the fraction of total funds supplied by the combination of retained earnings, depletion and depreciation. Rather, we must look for a leveling off of the relative importance of these internally generated funds as a component of total sources of funds.

Let us now turn to another source: current and other liabilities. The increase in current and other liabilities, which amounted to some $50 billion in the decade of the 1950's, is a normal source of short-term or temporary financing, particularly in periods of business expansion. Trade payables and other liabilities should increase with the volume of business. In the 1950's, however, the U. S. Treasury cut down the duration of its temporary financing, through the tax accrual account, during periods of rising profits. This is the well-known program of acceleration of tax payments. But now this program has been completed and the effects of this change in the composition of current liabilities have presumably already been felt. This is another way of saying that tax borrowing from the commercial banks has become a recurrent regular phenomenon.

Turning now to the sources of funds which come from the money and capital markets, we observe that these external sources amounted to slightly under one quarter of the total during the decade of the 1950's. Of this roughly $94 billion supplied by the money and capital markets, the increase in short-term bank loans represented just over 13%. Since current assets, even after you deduct the increase in trade payables, increased by about seven times the increase in bank loans, it is hard to see that there was any deterioration in the credit position of nonfinancial corporations. They surely have not exhausted their capacity to borrow at short term.

Long-term borrowing in the form of corporate bonds provided 48% of this $94 billion from external sources, and other long-term debt, in the form of bank term loans and mortgage financing, provided about 15%. During the 1950's each dollar of long-term debt incurred was matched with almost $2 of retained profits plus new equity securities sold for cash, so again there does not seem to have been an impairment of the borrowing power of business, at least when we look at business in the aggregate.

We may say, I think fairly, that business enters the 1960's with its credit standing unimpaired. It has the credit worthiness to qualify for loans and investments by the major financial intermediaries. What these institutions will be able and willing to supply is the topic to which my fellow panelists will address themselves. They will also, I hope, deal with the question of whether business will sell more equity securities in the years ahead. In the 1950's, net new stock issues provided about 24% of the funds obtained from the money and capital markets. If we use the trend of stock prices as a simple indicator, we may perhaps conclude that the equity market could have supplied even a larger share of business requirements had corporate financial officers decided to draw more heavily upon it.

There is one other source of funds which does not get into the total but which was very important in the 1950's. This is the condition of high liquidity with which business corporations entered the decade. At the start of the 1950's, you will recall, cash and U. S. government securities were equal to cover 70% of current liabilities. At the end of the decade, this liquidity ratio was down to less than 45%. It is hard to say how far business can go in economizing in the use of cash balances, but it has appeared from time to time that there is relatively little room left for further reductions in liquidity.

Looking at the past decade, we observe that business increased its sales by about a quarter, with little in the way of additions to liquid assets. It seems fair to conclude that further reductions in corporate liquidity positions will not serve as an important factor in easing the need for funds for business expansion in the 1960's.

What can we conclude, then, on this question of whether business will be more or less dependent on the money and capital markets in the 1960's? On balance, it appears that the proportion of funds provided from internal sources will not continue to increase. In 1959, retained profits and depreciation provided about 60% of all sources compared with less than 50% in the boom years of the early 1950's. We should not, for the reasons given, project this fraction at 65% or 70% for the late 1960's. Rather, it seems more reasonable to assume that these combined sources of internally generated funds will provide only a very modestly higher share of the total. This implies heavy demands on the money and capital markets in periods of broad economic expansion. It suggests that the participants in these markets, institutions and individuals alike, have a major task of gathering funds for the business sector in the years ahead.

Two factors, however, are likely to ease the task. In the first place, the overstatement of profits and hence the overtaxation of true earnings which characterized the early 1950's because of the inadequacy of allowable depreciation charges has largely passed. The liberalization of depreciation provisions and the catching up with the rise in the prices of capital goods have had the effect of lightening the tax load.

Secondly, we have—or at least we hope we have—become more successful in coping with inflationary pressures; therefore the dollars provided to business corporations have not been losing their purchasing power at such a rapid rate as was true during portions of the 1950's. If we are able to achieve our national goal of growth without inflation, corporations should receive some considerable relief from what has been their recurring problem, sometimes referred to as the rising cost of corporate living, or the rising cost of corporate investment. Dollars which they generate, it seems, will command more resources in real terms. If all goes reasonably well, therefore, business corporations will need less in the way of internally and externally provided funds to contribute effectively to economic growth. We can think of restraint on the upward pressure of prices as equivalent to restraint on the pressures operating in the money and capital markets.

I suppose I am basically optimistic on this score, on our ability to achieve our goal. It is sobering to think of what will be required in the 1960's for the most effective functioning of our saving and investment process in financing business expansion. We shall require, in addition to effective monetary and fiscal policies, a willingness to rely on market forces for the allocation of funds among different users. We shall probably not be able to fulfill all the dreams of the housing promoters, the advocates of mammoth public works programs, and the optimists among business spenders simultaneously. Our money and capital markets really do an extraordinarily fine job of channeling funds to the most effective users. I hope that these markets will continue to have the opportunity to perform this function in the 1960's. If they are afforded this opportunity, I think we can all share my feeling of optimism in the outlook for financing business expansion.

2

John D. Wilson
VICE PRESIDENT
THE CHASE MANHATTAN BANK

The Role of the Banks

MY TASK is to look ahead at the role of the banks in financing business in the 1960's. I must confess that I have approached this assignment with a certain degree of trepidation, for it seemed to me that my old friend, Roger Murray, drew the choice spot this morning, and knowing his great competence and thoroughness, I was not sure that there would be much left for me to say. But I finally decided that he really could not exhaust the subject in the time limit allotted to him, and that I should proceed as planned. At any rate, the future is usually, with some significant modifications, an extension of the recent past; so I thought that I would look first at just what banks did accomplish during the 1950's in the way of financing business.

The record in this regard is quite impressive. Bank loans to commerce and industry (including sales finance companies) increased by 170% in the decade, or an average of more than 10% a year. This was a somewhat more rapid rate of increase than that for bank loans to all types of customers, and it was almost double the rate of advance that occurred in the economy generally. At the end of the decade bank loans accounted for some 17.5% of all corporate debt; whereas ten years earlier the proportion had only been 14.5%.

The great expansion in bank loans during the 1950's was only possible because of a substantial increase in loan/deposit ratios—that is, banks were willing to sell off part of their securities and to use those funds, as well as all new deposits, for the purpose of making loans. The actual growth of deposits during the decade was strongly influenced by the Federal Reserve, and the rise in demand deposits, in particular, was extremely slow after 1954—little more than 1½% a year. This of course was the result of a deliberate policy of active credit restraint, carried out by the monetary authorities in an effort to curb inflationary pressures. However, bank *loans* relative to deposits, were not large at the start of 1950 (some 31%) and banks had an incentive to substitute loans for government securities. By the end of the decade the ratio of loans to net deposits had risen to 54%. In the main centers the ratio was considerably higher and today in New York City banks it is close to 70%.

It is fair to say that banks did not foresee in the early 1950's a loan increase as great as they finally realized; nor did they foresee loan/deposit ratios climbing to their present heights. The problem over many years—during the 1930's, the 1940's and even until the mid-1950's—had been to build up loan portfolios with loans of proper quality. Bankers used ingenuity and imagination in developing new outlets for bank credit over this period. Term loans were developed, revolving credits and a whole host of loans were tailored to meet the needs of specific businesses: oil production loans, mortgage warehousing loans for construction, and loans with payoffs geared to the flow of depreciation for the purchase of machinery—to name a few. Nor should we ignore the many uses of installment credit devised for small business. As a result, the nature of bank credit for business had come to be considerably modified from the old textbook version of such credit as existed for example in the 1920's. Rather than bank loans being almost exclusively of a short-term character, used largely for financing inventories and receivables, a sizable proportion have come to be term loans, amortized on an orderly basis over periods of one to five years, or even longer. Moreover, many of these are in the nature of capital loans. At the time of the last survey by the Federal Reserve, close to 40% of all business loans fell in the term category.

So much then for the recent past—the background. What about the future? Can we expect the pattern of the 1950's to repeat itself in the decade ahead? I think it is clear that in some significant respects, at least, it is not likely to do so. For one thing, I doubt that banks would be able to handle the same *percentage* advance in loans during the 1960's. They will not have the funds to do so. For another, I have an idea that the *demand* on the part of business for bank credit, although continuing strong, may not be quite so pressing in the 1960's as it was through much of the 1950's.

Let's consider the demand aspect first. As I indicated, business loans in the 1950's increased at a rate almost twice as great as the gross national product—an annual average increase of more than 10%, as against an average increase in GNP of around 6%. But the economy through much of the 1950's suffered from a strong tendency toward inflation; more than a third of the rise in GNP was the result of higher prices. And inflation is apt to increase the demand for bank credit beyond what it might otherwise be. Higher costs for raw materials, payrolls, the replacement of equipment— all require more cash, and at the outset, at least, business must go to the banks to get it.

I have hopes that the nation has learned a lesson in the 1950's, and that we shall be more successful in curbing inflation in the period ahead. Experience in the last two years suggests that this may well be the case. Moreover, there are other factors that may tend to dampen demand for bank loans by business: corporate debt ratios have risen considerably over the past decade; interest rates are also higher. At the same time, banks won't be reaching out for loans to the same degree as in the 1950's. Given all these circumstances I would expect the increase in bank loans to fall more closely in line with the rise in economic activity generally, and certainly not to rise twice as rapidly as GNP.

As a matter of fact, it is not unreasonable to expect bank loans to business to rise somewhat parallel with the increase in the gross national product. That will be the case particularly if private enterprise, and not government, is to power the advance in the economy, as I am anticipating will occur. In these circumstances the actual expansion of bank loans to business would still be substantial. Let us suppose, for the sake of example, that the nation continues to experience a small degree of inflation (say 1% annually) and that the increase in bank loans to business averaged out to 5% a year—half the *rate* of the 1950's, but somewhat similar to the potential at which GNP in current prices could advance. We would then find that total loans to commerce and industry (including finance companies) ten years hence might amount to no less than $77 billion. The increase for the decade would be on the order of $30 billion—a slightly larger expansion in absolute terms than occurred in the past decade. At the same time we must remember that banks have obligations to other customers as well, and that the advance in mortgages and consumer credit in particular may prove to be sizable in the 1960's.

The question then arises as to whether banks will, in fact, be able to take care of needs of this magnitude, and especially the needs of business. I believe that they can, but only if certain conditions are met. For one thing, the monetary authorities will have to permit a considerably greater increase in bank deposits (that is, in demand deposits or the money supply) than has been the case in recent years. At the same time, banks will have to compete more vigorously for savings and time deposits, particularly vis-à-vis the savings and loans. Then again, I believe that in periods of cyclical expansion, banks must be prepared to see even higher loan/deposit ratios develop than they have recently experienced. And finally, in the circumstances that seem likely to exist, customers should not be surprised if the tendency to modify loan policies which has been apparent over the past several years should continue.

Let me say just a brief word about each of these matters. First as to deposits and the money supply, it seems reasonable to anticipate that the Federal Reserve will permit the money supply to grow more rapidly in coming years than has been the case in the recent past. Since 1954 the money supply has risen an average of 1½% a year; whereas the gross national product in current prices has advanced 6%. The economy has now pretty well grown up to the excess money supply created during the war. Velocity has increased and excess liquidity has been largely squeezed out of the system. I would not be surprised to see an increase in demand deposits on the average in coming years of something better than 3%. I might add as an afterthought that the New York City banks may continue to grow more slowly than the rest of the country, which will act to complicate their problems. (These banks now hold about 26% of all commercial and industrial loans.) I would hope that some reduction in reserve requirements might come along to help on that score.

More troublesome in some respects is the outlook for savings and time deposits. Since 1958 the commercial banks have been losing relative position in that end of their business. They have not been able to compete effectively with the savings and loans, let alone with the savings banks. Moreover, New York City banks have been hampered in their competition for foreign time deposits. Part of the trouble lies in the artificial ceiling which the Federal Reserve has held over the rate banks can pay for deposits under Regulation "Q." If business remains relatively strong in the 1960's—and I am assuming here that it will, except for periods of cyclical downturn —then some change eventually should be made in Regulation "Q." It is surprising when one looks ahead what a difference this could make to savings and time deposits of banks over an extended period.

Yet even with a change in Regulation "Q," and a faster growth in demand deposits, my judgment is that banks may not be able to meet the peak demand for loans in the 1960's without a further advance in loan/deposit ratios. This would only be the case, of course, in periods of strong cyclical expansion. I don't think we can say here today what the maximum loan/deposit ratio might be. This varies with a whole host of factors and of course it differs widely as between different banks. It does seem pretty clear, however, that the ratio can move higher, particularly for the banking system as a whole, although we certainly shall not see any increase in this respect which compares in degree with that of the 1950's.

One of the major considerations here today, it seems to me, is what these higher loan/deposit ratios may mean in terms of lending policy. They suggest that banks will have to look ahead consistently to the possibility at some stage of tight money; this means that banks must continue to be more highly selective in their lending, and it means that in periods of cyclical expansion, bank interest rates may be relatively high in order to assist in the process of selectivity. By all this I don't want to imply that banks will not be able to take care of their customers. They will always do that. Nor will they cease looking for new business. They will always desire and welcome new business. But unlike the situation a decade ago, there will be less reaching out for new credits simply to build loan portfolios. Banks want new business to be well-rounded business, involving a deposit relationship as well as a loan relationship. In cases where this is not possible, loan demands quite naturally will hold a lower priority.

And yet there are always exceptions to any rule. I believe we shall find such exceptions particularly in the case of loans to small business, including of course installment loans. Banks generally realize that they have an obligation to all elements of the community of which they are a part, and at times when credit becomes scarce the welfare of the community as a whole is a powerful consideration in allocating loan funds. At such times small business particularly is very often given special consideration.

I think we shall find, too, that the trend toward term loans may be further eased. Already many banks have tended to shorten the average length of term portfolios, and to seek a somewhat higher proportion of short-term credits. I believe this tendency will continue. Not that banks will go back to the 1920's in this respect. Term loans are here to stay, and very much so. They fulfill a vital function in the highly industrialized type of society which we now have—a function in which banks recognize they have an important role to play.

Banks, from their earliest days, have been a mainstay of credit for business. George Champion, the President of our bank, likes to say that bank credit provides the life blood for free enterprise. There is a great deal to be said for that. One thing is certain—in the

1960's business will continue to stand at the top of the priority list of banks for service. Perhaps the percentage expansion of loans will not be as great. As we have seen, in all likelihood it cannot be. But no good customer, with a proper loan demand, is likely to be neglected.

3

George T. Conklin, Jr.

SENIOR VICE PRESIDENT
THE GUARDIAN LIFE INSURANCE COMPANY OF
AMERICA

The Next Decade for Insurance Companies

THE LIFE INSURANCE INDUSTRY represents the pooled savings of millions of small individuals and, in total, comprises by far the largest single fund of capital for long-term purposes in our economy. At the end of 1959, it is estimated that the assets of the industry totaled approximately $113,600,000,000, or almost twice as large as the next largest savings institution, the savings and loan associations.

In addition to being the largest pool of long-term capital, the life insurance industry is also the most diversified of all of the forms of investment. There is virtually not a single field of investment in which the life insurance companies at one time or another do not invest their funds—whether it be in the ownership of barges plying the Mississippi, or tankers plying the ocean, or fleets of automobiles which they own, railroad tank cars, industrial equipment of all types; even schools, or the more usual outlets such as bonds and mortgages of all categories, preferred stocks, and to a minor degree, equities.

To bring into perspective the importance of life insurance companies in the capital markets in the decade of the 1950's, the assets of the life insurance industry increased during this period approximately $50 billion and thus provided this amount of net funds. On a gross basis, the funds provided to the economy by the life insurance industry totaled somewhere in the area of $100 billion, and this reflects not only the savings of policyholders but the supplementing of this source by the sales of existing securities —for example, liquidation of governments and the amortization and prepayments of existing investments. Of this total flow slightly over $50 billion went into the mortgage field, primarily residential mortgages reflecting the tremendous demands of the postwar housing boom. A little less than $50 billion went into the securities of business and industry, on a gross basis.

At the end of 1959, just to give you some idea of the distribution of existing assets, the industry held approximately $16.5 billion of public utility bonds, $25.1 billion of industrial and miscellaneous bonds, $6.9 billion in U. S. Governments, $3.8 billion in railroads, $4.6 billion in preferred and common stocks, of which common was about $3 billion, $37 billion in mortgages and about $3.6 billion in real estate.

The life insurance companies, it should be stressed, are the most important suppliers of debt capital to business and industry. The corporate bond market today is almost exclusively an institutional market; individual purchases of corporate bonds are relatively negligible. Three institutions dominate the corporate bond market —the life insurance companies, the corporate pension funds and the state and local government pension funds. To give an example of their relative importance in the market, in 1959 there was an estimated net increase in corporate fund debt outstanding of about $4 billion. The life insurance companies' net purchases amounted to $2 billion; the corporate pension funds, $1.5 billion; and the state-local funds, approximately $900 million. That totals up to $4.4 billion in these three institutions. These three institutions, alone, took more than the complete net addition to corporate bonds in the year 1959, thus taking over holdings, for example, of some $400 million from other investors.

The corporate bond market may, in turn, be broken down into two sectors—the public sector and the private sector (or the direct placement sector, as we like to call it) and this is a very fundamental distinction. People who think in terms of a completely homogeneous bond market often draw a sadly wrong conclusion regarding trends in the capital market because the two markets can be quite different. The capital market today is characterized by a great degree of compartmentalization, with some funds locked up in certain areas and unavailable to other areas. Life insurance funds contrast with these locked-up funds because they can flow in any direction, with the exception of heavy investment in equity.

The dominant institutions in the public market, which is primarily the public utility market, are the state and local pension funds, supplemented to some degree by the corporate pension funds. The life insurance companies make very few purchases in the public market. They concentrate about 90% of their purchases in direct placements. The reason for this is simple—they believe that they get better values there. They do get better values in terms of more adequate protection against refunding at lower interest rates, such as almost all public issues are woefully exposed to, and secondly, because more attractive yields are available elsewhere. This is an example of the compartmentalization of the debt. The public utility companies, particularly the electric companies, enjoy a trapped sort of market in the form of the state and local pension funds. These funds have only recently graduated from investment in U. S. government securities and have been given the tremendous latitude, in some cases, of investing in double-A and triple-A bonds. Having little other alternative they are forced, in effect, if they are going to purchase any corporate bonds, to buy the type available in the public market—namely, the electric utility bonds, which are relatively lower in yield because of this fact.

The life insurance companies, as I have implied, invest dominantly, almost wholly, in fixed-income securities. Their investments in common stocks are less than 3% of assets. There is no reason, basically, why insurance companies should not invest in common stocks. Of all the investment institutions, life insurance companies are ideally suited to invest in common stocks, with their virtually assured supply of funds year in and year out. But the restrictions against surplus accumulation and the regulations requiring the evaluation of common stocks at market preclude a heavy equity investment on the part of life insurance companies at the present time.

Let us now turn to the behavior of the life insurance industry as to savings. Life insurance savings have increased year in and year out for more than 60 years, in good times and bad, even through the depression of the 1930's. The rate of increase has been remarkably constant for such a long span of years, ranging usually between 6% and 8.5% per annum. It deviated substantially from that on the up side in the tremendous life-insurance boom of the 1920's and on the down side in the depression years (1931, 1932 and 1933). It deviated also on the down side in recent years. For the past 15 years, the trend of the *rate* of *increase* in savings through life insurance has been definitely downward. There has been no absolute decrease but the trend in the increase has steadily declined in the past 15 years, with few interruptions, and in 1959 the rate of increase was approximately 5.25%—one of the lowest percentage increases in the history of the industry, excluding the depression period of the 1930's.

This is disturbing, naturally. Even more important perhaps is the fact that life insurance savings have lost ground, relatively and rapidly, to other types of savings institutions, dropping from about 50% of a selected group of savings institutions in 1948 to approximately 25% of that same group in 1958, a drop of one half in the relative share of importance among the financial intermediaries of that kind within a decade. This is certainly a very striking change, and it is one of particular significance for business and industry, since the life insurance industry is so vitally important in providing capital to business and industry. And the point is made more cogent when one realizes that the fastest rate of increase by any institution by far was that of the savings and loan institutions during the postwar period, an increase which has been actually phenomenal in 1959. Their increase in assets in that year was the largest of any institution of any kind, totaling more than $7 billion. The implication of this in our economy is very important when we realize that *none* of these funds finds their way into the securities of industry. They are legally tied into residential mortgages almost 100%.

The reasons for the relative decline in savings through life insurance are too numerous to go into detail here, but let me mention a few of them. The most significant has been a relative and definite decline in the importance of the savings element in life insurance itself, which has taken place through the purchase of increasing amounts of term insurance (reminiscent of the speculative period of the 1920's when the slogan was, "Buy term and invest the rest"), through increases in policy loans and surrenders to realize upon guaranteed cash values, and lastly through decreases in funds left on deposit.

These trends, in turn, have reflected a public psychology which permeated the country, based upon the fear of inflation, with the consequent aversion to the fixed form of savings applied in life insurance. This has been accompanied, on the other hand, with the luring and the strong appeal to policyholders, and to others in the economy, to invest their funds directly by virtue of the unprecedented stock market boom of the 1950's, and by virtue of the higher interest rates currently available, relative to the average rates which are realized by insurance companies and credited to policyholders. The average rate is a product not only of the present but of the past, and this difference between current interest rates and the average rate has led people to take funds out to invest currently.

The second important reason has been that competition of other methods of providing security, both government and private, has undoubtedly cut into life insurance savings. In particular, the growth of noninsured pension plans has reduced the rate of growth which might otherwise have been expected by the life insurance companies. This has taken place predominantly because of the greater investment flexibility accorded this type of noninsured plan to invest heavy amounts in equity, accompanied by a substantial tax advantage enjoyed until recently.

Thirdly, there has been a severely competitive war going on in life insurance for the past decade. The result, as in all extreme competition, has been a cutting of prices and the reduction of gross premiums of life insurance. These are some of the major factors that have been behind this slowdown in the rate of growth of life insurance assets and life insurance savings.

Looking into the next decade and projecting the trends and forces that were at work during the 1950's, one might well come up with an asset figure for the industry in 1970 of some $193 billion compared with $113 billion in 1960—an increase of approximately $80 billion compared with $50 billion in the 1950's. This, in turn, would imply funds available for the economy from the life insurance industry on a gross basis of some $150 billion compared with $100 billion during the 1950's.

Consequently, when people talk about declining rates of growth of insurance savings, be careful that you do not lose sight of the fact that in absolute terms such savings will still be growing very substantially. Some people, on hearing talk of declining rates, rush to the conclusion that life insurance companies are going to have less money to invest. This is not the case. The trend in the amounts will certainly be much greater. It is the rate of increase that will be less.

A gross increase in the 1960's of $150 billion would imply a further decline in life insurance relative to other intermediaries and a futher deceleration of the rate of increase in life insurance savings. Any such projection of life insurance savings or assets ten years in the future is more hazardous today than it would have been many times in the past. Often in the past, it was one of the easiest variables to predict and project because of its regularity. However, the forces of the 1950's, operating to produce these results, may well be subject to considerable change in intensity, and even direction. It is quite possible, therefore, that the figure I cite of $193 billion could be very much on the low side by as much as $25 billion or more. It is my feeling that changes may well take place in these trends, and I would like to cite some reasons.

I have already mentioned that one of the basic factors affecting insurance savings in the 1950's was the question of inflation and the consequent, almost heedless, escape to the equity market on the part of policyholders and others. Provided that policies similar to those now followed by the Administration and by the Federal

Reserve Board are kept in effect in the 1960's, inflation is bound to be very much less a factor in the 1960's, and it is quite possible that the discipline of the international money market may force us to keep policies somewhat akin to those that have been adopted in recent years. It is certainly an even bet that inflation will be very much less an important problem, certainly always a threat, but a very much less important problem in the 1960's than in the 1950's, and this in itself would imply a very considerable re-evaluation of the position of equities versus fixed income securities implied in life insurance. Possibly even more important, the investment performance of equities in the late 1960's compared to fixed income investments cannot possibly be anywhere near as brilliant as it was during the period of the 1950's.

Without going into too much detail, a good equity performance in the 1960's is going to be dependent upon astute investment judgment in the selection of securities, and it is not going to be the result of the mere holding of common stocks (almost indiscriminately). The latter applied during most of the 1950's. When I look at the investment judgments in the market as evidenced in the 1950's and possibly typified by the tremendous vogue of the oil stocks as the premier growth stocks in almost every single portfolio (up to and past the date at which it is discovered that they are no longer such an industry), I feel that the requirement of astute selection of securities in the 1960's is going to lead to some acute disappointments in equity performance of average individuals and institutions. This is likewise going to lead to a reappraisal of the equity versus the fixed-income type of security typified by life insurance.

The interest-rate differential between new funds available on the market and the average rate credited by life insurance companies is purely a statistical phenomenon and it will disappear, modify, and may even reverse itself and be a force in the other direction. Thus this reason for taking funds from life insurance companies versus investing them outside will disappear during the 1960's and will no longer be an operative force. Lastly, the competitive disadvantages of the insured pension funds compared to noninsured pensions will be gradually removed in the 1960's, which could slow and possibly even reverse this trend which has been unfavorable to life insurance companies.

For these and other reasons, all of which represent controversial, debatable viewpoints, I am of the view that the adverse trends of the past decade in life insurance savings will slow down and may possibly be reversed, in which case a materially higher asset figure would be indicated for 1960 and a higher flow of funds for investments during the 1960's.

As to the channeling of life insurance funds during the 1960's, I do not foresee any substantial changes in the major underlying forces governing investment policies. Life insurance companies will continue to invest dominantly in the private sector; they will continue to cover the waterfront of all investment outlets, and they will continue to shift and channel funds from one field to another as the demand and the relative attractiveness changes, as they should in a properly functioning capital market. They will continue to insist upon adequate call protection, and they will continue to invest primarily in direct placements and mortgages. Over the period, changes in regulations regarding valuation and legal permission governing common stocks promise to increase the equity investment of life insurance companies during the 1960's, but I foresee nothing more than a moderate increase at the present time. Present increased taxation of life insurance will lead to greater interest in tax-exempt securities and in corporate preferred stocks during the 1960's, but this likewise will not be a factor of major importance from the standpoint of the industry as a whole.

All in all, it appears likely though by no means certain that the life insurance industry will continue in the 1960's to be the major supplier of capital to business and industry in our economy.

Ragnar D. Naess

4

SENIOR PARTNER
NAESS & THOMAS

The Stock Market: Perspectives and Potentials

I SHALL DISCUSS the stock market in the 1960's in terms of its potentials—what it can do—and its contributions to the capital market. Then we shall review the character of the stock market and the changes it is going to undergo during the next ten years. But the first thing I want to say is that the stock market reflects very sensitively the fears and ambitions, expectations and hopes of millions of investors, and hence it is the barometer of changing events, particularly economic.

I wish to take you back ten years and describe what the stock market looked like, or what the future looked like for the stock market, in the eyes of the average investor in the beginning of the decade of the 1950's, on January 1, 1950. The Dow-Jones industrial average was about 200. In 1950 earnings of the companies in the Dow-Jones averaged about $30 a share, so it was selling around 7½ times the earnings. It paid dividends of about $15, yielding about 7.5%. Many stocks yielded 9%, 10%, 11% and 12%. This, of course, shows that the market was very, very low. Why was it so low? Because people had no confidence in the future. Many people thought we would have a depression following the war. It was generally assumed that commodity prices would collapse because they always did after major wars. In addition to that, we were very fearful that we would have a third world war. In fact, the Korean war started in 1950. Common stocks were on the bargain counter.

My point is that we did not have a depression, we had a boom. Commodity prices did not collapse following the 100% increase over the prewar year 1939. They increased further. We did not have a third world war. We had small wars that stimulated the economy and led us to build a defense establishment which was of colossal magnitude. The prevalent opinion on these very important scores was 100% wrong. People thought that stocks would never again yield 3% and 4%; they thought that stocks would always yield 5%, 6% and 7% for the reason that the outlook was so bleak, and on that score there was a great misapprehension.

I will only add that if you go back every decade for the last several decades, whether you take the beginning of the 1920's, the beginning of the 1930's, the beginning of the 1940's or the beginning of the 1950's, you can only draw the conclusion that the tendency is to go on historic precedents, or to project concurrent trends to make conclusions; and in every instance those conclusions were proved to be far away from the mark. I believe right now that the 1960's will be very different from the 1950's.

In the decade of the 1950's, the Dow-Jones went up from 200 to 685. That is nearly three and a half times. It started on a 7½% yield basis, and it ended on a 3% yield basis. Stocks that yielded 10% now yield 2% and 3%.

What were the factors that made for this gigantic rise in stock prices? We rebuilt Europe by pouring funds into it. We rebuilt our own economy, in the sense that we had a tremendous deferred demand for all kinds of goods and services—consumers' goods, capital goods. We had a technological revolution unequalled up to that time, with the astounding development in research and in new technology during and following the war on which we capitalized. We had an inflationary trend which was also unprecedented, with wage rates in a continuous rising trend. Corporations got the habit of increasing wage rates every year, requiring great confidence in the future—a sharp departure from past poliices. This led to a substantial increase in costs, and therefore to an upward cost-price spiraling.

All these developments represent a combination of circumstances which I just cannot believe can be duplicated, when we look into the 1960's. In the 1960's we cannot expect anything like the performance of the 1950's.

That does not mean that I am at all pessimistic about the 1960's. I think the 1960's will be a good period, and that with the changes in social and economic background of the last 30 or 40 years we are not going to have any serious depression. That is unlikely, and in itself is important. It does not mean that we are not going to have more serious declines in business, perhaps, than we had since the war, but essentially we are not going to have a catastrophic depression. We are no longer able to suffer the readjustments that come from a severe depression. Instead, we made the readjustments by inflating, which is much less painful for most people.

If we look ahead, then, what can we expect? We make very careful estimates of the long trend of earnings and dividends and our estimate suggests that the Dow-Jones earnings per share will rise from something like $37 a share in 1960 to somewhat over $60 a share in 1970. Dividend payments have been very conservative relative to earnings and I think they will be less conservative. If they are $21 or so in 1960, they may perhaps be $35 or $36 in 1970. These are just figures to indicate the magnitude of the possibilities.

If that is the case—and I do not say that this is unreasonable—it means that the Dow-Jones industrial average in 1970, under normal conditions such as I have outlined, might be between 850 and 900. If people are extremely bullish in the future as they are today, in terms of stock prices, the Dow-Jones can be 1100 or maybe even 1200; and if they are very bearish and business is in a declining trend, it could be as low as 600, which is about the level today. In any case, that is again a gain of 40% to 50% of the anticipated average level which surely is modest in relation to that of the 1950's.

What I have said so far about the stock market and its potentials is relatively unimportant because I have not yet come to the really important items. Number one is this: The common stock market has not been very important as a source of funds for financing in the 1950's, for the simple reason that the tax laws made it far better to finance by bonds, where interest can be deducted and charged as an expense. With the low yields on common stocks today, and with higher interest rates than those of the 1950's, there is a better chance that common stocks will become more important to finance industry than they have been.

Convertible bonds have also become more important, relatively speaking, than in the past, and I think that will continue. Both common stocks and convertible bonds will become more widely used as vehicles for new financing, but I cannot believe that the common stock market in the future, any more than in the past, will become one of the most important sources of financing. That, however, does not mean that the common stock market as an institution is not of significance in helping industry to finance. Actually it is a place where smaller companies can introduce and distribute their common stocks and thereby become better known and able to obtain financing more easily. In this fashion the common stock market has been of enormous importance in the 1950's. When we see the number of common stocks now listed and which is growing continuously on the organized exchanges, we are amazed. This trend will continue.

The common stock market, then, is a very vital element in our economy. I believe that many stocks of companies that have been considered highly desirable, which have really become institutional holdings and are considered top-notch quality, will lose investment standing in the 1960's, and many companies that we do not know so well today will gain investment standing. Of course, this happens all the time. My point is that it is going to happen more often in the 1960's. If instead of calling the years of the 1960's the Roaring Sixties we call them the Decade of Intense Competition, I think we will describe the outlook well. We have, then, a situation where selection is going to be of the utmost importance, which comes back to the point I have just made. There will be many "unknown" companies which will become important, require capital and by reason of the fact that the stocks are on the organized exchanges, be able to get such capital more readily. On the other hand, there will be many large companies whose stocks are on the exchanges which will not need so much capital because they are not quite so dynamic as they used to be. There will thus be introduced this new element (which is really not new, but merely intensified in the 1960's) of a problem that faces all investors and reflects the conditions that will exist—namely disappointment in the performance of stocks that formerly had a wonderful performance and standing. These "disappointed" investors lack the perceptiveness to realize that such companies must enter new fields that are more promising and dynamic and thus need new capital. This is an old, old story, but it is going to be magnified and be the key to a successful investment policy in the 1960's. In the 1950's you could buy the name stocks, sit on them and get rich. You will not be able to do that in the 1960's in most cases.

What are the fields in the 1960's that are going to come to the fore and become more important and to which investors will turn? These fields are known; I am not trying to pull out of the hat new fields for investment. It is just a matter of appreciating that they will continue to be very attractive for investment. They will need a lot of money and they will be able to get that money in financing by reason of their high investment standing. I will mention just a few.

In the field of raw materials, we obviously still have ahead of us large and growing demands for aluminum, fiberglass, plastics and new materials which will grow in importance in relation to the older materials with which we are familiar. Here is a list of industries that need more capital—the aluminum industry, for example, the glass-fiber industry, and certainly the chemical industry, particularly in terms of plastics. These are investment outlets that will fare well in the stock market, will need new capital, and will get it.

Certain types of products that are related to construction and building certainly will have a dynamic prospect. I have in mind air-conditioning; the control of temperature and humidity is a field of great potential that will do well and require a lot of capital, which it will get.

The drug industry still has a phenomenal future. The potentials of the solution of the problems of disease are enormous. That industry, of course, will also need more new capital. It has a large profit margin and generates a good deal of money internally, but it will have to go to the market to obtain more capital. And this brings up the important question: Will the drug industry be allowed to make the money they have to make in order to do the research and take the risks they have to take? I think it will be allowed to do it, but one never knows. If it is not allowed to, it is going to lose some of its dynamic character and certainly some of its investment rating.

The next field, and one that really stands above all the others, is the field of electronics, which is really not an industry. It is a way of life for all industry, so we must deal with it as a completely revolutionary concept in human activity. I do not care whether it is educational, defense, transportation, industrial control or labor-saving devices in white-collar offices—electronics represents a completely new way of doing things throughout human activity. Here is an industry that compares with or even exceeds in potentials the chemical industry of 30 or 40 years ago. Electronics firms are going to be extremely hungry for capital. That is why they just cannot show much earnings, because they reinvest continuously such an enormous amount of funds that they cannot show earnings. This is one reason the stock sells so high, and allowance should be made for this fact in judging the prices of the stocks.

The life insurance business has been a pet of mine for many years, and I still believe that this industry must be considered as highly dynamic. Another new field which we really have not lived in for long is the leisure-time activities field. The point here is not only that the companies catering to leisure-time activities will need much capital and will grow—it is also the effect of this field on other companies that is important. For example, the automobile has lost some of its status as a symbol of the family standing, as a means of recreation; it has become more a means of transportation. The average family now likes boats, do-it-yourself tools, travel, entertainment, television and so on. Here is a whole field which, I think, will be dynamic, popular, and will do very well.

The office equipment field is a staggering field and will need a lot of capital and will grow and be very dynamic. The field of publishing looks very favorable with educational demands and increased population over the decade ahead, and the electric power industry should also continue dynamic. There are other fields, but perhaps I have already mentioned enough.

The reverse of the above is that some of the older fields have become less desirable and need less funds. Unfortunately there is a tendency for government agencies to become more interested in controlling business, and there are increasing problems for many companies that tend to retard their growth. Take the airlines, which are in a really wonderful business and should be profitable. They have untold troubles. You are familiar with them, and I do not have to repeat them. Their investment status is very poor, and they cannot get much financing done without paying a lot for it, and this is a very unfortunate thing.

The most promising and dynamic fields of endeavor will continue to be capitalized in the market at very high premiums. That has been true for a long time, and will continue to be true because of the limited number of really great and outstanding companies. The fields that are less desirable will continue to be capitalized at a relative discount, and these fields are likely to include such important industries as automobiles and oil, which are faced with serious difficulties, certainly in part due to their own lack of statesmanship during the last few years. In the 1960's, their earnings may be capitalized at far less optimistic rates of capitalization as compared with those applied to the stocks of more dynamic companies than was the case in the 1950's. The more promising industries, such as electronics, or leisure-time and others, will continue to demand high prices in relation to earnings and will therefore naturally be able to finance their requirements on very attractive terms.

In conclusion, as we look ahead in the 1960's we should not think too much about the general level of stock prices. Stock prices should advance moderately, and barring a depression (which I do not think we will have) the potentials on the down side are not very serious. I believe we will go through the period we are now in with no more than a moderate readjustment in business, and then go forward again in 1962 and 1963.

The up-side potentials are not very great, either. Let us forget about the general market, so to speak, and find out what are the most promising industries. This is where the stock market will exert its greatest constructive effort in providing capital. It will provide new capital to the coming companies that are young, growing, dynamic and in need of capital.

5

Discussion

QUESTION: I would like to direct a question as to the liquidity of both corporations and banks. In the past year or so the banks definitely lost liquidity. They have lost it to the corporations. The corporations have increased their liquidity. The banks, as has been indicated very clearly, show that they are 70% loaned in New York City. Some indication was made in the talks that the percentage might rise in the future. If we do not have the chance of gaining deposits—and that seems to be a little difficult—perhaps it would devolve upon the corporations to divest something of their liquidity, and here is where the real question comes in.

Today there are outstanding $41,160,000,000 of Treasury bills. Of that, there are owned by other than the banks, Federal Reserve, the Treasury, and the insurance companies, something like $33 billion. If we are to advance and take care of this future growth, will not the corporations have to divest themselves of that liquidity, which must be purchased in turn by the Federal Reserve System, in order to give us the growth in the banking system that will take care of the capital demands upon the banks?

MR. WILSON: First, I do not think, so long as the interest-rate structure is relatively high, that we can expect corporations to hold larger cash balances with banks than they actually need. I do not believe that we can turn the clock back in the banking world to the 1930's, the 1940's and the early 1950's in this regard.

At the same time, I think that the cash requirements of corporations are such that they cannot cut back on their bank deposits, relatively, to the same extent in the future as they have in the past. I doubt very much that they will be able greatly to reduce the amount of cash which they now hold. On the contrary, as business expands, they will have to increase this cash. This is one of the reasons I believe we shall see a greater growth in bank deposits in the country in this next decade than we experienced in the past. I doubt, however, that the growth is going to be achieved by corporations decreasing the absolute amount of their Treasury holdings in this period.

I think we can achieve this greater growth in the money supply, in part, through a reduction in reserve requirements, and that we shall see a reduction in reserve requirements over the coming decade. We can also achieve the growth in money supply to some extent through open-market operations that might involve the divestment of government securities by investors other than corporations.

I think, too, that if the government should find it necessary to run a deficit on balance over the length of the decade—in other words, if we should find that the government debt is higher at the end of the decade than it is at the beginning—that, too, will enlarge the opportunity for open-market operations and also for a growth in bank deposits through some increase in bank security holdings. I would not be a bit surprised if we do find at the end of the 1960's a somewhat larger volume of government debt than we have today, although I hope that it is not increased greatly.

Thus I believe there are a number of ways that are open here for a larger increase in bank deposits during the 1960's than we had during the 1950's—ways that would not require corporations to divest themselves of Treasury securities which they now hold. At the same time, I want to repeat that I do not think that corporations can conserve on cash in the 1960's to the same extent that they did in the 1950's. After all, conserving on cash is only another way of saying that velocity of circulation is increasing. We now find that the velocity of circulation is again beginning to approach the peak reached in the 1920's and it probably cannot go much higher.

QUESTION: This question is again to Mr. Wilson and it is about term loans and it has a Canadian slant. There will be a 30-second preamble to my question, Mr. Chairman.

We have banking problems in Canada that are broadly the same you have been coping with here. We do have, however, only nine chartered banks, eight of those very large bank organizations. The relationship between the central bank and the commercial banks is therefore very close, very informal, and a lot of lunch-table technique. We do not have any legal maximum on the rate of interest that we may pay, but for nigh onto a hundred years we have had a legal maximum on the rate of interest we may charge. That is the preamble.

We got into the term-loan business in Canada at about the same time it began to develop here and, I think, for substantially similar reasons. Our loan ratios were low. We were in effect merchandising lending techniques. Looking at it in retrospect, apart from the yields that you see on your books—which are a little depressing now —I think it is a fair statement that by and large most of the term-loan business that we were doing at that time was business that could just as readily and just as efficiently have been handled by the investment-dealer organization, and under conditions that would not have led to an expansion of bank credit.

I mentioned the close contact with our central bank. Apparently it, too, arrived at the same view and, on several occasions since the late 1940's and early 1950's, the central bank suggested to the chartered banks that they stay out of the term-loan field and leave it to the investment dealers, and that the financing of capital expenditures by creation of bank credit was not, in their view, a proper activity for a banking system, particularly under conditions when money was tight. The last time that suggestion was made to us was in 1955. That rate still runs, except in the case of very small term loans.

I was interested to read that my good friend, Mr. Alfred Hayes, President of the Federal Reserve Bank of New York, is now suggesting to the banks here that they should think in terms of a penalty rate in term loans, to persuade borrowers out into the somewhat chillier wind of the bond market.

In Canada, we have pretty much that same thing going on without the penalty rate. Our very adaptable investment dealers have again picked up the ball. We have had a very active development in the commercial paper market, not the same term as a term loan, but the paper rolls over and fulfills the same function.

Now I come to my question, which is this: If we go on the assumption that through the 1960's the banks may still be faced with a problem of allocating scarce resources, would you agree that a term-loan activity is probably the most readily dispensable activity on the part of a banking system, dispensable both from the standpoint of proper functioning of banking in terms of a tight situation, and also because it is the kind of activity that is most likely and most readily picked up by other financial intermediaries?

MR. WILSON: I did indicate, I believe, that the trend toward term loans would ease. In other words, it is my personal judgment—and I might say that it is not shared by everybody within our bank—that we probably will experience over the decade pressure to get into a larger proportion of short-period loans, as opposed to medium-term loans. But I think this is quite different from saying that we shall get out of the term-loan business almost altogether.

I think that the American economy is somewhat different from the Canadian economy, in several significant respects. We are much less dependent on agriculture in this country than is Canada. We are much less of a natural-resource economy than is Canada. An agricultural and natural-resource economy, I believe, creates short-term credit needs to a relatively greater extent than does a highly industrialized economy.

In this regard there has been a fundamental change in the American economy since the earlier decades in the century, and some of the older officers around our bank stress this. George Champion, our president, who traveled through the South for our Bank for many years, points out that today the American economy is highly industrialized, and that as a result there is not the same degree of seasonal activity—activity which tends to create short-term credit demands. You have the government holding large stocks of agricultural commodities, which itself reduces the need for short-term credit. In this instance, the government holds inventories which might otherwise be held by business. In contrast, we have today an industrialized society where working capital needs—the need for financing inventories and receivables—do change with the business cycle but not seasonally, at least not to the same extent as in the past. As a result, the demands that come upon banks are to a considerable extent demands of a capital nature. They are demands for increased funds, not only for machinery and fixed assets but also for increased working capital on a permanent basis.

I might say finally that perhaps the United States banking system has provided some of the term-loan capital needed in Canada and which the Canadian banks have not been in a position to provide. American banks have done this through the provision of term loans to American companies which have made very heavy investments in Canada. I know our own bank has done this.

For all these reasons, but principally because I think the American economy of the 1960's is going to be a highly industrialized economy, the increased bank credit to business will continue to take the form of term loans as well as short-period loans, although to a somewhat smaller degree than was the case in the 1950's.

QUESTION: George Conklin mentioned that he thought the life insurance industry would do relatively better in relation to pension funds than it has in the past decade. I was just wondering what some of his reasoning was in this field.

MR. CONKLIN: Mainly because of the removal of disadvantages that have existed in the past—which, I think will gradually be removed, either through appropriate legislation in the States or for, example, in the case of taxation—the advantage that the insured pension funds have had has essentially been removed now by the new tax law. It may well be, also, that special methods will be derived for group annuities and pensions, whereby investments in common stock comparable to the corporate pension funds may be permitted on the part of life insurance companies, if this is required or desired by the corporation.

In other words, I think that increasingly in the future the life insurance companies will be enabled to perform the same services as the banks in this respect. I see no reason, therefore, why they should not be able to get a better share of the business than in the last ten years.

Finally, I believe that the investment performance of equities in the 1960's will be much less glamorous than in the 1950's, and many corporations with noninsured pension funds may be heavily disappointed in the investment results achieved by corporate trustees.

CHAIRMAN SHIELDS: How long will it be before the reinvestment factor will have the effect of lifting earning rates in the insurance companies close to the market rates?

MR. CONKLIN: That depends on how far and how fast the rates keep going. If they should level out at this rate, it would not be more than another several years before they approach the market rates. The earning rates have been moving up very sharply in the last three years. The practical answer is, within a few years.

CHAIRMAN SHIELDS: As that develops, the cost of insurance might come down and that may be an incentive for more sales.

MR. CONKLIN: Yes, it may.

CHAIRMAN SHIELDS: Dr. Murray, could we see a significant increase in the rate of savings? We are providing more incentive for saving than we did in the 1950's or 1940's or 1930's. We are moving millions of our families from an income bracket where they could not save if they wanted to, to a bracket where they can and customarily do save. And we have just gotten into high gear three very powerful and rapidly growing savings mechanisms—the pension funds, the savings and loan associations, and the mutual open-end funds. Could we as a result have an increase in the rate of savings in the United States in the decade ahead?

DR. MURRAY: I think there are strong reasons to believe that we can have precisely that. You have mentioned the principal factors in such a development: new institutions that are very vigorous, and, in certain cases, have very effective and aggressive promotions behind them. The fact is that if we do have the vigorous growth in the economy which we all look for, our savings flow is really hard to visualize. We can talk about the demands for funds and we are impressed by them. We do not always look at the other side of the coin. If we develop this rate of economic activity, we will simultaneously be generating a very, very large flow of savings. It is even possible that we might see in the 1960's a rise in the long-term level of the savings ratio in the American economy. As you know, the ratio of the savings to income has been relatively constant over a long period, 50 to 75 years. It may be that we are in the process, partly as the result of institutional influences, of a modest increase in that savings ratio.

MR. CONKLIN: I rather differ from that viewpoint. After all, we have been in a period of rapid growth in our economy, the Dynamic Fifties, and we have been in a period when new institutions have come to the fore very rapidly, institutions for savings, and the savings rate has not tended to appreciably depart from the long-term rate. If there has been any trend it has been somewhat downward. I think it would be unusual if it did turn upward, and if it does it might cause some very serious problems, at least for the intermediate term.

QUESTION: I see in my notes that current assets increased seven times short-term loans from 1950 to 1960, and I also note that cash and securities decreased in relation to current liabilities from 70% to 45%, and I was wondering if I have those notes right in the first place. If they are right, what happened to the money? Did it go into inventory, and will that perhaps be liquidated in the 1960's?

DR. MURRAY: There was a large increase in the book value of inventory, part of which was price, but there is a striking increase in corporate receivables that is observable over the period of the 1950's. If you relate receivables to sales or use any other ratio, you will observe that receivables have risen markedly in corporate enterprise. Most people recognize in this the fact that corporate enterprise is financing noncorporate business to an increasing extent—that is, the corporate enterprise is providing an increasing volume of credit relative to economic activity to noncorporate business, and this has been a major factor in the rise of the corporate receivables.

The other factor is, of course, more liberal extension of consumer credit by business.

QUESTION: Mr. Naess, would you compare the potential support to the stock market from the financial institutions in the 1960's as compared with the 1950's?

MR. NAESS: I think that the financial support of the stock market from financial institutions in the 1960's will continue to be very great. I feel that the flow of funds into stocks from financial institutions will really be the dominating factor in the stock market. When you think of the increase in the number of profit-sharing plans and of pension funds—not to mention mutual funds and life insurance companies—I believe that there is going to be a great demand for good common stocks. If anything, there will be a shortage of good common stocks in relation to the demand for common stocks, and the idea of ownership of common stocks, which has become so imbedded in the last few years in the American consciousness, will continue to grow and become more important. As I said, the support of the stock market from financial institutions will be a very important item.

CHAIRMAN SHIELDS: John Wilson wants to ask a question.

MR. WILSON: I looked at these very interesting projections that Ragnar Naess made regarding the Dow-Jones average earnings and the average itself. It seems to work out that he looks for a price-earnings ratio of around 15 times. That, of course, is rather high historically, and I just want to ask him whether or not he regards such a ratio as now being normal.

MR. NAESS: I think, historically, the times earnings have been between 13 and 14 for many years. When I said that the Dow may be 850 to 900, I had in mind earnings of maybe $60 a share, and I think that comes out about 14. I believe chances are that we will have stocks selling somewhat higher in relation to earnings than we did in the past, for the reasons that I mentioned. And the fact is, if we look back far enough, 70 or 80 years, there has been some increase in the times earnings, some decline in the dividend. However, I have not assumed much of an increase in my projection.